Beginning Python Visualization

Crafting Visual Transformation Scripts

Second Edition

Shai Vaingast

Apress®

Beginning Python Visualization

ISBN-13 (pbk): 978-1-4302-0053-7

ISBN-13 (electronic): 978-1-4302-0052-0

Publisher: Heinz Weinheimer
Lead Editor: Steve Anglin
Development Editor: Linda Laflamme
Technical Reviewer: Leigh Sheneman
Editorial Board: Steve Anglin, Mark Beckner, Ewan Buckingham, Gary Cornell, Louise Corrigan,
    James T. DeWolf, Jonathan Gennick, Robert Hutchinson, Michelle Lowman, James Markham,
    Matthew Moodie, Jeff Olson, Jeffrey Pepper, Douglas Pundick, Ben Renow-Clarke, Dominic Shakeshaft,
    Gwenan Spearing, Matt Wade, Steve Weiss
Coordinating Editor: Anamika Panchoo
Copy Editor: Patrick Meader
Compositor: SPi Global
Indexer: SPi Global
Artist: SPi Global
Cover Designer: Anna Ishchenko

Distributed to the book trade worldwide by Springer Science+Business Media New York, 233 Spring Street, 6th Floor, New York, NY 10013. Phone 1-800-SPRINGER, fax (201) 348-4505, e-mail orders-ny@springer-sbm.com, or visit www.springeronline.com. Apress Media, LLC is a California LLC and the sole member (owner) is Springer Science + Business Media Finance Inc (SSBM Finance Inc). SSBM Finance Inc is a Delaware corporation.

For information on translations, please e-mail rights@apress.com, or visit www.apress.com.

Apress and friends of ED books may be purchased in bulk for academic, corporate, or promotional use. eBook versions and licenses are also available for most titles. For more information, reference our Special Bulk Sales–eBook Licensing web page at www.apress.com/bulk-sales.

Any source code or other supplementary materials referenced by the author in this text is available to readers at www.apress.com. For detailed information about how to locate your book's source code, go to www.apress.com/source-code/.

This book is dedicated to my wife, Orna Vaingast

Contents at a Glance

Contents

About the Author

Shai Vaingast has been an engineer, an engineering manager, and a director of engineering since 1993. He has worked in the defense industry and in the medical device industry while being heavily involved with data processing and visualization. He has several patents.

About the Technical Reviewer

Leigh Sheneman is a Graduate Research Assistant in the BEACON Center for the Study of Evolution in Action at Michigan State University. She has spent many years helping non-profit organizations develop interactive applications that focus on efficiency. Sheneman holds degrees from Texas A&M University and The University of Texas at Tyler. She blogs on a wide range of topics at leighsheneman.com.

Acknowledgments

I'd like to thank the following individuals for their contributions to the first edition of the book (in alphabetical order): Shai Ayal, C.Titus Brown, Ehud Cohen, Bryan Crouse, Kylie Johnston, Michelle Lowman, Rich Lundeen, Frank Pohlmann, Ami Saguy, Sam Saguy, Janet Vaingast, Motty Vaingast, Orna Vaingast, and Arnon Zeira.

I would also like to thank the following individuals for their contributions to the second edition of the book (in alphabetical order): Alex Elberg, Linda Laflamme, and Leigh Sheneman.

Introduction

I have always been drawn to math and computers, ever since I was a kid playing computer games on my Sinclair ZX81. When I attended university, I had a special interest in numerical analysis, a field that I feel combines math and computers ideally. During my career, I learned of MATLAB, widely popular for digital signal processing, numerical analysis, and feedback and control. MATLAB's strong suits include a high-level programming language, excellent graphing capabilities, and numerous packages from almost every imaginable engineering field. But I found that MATLAB wasn't enough. I worked with very large files and needed the ability to manipulate both text and data. So I combined Perl, AWK, and Bash scripts to write programs that automate data analysis and visualization. And along the way, I've developed practices and ideas involving the organization of data, such as ways to ensure file names are unique and self-explanatory.

With the increasing popularity of the Internet, I learned about GNU/Linux and the open source movement. I've made an effort to use open source software whenever possible, and so I've learned of GNU-Octave and gnuplot, which together provide excellent scientific computing functionality. That fit well on my Linux machine: Bash scripts, Perl and AWK, GNU-Octave, and gnuplot.

Knowing I was interested in programming languages and open source software, a friend suggested I give Python a try. My first impression was that it was just another programming language: I could do almost anything I needed with Perl and Bash, resorting to C/C++ if things got hairy. And I'd still need GNU-Octave and gnuplot, so what was the advantage? Eventually, I did learn Python and discovered that it is far better than my previous collection of tools. Python provides something that is extremely appealing: it's a one-stop shop—you can do it all in Python.

I've shared my enthusiasm with friends and colleagues. Many who expressed interest with the ideas of data processing and visualization would ask, "Can you recommend a book that teaches the ideas you're preaching?" And I would tell them, "Of course, numerous books cover this subject! But they didn't want numerous books, just one, with information distilled to focus on data analysis and visualization. I realized there wasn't such a title, and this was how the idea for this book originated.

What's New in the Second Edition

Aside from using the most up-to-date version of Python that supports all the visualization packages (version 3.3 at the time of the writing the second edition), I've also introduced the following additional content:

- 3-D plots and graphs
- Non-rectangular contour plots
- *Matplotlib's basemap* toolkit
- Reading and writing MATLAB binary files
- Reading and writing data to *NumPy* arrays
- Reading and writing images to *NumPy* arrays
- Making movies
- IPython, IPython Notebook, and Spyder development environments

Who This Book Is For

Although this book is about software, the target audience is not necessarily programmers or computer scientists. I've assumed the reader's main line of work is research or R&D, in his or her field of interest, be it astrophysics, signal and image processing, or biology. The audience includes the following:

- Graduate and PhD students in exact and natural sciences (physics, biology, and chemistry) working on their thesis, dealing with large experimental data sets. The book also appeals to students working on purely theoretical projects, as they require simulations and means to analyze the results.

- R&D engineers in the fields of electrical engineering (EE), mechanical engineering, and chemical engineering: engineers working with large sets of data from multiple sources. In EE more specifically, signal processing engineers, communication engineers, and systems engineers will find the book appealing.

- Programmers and computer enthusiasts, unfamiliar with Python and the GNU/Linux world, but who are willing to dive into a new world of tools.

- Hobbyist astronomers and other hobbyists who deal with data and are interested in using Python to support their hobby.

The book can be appealing to these groups for different reasons. For scientists and engineers, the book provides the means to be more productive in their work, without investing a considerable amount of time learning new tools and programs that constantly change. For programmers and computer enthusiasts, the book can serve as an appetizer, opening up their world to Python. And because of the unique approach presented here, they might share the enthusiasm the author has for this wonderful software world. Perhaps it will even entice them to be part of the large and growing open source community, sharing their own code.

It is assumed that the reader does have minimal proficiency with a computer, namely that he or she must know how to manipulate files, install applications, view and edit files, and use applications to generate reports and presentations. A background in numerical analysis, signal processing, and image processing, as well as programming, is also helpful, but not required.

This book is not intended to serve as an encyclopedia of programming in Python and the covered packages. Rather, it is meant to serve as an introduction to data analysis and visualization in Python, and it covers most of the topics associated with that field.

How This Book Is Structured

The book is designed so that you can easily skip back and forth as you engage various topics.

Chapter 1 is a case study that introduces the topics discussed throughout the book: data analysis, data management, and, of course, data visualization. The case study involves reading GPS data, analyzing it, and plotting it along with relevant annotations (direction of travel, speed, etc.). A fully functional Python script will be built from the ground up, complemented with lots of explanations. The fruit of our work will be an eye-catching GPS route.

If you're new to data analysis and visualization, consider reading Chapter 2 first. The chapter describes how to set up a development environment to perform the tasks associated with data analysis and visualization in Python, including the selection of an OS, installing Python, and installing third-party packages.

If you're new to Python, your next stop should be Chapter 3. In this chapter, I swiftly discuss the Python programming language. I won't be overly rehashing basic programming paradigms; instead I'll provide a quick overview of the building blocks for the Python programming.

Regardless of your Python programming experience, I highly encourage you to read Chapter 4 before proceeding to the next chapters. Organization is the key to successful data analysis and visualization. This chapter covers organizing data files, pros and cons of different file formats, file naming conventions, finding data files, and automating file creation. The ideas in Chapter 4 are used throughout the book.

From there on out, you have several options. If you intend to process text and data files, proceed to Chapter 5. Chapter 5 covers text files from all aspects: I/O operations, string processing, the csv module, regular expressions, and localization and internationalization. If Chapter 5 leaves you wanting to know more about file processing, proceed to Chapter 10. Chapter 10 includes advanced file processing topics: binary files, command-line arguments, file and directory manipulation, and more. Both Chapters 5 and 10 are augmented with numerous examples.

If graphs and plots are your heart's desire, skip directly to Chapter 6. In Chapter 6 I examine *matplotlib* and explore its capabilities.

If you're interested in the numerical aspects of data, it is advised you read Chapter 7 first. Chapter 7 discusses the basic building blocks for scientific computing. Chapter 8 builds on Chapter 7 and includes more advanced topics such as numerical analysis and signal processing.

Image processing is an important aspect of data processing. Chapter 9 deals with tools available as part of the Python Imaging Library (*Pillow*) package and shows how to further expand the package and perform more complex image processing tasks.

Chapter 10 includes advanced file processing topics including binary files and random access, object serialization, command line parameters, file compression and more.

Finally, the Appendix provides additional source code listings used in the book.

Downloading the Code

The source code for this book is available to readers at www.apress.com in the Downloads section of this book's home page. Please feel free to visit the Apress web site and download all the code there. You can also check for errata and find related titles from Apress.

Contacting the Author

You can contact me at shai.vaingast@gmail.com.

CHAPTER 1

■ ■ ■

Navigating the World of Data Visualization

A Case Study

As an engineer, I work with data all the time. I parse log files, analyze data, estimate values, and compare the results with theory. Things don't always add up. So I double-check my analysis, perform more calculations, or run simulations to understand the results better. I refer to previous work because the ideas are similar or sometimes because they're dissimilar. I look at the graphs and realize I'm missing some crucial information. So I add the missing data, but it's noisy and needs filtering. Eventually, I realize my implementation of the algorithm is poor or that there is a better algorithm with better results, and so it's back to square one. It's an iterative process: tweak, test, and tweak again until I'm satisfied with the results.

Those are the tasks surrounding research and development (R&D) work. And to be honest, there's no systematic method. Most of the time, research is organized chaos. The emphasis, however, should be on "organized", not "chaos". Data should be analyzed and presented in a clear and coherent manner. Sources for graphs should be well understood and verified to be accurate. Algorithms should be tested and proven to be working as intended. The system should be flexible. Introducing new ideas and challenging previous methods should be easy, and testing new ideas on current data should be fast and efficient.

In this book I will attempt to address all the topics associated with data processing and visualization: managing files and directories, reading files of varying formats, and performing signal processing and numerical analysis in a high-level programming language similar to MATLAB and GNU-Octave. Along the way, I will teach you Python, a rich and powerful programming language.

In a nutshell, *Beginning Python Visualization* deals with the processing, analysis, manipulation, and visualization of data using the Python programming language. The book covers the following:

- Fundamentals of the Python programming language required for data analysis and visualization.

- Data files, format, and organization, as well as methods and guidelines for selecting file formats and storing and organizing data to enable fast, efficient data processing.

- Readily available Python packages for numerical analysis, signal and image processing, graphing and plotting, and more.

To demonstrate what's possible, this chapter will present a case study of using Python to gather GPS data, analyze the data prior to visualization, and plot the results.

1

Before we begin, however, you should understand a few fundamentals about Python. Python is an *interpreted* programming language. This means that each command is first read and then executed. This is in contrast to compiled programming languages, where the entire program is evaluated (compiled) and then executed. One of the important features of interpreted programming languages is that it's easy to run them interactively. That is, you can perform a command, examine the results, perform more commands, examine more results, and so on. The ability to run Python interactively is very useful, and it allows you to examine topics as you learn them.

It's also possible to run programs, referred to as *scripts*, non-interactively in Python, and there are several ways to do that. You can run scripts from the interactive Python prompt by issuing the command exec(open('scriptname.py').read()). Or you can enter python scriptname.py at the command-line interface of your operating system. If you're using IPython, you can issue the command run scriptname.py instead; and if you're running IDLE, the Python GUI, you can open the script and press **F5** to execute it. The .py extension is a common convention that distinguishes Python scripts from other files. The case study described in this chapter takes advantage of scripts, as well as running Python interactively.

■ **Note**   It is important to be able to distinguish between interactive sessions and Python scripts. When code starts with >>>, it means that the code was run on Python interactively. In cases where the ellipsis symbol (. . .) appears, it means that the code is a continuation of a previously interactively entered command. Lines of text following the symbols . . . or >>> are Python's response to the issued command. A code listing that does not start with >>>is a script written in an editor; in order to execute it, you will have to save it under scriptname.py (or some other name) and execute it as described previously.

Gathering Data

We spend considerable time recording and analyzing data. Data is stored in various formats depending on the tools used to collect it, the nature of the data (e.g., pictures vs. sampled analog data), the application that will later process the data, and personal preferences. Data files are of varying sizes; some are very large, others are smaller but in larger quantities. Data organization adds another level of complexity. Files can be stored in directories according to date, grouped together in one big directory or in a database, or adhere to a different scheme altogether. Typically, the number of data files or the amount of data per file is too large to allow skimming or browsing with an editor or viewer. Methods and tools are required to find the data and analyze it to produce meaningful results. As you'll soon see, Python provides all the tools required to do just that.

Case Study: GPS Data

You just got a USB GPS receiver for your birthday! You'd like to analyze GPS data and find out how often you exceed the speed limit and how much time you spend in traffic. You'd like to track data over a year, or even longer. You decide to record, analyze, and visualize the GPS data in Python.

Some hardware background: most USB GPS receivers behave as serial ports (this is also true for Bluetooth GPS devices). This means that once a GPS is connected (assuming it's installed properly), reading GPS data is as simple as opening the COM port associated with the GPS and reading the values. GPS values are typically clear text values: numbers and text. Of course, if you're planning on recording GPS data from your car, it would make a lot of sense to hook it up to a laptop rather than a desktop.

■ **Note** If you wish to follow along with the remainder of the chapter by issuing the commands yourself and then viewing the results, you might first want to refer to Chapter 2 and set up Python on your system. That said, it's not necessary, and you can follow along to get an understanding of the book and its purpose. In fact, I encourage you to come back to this chapter and read it again after you've had more experience with Python.

To be able to access the serial port from Python, we'll use the *pySerial* module. *pySerial,* as the name suggests, allows seamless access to serial ports (the module *pySerial* requires downloading and installing; see Chapter 2 for details). To use *pySerial*, we must first read the module to memory, that is, we must import it using the `import` command. If all goes well, we'll be presented with the Python prompt again.

```
>>> import serial
```

Scanning Serial Ports

Next, we need to find the serial port parameters: the baud rate and the port number. The baud rate is a GPS parameter, so it's best to consult the GPS manual (don't worry if you can't find this information, I'll discuss later how to "guess" what it is). The port number is determined by your operating system. If you're not sure how to find the port number—or if the port number keeps changing when you plug and unplug your GPS—you can use the following code to identify active serial ports (see Listing 1-1a).

Listing 1-1a. Scanning Serial Ports (Linux)

```
>>> from serial.tools.list_ports import comports
>>> comports()
```

```
[('/dev/ttyS3', 'ttyS3', 'n/a'), ('/dev/ttyS2', 'ttyS2', 'n/a'), ('/dev/ttyS1',
'ttyS1', 'n/a'), ('/dev/ttyS0', 'ttyS0', 'n/a'), ('/dev/ttyUSB0',
'Company name and device info should be here', 'USB VID:PID=xxxx:yyyy')]
```

Listing 1-1a tells us that there are four serial ports named /dev/ttySn, where n is an integer less than or equal to 3. There is also a port named /dev/ttyUSB0, and this is the port I'm looking for.

In Windows the code looks slightly different. The reason: the function `comport()` returns a *generator expression* instead of a list of available ports (you will learn more about generator expressions in Chapter 3). Listing 1-1b shows the Windows version of the script.

Listing 1-1b. Scanning Serial Ports (Windows)

```
>>> from serial.tools.list_ports import comports
>>> >>> list(comports())
```

```
[('COM6', 'Company name and device info', 'USB VID:PID=xxxx:yyyy')]
```

This is a rather quick introduction to Python! First, let's dissect the code line-by-line. The first line, `from serial.tools.list_ports import comports`, allows us to access a function named `comports()`. By using the `import` command, we load the function `comports()` and are able to use it. The function `comports()` is part of a module (a module is a collection of functions and data structures) named *tools*. The package *serial* is a collection of modules associated with the serial port, one of which is *tools*. Accessing modules within packages is performed using the dot operator. This is something you'll see a lot of in Python: `from package.module import function` (see Chapter 3 for more on this topic).

The second line calls the function `comports()`; in both the Linux and the Windows versions, it returns a list of available serial ports. In the Linux version, the list is returned by calling the function `comports()` directly. In the Windows version, a rather more complex mechanism is used, called a generator expression. This is a rather advanced topic and is discussed in Chapter 3, so we will skip it for now. In both versions, the list is composed of pairs of values. The first value is the location of the serial port, and the second is a description. Write down the serial port location; you'll need it for the next section.

Recording GPS Data

Let's start gathering data. Enter the code in Listing 1-2 and save it in the file, record_gps.py.

Listing 1-2. record_gps.py

```python
import time, serial

# change these parameters to your GPS parameters
port = '/dev/ttyUSB0'  # in Windows, set this to 'COMx'
ser = serial.Serial(port)

ser.baudrate = 4800
fmt = "../data/GPS-%4d-%02d-%02d-%02d-%02d-%02d.csv"

filename = fmt % time.localtime()[0:6]
f = open(filename, 'wb')
while True:
    line = ser.readline()
    f.write(line)
    print(line)
```

■ **Note** If your GPS does not support access through the serial port and you would like to follow along with this chapter, you can download an example data file from the official website for this book and continue with that.

This time, we've imported another module: *time*. The *time* module provides access to date and time functions, and we'll use those to name our GPS data files. We also introduce an important notion here: comments! Comments in Python are denoted by the # sign and are similar to C++ double slash notation, //. Everything in the line from that point onward is considered a remark. If the # sign is at the beginning of a line, then the entire line is a remark, usually describing the next line or block of code. The exception to the # sign indicating a remark occurs when it is quoted inside a string, as follows: "#".

Don't forget to change the value of the variable port to point at your serial port location as returned from the port scanning code in Listing 1-1. You should also set the proper baud rate. Determining the baud rate is not complex, but it's best to consult the manual. Mine turned out to be 4800; if you're not sure of yours, you can tweak this parameter. The script record_gps.py will print the output from the GPS onscreen so you can change the baud rate value (try the values 1200, 2400, 4800 and 9600) until you see some meaningful results (i.e., text and numbers).

Running record_gps.py (I'll get to how it works soon) yields GPS data:

```
>>> exec(open('record_gps.py').read())
```

```
$GPRMC,140053.00,A,4454.1740,N,09325.0143,W,000.0,128.7,300508,001.1,E,A*2E
$GPGGA,140053.00,4454.1740,N,09325.0143,W,1,09,01.1,00289.8,M,-030.7,M,,*5E
$GPGSA,A,3,21,15,18,24,26,29,06,22,,03,,,02.0,01.1,01.7*04
$GPGSV,3,1,12,21,75,306,40,15,59,075,46,18,57,269,49,24,56,115,46*79
$GPGSV,3,2,12,26,48,059,43,29,27,188,48,06,25,308,41,22,18,257,33*7D
$GPGSV,3,3,12,08,14,060,,03,11,320,32,09,06,144,,16,04,311,*7C
$GPRMC,140054.00,A,4454.1740,N,09325.0143,W,000.0,128.7,300508,001.1,E,A*29
$GPGGA,140054.00,4454.1740,N,09325.0143,W,1,09,01.1,00289.8,M,-030.7,M,,*59
$GPGSA,A,3,21,15,18,24,26,29,06,22,,03,,,02.0,01.1,01.7*04
```

Data is being recorded to file as it is displayed. When you wish to stop viewing and recording GPS data, press **Ctrl+C**. If you're running in an interactive Python, be sure to close the serial port once you issue **Ctrl+C**, or you won't be able to rerun the script record_gps.py. To close the port, issue the following command:

```
>>> ser.close()
```

It's also a good idea to close the file:

```
>>> f.close()
```

Let's take a closer look at record_gps.py, to gain insight into how it works. The heart of the script lies in the following lines of code:

```
while True:
    line = ser.readline()
    f.write(line)
    print(line)
```

This is a straightforward implementation. The first line, while True:, instructs that the following block should be run indefinitely; that is, in an infinite loop. That's why you need to press **Ctrl+C** to stop recording. The next three lines are then executed continuously. They read a line of text from the serial port, store it to file, and print it to screen. Reading GPS data is carried out by the command line = ser.readline(). Writing that data to a file for later processing is done by f.write(line). Printing the data to screen so the user has some visual feedback is done with print(line).

■ **Note**   The indentation (the number of spaces) in Python is important because it groups commands together. This is also true when using Python in an interactive mode. All lines with the same indentation are considered one block. Python's indentation is equivalent to C/C++ curly braces—{}.

Data Organization

Let's turn to selecting file format, file naming conventions, and data location. There isn't a single, good solution that fits all cases, but the methodologies and ideas are simple. The method I'll use here is based on file names. I'll show you how to name data files in a way that lends itself easily to automatic processing later on.

File Format

A file format is a set of rules describing the contents of a file. For the GPS problem, we'll choose the Comma Separated Values (CSV) file format. CSV files are text files with values separated by commas, as in this example:

```
$GPGSV,3,2,12,06,43,096,37,07,41,291,38,16,39,052,32,27,34,291,34*76
$GPGSV,3,3,12,19,26,152,35,08,06,280,,10,00,337,,00,00,000,*74
$GPRMC,233547.32,A,4455.6446,N,09329.3400,W,030.1,272.5,040608,001.1,E,A*2E
$GPGGA,233547.32,4455.6446,N,09329.3400,W,1,06,02.8,00299.0,M,-030.7,M,,*5A
```

CSV is a popular format recognized by most spreadsheets; database applications; and, of course, text editors, seeing as they're really just text files. As it turns out, the data the from most USB-GPS receivers is already comma separated, so all that's required is to save this information to a file, as-is.

File Naming Conventions

Now let's look at how to select proper file names for our data files. File names should be unique, so that files won't be accidentally overwritten. File names should also be descriptive; that is, they should tell us something about the contents. Lastly, we'd like the file name extension to tell us how to view the file. The latter is typically achieved by selecting a proper extension—.csv, in our case. Here are the naming conventions I chose for this example:

- File names holding GPS data will start with the text "GPS-".

- Next will come the date and time in ISO format, with the separating colons omitted and a hyphen between the date and time: YYYY-mm-dd-HH-MM-SS, where YYYY stands for year, mm for month, dd for day, HH for hours, MM for minutes, and SS for seconds. In cases where a value is one digit and two digits are required, the value will be padded with a preceding zero. For example, the month of May will be denoted by 05, not 5. For additional information regarding the ISO format, refer to ISO 8601, "Data elements and interchange formats—Information interchange—Representation of dates and times" (http://www.iso.org).

- All files will have a .csv extension.

Following these conventions, a file name might look like this:

```
GPS-2008-05-30-09-10-52.csv
```

Data Location

This is where we store data files:

- All data files are stored in the directory, `data`. All scripts are stored in directory, `src`. Both directories are under the same parent directory, `Ch1`. So, a relative path from `src` to `data` is `../data`. We'll follow this convention throughout the book.

- It's also a good idea to add a `Readme.txt` file. Readme files are clear text files describing the contents of a directory, in as much detail as deemed reasonable. Such files typically describe the data source, data acquisition system, person in charge of data gathering, reason for gathering the data, and so on. Here's an example:

```
Data recorded from a USB GPS receiver, connected to a Lenovo laptop T60.
Data was gathered via the serial port stored to clear text files (CSV).
Measurements were taken to estimate speed and time spent in traffic.
Gathered by Shai Vaingast.
Date: throughout 2008, see file timestamps.
```

Data Analysis

Once the data is organized and accessible in files, the next step is to extract information. Information can be a value, a graph, or a report pertaining to the problem at hand.

The idea is to use Python's scripting abilities and the wide range of readily available packages to write a fully automated application to process, analyze, and visualize data. Scripts are small pieces of code that are written relatively quickly in a high-level programming language. The key word here is productivity, the ability to change and test algorithms and extract results fast. Scripts might not be highly efficient in terms of processing speed, but written properly, they should not slow down running times. For example, a script might generate graphs or search the hard drive for data files, analyze log files, and extract the maximum and minimum temperatures. In our case, of course, we'll use them to analyze GPS data.

In our GPS case study, we'll use the following algorithm:

1. Compile a list of all the data files.

2. For each file:

    a. Read the data.

    b. Process the data.

    c. Plot the data.

Walking Directories

To compile a list of all the files with GPS data, we use the function os.walk() provided with the module *os*, which is part of the Python Standard Library. To use *os*, we issue import os:

```
>>> import os
>>> for root, dirs, files in os.walk('../data'):
...     print(root, dirs, files)
...
```

```
../data [] ['GPS-2008-05-30-09-00-50.csv', 'GPS-2008-05-30-09-10-52.csv',
'Readme.txt']
```

■ **Note**   To be able to change directories within the Python interpreter, first issue import os. Then, to change to a directory, issue os.chdir(directory_path). To list directory contents, you can use os.listdir(directory_path). Some interpreters, like IPython, let you use, among other enhancements, shell-like commands such as cd and ls, which add considerable usability.

The function os.walk() iterates through the directory data and its subdirectories recursively, looking for files and folders, and then storing the results in variables root, dirs, and files. The second line prints out the root directory for the search. In our case, that means ../data (notice the relative path), then the subdirectories, and lastly, the files themselves, in a list. I've only recorded two data files thus far; but over time, more data is added to this folder, and the number of files can increase substantially. Since we have no subdirectories in folder data, the output corresponding to dirs should be an empty list, which is denoted by [].

Using the function os.walk() is a bit of overkill here. In our case, directory data doesn't have any subdirectories, and we could have just as easily listed the contents of the directory using the os.listdir() function call, as follows:

```
>>> os.listdir('../data')
```

```
['GPS-2008-30-05-09-00-50.csv', 'GPS-2008-30-05-09-10-52.csv', 'Readme.txt']
```

However, os.walk() is very useful. It's not uncommon to have files grouped together in directories. And within those directories, you might have subdirectories holding still more files. For example, you might want to group files in accordance with the GPS that recorded the data. Or if another driver is recording GPS data, you might want to put that data in a separate subdirectory within your data directory. In those cases, os.walk() is exactly what's needed.

Now that we have a list of all the files in directory data, we can process only those with the .csv extension. We can do this using the endswith() function, which checks whether a string ends with "csv". Files that do not end with "csv" are skipped using the continue command: continue instructs the for loop to skip the current execution and proceed to the next element. Files that do end with "csv" are read and processed. To create a full file name path from the directory and the file name, we use the function os.path.join(), as shown in Listing 1-3.

Listing 1-3. Processing Only CSV Files

```
for root, dirs, files in os.walk('data'):
    for filename in files:
        # create full file name including path
        cur_file = os.path.join(root, filename)
        if filename.endswith('csv'):
            y = read_csv_file(cur_file)
        else:
            continue

    # only files with the .csv extension from here on
```

Reading CSV Files

Our next step is to read the files. Again, we turn to Python's built-in modules, this time the *csv* module. Although the CSV file format is quite popular, there's no clear definition, and each spreadsheet and database employs its own "dialect." The files we'll be processing adhere to the most basic CSV file dialect, so we'll use the default behavior of Python's *csv* module. Since we'll be reading several CSV files, it stands to reason that we should define a function to perform this task. Listing 1-4 shows this function.

Listing 1-4. A Function to Read CSV Files

```
def read_csv_file(filename):
    """Reads a CSV file and return it as a list of rows."""

    data = []
    for row in csv.reader(open(filename)):
        data.append(row)
    return data
```

The first line defines a function named read_csv_file(). CSV file support is introduced with the *csv* module, so we have to import csv before calling the function. The function takes one variable, filename, and returns an array of rows holding data in the file. In other words, every line read is processed and becomes a list, with every comma-separated value as one element in that list. The function returns an array of such lists, as in this example:

```
>>> import csv
>>> x = read_csv_file('../data/GPS-2008-06-04-09-03-45.csv')
>>> len(x)
```

3683

```
>>> x[10]
```

```
['$GPGSV', '3', '3', '12', '29', '10', '040', '', '16', '01', '302', '', '26', '01',
'037', '', '00', '00', '000', '*72']
```

```
>>> x[1676]
```

```
['$GPGSV', '3', '1', '12', '21', '86', '258', '43', '18', '66', '286', '20', '15', '50',
'059', '45', '24', '44', '126', '43*72']
```

len(x) tells us the size of the array of lists. It's also a crude way for us to ensure that data was actually read into the array.

The second line in the function is called a *docstring*, and it is characterized by three quotes (""") surrounding the text in the following manner: """dosctring""". In this case, a docstring is used to document the function; that is, it enables us to explain what it does. Issuing the command help(funcname) yields its docstring:

```
>>> help(read_csv_file)
```

```
Help on function read_csv_file in module __main__:

read_csv_file(filename)
    Reads a CSV file and return it as a list of rows.
```

You should use help() whenever you need a reminder of what a function does. help() can be invoked with functions as well as modules. For example, the following invokes help on module *csv*:

```
>>> help(csv)
```

```
Help on module csv:

NAME
    csv - CSV parsing and writing.

DESCRIPTION
    This module provides classes that assist in the reading and writing
    of Comma Separated Value (CSV) files, and implements the interface
    described by PEP 305.  Although many CSV files are simple to parse,
    the format is not formally defined by a stable specification and
    is subtle enough that parsing lines of a CSV file with something
    like line.split(",") is bound to fail.  The module supports three
    basic APIs: reading, writing, and registration of dialects.
```

The line data = [] declares a variable named data and initializes it as an empty list. We will use data to store the values from the CSV file.

The *csv* module helps us read CSV files by automating a lot of the tasks associated with reading them. I will discuss CSV files and the *csv* module in more detail in Chapters 4 and 5; this chapter will only provide an overview.

Here are the steps for reading CSV files with the *csv* module:

1. Open the file for reading.

2. Create a csv.reader object. The csv.reader object has functions that help us read CSV files.

   a. Using the csv.reader object, read the data from the file, a row at a time.

   b. Append every row to the variable data.

3. Close the file.

Let's try this, a step at a time:

```
>>> import csv
>>> f = open('../data/GPS-2008-06-04-09-03-45.csv')
>>> cr = csv.reader(f)
>>> for row in cr:
...     print(row)
```

```
['$GPGSA', 'A', '3', '21', '18', '15', '24', '', '22', '', '', '', '', '', '',
'03.5', '02.2', '02.7*09']
['$GPGSV', '3', '1', '12', '21', '86', '267', '39', '18', '66', '286', '44',
'15', '51', '060', '43', '24', '45', '125', '30*7A']
['$GPGSV', '3', '2', '12', '06', '28', '300', '33', '22', '27', '265', '31',
'03', '18', '312', '27', '29', '15', '185', '31*7C']
['$GPGSV', '3', '3', '12', '09', '15', '138', '31', '16', '00', '301', '',
'19', '00', '332', '', '00', '00', '000', '*70']
['$GPRMC', '140706.24', 'A', '4455.6241', 'N', '09328.0519', 'W', '011.4',
'152.7', '040608', '001.2', 'E', 'A*25']
['$GPGGA', '140706.24', '4455.6241', 'N', '09328.0519', 'W', '1', '04', '03.0',
'00295.1', 'M', '-030.7', 'M', '', '*51']
['$GPGSA', 'A', '3', '21', '18', '15', '24', '', '', '', '', '', '', '', '',
'08.9', '03.0', '08.4*04']
```

```
>>> f.close()
```

First, we open the data file and assign it to variable f. The opened file can now be referred to by the variable f. Next, we create a `csv.reader` object, `cr`. We associate the `csv.reader` object, `cr`, with the file f. We then iterate through every row of the `csv.reader` object and print that row. Lastly, we close the file by calling `f.close()`. It is considered good practice to close the file once you're done with it; but if you neglect to do so, Python will close the file automatically once the variable f is no longer in use.

■ **Note** You may, after issuing the commands, receive an error similar to this: `UnicodeEncodeError: 'charmap' codec can't encode character '\uABCD'`. If this happens, open the GPS file in a text editor and make sure the file contains proper alpha-numeric characters. Be sure to delete lines with non-alpha-numeric characters.

Python also lets you implement *cascade functions*, where you can call new functions based on the results of other functions. This process can be repeated several times. Cascading (usually) adds clarity and produces more elegant scripts. In our case, the variable f isn't really important to us, so we discard it after we attach it to a `csv.reader` object. Instead of the preceding code, we can write the following, by cascading the functions:

```
>>> cr = csv.reader(open('../data/GPS-2008-06-04-09-03-45.csv')):
>>> for row in cr:
...     print(row)
```

The same holds true for variable `cr`, for which we can cascade several functions and generate a more compact line of code:

```
>>> for row in csv.reader(open('../data/GPS-2008-06-04-09-03-45.csv')):
...     print(row)
```

While the script might be shorter, there's no performance gain. It is therefore suggested that you cascade functions only if it adds clarity; there's a good chance you'll be editing this code later on, and it's important to be able to understand what's going on. In fact, not cascading functions might be useful at times because you might need access to intermediate variables (such as `f` and `cr` in our case).

The `csv.reader` object converts each row we read into a row of fields, in the form of a list. That row is then appended to a list of rows and stored in the variable `data`.

■ **Note** By now, you've seen the dot symbol (.) used several times. Its use might be a bit confusing, so an explanation is in order. The dot symbol is used to access function members of modules, as well as function members of objects (classes). You've seen it in member functions of modules, such as `csv.reader()`, but also for objects, such as `f.read()`. In the latter, it means that the file object has a member function `read()` and that the function is called to operate on variable `f`. To access these functions, we use the dot operator. We'll touch on this again in Chapter 3. Lastly, we use the ellipsis symbol (...) to denote line continuation when interactively entering commands in Python.

Analyzing GPS Data

Also known as NMEA 0183, the GPS format contains many header stamps, some of which hold useful information for our task. Let's take a closer look at the GPS data:

- Each row seems to start with a text header stamp, beginning with the characters $GP.
- There are several header stamps (e.g., $GPGSA and $GPRMC).
- Additional values follow the header, most of which are numeric.

■ **Note** NMEA stands for the National Marine Electronics Association; see `http://www.nmea.org` for more information. The NMEA 0183 data format is described at `http://www.gpsinformation.org/dale/nmea.htm`.

As mentioned earlier, several $GP header stamps appear in our data files, but we need to determine which ones exactly are relevant to us. First, it would be nice to know which header stamps from the NMEA standard are even present in our data files. One option would be to open the files, look for the headers, and jot down every new header once we see it. Another, of course, would be to use Python to do that for us.

Python is a very high-level programming language. As such, it has built-in support for *dictionaries* (also known as associative arrays in Perl), which are data structures that have a one-to-one relationship between a key and a value, very much like real dictionaries. Traditional dictionaries, however, often have several values for a key; that is, they have several interpretations (values) for one word (key). You can easily implement this in Python using the dictionary object, `dict`, as well by assigning a list value to a key. That way, you can have several entries per one key, because the key is associated with a list that can hold several values. In reality, it's still a one-to-one relationship, but enough about that for now. I'll cover dictionaries in more detail in future chapters. What we want to do here is use a dictionary object to hold the number of times a header is encountered. Our key will be the GPS header stamp, and our value will be a number that indicates occurrence. We'll increment the value whenever a key is encountered, as shown in Listing 1-5.

Listing 1-5. Function list_gps_commands( )

```
def list_gps_commands(data):
    """Counts the number of times a GPS command is observed.

Returns a dictionary object."""

    gps_cmds = dict()
    for row in data:
        try:
            gps_cmds[row[0]] += 1
        except KeyError:
            gps_cmds[row[0]] = 1

    return gps_cmds
```

There are few things to keep in mind about this function. First, the docstring spans multiple lines, which is one of the key benefits of docstrings. Docstrings will display all the spaces and line breaks as shown in the function itself. Second, we initialize a variable, gps_cmds, to be our dictionary. We then process every list in the GPS data: we only care about the first element of every row, as that's the value that holds the GPS header stamps. We then increment the value associated with the key: gps_cmds[row[0]] += 1. We use the += operation to increment the value by 1, similar to how it's done in C (Python, however, does not use the ++ operator). If the key does not exist, which will happen whenever we encounter a new header stamp, an exception will be raised. We catch the exception with our except KeyError statement. In the case of an exception, we set the dictionary value associated with the key to 1.

We can write the function list_gps_commands() even more compactly using the dictionary method get(); see Chapter 3 for details.

Let's analyze some GPS data:

```
>>> x = read_csv_file('../data/GPS-2008-05-30-09-00-50.csv')
>>> list_gps_commands(x)
```

```
{'$GPGSA': 282, '$GPGSV': 846, '$GPGGA': 282, '$GPRMC': 283}
```

It turns out there are four distinct GPS headers being generated by my GPS. Of those, only two interest us: $GPGSV, which holds the number of satellites in view (Hey! It's really important!); and $GPRMC, which holds location and velocity information.

What we'd like to do is code a function that takes the GPS data and, whenever the header field is $GPGSV or $GPRMC, extracts the information and stores it in numerical arrays that will be easier to manipulate later on. Numerical arrays are introduced with the *NumPy* module, so we have to import numpy. Since we'll be using a lot of the functionality of *NumPy*, *SciPy*, and *matplotlib*, an easier approach would be to import pylab, which imports all these modules, as follows:

```
>>> from pylab import *
```

■ **Note**   The name *PyLab* comes from Python and MATLAB. The *PyLab* module provides MATLAB-like functionality in Python.

Extracting GPS Data

In the case of a $GPGSV header, the number of satellites is the fourth entry. In the case of a $GPRMC header, we have a bit more interesting information. The second field is the timestamp, the fourth field is the latitude, the sixth field is the longitude, and the eighth field is the velocity. Again, refer to the NMEA 0183 format for more details. Table 1-1 summarizes the fields and their values in a $GPRMC line.

Table 1-1. *$GPRMC Information (Excerpt)*

Field Name	Index	Format
Header	0	$GPRMC (fixed)
Timestamp	1	*hhmmss.ss*
Latitude	3	*DDMM.MMM*
Longitude	5	*DDDMM.MMM*
Velocity	7	*VVV.V*

We need to keep in mind some caveats regarding the information in $GPRMC. For example, let's look at the timestamp of an arbitrary line:

```
>>> x[12]
```

```
['$GPRMC', '140055.00', 'A', '4454.1740', 'N', '09325.0143', 'W', '000.0',
'128.7', '300508', '001.1', 'E', 'A*28']
```

In this output, the timestamp appears as '140055.00'. This follows the format *hhmmss.ss* where *hh* are two digits representing the hour (it will always consist of two digits—if the hour is one digit, say 7 in the morning, a 0 will be added before it), *mm* are two digits representing the minute (again, always two digits), and *ss.ss* are five characters (four digits plus the dot) representing seconds and fractions of seconds. There's also a North/South field, as well as an East/West field. Here, for simplicity, we assume northern hemisphere, but you can easily change these values by reading the entire $GPRMC structure.

■ **Note** In the ISO time format, we've used *HHMMSS* to denote hours minutes and seconds. In this case, we follow the convention in NMEA, which uses *hhmmss.ss* for hours, minutes, and seconds, and then sets *DD* and *MM* to angular degrees and minutes.

The timestamp string is a bit hard to work with, especially when plotting data. The first reason is that it's a string, not a number. But even if you translate it to a number, the system does not lend itself nicely to plotting because there are 60 seconds in a minute, not 100. So what we want to do is "linearize" the timestamp. To achieve this, we translate the timestamp as seconds elapsed since midnight, as follows: $T = hh * 3600 + mm * 60 + ss.ss$.

The second issue we have is that *hh*, *mm*, and *ss.ss* are strings, not numbers. Multiplying a string in Python does something completely different than what we want here. In this case, we have to first convert the strings to numerical values. Specifically, we want to use floating point numbers (i.e., float) because of the decimal point in the string representing the seconds. This all folds nicely into the following:

```
>>> row = x[18]
>>> row
```

```
['$GPRMC', '140056.00', 'A', '4454.1740', 'N', '09325.0143', 'W', '000.0',
'128.7', '300508', '001.1', 'E', 'A*2B']
```

```
>>> float(row[1][0:2])*3600+float(row[1][2:4])*60+float(row[1][4:6])
```

```
50456.0
```

The operator [ ] denotes the index, so row[0] is the header, and row[1] is the second field of row (counting starts at zero), which is a string. The first two characters of a string are denoted by [0:2]; cutting characters from a string is known as ***string slicing***. So, to access the first two characters of the first field, we write row[1][0:2]. Upcoming chapters will include more about strings and the methods available for slicing them.

Next, we tackle latitude and longitude. We face the same issue as with the timestamp, only here we deal with degrees. Latitude follows the format *DDMM.MMM*, where *DD* stands for degrees and *MM.MMM* stands for minutes. This time, we will use degrees; converting the minutes to degrees make the later calculations simpler to follow. To translate the latitude into decimal degrees, we need to divide the minutes by 60:

```
>>> row = x[18]
>>> row
```

```
['$GPRMC', '140056.00', 'A', '4454.1740', 'N', '09325.0143', 'W', '000.0',
'128.7', '300508', '001.1', 'E', 'A*2B']
```

```
>>> float(row[3][0:2])+float(row[3][2:])/60.0
```

```
44.9029
```

For latitude information we require the fourth field, hence row[3]. This example also introduces another notation, [2:], which refers to the slice of the string from the third character until the end.

It's important to know that since Python 3.x the default behavior of division has changed. In Python 2.x, the default division was integer division. In Python 3.x, the default division is a floating-point division. The results from issuing the expression 100/60 return two different results in Python 2.x and Python 3.x, as follows:

In Python 2.x, dividing 100 by 60 returns the following result:

```
>>> 100/60
```

```
1
```

In Python 3.x, it returns the following:

```
>>> 100/60
```

```
1.6666666666666667
```

To ensure a floating point division in Python 2.x, as common practice, it is a good idea to add a decimal point, i.e., `100/60.0` (notice the dot zero). Adding a decimal point also works in Python 3.x (although it's not needed because floating-point division is the default). But what if you'd like to perform an integer division in Python 3.x? The answer is simple: use an integer division operator, denoted by `//`:

```
>>> 100//60
```

```
1
```

In this book, we will use Python 3.x's default floating-point division.

It's also possible to use the function `int()` to cast values to integer values, as follows:

```
>>> int(100/60)
```

```
1
```

Longitude information is similar to latitude with a minor difference: longitude degrees are three characters instead of two (up to 180 degrees, not just up to 90 degrees), so the indices to the strings are different.

Listing 1-6 presents the entire function to process GPS data.

Listing 1-6. Function process_gps_data( )

```python
NMI = 1852.0
def process_gps_data(data):
    """Processes GPS data, NMEA 0183 format.

Returns a tuple of arrays: latitude, longitude, velocity [km/h],
time [sec] and number of satellites.
See also: http://www.gpsinformation.org/dale/nmea.htm.
    """

    latitude   = []
    longitude  = []
    velocity   = []
    t_seconds  = []
    num_sats   = []

    for row in data:
        if row[0] == '$GPGSV':
            num_sats.append(float(row[3]))
        elif row[0] == '$GPRMC':
            t_seconds.append(float(row[1][0:2])*3600 + \
```

```
                float(row[1][2:4])*60+float(row[1][4:6]))
        latitude.append(float(row[3][0:2]) + \
            float(row[3][2:])/60.0)
        longitude.append((float(row[5][0:3]) + \
            float(row[5][3:])/60.0))
        velocity.append(float(row[7])*NMI/1000.0)

return (array(latitude), array(longitude), \
    array(velocity), array(t_seconds), array(num_sats))
```

Here are some notes about the process_gps_data() function:

- NMI is defined as 1852.0, which is one nautical mile in meters and also one minute on the equator. The reason the constant NMI is not defined in the function is that we'd like to use it outside the function, as well.

- We initialize the return values latitude, longitude, velocity, t_seconds, and num_sats by setting them to an empty list: [ ]. Initializing the lists creates them and allows us to use the append() method, which adds values to the lists.

- The if and elif statements are self-explanatory: if is a conditional clause, and elif is equivalent to saying "else, if." That is, if the first condition didn't succeed, but the next condition succeeds, execute the following block.

- The symbol \ that appears on the several calculations and on the return line indicates that the operation continues on the next line.

- Lastly, the return value is a tuple of arrays. A *tuple* is an immutable sequence, meaning you cannot change it. So tuple means an unchangeable sequence of items (as opposed to a list, which is a mutable sequence). The reason we return a tuple (and not a two-dimensional array) is that we might have different lengths of lists to return: the length of the number of satellites list may be different than the length of the longitude list, since they originated from different header stamps.

Here's how you call process_gps_data():

```
>>> y = read_csv_file('../data/GPS-2008-05-30-09-00-50.csv')
>>> (lat, long, v, t, sats) = process_gps_data(y)
```

The second line introduces sequence unpacking, which allows multiple assignments. Armed with all these functions, we're ready to plot some data!

Data Visualization

Our next step is to visualize the data. We'll be relying on the *matplotlib* package heavily. We've already imported *matplotlib* with the command from pylab import *, so there's no additional importing needed at the moment. It's time to read the data and plot the course.

Our first problem is that the information is given in latitude and longitude. Latitude and longitude are spherical coordinates, that is, those are points on a sphere, the earth. But we want a map-like plot, which uses Cartesian coordinates; that is, *x* and *y*. So first we have to transform the spherical coordinates to Cartesian coordinates. We'll use the quick-and-dirty method shown in Listing 1-7 to do this; this approach is actually quite accurate, as long as the distances traveled are small relative to the radius of the earth.

Listing 1-7. "Quick-and-Dirty" Spherical to Cartesian Transformation

```
x = longitude*NMI*60.0*cos(latitude)
y = latitude*NMI*60.0
```

To justify this to yourself, consider the following reasoning: As you go up to the North Pole, the circumference at the location you're at gets smaller and smaller, until at the North Pole it's zero. So at latitude 0°, the equator, each degree (longitude) means more distance traveled than at latitude 45°. That's why x is a function of the longitude value itself, but also of the latitude: the greater the latitude, the smaller a longitude change is in terms of distance. On the other hand, y, which is north to south, is not dependent on longitude.

The next thing to understand is that the earth is a sphere; and whenever we plot an x-y map, we're only really plotting a projection of that sphere on a plane of our choosing. Hence, we denote it by *(px,py)*, where *p* stands for "projection." We'll take the southeastern-most point as the start of the GPS data projection: *(px,py) = (0,0)*. This translates into the code shown in Listing 1-8.

Listing 1-8. Projecting the Traveled Course to Cartesian Coordinates

```
py = (lat-min(latitude))*NMI*60.0
px = (long-min(longitude))*NMI*60.0*cos(D2R*latitude)
```

Some things to note include:

- Variables py and px are arrays of floating-point values. With *NumPy*, we can operate on entire arrays seamlessly.

- D2R is a constant equal to $\pi/180$, converting degrees to radians.

- To set the y-axis at the minimum latitude and the x-axis at the minimum longitude, we subtract the minimum latitude and minimum longitude values from latitude and longitude values, respectively.

GPS Location Plot

Now comes the moment we've been waiting for: plotting GPS data. To be able to follow along and plot data, be sure to define the functions read_csv_file() and process_gps_data() as previously detailed and set the file name variable to point to your GPS data file. I've suppressed *matplotlib* responses, so that the code is easier to follow:

```
>>> filename = 'GPS-2008-05-30-09-00-50.csv'
>>> y = read_csv_file('../data/'+filename)
>>> (lat, long, v, t, sats) = process_gps_data(y)
>>> px = (long-min(long))*NMI*60.0*cos(D2R*lat)
>>> py = (lat-min(lat))*NMI*60.0
>>> figure()
>>> gca().axes.invert_xaxis()
>>> plot(px, py, 'b', label='Cruising', linewidth=3)
>>> title(filename[:-4])
>>> legend(loc='upper left')
>>> xlabel('east-west (meters)')
>>> ylabel('south-north (meters)')
>>> grid()
>>> axis('equal')
>>> show()
```

Figure 1-1 shows the result, which is rather pleasing.

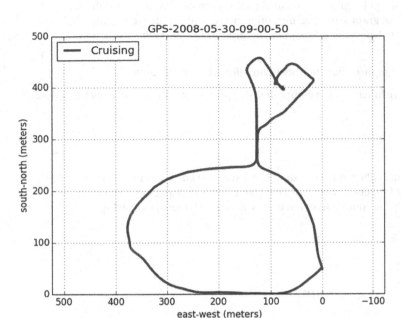

Figure 1-1. GPS data

We've used a substantial number of new functions, all part of the *matplotlib* package: plot(), grid(), xlabel(), legend(), and more. Most of them are self-explanatory:

- xlabel(string_value) and ylabel(string_value) prints a label on the x- and y-axis, respectively. We use title(string_value) to print a caption above the graph. The string value in the title is the file name up to the end, minus four characters (so as to not display ".csv"). We accomplish this by using string slicing with a negative value, which means "from the end."

- legend() prints the labels associated with the graph in a legend box. legend() is highly configurable (see help(legend) for details). The example plots the legend at the top-left corner.

- grid() plots the grid lines. You can control the behavior of the grid quite extensively.

- plot() requires additional explanation because it is the most versatile. The command plot(px, py, 'b', label='Cruising', linewidth=3) plots px and py with the color blue as specified by the character 'b'. The plot is labeled "Cruising"; so later on, when we call the legend() function, the proper text will be associated with the data. Finally, we set the line width to 3.

- The function axis() controls the behavior of the graph axis. Normally, I don't call the axis() function because plot() does a decent job of selecting the right values. However, in this case it's important to visualize the data properly. That means we need both the x- and y-axes with equal increments, so the graph is true to the path depicted. This is achieved by calling axis('equal'). There are other values to control axis behavior, as described by help(axis).

- Lastly, `gca().axes.invert_xaxis()` is a rather exotic addition. It stems from the way we like to view maps and directions. In longitude, increasing values are displayed from right to left. However, in mathematical graphs, increasing values are typically displayed from left to right. This function call instructs the x-axis to be incrementing from right to left, just like maps.

- When we're done preparing the graph, calling the `show()` function displays the output.

Matplotlib, which includes the preceding functions, is a comprehensive plotting package, and it will be explored in greater detail in Chapter 6.

Annotating the Graph

We'd like to add some more information to the GPS graph. For example, we'd like to know where we stopped and where we were speeding. For this we use the function `find()`, which is part of the *PyLab* package. The function `find()` returns an array of indices that satisfy the condition. In our case, we want to know the following:

```
>>> STANDING_KMH = 10.0
>>> SPEEDING_KMH = 50.0
>>> Istand = find(v < STANDING_KMH)
>>> Ispeed = find(v > SPEEDING_KMH)
>>> Icruise = find((v >=STANDING_KMH) & (v <= SPEEDING_KMH))
```

We also calculate when we're cruising (i.e., not speeding nor standing) for future processing.

To annotate the graph with these points, we add another plot on top of our current plot. However, this time we change the color of the plot, and we use symbols instead of a solid blue line. The combination `'sg'` indicates a green square symbol (g for green, s for square); the combination `'or'` indicates a red circle (r for red, o for circle). I suggest you use different symbols for standing and speeding, not just colors, because the graph might be printed on a monochrome printer. The function `plot()` supports an assortment of symbols and colors; consult with the interactive help for details. The values we plot are only those returned by the `find()` function:

```
>>> plot(px[Istand], py[Istand], 'sg', label='Standing')
>>> plot(px[Ispeed], py[Ispeed], 'or', label='Speeding!')
>>> legend(loc='upper left')
```

Figure 1-2 shows the outcome.

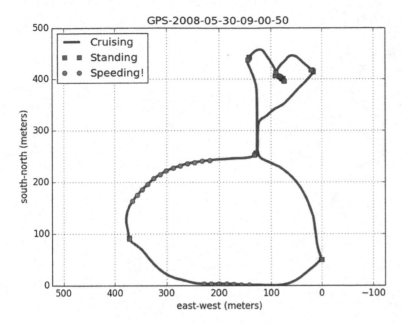

Figure 1-2. *GPS data with additional speed information*

We'd also like to know the direction the car is going. To implement this, we'll use the text() function, which allows us to write a string to an arbitrary location in the graph. So, to add the text "Hi" at location (10,10), we issue the command text(10, 10, 'Hi'). One of the nice features of the text() function is that we can rotate the text at an arbitrary angle. To plot "Hi" at location (10,10) at 45 degrees, we issue text(10,10, 'Hi', rotation=45). Our implementation of heading information involves rotating the text ">>>" at the angle the car is heading. We'll only do this ten times, so as not to clutter the graph with ">" symbols. Calculating the direction the car is heading at a given point, i, is shown in Listing 1-9.

Listing 1-9. Calculating the Heading

```
dx = px[i+1]-px[i]
dy = py[i+1]-py[i]
heading = arctan2(dy, dx)
```

Although we could have calculated the heading using arctan(dy/dx), I chose to use the function arctan2(dy,dx) instead. The benefits of using arctan2() over arctan() are twofold: 1) there's no division that might cause a divide-by-zero exception in case dx is zero, and 2) arctan2() preserves the angle from -180 degrees to 180 degrees, whereas arctan() produces values between 0 degrees and 180 degrees only. The following code adds the direction symbols:

```
>>> for i in range(0, len(v), len(v)//10-1):
...     text(px[i], py[i], ">>>", \
...         rotation = arctan2(py[i+1]-py[i], -(px[i+1]-px[i]))/D2R, \
...         ha='center')
```

Notice that I've used integer division to calculate the ten indices as follows: len(v)//10-1. The reason: indices to arrays must be integers, not floats (there's no 1.37th element in an array).

Figure 1-3 shows the resulting graph.

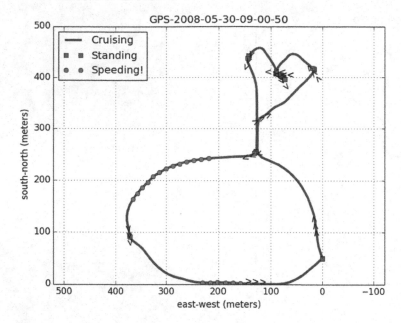

Figure 1-3. *GPS graph with heading*

Velocity Plot

We now turn to plotting a graph of the speed. This is a lot simpler:

```
>>> figure()
>>> t = (t-t[0])/60.0
>>> plot(t, v, 'k')
>>> plot([t[0], t[-1]], [STANDING_KMH, STANDING_KMH], '-g')
>>> text(t[0], STANDING_KMH, \
...     " Standing threshold: "+str(STANDING_KMH))
>>> plot([t[0], t[-1]], [SPEEDING_KMH, SPEEDING_KMH], '-r')
>>> text(t[0], SPEEDING_KMH, \
...     " Speeding threshold: "+str(SPEEDING_KMH))
>>> grid()
>>> title('Velocity')
>>> xlabel('Time from start of file (minutes)')
>>> ylabel('Speed (Km/H)')
>>> show()
```

We start by opening a different figure with the figure() command. We proceed by changing the timescale units to minutes, a value easier for most humans to follow than seconds. Selecting the proper units of measurement is important. Most people will find it easier to follow the sentence "I drove for 30 minutes" as opposed to "I drove for 1800 seconds." We also set the time axis to start at t[0]. Next, we plot the velocity as a function of the time, in black. Good graphs require annotation, so we choose to add two lines describing the thresholds for standing and speeding, as well as text describing those thresholds. To generate the text, we combine the text "Standing threshold" with the threshold value (after casting it to a string with str()) and use the + operator to concatenate strings. Last, of course, come the title, *x* and *y* labels, and grid. Figure 1-4 shows the final result.

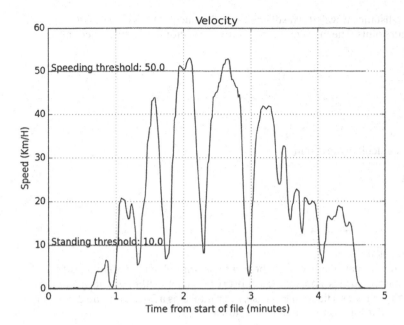

Figure 1-4. *Velocity over time*

Subplots

We'd also like to display some statistics. But before we do that, it would be preferable to combine all these plots (GPS, velocity, and statistics) into one figure. For this, we use the subplot() function. subplot() is a *matplotlib* function that divides the plot into several smaller sections called subplots and selects the subplot to work with. For example, subplot(1, 2, 1) informs subsequent plotting commands that the area to work on is 1-by-2 subplots and that the currently selected subplot is 1; in other words, it is half of the left side of the plot area. subplot(2, 2, 2) will choose the top-right subplot; subplot(2, 2, 4) will choose the lower-right subplot. A selection I found most readable in this scenario is to have the GPS data take half of the plot area, the velocity graph a quarter, and the statistics another quarter. Each subplot() call should be done prior to calling the plotting commands (e.g., plot()).

Text

Sometimes, the best way to convey information is using text, not graphics. We'll be limiting our work to the statistics quarter for this section. Our first task is to get rid of the plot frame and the *x* and *y* ticks. We just want a plain canvas to display text on. We can achieve this by issuing the following:

```
>>> subplot(2, 2, 4)
>>> axis('off')
```

The first call to subplot() selects our region of work as the lower-right quarter. The second line removes the axes and hides the frame box.

It's time to calculate some statistics. It appears that GPS data is being sent in regular intervals, typically one second. So, to calculate the time spent standing, in seconds, we calculate the length of the vector Istand. Likewise, to calculate the time speeding, we can calculate the length of Ispeed. To estimate how much these were in percent values, we divide the length of the Istand and Ispeed vectors by the length of the velocity vector and multiply by 100. To calculate the average speed, we use the mean() function, which is part of *PyLab*.

We also would like to calculate the total distance traveled. The distance can be calculated as the sum of the distances between each two consecutive data points. The function `diff()` returns a vector of the differences of the input vector:

```
>>> diff([1, 4, 0, 2])
```

```
array([ 3, -4,  2])
```

This is really useful because we can now calculate the distance:

```
>>> sum(sqrt(diff(px)**2+diff(py)**2))
```

```
1652.1444099624528
```

This, in turn, yields the total distance traveled.

To automate the whole process of printing the statistics, we store the text to be printed in the variable `stats`, a list of strings. We also use a method of formatting strings similar to C's `printf()` function, although the syntax is a bit different. `%s` indicates a string, while the `%f` indicates a float. In our case, `%.1f` indicates a float with one digit after the decimal point, and `%d` indicates an integer. The following generates the statistics text:

```
>>> Total_distance  = float(sum(sqrt(diff(px)**2+diff(py)**2))/1000.0)
>>> Stand_time  = len(Istand)/60.0
>>> Cruise_time = len(Icruise)/60.0
>>> Speed_time  = len(Ispeed)/60.0
>>> Stand_per   = 100*len(Istand)/len(v)
>>> Cruise_per  = 100*len(Icruise)/len(v)
>>> Speed_per   = 100*len(Ispeed)/len(v)
>>> Stats=['Statistics', \
...     '%s' % filename, \
...     'Number of data points: %d' % len(y), \
...     'Average number of satellites: %d' % mean(sats), \
...     'Total driving time: %.1f minutes:' % (len(v)/60.0), \
...     '    Standing: %.1f minutes (%d%%)' % \
...     (Stand_time, Stand_per), \
...     '    Cruising: %.1f minutes (%d%%)' % \
...     (Cruise_time, Cruise_per), \
...     '    Speeding: %.1f minutes (%d%%)' % \
...     (Speed_time, Speed_per), \
...     'Average speed: %d km/h' % mean(v), \
...     'Total distance travelled: %.1f Km' % Total_distance ]
```

To print the text on the canvas, we again use the `text()` function. This time, we use a `for` loop, iterating over every string of the `stats` list:

```
>>> for index, stat_line in enumerate(reversed(stats)):
...     text(0, index, stat_line, va='bottom')
...
>>> plot([index-.2, index-.2])
>>> axis([0, 1, -1, len(stats)])
```

We've introduced two new functions. One is reversed(), which yields the elements of stats, in reversed order. The second is enumerate(), which returns not just each row in the stats array, but also the index to each row. So when variable stat_line is assigned the value 'Average speed...', the variable index is assigned the value 8, which indicates the ninth row in stats. The reason we want to know the index is that we use it as a location on the y-axis. Lastly, the vertical alignment of the text is selected as bottom, as suggested by the parameter va='bottom' (va is short for vertical alignment).

Tying It All Together

Finally, Listing 1-10 shows the combined code to analyze and plot all GPS files in directory data.

Listing 1-10. Script gps.py

```
from pylab import *
import csv, os

# constant definitions
STANDING_KMH = 10.0
SPEEDING_KMH = 50.0
NMI = 1852.0
D2R = pi/180.0

def read_csv_file(filename):
    """Reads a CSV file and return it as a list of rows."""

    data = []
    for row in csv.reader(open(filename)):
        data.append(row)
    return data

def process_gps_data(data):
    """Processes GPS data, NMEA 0183 format.

Returns a tuple of arrays: latitude, longitude, velocity [km/h],
time [sec] and number of satellites.
See also: http://www.gpsinformation.org/dale/nmea.htm.
    """

    latitude    = []
    longitude   = []
    velocity    = []
    t_seconds   = []
    num_sats    = []

    for row in data:
        if row[0] == '$GPGSV':
            num_sats.append(float(row[3]))
        elif row[0] == '$GPRMC':
            t_seconds.append(float(row[1][0:2])*3600 + \
                float(row[1][2:4])*60+float(row[1][4:6]))
```

```python
        latitude.append(float(row[3][0:2]) + \
            float(row[3][2:])/60.0)
        longitude.append((float(row[5][0:3]) + \
            float(row[5][3:])/60.0))
        velocity.append(float(row[7])*NMI/1000.0)

    return (array(latitude), array(longitude), \
        array(velocity), array(t_seconds), array(num_sats))

# read every data file, filter and plot the data
for root, dirs, files in os.walk('../data'):
    for filename in files:
        # create full filename including path
        cur_file = os.path.join(root, filename)
        if filename.endswith('csv'):
            y = read_csv_file(cur_file)
        else:
            continue

        # only files with the .csv extension from here on

        # process GPS data
        (lat, long, v, t, sats) = process_gps_data(y)

        # translate spherical coordinates to Cartesian
        py = (lat-min(lat))*NMI*60.0
        px = (long-min(long))*NMI*60.0*cos(D2R*lat)

        # find out when standing, speeding or cruising
        Istand = find(v < STANDING_KMH)
        Ispeed = find(v > SPEEDING_KMH)
        Icruise = find((v >=STANDING_KMH) & (v <= SPEEDING_KMH))

        # left side, GPS location graph
        figure()
        subplot(1, 2, 1)

        # longitude values go from right to left,
        # we want increasing values from left to right
        gca().axes.invert_xaxis()

        plot(px, py, 'b', label=' Cruising', linewidth=3)
        plot(px[Istand], py[Istand], 'sg', label=' Standing')
        plot(px[Ispeed], py[Ispeed], 'or', label=' Speeding!')

        # add direction of travel
        for i in range(0, len(v), len(v)//10-1):
            text(px[i], py[i], ">>>", \
                rotation=arctan2(py[i+1]-py[i], -(px[i+1]-px[i]))/D2R, \
                ha='center')
```

```
# legends and labels
title(filename[:-4])
legend(loc='upper left')
xlabel('east-west (meters)')
ylabel('south-north (meters)')
grid()
axis('equal')

# top right corner,  speed graph
subplot(2, 2, 2)

# set the start time as t[0]; convert to minutes
t = (t-t[0])/60.0
plot(t, v, 'k')

# plot the standing and speeding threshold lines
plot([t[0], t[-1]], [STANDING_KMH, STANDING_KMH], '-g')
text(t[0], STANDING_KMH, \
    " Standing threshold: "+str(STANDING_KMH))
plot([t[0], t[-1]], [SPEEDING_KMH, SPEEDING_KMH], '-r')
text(t[0], SPEEDING_KMH, \
    " Speeding threshold: "+str(SPEEDING_KMH))
grid()

# legend and labels
title('Velocity')
xlabel('Time from start of file (minutes)')
ylabel('Speed (Km/H)')

# right side corner, statistics data
subplot(2, 2, 4)

# remove the frame and x/y axes. we want a clean slate
axis('off')

# generate an array of strings to be printed
Total_distance  = sum(sqrt(diff(px)**2+diff(py)**2)/1000.0)
Stand_time  = len(Istand)/60.0
Cruise_time = len(Icruise)/60.0
Speed_time  = len(Ispeed)/60.0
Stand_per   = 100*len(Istand)/len(v)
Cruise_per  = 100*len(Icruise)/len(v)
Speed_per   = 100*len(Ispeed)/len(v)
stats = ['Statistics', \
'%s' % filename, \
'Number of data points: %d' % len(y), \
'Average number of satellites: %d' % mean(sats), \
'Total driving time: %.1f minutes:' % (len(v)/60.0), \
'    Standing: %.1f minutes (%d%%)' % \
(Stand_time, Stand_per), \
```

```
'    Cruising: %.1f minutes (%d%%)' % \
(Cruise_time, Cruise_per), \
'    Speeding: %.1f minutes (%d%%)' % \
(Speed_time, Speed_per), \
'Average speed: %d km/h' % mean(v), \
'Total distance traveled: %.1f Km' % Total_distance ]

# display statistics information
for index, stat_line in enumerate(reversed(stats)):
    text(0, index, stat_line, va='bottom')

# draw a line below the "Statistics" text
plot([index-.2, index-.2])

# set axis properly so all the text is displayed
axis([0, 1, -1, len(stats)])
show()
```

Figure 1-5 shows the final results.

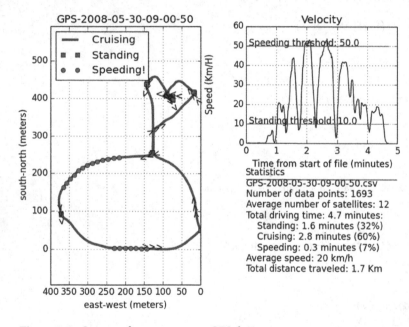

Figure 1-5. *Output of gps.py on some GPS data*

Final Notes and References

The GPS problem described here is research and development in nature: a computation and an intermediate result, not an end product. Research, or R&D work, especially feasibility studies, requires rapid responses. This means using readily available tools as much as possible and combining them to get the job done. If those tools are inexpensive, or free, that's yet another reason to use them.

Throughout the book, we will examine different packages and modules and show how they may be used to perform data analysis and visualization. The theme we'll be following is open software, including software published under the GNU Public License (GPL) and Python Software Foundation (PSF) license. Examples of these tools include GNU/Linux and, of course, Python.

There are several benefits to developing data analysis and visualization scripts in Python:

- Developing and writing code is quick, which is appealing for research work.

- Readily available packages further increase productivity and ensure accurate results.

- Scripts introduce automation. Modifying an algorithm is easily done.

Scripts will be numerous and explained in detail, and I aim to cover most of the issues you are likely to encounter in the real world. Ranging from simple one-liners to the more complex, examples include scripts written in Python to deal with binary files, to combine data from different sources, to perform text parsing, to use high-level numerical algorithms, and much more. We'll pay special attention to data visualization and how to achieve pleasing results in Python. First though, you have to get the Python environment up and running, which will be covered in the next chapter.

If you'd like to read more about Python in general (and not necessarily for data analysis and visualization), the Python official web site is an excellent resource:

- Python Programming Language—Official Website, `http://www.python.org`

Other references used in this chapter include:

- *pySerial*, `http://pyserial.sourceforge.net/`

- "Data elements and interchange formats—Information interchange—Representation of dates and times", `http://www.iso.org`

- NMEA 0183, `http://www.nmea.org` and `http://www.gpsinformation.org/dale/nmea.htm`

CHAPTER 2

■ ■ ■

The Environment

Tools of the Trade

Chapter 1 demonstrated Python at work in a case study involving the collection, analysis, and visualization of GPS data. To put Python to work yourself, you first need to build your own development environment. This chapter will walk you through the various software components you need and help you weigh your installation options. Unless you're already familiar with Python and have the packages we used in Chapter 1 installed, read on.

Setting up a solid environment to analyze and visualize data requires general-purpose software components, as well as Python and some additional Python packages for data analysis and visualization. For general software, you will need:

- An operating system (OS)
- A text editor in which to write the code
- An image viewer
- Tools to present and view the results
- A version-control system

In the following sections we'll examine your options for these components more closely, and I'll recommend a few that can improve productivity. If you're already comfortable with another general-software component, by all means use it over the one suggested here. The Python-specific components discussed, on the other hand, are tools required to run the examples in the book. Whenever a component is a required component, I'll clearly say so. The chapter introduces the various software components in a linear fashion, building from the ground up—first the OS, then Python and Python packages, and lastly, the supporting software components.

■ **Note**   Although this chapter is organized in a linear fashion, feel free to skip the general-software components section if you already know what applications you'll be using. You should, however, ensure you have the Python-specific components properly installed; code presented in the book assumes that is the case.

Operating Systems

The development environment is built upon an operating system. For this foundation, your choices are a UNIX-based operating system (such as GNU/Linux and Mac OS X) or Windows. We'll focus on Linux and Windows, but because Mac OS is a UNIX-based operating system, most of the discussions regarding Linux apply to it, as well. For a complete list of supported operating systems, see the Python website (https://www.python.org), which is an excellent resource for all things Python.

GNU/Linux

Linux is a generic term that describes UNIX-like operating systems based on the Linux kernel. A Linux distribution is a collection consisting of the Linux kernel, along with additional software packages that together provide a full OS. Most distributions provide more than a basic OS functionality; they provide additional software packages such as multimedia applications, games, office productivity suites, and much more. A considerable portion of the packages in most Linux distributions is based on the GNU project (http://www.gnu.org)—hence, the term GNU/Linux.

There are a large number of Linux distributions (distros) available today, including (but not limited to) the following:

- Fedora project: https://www.fedoraproject.org

- Debian: https://www.debian.org

- Ubuntu: http://www.ubuntu.com

- Gentoo: http://www.gentoo.org

Most of these are excellent distributions. If you plan on going the Linux route, spend some time to acquaint yourself with these distributions, so you can decide on the one that best suits your needs (or perhaps better still, your personality). For a side-by-side comparison of various Linux distributions, refer to http://en.wikipedia.org/wiki/Comparison_of_Linux_distributions.

It is especially important that you know how to install applications in the Linux distribution of your choice. Most distributions come with a package-management tool (e.g., rpm/PackageKit/Yum on Fedora, apt-get/APT on Debian/Ubuntu, and emerge/Portage on Gentoo) that enables downloading applications and installing them on your Linux OS. Typically, package-management tools synchronize with an online repository and enable downloading and upgrading software. They also take care of any version conflicts and perform the actual installation tasks such as copying files and updating system information.

As a general rule, you should opt for using your Linux distribution's built-in package-management tool to install the software components discussed in this chapter, with Python and its packages included, over a manual install; this will ensure a stable Linux system. If a desired software application is not available via your Linux distribution's package-management tool, you can manually install that application. This is not a trivial task and requires some Linux expertise. (On the other hand, manually installing Python packages is straightforward, as you'll learn later in the "Manually Installing a Python Package" section.)

Windows

Of the Windows versions available today, opt for a version that is currently supported by Microsoft. Unlike with Linux, after selecting Windows as the OS, you still need to choose the exact environment on which to run Python. The three main options are:

- Stand-alone (natively)

- Cygwin

- Virtual machines (VMs)

Stand-Alone (Natively)

Unless you have a strong reason against it, this should be your preferred choice if you intend on using Windows: installing Python natively without an additional environment. It's less of a hassle to install, your code will run faster, and it's easy to copy and paste from Python directly to documents. Python comes as an executable file with an installer application. After downloading it, double-click the executable and install Python (more on Python installation shortly). Most other packages we'll be dealing with also come bundled in this fashion, so installing them should be simple, as well.

If you'd like to install a package that doesn't come with an installer, you'll have to consult with that package's documentation. By the way, regardless of whether you choose a stand-alone approach or one of the other methods suggested next (or Linux), there are bound to be packages that require a manual installation, so knowing how to do a manual package install is of value.

Cygwin

The Cygwin (http://www.cygwin.com) environment runs in Windows and provides UNIX-like functionality. It is an excellent software product, even if you are a devoted Windows user.

Cygwin comes with a GUI installer that runs on Windows. The Cygwin Net Release Setup Program allows you to select and install software packages. Please note that there are two versions of Cygwin, the 64-bit version and the 32-bit version; ensure that you are installing the correct version for your OS. The Cygwin installer is actually a package-management tool, just like any other package-management tool in most Linux distributions. As you browse through the list of packages, you'll realize there's an extensive selection to choose from; however, that should not deter you. Install the default options knowing you can always go back and add or remove applications; it's as simple as rerunning the Cygwin installer. After installing Cygwin, run it via Start ➤ All Programs ➤ Cygwin ➤ Cygwin Terminal.

Cygwin provides a great number of additional open source software packages, including Python. If you want additional functionality—bash shell, SSH, editors, viewers, version-control systems, X functionality, and more—then Cygwin is an excellent choice. The downside is that it is a bit more complex for a less-experienced user than the stand-alone approach. There's also a small performance hit using Cygwin compared with a native installation. For example, on my computer, a simple for loop summing values was 20 percent slower in Python on Cygwin compared with a native Python installation.

■ **Note**   Cygwin treats drives differently than Windows, as it follows a UNIX directory structure. If you installed Cygwin under c:\cygwin, then this directory is usually denoted as the topmost directory: /. To access directories outside c:\cygwin, use the following notation: /cygdrive/disk or disk:/. For example, if a file is located in c:\data, it is accessible in Cygwin as /cygdrive/c/data or c:/data.

Virtual Machines

The third option, which is a bit more exotic, is running a virtual machine (VM). A virtual machine allows you to run a Linux OS (or another OS for that matter) in the host operating system, which is in this case Windows or Mac OS. This option is for the more experienced user: installing and configuring a VM is not an easy task.

Whenever I want to cross develop—that is, to develop an application that needs to run on both Windows and Linux—I'll develop in Windows and run a Linux VM in Windows. This way, I can easily check the code in both operating systems without switching computers. Another advantage of VMs is familiarity with applications from both Windows and Linux: VMs allow you to use both applications on the same computer.

On Windows, there are several VMs available today:

- Oracle VM VirtualBox (https://www.virtualbox.org/). VirtualBox is free for personal use; see Oracle's licensing FAQ (https://www.virtualbox.org/wiki/Licensing_FAQ) for details.

- VMware (http://www.vmware.com). This VM also has a free version, named VMware Player.

- Parallels (http://www.parallels.com) for MacOS. Parallels is commercial software.

■ **Tip** Running a virtual machine might be a good option if you just want to try out Linux in general, but don't want to go the full route of installing an OS. If that is the case, there is also the option of running a live CD, which basically means booting a full-fledged Linux OS from CD-ROM. There's quite a large number of live CDs available today; one well-known option is Knoppix (`http://knoppix.net/`).

One of the downsides of using a VM is that you pay a price in performance. That said, VM implementations and the increasing power of computing have made this a relatively small price to pay.

Choosing an Operating System

Which operating system is the strongest foundation for Python? From a data analysis and visualization perspective, Linux is a perfect match. The main reason is that Linux comes with a strong command-line interface (CLI) compared with Windows, which relies heavily on a graphical user interface (GUI).

When you're working with a significant number of files, a CLI wins hands down over a GUI. Consider renaming a large number of files, say, pictures you took on your last vacation. Most cameras generate files that follow a sequential naming scheme: DSB00001.jpg, DSB00002.jpg, and so forth, which is rather cryptic. You, on the other hand, would like to rename these files to something a bit more informative, such as Vacation2014-03-20-NNNNN.jpg, where NNNNN is the running index. So a file named DSB00002.jpg will now be named Vacation2014-03-20-00002.jpg. You can perform this task with both a GUI and a CLI:

- With the GUI approach, you must point, click, and type a new name for each and every file. This might be perfectly reasonable for a small number of pictures; but as the number increases, the task becomes tedious and time consuming.

- The CLI approach is to write a command to rename all the files at once. If you're familiar with Bash, you might issue the following:

  ```
  $ for fn in DSB*.jpg; do mv $fn ${fn/DSC/Vacation2014-03-20-}; done
  ```

(There are lots of ways to do it with a CLI, and this is just one I prefer. I will not be discussing Bash in the book.) For a handful of pictures, this seems like overkill; once the number of files increases, however, the CLI approach is a significant time saver.

Of course, renaming files is a simple task, one that Windows also supports via its command prompt (which is the Windows version of a CLI). However, even this simple task is not trivial in Windows, unless you install additional software or write some code to perform the task (although recent versions of Windows also introduce shell capabilities enabling both GUI and CLI interfaces). For more complex data-management tasks, a CLI-centric approach is much better than a GUI. An operating system built around a CLI is usually a better choice for managing data files.

■ **Note** There isn't a right or wrong choice, whatever OS you elect to go with—the concepts (and code) presented in this book will work just fine.

Here are some things to consider when choosing an OS:

- Linux is a stable and able operating system. The benefits of using Linux include low cost (typically, none), solid CLI, and an active and supportive community. The main disadvantage with Linux is that, if you're not familiar with the OS, there is a learning curve—although, with today's distributions, the curve has leveled off significantly. Also, support for hardware isn't as all-encompassing as is the case in Windows. This might prove a serious disadvantage if your work involves using an already existing piece of hardware that isn't supported in Linux to generate data.

- Windows is a widely popular operating system. Most users have experienced working in Windows to some degree, so the learning curve is very shallow, if any. Support for hardware is very good; most hardware vendors target Widows as their primary OS. The drawbacks of using Windows are lack of a strong CLI, as well as the cost of the OS and additional software applications.

- Mac OS is quite popular and for a reason: it combines the GUI experience with UNIX power. Although it's relatively new in the data analysis and visualization scene, due to those two traits, I have a feeling you'll see more and more of Mac OS being used. The downsides to the Mac OS are cost and its support for legacy hardware.

Table 2-1 summarizes the pros and cons of each OS choice.

Table 2-1. *Linux, Windows, and Mac OS as Development Environments for Data Processing and Visualization*

	Linux	**Windows**	**MacOS**
CLI	Very good (native)	Good (with Python)	Very good (native)
Applications	Full (mostly free)	Full (possible additional cost)	Full (possible additional cost)
Learning curve	Steep	Gentle	Gentle
Cost	Low	Medium	Medium
Hardware support	Good	Very good	Medium
Stability	Very good	Very good	Very good

Then Again, Why Choose? Using Several Operating Systems

The nice thing about Python is that it eliminates the operating system from the equation. Python is a complete environment, with a "batteries-included" approach: you should be pretty much good to go, out of the box, after installing Python; the standard library provides full functionality. What that means is that all of a sudden, Windows has a strong CLI as well: the Python interpreter. With that in mind, the selection of an OS becomes more of a personal preference than anything else. For example, I use both Linux and Windows for data analysis and visualization: my Linux machine is a stationary home server, so I can't use it to record GPS data when driving; my laptop runs Windows and does that for me.

If you require more UNIX-like functionality than Python provides, but would still like to use Windows, you can opt for Cygwin, which provides a host of GNU tools ported to Windows. In fact, I use Cygwin's X server and connect to my Linux machine if I need some GUI interactive work (the Linux machine is tucked under the desk and has no monitor).

If you plan on installing both Windows and Linux to analyze data on the same computer, which is called dual-booting, think about how you're going to transfer data between the Linux and Windows partitions. There are several ways: having a shared partition that both Linux and Windows can handle (FAT32, NTFS on some), transferring files through a USB device, or even networking to another machine. Each has its benefits, but remember that you might be dealing with a large number of files, so it would be best if you could access the data on a shared resource.

■ **Caution** Installing an OS is a time-consuming task, taking twice as long if you intend to dual-boot. You should consult with the Linux documentation of your distribution on how to best achieve dual-booting; this is especially true when deciding which OS (Linux or Windows) you should install first. Dual-booting is an advanced topic and is not suggested for the beginner.

Using a dual-boot system can be annoying at times, especially since you have to reboot to switch operating systems. In addition, the installation process is a bit risky. You could lose data while repartitioning the hard disk, for example (although this scenario can be avoided, if you know what you're doing). To minimize your annoyance and risk, a VM is a good alternative: data is safe from repartitions, and actual reboots are not required. My PC is strong enough to run Linux as a VM in Windows with excellent performance. If you'd like to use this setup, again, think about how you're going to share data between the host OS and the target OS. A common (and good) approach is to transfer files using a virtual network interface. Another option is to use shared folders such as the one provided with Oracle's VirtualBox guest additions.

On Mac OS, these solutions are somewhat less necessary; Mac OS is already a UNIX-like OS.

The Python Environment

By now you should have already selected and installed the OS of your choice. You should also be comfortable with downloading and installing packages. It's now time to install Python. This section discusses the installation of Python and Python packages to enable programming data analysis and visualization scripts. Chapter 3 provides a more detailed discussion on using Python both in an interactive shell and to run stand-alone application. Here, I'll be focusing on Python distributions, Python IDEs, and Python packages.

■ **Note** Modules are Python files. Packages are collections of modules that reside in a directory (modules in a package also share an additional __init__.py file). In this book, whenever I talk about a package or a module, I use italics. Examples of packages are *SciPy* and *NumPy*. Examples of modules are *time* and *random*. For information on importing modules and packages see Chapter 3, "The import Statement."

Versions

The main Python version I'll be covering in this book is Python version 3.3. As a general rule, you should opt for the most updated Python version. Unfortunately, that's not always possible:

- At the time of writing, Python 3.4 was released. However, not all the packages used in the book have caught up yet, so I've had to stick with Python 3.3.

- Some operating systems, such as the Gentoo Linux distribution, rely heavily on Python for system administration, and upgrades require extensive testing to ensure the system is stable. So although a new release of Python becomes available, you might not be able to use it yet. There are workarounds to that, such as installing several versions of Python on one machine; again, refer to your Linux distribution for further information, as this topic is beyond the scope of this chapter.

Before upgrading to a more recent version of Python, be sure all the packages you'll be using support the new version. Write down all the packages you'll be using along with version numbers. Also, be sure to take special note of the following:

- The OS you're using, whether it's Windows, Linux or MacOs.

- Is your OS 64-bit or 32-bit? Typically, 64-bit package versions have the text `amd64` or `x86-64` in the download filename; 32-bit versions have the text `win32` (Windows) or `x86` (Linux) in the download filenames.

- The exact Python version. For example, if you're downloading *NumPy* version 1.8, make sure you download the version of *NumPy* compiled for Python 3.3.

A good starting point to look for the most updated Python packages is PyPI—the Python Package Index, `https://pypi.python.org/pypi`. Table 2-2 summarizes the versions of Python and its packages used in this book.

Table 2-2. *Versions of Python and the Python packages used in this book*

Package	Version	Use	Notes
Python	3.3.5	The main Python language software	On Windows, I've had to select the option *"Install just for me"* for the installer to work properly. I've also selected the option *"Add python.exe to the Path"* so that double-clicking a Python script would automatically run that script.
NumPy	1.8.1	Powerful numerical data structures and algorithms	
SciPy	0.13.3	Additional scientific packages	Opt for the superpack download.
IPython	2.0.0	An enhanced Python shell	On Windows, I've also had to install *setuptools* (version 3.4.4) and *pyreadline* (version 2.0). For IPython notebook functionality (see the IPython notebook section), you'll also need *pyzmq* (version 14.1.1), *jinja2* (version 2.7.2), *Markupsafe* (version 0.21), and *tornado* (version 3.2).
Matplotlib	1.3.1	Graphs and plots	You'll also have to install *dateutil* (version 2.2), *pyparsing* (version 2.0.2), and *six* (version 1.6.1).
Pillow	2.4.0	Image processing	
pySerial	2.7	Serial port (USB-GPS data example in Chapter 1)	

The code presented in this book will work on most 3.x versions with little to no changes at all. As for 2.x versions, minor adjustments should be made; most notably, you'll need to replace the division operator (`/`) with the integer-division operator (`//`) (or vice-versa) because the default behavior of division of numbers is different (see the section, "Extracting GPS Data" in Chapter 1 for more information). Alternatively, you can add the line from `__future__` import `print_function, division` to use the scripts in the book with Python version 2.x.

If Table 2-2's list is too intimidating, opt for installing a Python distribution with all these packages included; see the section "Python Distributions with Scientific Packages" later in this chapter for suggestions.

■ **Note** Always make sure you're downloading and installing a version of a package that is compatible with the version of Python you're using. Some packages keep older versions if you need them for compatibility reasons.

Python

You can download a Python implementation for your specific OS from https://www.python.org/downloads/. Read carefully and select the download that fits your OS. Again, if you're running a Linux OS, opt for using that system's package-management tool over downloading and installing from the Python website. The same applies for Cygwin: use the Cygwin installer if you can. On Windows, the common practice is to use the Python binaries distributed with an installer from the preceding URL. Although you can install Python from source code—that is, you can download the source code and compile it on your OS—I haven't found a reason to do this other than to satisfy my curiosity that the code does indeed compile properly.

If you are wondering about Jython (an implementation of Python written purely in Java, see http://www.jython.org) or IronPython (an implementation of Python on Microsoft's .NET platform, see http://ironpython.net/), I'm afraid they're not good options for this book. A lot of the code and examples rely heavily on packages that do not run on Jython or IronPython. Other alternative Python implementations can be found at the Python website at https://www.python.org/download/alternatives/; again these alternatives are not covered in this book.

Python Distributions with Scientific Packages

Another option is to use a Python distribution that already bundles a significant number of the Python packages we'll be using. These are a good option if you don't want the hassle of installing individual packages, or if you can't wait to be past the installation phase and up and running code. Here's a list of options:

- Enthought Canopy: https://www.enthought.com/products/canopy/

- Python(x,y): https://code.google.com/p/pythonxy/

- WinPython: http://winpython.sourceforge.net/

- Anaconda: https://store.continuum.io/cshop/anaconda/

If you choose a Python distribution with scientific packages, you can skip the sections later in the chapter related to Python Integrated Development Environment, *SciPy*, *NumPy*, *matplotlib*, and IPython. A Python distribution that includes scientific packages will include these packages out of the box.

Python Integrated Development Environments

An integrated development environment (IDE) is, simply put, an application that helps programmers write code. Typically an IDE is composed of the language engine (Python), an editor, a debugger, documentation, and possibly additional productivity tools. While it is by all means possible to use Python without an IDE, using one will greatly increase your productivity and will enable a faster learning pace.

There are several Python IDEs available; of these, we'll explore IDLE, IPython (my personal favorite), IPython Notebook, and Spyder.

IDLE

IDLE (`https://docs.python.org/3.3/library/idle.html`) is a cross-platform Python GUI IDE. If you installed from Windows binaries, IDLE is automatically installed; access it via Start ➤ All Programs ➤ Python 3.3 ➤ IDLE (Python GUI). IDLE is a capable IDE with the following features: seamless integration with the Python interpreter, an editor, a debugger, and a help system. It's an excellent environment to get up and running with, especially if you're new to programming.

One of the benefits of using IDLE is that you can write code in an editor (File ➤ New File or **CTRL-N**), specifically designed for Python, and then quite easily execute it in IDLE by pressing **F5**. With a CLI approach, you'd have to invoke Python with the file you'd like to execute (more on this in Chapter 3).

IPython

As you start working with a CLI, you'll realize there are some things you'd really like enhanced. IPython (`http://ipython.org/`) provides an enhanced interactive Python shell. I highly recommend it, mostly because data analysis and visualization is interactive in nature. IPython is supported on most platforms. Here's a short list of the added features that come with IPython:

- Tab completion, which involves the completion of variables, functions, methods, attributes, and file names. Tab completion is achieved with the GNU Readline library (`http://cnswww.cns.cwru.edu/php/chet/readline/rltop.html`) and is highly addictive. It's very hard to go back to a regular CLI after you've been exposed to GNU Readline.

- Command history capabilities: issue the command `history` for a full account of the commands you've recently typed. You can copy and paste those into a Python script and save time and effort.

- Seamless integration with system shell: you can use `ls -l` or `cd /home/user`, for example.

- Colored output.

IPython is not required but is *highly recommended*. It is my personal favorite enhancement application for writing code in Python.

IPython comes bundled with an installer for Windows and is available on most package-management tools, as well as on Cygwin. Depending on your OS, you might need to install GNU Readline; on Windows, you'll also need to install PyReadline (`http://ipython.org/pyreadline.html`). Consult with IPython's installation documentation.

■ **Note**   IPython should be installed after Python, GNU Readline, and PyReadline are installed.

CHARACTER COMPLETION WITH IPYTHON AND GNU READLINE

Character completion with GNU Readline is a welcome addition to an interactive CLI. With IPython, character completion can be used to complete the following:

- Names of variables

- Names of methods and attributes

- File names

To invoke character completion, start by spelling out the first few characters of the word you wish to write, and then press the **Tab** key to have GNU Readline try and complete the word for you. The following is from IPython:

```
In [1]: s = "A string"

In [2]: s.is
s.isalnum       s.isdigit        s.isnumeric    s.istitle
s.isalpha       s.isidentifier  s.isprintable  s.isupper
s.isdecimal     s.islower        s.isspace
In [2]: s.is
```

After typing s.is, I pressed the **Tab** key and was presented with a list of options. Had I spelled the word s.isdi and pressed **Tab**, the entire s.isdigit would have appeared automatically at the prompt.

The way GNU Readline works is that it tries to complete the word by searching for a variable, function, method, attribute, or file name that matches the typed characters. In case of one option, that word is automatically spelled out at the prompt. In case of several options, all the options are displayed. To select which of the options you'd rather have completed, supply the next character and then press **Tab** again. If there are no matches to the typed word, nothing happens.

You can also use the character completion feature to explore methods and attributes of a class, or any other namespace for that matter. In the following listing, I pressed the **Tab** key after entering a. (notice the dot):

```
In [1]: a = dict()

In [2]: a.
a.clear      a.fromkeys    a.items    a.pop      a.setdefault    a.values
a.copy       a.get         a.keys     a.popitem  a.update
```

IPython Notebook

An exciting and relatively new feature to IPython is IPython Notebook (see http://ipython.org/notebook.html). IPython Notebook provides a web-based interactive Python scripting environment capable of both executing code and embedding graphs. Furthermore, it lets you share a notebook with readers via the IPython Notebook viewer (see http://nbviewer.ipython.org/) or export the notebook to other formats such as PDF or HTML. Figure 2-1 shows an example.

IPython Notebook is installed automatically when you install IPython. However, for IPython Notebook to work properly, the following packages must also be installed (they provide the web-based functionality, as well as HTML templates):

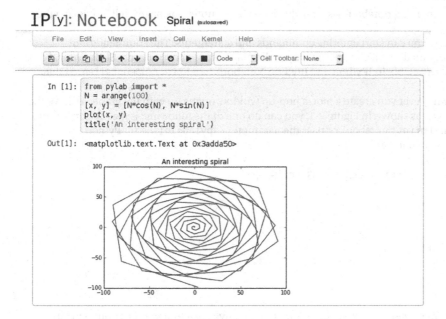

Figure 2-1. *The IPython Notebook*

- Package *pyzmq*, see https://github.com/zeromq/pyzmq

- Package *jinja2*, see http://jinja.pocoo.org/

- Package *markupsafe*, see https://github.com/mitsuhiko/markupsafe

- Package *tornado*, see http://www.tornadoweb.org/

Once you start IPython Notebook, the first screen you'll see is similar to the one shown in Figure 2-2.

You can either create a new notebook by clicking the New Notebook button, or you can click an already active notebook. In the preceding example, the active notebooks are titled *Spiral* and *Untitled0*. You can close notebooks

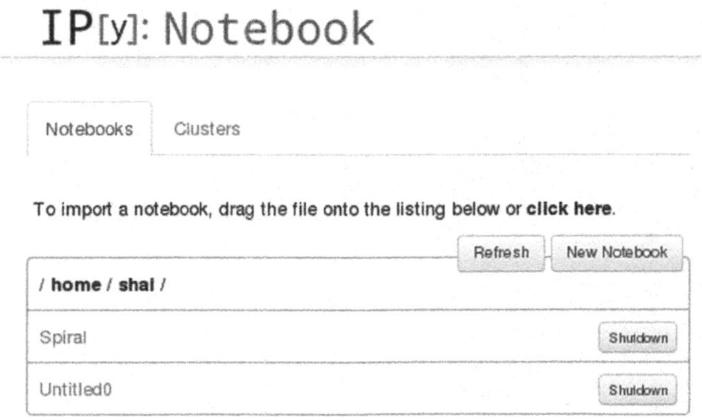

IP[y]: Notebook

Notebooks   Clusters

To import a notebook, drag the file onto the listing below or **click here**.

Refresh   New Notebook

/ home / shai /

Spiral   Shutdown

Untitled0   Shutdown

Figure 2-2. *The IPython dashboard*

by clicking the button Shutdown. Renaming notebooks is typically done via the notebook page itself by clicking the notebook name.

After you've created a notebook, you can start entering commands and statements. The commands and statements aren't evaluated (i.e., executed) until you run the cell via the play button above or press **Shift-Enter**. For a quick reference sheet of commands available in IPython and IPython Notebook, see http://damontallen.github.io/IPython-quick-ref-sheets/.

The default behavior is that, whenever you create a plot, a pop-up window opens up with the graph. To have the graph embedded within the webpage, as shown in Figure 2-1, you can do one of the following: issue the command %pylab inline as the first command in your notebook or pass the parameter --pylab=inline to IPython.

In Windows, that looks like this (in one line):

```
C:\Python33\python.exe "C:\Python33\scripts\ipython3-script.py"
notebook --pylab inline
```

And in Linux, it looks like this:

```
$ ipython notebook --pylab inline
```

Spyder

Spyder (http://code.google.com/p/spyderlib/) is an open source Interactive Development Environment (IDE) dedicated for Python. It is full of features and runs on most operating systems. Spyder has a built-in editor with syntax coloring, code completion, debugger support, and much more. It is an excellent IDE to work with.

There are several ways to install Spyder (see Figure 2-3): using one of the Python distributions with scientific packages such as Python(x,y), WinPython, or Anaconda (see previously in this chapter); using binary installers; or manually installing from source. If you're manually installing in Windows, the packages *PySide* (http://qt-project.org/wiki/PySide), *pyzmq* (https://github.com/zeromq/pyzmq), and *pygments* (http://pygments.org/) are also required. Again, if you're going with a Python distribution with scientific packages, then you don't need any additional package.

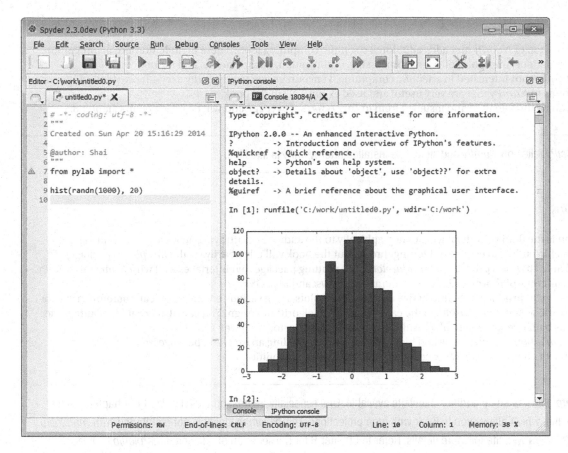

Figure 2-3. *The Spyder IDE*

Scientific Computing

A significant portion of the book is dedicated to the processing of data prior to visualization. Two packages help us achieve that end: *NumPy* and *SciPy*. *NumPy* will be discussed in Chapter 7, and *SciPy* will be reviewed in Chapter 8. These two packages, combined with *matplotlib*, behave similarly to most high-end math packages, such as the open source GNU Octave (http://www.octave.org) and the commercial MATLAB (http://www.mathworks.com). In fact, there's even a name for these three packages working together: *PyLab*, which is a combination of Python and MATLAB. *SciPy*, *NumPy*, and *matplotlib* are all open source software packages and are required to run the code presented in the book.

NumPy

NumPy provides a powerful N-dimensional array that is the basis for most of the data processing we'll perform. You've already seen it in action in the GPS example in Chapter 1. *NumPy* also provides additional numerical capabilities: linear algebra, Fourier transforms, and more.

NumPy is a mature and stable package and can be downloaded and installed from http://www.numpy.org/. *NumPy* will be discussed in Chapter 7 and Chapter 8.

SciPy

SciPy builds on top of *NumPy* and adds additional scientific computing tools. These include numerical integration, differential equations, interpolation, signal processing, optimization, linear algebra, and more.

Even if you're not interested in scientific computing, I encourage you to give *SciPy* a try—it provides additional utility functions to *NumPy* that are very useful and used extensively in the book.

SciPy can be downloaded and installed from `http://www.scipy.org/` and will be reviewed in Chapter 8.

■ **Note**   *SciPy* relies on *NumPy* and should be installed after *NumPy* is installed.

Matplotlib

Visualization is the final step, displaying data graphically to the audience, portraying an idea, and capturing information efficiently and elegantly. Plotting throughout the book will rely heavily on the *matplotlib* package, maintained at `http://matplotlib.org/`. *Matplotlib* is a plotting package that interfaces well with *NumPy* and *SciPy*. The package is cross-platform and works on Linux, Windows, and Mac OS.

Matplotlib can produce both interactive and file-based plots using various engines. You can therefore use it for interactive work, which is very useful in the early stages of an algorithm design. You can also use it in an automatic mode such as batch processing to plot results to, say, a shared directory or a web server.

Matplotlib is both simple to use and highly customizable, yielding an excellent package for our purposes. It allows a range of plot types and has excellent graph annotation capabilities.

■ **Tip**   *Matplotlib* has some additional toolkits available. One especially interesting toolkit in light of Chapter 1 is the *basemap* toolkit, which allows you to work with map projections. The *basemap* toolkit is not distributed with *matplotlib;* refer to *matplotlib*'s website for more details. Refer to Chapter 6 for a discussion of additional *matplotlib* toolkits.

Image Processing

Image processing provides the final piece of the puzzle. It is an important part of data visualization and will be discussed extensively in Chapter 9. We'll be using a fork of the Python Imaging Library (PIL) named *Pillow* to provide image-processing support.

Pillow enhances Python with excellent image-processing capabilities. It supports most popular image file formats and provides a wealth of functions for manipulating image data. *Pillow*, combined with *NumPy*, provides a very capable image-processing environment for Python.

PySerial

In Chapter 1, we used *pySerial* to capture GPS data through the serial port. *PySerial* is available at `http://pyserial.sourceforge.net/`. Whenever you need access to a serial port, *PySerial* is an excellent candidate to use.

Manually Installing a Python Package

As mentioned previously, some Python packages do not come with a stand-alone installer. In that case, you'll have to perform a manual install. Not to worry, this is easier than it sounds.

As a general rule, it's best to read the documentation and follow the instructions. That said, most Python packages require a similar set of steps to install:

1. Download the package.

2. Unpack the package to a temporary directory. Most packages are distributed as compressed files, with extensions such as `.tar.gz` or `.zip`, or even self-extracting `.exe` files. You'll need to unpack the package to a temporary directory. Occasionally, files having the extension `.tar.gz` are downloaded as `.tar.tar`. If that is the case, rename the file with the extension `.tar.gz` and continue to unpack as you normally would.

3. Run `python setup.py install` in the temporary directory. Of course, this has to be done after Python is installed and working properly on your system.

For example, the steps I took to install *pySerial* on Cygwin were as follows:

```
$ tar -zxvf pyserial-2.7.tar.gz
$ cd pyserial-2.7
$ python setup.py install
```

The first command unpacks the downloaded file to a newly created directory named `pyserial-2.7`; the creation of the new directory is done automatically by the application `tar` and is reported to the user. If you're running Windows (and not Cygwin), you can use a native Windows utility, such as 7-Zip (`http://www.7-zip.org/`), to unpack the files; the `tar` application is available in Linux and usually comes preinstalled with the OS. The second command changes directory to the temporary directory. The third command performs the installation and ensures the package is properly installed.

You can also use the *setuptools* package (which includes the easy_setup tool), available from `https://pypi.python.org/pypi/setuptools`. This package gives you better control over installing and maintaining packages, especially packages that depend on other packages. Another benefit of the package is that you can also install Python packages on machines where you don't have root (superuser) permissions.

Installation Summary

Table 2-3 summarizes the Python packages discussed previously and indicates which software is required to run the examples in the book.

Table 2-3. *Package Installation Summary*

Software/Package	Functionality	Required?
Python	Python programming language	Yes
IDLE	Python IDE	No
IPython, Readline	Python CLI enhancements	No
IPython notebook	Web-based Python environment	No
Spyder	Python IDE	No
NumPy	N-dimensional arrays and math package	Yes
SciPy	Scientific tools	Yes
Matplotlib	Plotting and graphing package	Yes
Pillow	A Python Imaging Library	Partial (Chapter 7 and 9)
PySerial	Serial interfaces	Partial (Chapter 1)

Additional Applications

By now you should have a working development environment that includes the OS of your choice, Python, and Python packages. We now turn to additional software applications to complete an environment for developing and running data analysis and visualization scripts in Python. This section suggests tools to augment the development environment from the open source software world. While there are excellent commercial applications as well, I will not be covering those. The suggested applications are perfectly good for me, but you might have your own preference, even applications that aren't mentioned here. By all means, use your favorites; this section is mostly intended for those who require some starting points.

Editors

The number one tool in a developer's arsenal is a text editor. Think of it as your Swiss Army knife: it can be used to read, write, or modify scripts; to view data files; as a scratchpad for ideas; and as a clipboard for intermediate copy and paste, among other uses. Basic text editors will soon frustrate you because some are limited in the size of files they can edit, others do not allow several open files, and yet others are missing syntax highlighting or bookmark capabilities.

Selecting the Proper Editor for You

Editors play a major role in your development environment. There's a bit of a learning curve with a new editor, so consider the following points when you select a text editor or switch from your current one:

- Ease of use: This one is obvious. Is the editor easy to use and intuitive? Is there a learning curve; and if so, how long will it take you to master?

- Multiple file editing: You might be dealing with a considerable number of script files or even examining data files in the editor. Having one application deal with all these files removes clutter from your desktop and is generally easier to handle.

- Maximum file size: What's the largest file you can open in the editor? Again, this is useful to know when you'd like to view large data files.

- Syntax highlighting: This feature displays reserved or specific syntax of a programming language in a different color or font, so that the code is easier to view. Most editors that support syntax highlighting have built-in support for several programming languages, including Python. This feature is handy as it will highlight possible syntax errors, as well as make the code more readable.

- Line numbering: Errors and warnings typically return line information where they occurred. Therefore, being able to know what line caused an error without counting lines is important. Some editors also support a jump-to-line command, which can be useful if your code is long. Lastly, line numbers are helpful when communicating with another person.

- Most recently used files list: This is a nice feature that allows you to easily access one of the files you've recently viewed or edited, without specifying its full path.

- Bookmarks: These enable easy navigation and are especially useful with large files.

- Macro support and macro recording: Macros and the ability to record and play back macros can boost productivity (see the sidebar "Recording Macros").

- Autocompletion: This feature is similar to character completion, described previously in the sidebar, "Character Completion in Readline" (but usually with a different keystroke, such as **Ctrl+Space**). It can boost productivity, but requires some getting used to.

- Other features: The preceding is a list of features I consider important. You might have different needs and different requirements, so jot them down and use those to select the proper editor for you.

RECORDING MACROS

Macro recorders are a quick and effective way to perform automation without actually writing code. Suppose you want to combine every two consecutive lines in a file into one line with && symbols in between. This is not easily done with a search and replace (unless your search and replace also supports new-line characters). Of course, you could write a Python script to do this, but let's suppose in this particular case there's no point in automation simply because you'll only do it once. This is exactly where you would use a macro recorder. The steps to follow are as follows:

1. Move your cursor to the beginning of the file (or press **Ctrl+Home** on some editors to get there).

2. Start your macro recorder and perform the following actions: press **End** to reach the end of the line, press **Del** to delete the line separator and combine the two lines into one long line, type &&, move down one line with the **Down-Arrow**, and press **Home** to get to the beginning of the next line.

3. Stop your macro recorder to finish the recording of your macro. This sequence combines two lines into one, adding && in between. Note that I've used the keyboard and not the mouse; this is important, as most macro recorders in editors don't support mouse recording.

4. Next, run the macro N times where N is the number of lines in the file divided by 2 (remember that you combine two lines per macro). Or, you can run that macro for each pair of lines you want to combine.

Some editors have the option to run the macro to the end of file. The following figure shows a macro recorder in Notepad++.

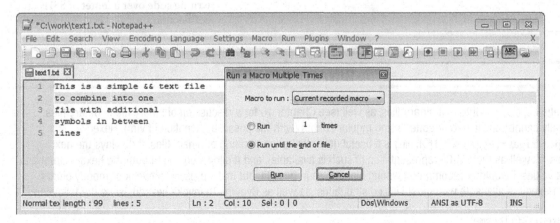

The macro is highly reliant on the location of the cursor. If you move the cursor to the end of the file and run the macro, you might get some unintended results.

A Short List of Text Editors

Table 2-4 presents a short list of some popular text editors. Use this table as a starting point in selecting an editor. This is not, by any means, a comprehensive list of available editors, so shop around and use the Internet to find more.

Table 2-4. *Short List of Open Source Editors*

Editor	OS/Environment	Notes
Notepad++ http://notepad-plus-plus.org/	Windows	Has all the features described previously in the chapter and more. Downside: available only in Windows. Sorry, Linux folks.
SciTE, Scintilla Text Editor http://www.scintilla.org/SciTE.html	Windows, X	A very good text editor, especially if you're developing on both Windows and X: you can use one editor for both platforms. It is lacking in the number of open files it allows and its macro recording capabilities.
GNU Emacs http://www.gnu.org/software/emacs/	Windows, Linux, X, Cygwin	A very rich editor. Runs on most any platform, including text-based CLI (Linux), X, and Windows, as well as Cygwin. Has a bit of a learning curve if you're new to Emacs.
Vim http://www.vim.org	Windows, Linux, X, Mac OS	A very rich editor that runs on most any platform; has most of the features described previously and more (e.g., a hex editor).
GNU Nano http://www.nano-editor.org/	Linux, Cygwin, Windows	A text based (nongraphical) lightweight editor. Missing some features, but makes up for that in size and performance. A good candidate when writing code over a telnet or SSH connection.

A BINARY EDITOR

Sometimes, it's useful to edit binary files, as well (see Chapter 10 for a discussion of binary files). Binary files typically cannot be viewed or edited using regular editors (with the possible exception of Vim). Hexedit (http://rigaux.org/hexedit.html) is a useful utility that allows editing of binary files. It displays the hex values, as well as their ASCII representation (if such is available), and it allows editing of both the hexadecimal and ASCII values. I wouldn't recommend writing binary files in hexedit, but instead use it to tweak or modify binary files. Hexedit is available with most Linux distributions, as well as Cygwin. To invoke hexedit, issue the following:

```
$ hexedit filename
```

While in hexedit, pressing **F1** will bring up a help screen. To exit hexedit without saving, press **Ctrl+C**.

Spreadsheets

Spreadsheets are excellent tools for data processing and visualization. The ease with which a user can import data from various file formats, organize it, and generate graphs is outstanding.

Comma-separated values (CSV, but also sometimes called character-separated values) is an extremely useful file format that is supported by virtually all spreadsheet applications. CSV files are used extensively in data analysis and visualization, and being able to edit them easily is a great benefit of spreadsheets.

Most spreadsheets come equipped with additional tools such as linear regression, statistical computations, financial functions, and more. A more experienced user may be able to use macros to automate tasks or to update results when new data is entered. Because of these features, spreadsheets will definitely complement your development environment.

Spreadsheets are not ideal for data processing, however. They're designed with an interactive point-and-click (GUI) user in mind, which makes them less natural at script automation. They're also limited in the amount of data they can process—you typically have to open the entire file in the spreadsheet, and that can be an issue with large files. Lastly, they lack inherent documentation—it's hard to capture and document the steps you took to reach a result.

Therefore, we will not be using spreadsheets in this book; however, I will mention their usage when appropriate. For example, it is of value to know how to export and import data to and from spreadsheets.

Two open source spreadsheet applications to consider are:

- Gnumeric (`http://www.gnumeric.org/`), a free spreadsheet.

- Calc (`https://www.libreoffice.org/`) is part of the LibreOffice project and is available on most platforms.

Word Processors

Finally, it might be of value to write a report or a presentation, displaying the results of your work. And you might want to publish the results in HTML or PDF format. Again, several open source applications are available, most notably the following:

- AbiWord (`http://www.abisource.com/`) is a word processing application available for Windows, GNU/Linux, and Mac OS.

- Writer (`https://www.libreoffice.org/`) is part of the LibreOffice project and is available on most platforms.

Image Viewers

If you plan on performing image-processing tasks, an image viewing utility is required. Even if you're not really performing an image-processing task—you're generating a graph in known file formats such as PNG and JPG, for example—an image viewing utility is still a must.

Windows has built-in support for most popular image formats. On Linux, both the GNOME and KDE desktop environments come with built-in image viewers. Plus, it's possible to open an image using a web browser both on Windows and Linux, as browsers also support most image formats. In other words, you don't need to install anything. Use your OS image viewer or web browser.

Version-Control Systems

A version-control system (VCS, also known as SCM for Software Configuration Management) enables management of several revisions of a document (or documents) with full history, tagging, and date capabilities. Most packages also support several developers working together simultaneously on the same file. A VCS enables you to go back to a previous working version, check the difference between the current version and an older one, or even view a version of the document based on date. It might hold such information as who edited the file or the tag assigned to the document to mark its status.

A VCS is increasingly recognized as a required tool for a team of developers. But even a solitary developer can benefit from using a VCS. These management systems are growing in popularity and for a good reason: they save time and help manage software projects. For this reason, they're good software to enhance your development environment. The downside of using a VCS is that it's not trivial to master and perhaps should be postponed until after you're comfortable with your programming environment. To help offset the complexity involved with VCSs, some also provide a GUI front end.

WORKING WITH A VERSION-CONTROL SYSTEM

In a nutshell, when you work with a version-control system, you follow four basic steps:

1. Check-out the project: create a local copy of the most updated version of the documents.

2. Update your local copy: edit source code, fix bugs, and add features.

3. Review your changes: make sure the right files are modified.

4. Commit changes: save the changes you've made in the version-control repository.

When you check out a document from the VCS repository, the system ensures you have the most updated version to work with. This is typically done once; and from there on, you update your local copy. You then modify your document, and once you're satisfied with the results, review the changes. Reviewing the changes can be done by performing a `diff` of the file you have with the copy in the repository. You then commit your changes (also known as checking in) and possibly add a description of the changes. Subsequent modifications follow steps 2 through 4.

The version-control system notifies you in case of a conflict. For example, suppose you checked out version 1 of the document, but by the time you wish to commit your changes, another developer has already checked in his version of the document: the system will alert you of a possible conflict because you're trying to update a document that is now version 2, whereas you were working on version 1.

The system also maintains a full history of the project. So even if you're the only person working on a project, the ability to go back to previous versions of the project is as simple as checking out an older revision. Most systems allow you to check out documents based on the date, revision, or even a tag that you've previously supplied. Because the system maintains such a complete history, most developers feel that you should commit changes as often as possible—you won't be negatively affecting "good" releases.

One final note: if you can, choose to use text files over binary files. Performing a `diff` on text files is supported by most VCS systems and is a valuable tool. With the binary version of the file (e.g., an executable), a `diff` yields very little information other than that the current version is not identical to the one in the repository.

Here's a set of commands I often use, working on a local copy I'm continually editing, once I'm done editing my local copy. With Mercurial, I issue the following:

```
$ hg status
$ hg commit filename
$ hg push
$ hg update
```

The first command checks the status of the project: which files are modified. The second and third commands check in the local copy and update the repository (where Mercurial stores the files). The last command ensures I have the most updated version of the project in my local directory.

In CVS, I follow a similar set of commands:

```
$ cvs diff
$ cvs commit
$ cvs update
```

Here are some pointers to several open source VCS software applications:

- CVS (http://www.nongnu.org/cvs/) is a widely popular system with several graphical user interfaces including web-based ones.

- Subversion (http://subversion.tigris.org/) is another widely popular system available on most platforms.

- Mercurial (http://mercurial.selenic.com/) is a lightweight VCS package designed for distributed projects.

- Git (http://git-scm.com/).

Example: Directory Structure for the Book

Version-control systems sound good in theory, but how does one work in practice? Consider this book as an example: while writing, I used a VCS system to control the documents, images, source code, and data for each chapter. I organized the directory structure, so that each chapter had a directory of its own named ChXX, with X being the chapter number. Within each directory corresponding to a chapter, I added four additional directories named doc, data, images, and src. I placed my writing in directory doc, my data files in directory data, images (such as those embedded in documents) in directory images, and source code in directory src.

```
Book
    Ch1
        data
        images
        src
        doc
    Ch2
        data
        images
        src
        doc
    ...
```

A side benefit of this directory structure is that it can help you envision how a project will look. If there's something important you realized in the first piece of code (in my case, the first chapter) but it doesn't really belong there, then simply dump the ideas and code in the relevant directory for future processing.

■ **Tip** This directory structure is also apparent in the source code listing. Since the source code resides in directory ChXX/src, and data files reside in directory ChXX/data, the relative path to directory data is ../data. Similarly, the relative path to directory images is ../images.

The reason I decided on using a VCS system for the book was quite simple. Because multiple editors were reviewing each document, the scenario was very similar to having several developers for one document. At any stage of the project, I'd hand over some documents of various revisions to editors, revisit others, and send reviewers yet a different version. Some editors would return responses to a revision that I'd already updated, and so I had to know which document they'd edited. Managing all the revisions of the documents was a lot easier with a version-control system. I could instantly view the status of each and every file; I could revert to an old version if needed, and I instantly knew which version I currently had in my local directory.

Licensing

Most of the software described in the chapter is open source and free (with the obvious exception of Windows and other commercial packages: MATLAB and VMware, to name a couple). That said, there are limitations on what you can do with open source software, especially if you intend to distribute your applications. Several software licenses exist, and I urge you to read each and every one. The same applies for commercial software: ensure you read the license agreement.

The following is a list of some of the license agreements of the software described in this chapter. It is neither complete nor comprehensive, and the licenses might change with time, so be sure to check the most recent license documentation:

- GNU licenses, including GPL and LGPL: These cover a substantial number of the packages described in this chapter: http://www.gnu.org/licenses/licenses.html.

- Linux distributions licenses: Refer to the respective web page of the distribution of your choice.

- Cygwin: Refer to the license documents installed in Cygwin, usually under c:\cygwin\usr\ share\doc\common-licenses or c:\cygwin64\usr\share\doc\common-licenses, as well as http://cygwin.com/licensing.html.

- VMware: http://www.vmware.com/.

- Python: https://docs.python.org/2/license.html.

- Enthought (EPD): https://www.enthought.com/.

- IPython: http://ipython.scipy.org/.

- *Matplotlib*: http://matplotlib.org/users/license.html.

- *SciPy*, http://www.scipy.org/scipylib/license.html.

- *NumPy*: http://docs.scipy.org/doc/numpy/license.html.

- *Pillow* (Python Imaging Library): http://pillow.readthedocs.org/en/latest/about.html.

- *PySerial*: http://pyserial.sourceforge.net/appendix.html.

- Scintilla and SciTE: http://scintilla.sourceforge.net/License.txt.

- Mercurial, http://mercurial.selenic.com/wiki/License.

- Subversion: http://subversion.tigris.org/license-1.html.

Final Notes and References

By now you should have a full development environment, one that provides all the tools of the trade. Experiment with your environment and get accustomed to it; in the following chapters, you'll be using it extensively.

Numerous Python packages are available, and more are being written every day. Two good sources of information on Python packages are:

- PyPI, the Python Package Index, https://pypi.python.org/pypi. This is an extensive repository for packages for Python.

- Unofficial Windows Binaries for Python Extension Packages, maintained by Christoph Gohlke, http://www.lfd.uci.edu/~gohlke/pythonlibs/. This site has many of the packages discussed as binary install files.

CHAPTER 3

■ ■ ■

Python for Programmers

The Building Blocks

Python is a very readable language. Assuming you've had some previous experience in programming, you should be able to read and understand the code presented in the book without much trouble. That said, this book would be incomplete without some coverage of the Python programming language.

In this chapter, I'll take you on a quick tour of the Python building blocks, providing short examples along the way. We'll start by going through the basics of invoking and using Python interactively and noninteractively, entering expressions, and running scripts. Next, we'll cover the basic building blocks of most modern programming languages: data types, structures, variables, printing, flow control, and functions. After a brief overview of object-oriented programming (OOP), we'll conclude with a discussion of modules and packages.

Keep in mind that there's much more to the full extent of the language than will fit in one chapter. Python topics not crucial for data analysis and visualization, I left out. If you would like to learn more about the Python programming language, the "Final Notes and References" section at the end of the chapter lists several Python-oriented books that are more comprehensive and should prove valuable resources.

From a book-design perspective, it stands to reason that this chapter appears in the beginning. But that shouldn't bind you; feel free to skip it and come back to it later and as often as necessary.

What Is Python?

In broad terms, Python is an open source, object-oriented, high-level programming language. (For a more detailed description, see http://www.python.org/about/.) Python has also developed a culture around it. You'll find such notions as "Pythonic" or "Easier to Ask Forgiveness than Permission" (EAFP) or the "batteries included" approach, which together prove that the Python is more than just a programming language. Many developers, so the rumors go, first use the language as a simple tool to solve a specific problem; but with time, they are absolutely captivated to the point they start writing haikus in Python. I'm afraid I'm not that artistic, so you won't be seeing any haikus in this book.

Here are the aspects of the language I view as the most important for using Python effectively for data analysis and visualization:

- *Open source*: Yes, I view this as one of the fundamental aspects about Python. Python—and its packages—have been developed by an active community. The language evolves and changes, providing a dynamic environment built on discussion, on actual needs, and on real problems people have to solve. This approach ensures a good language that hopefully will withstand the test of time.

- *Ease of learning*: It's easy to learn Python, especially if you're familiar with other programming languages—Python combines the best of several programming languages and programming paradigms in one.

- *"Batteries included"*: Python includes a great number of libraries as part of the standard library (several will be explored in this book). Additional packages can be installed and used seamlessly. You should be able to do most, if not all, of the work associated with data analysis and visualization without ever leaving the Python environment.

- *Versatility*: Python is versatile in that it supports both the early stages of development, as a rapid application development tool, and later phases of the project, when more structured programming paradigms are required.

- *Interactive nature*: The ability to run Python interactively gives you great flexibility. More about this in the next section.

Because I think it's easier to show what Python is than to try to define it, let's get to work.

Interactive Python

The ability to run Python interactively, with a command-line interface (CLI), is an envious ability. Using the interactive CLI enables you to understand of the workings of the programming language as well as your code as you write it. As you write code and execute commands, you receive feedback immediately. The feedback provided allows you to examine the results and see whether what you had in mind was actually what happened; that is, it lets you determine whether you wrote the Python code properly. It's not a new concept; the first programming environment I ever used was also interactive in nature: Basic in Sinclair's ZX-81 (see `http://en.wikipedia.org/wiki/Zx-81` for some nostalgia). At times, when I write C code, I just wish I could do the same now as I did then.

The interactive nature of Python is elegantly introduced by its creator, Guido van Rossum, in his "Python Tutorial" available at `https://docs.python.org/3.3/tutorial/`. We'll begin this chapter with a short introduction to running Python interactively, from a data analysis and visualization perspective.

Invoking Python

How you invoke Python depends on your platform:

- In Windows, assuming you've installed the binaries, click Start ➤ All Programs ➤ Python 3.3 ➤ Python (command line) or IDLE (Python GUI) if you prefer a GUI environment. You might have a newer version by now.

- In Windows, under Cygwin, start a Cygwin bash shell and issue the following command:

  ```
  $ python
  ```

- In Linux, open a terminal and issue the same command:

  ```
  $ python
  ```

- To exit Python, either press **Ctrl+D** or enter this:

  ```
  >>> exit()
  ```

Entering Commands

After starting Python in interactive mode, you're presented with version information and a short list of introductory commands: `help`, `copyright`, `credits`, and `license`. You're also presented with the Python prompt `>>>`.

■ **Note** Whenever you encounter the >>> prompt in any listings in the book, it is meant to indicate that the command was issued interactively with the Python interpreter, and you should try it yourself by repeating the same command in your Python interpreter. Similarly, when you encounter three dots (...) at the beginning of a line of code, it means that this is a continuation of the text entered interactively in the previous line.

Issue any of the these commands by entering the command name and pressing **Enter** (from now on, I'll refrain from mentioning to press **Enter** or discussing how to erase characters; I assume you know how to use a CLI). Here's the output from issuing the help command:

```
>>> help
Type help() for interactive help, or help(object) for help about object.
```

Python's CLI allows entering statements and evaluating expressions. Some basic ones are described here. Try them to get a feel for the interactive nature of Python:

```
>>> 1+2+3+4+5+6+7+8+9
```

```
45
```

```
>>> 22*2
```

```
44
```

```
>>> a = 4
>>> a*4
```

```
16
```

```
>>> 'a'*4
```

```
'aaaa'
```

```
>>> sqrt(a)
```

```
Traceback (most recent call last):
  File "<stdin>", line 1, in <module>
NameError: name 'sqrt' is not defined
```

The first couple of lines use Python to do basic arithmetic. One of the benefits of using interactive Python as opposed to using a calculator is that you can edit your previous entries easily; simply press the **Up-Arrow** key to scroll through previous entries you've made and edit them. Plus, you can retrace your steps and find a typo. But that's hardly the reason for using Python, just an added bonus.

The third line is an assignment: it assigns the value 4 to the variable a. The next line prints out the value of a times 4. You'll learn more about variables, functions and statements soon; but for now, let's examine the interactive environment and get you up to speed on how to work with it efficiently.

The following line shows Python's string capabilities. A string is typically enclosed in quotes, so the next command multiplies the string 'a' by 4. Which is exactly that: 'a' multiplied four times results in 'aaaa'—pretty cool.

The last line shows what happens when the interpreter encounters a problem: it raises an exception and reports the reason back to the user. In this particular case, the interpreter doesn't know of the function sqrt(); this can be easily remedied if we import the function by issuing from math import sqrt—but we'll cover that later.

The Result Variable

Whenever Python executes a statement, the result is stored in a special variable named _. This is useful when you're doing some manual calculations:

```
>>> 1+2+3+4+5+6+7+8+9
```

```
45
```

```
>>> _
```

```
45
```

```
>>> _ + 10
```

```
55
```

```
>>> _
```

```
55
```

```
>>> _ / 5
```

```
11.0
```

The result variable keeps on being updated, as shown in this example, so bear that in mind.

The Interactive Help System

The interactive help system is a valuable tool both when learning the language and when programming. Python has a considerable number of functions, modules, and packages, so a help system is a must. As the name suggests, the help system is an interactive system. Invoking it is straightforward (notice the required empty parentheses):

```
>>> help()
```

Enter quit to exit the system. Enter a function name to read about it (e.g., print).

If you enter sqrt, the help system will respond that there's no documentation regarding sqrt. The reason for this is that sqrt is part of the *math* module; to view its help information, you'll have to enter math.sqrt instead. Refer to the "Modules and Packages" section later in this chapter for more in-depth discussion about modules.

You can also view specific function help (noninteractively) using help(function):

```
>>> help(print)
```

```
Help on built-in function print in module builtins:

print(...)
    print(value, ..., sep=' ', end='\n', file=sys.stdout, flush=False)

    Prints the values to a stream, or to sys.stdout by default.
    Optional keyword arguments:
    file:  a file-like object (stream); defaults to the current sys.stdout.
    sep:   string inserted between values, default a space.
    end:   string appended after the last value, default a newline.
    flush: whether to forcibly flush the stream.
```

In reality what happens when you issue the command help(function) is that that function's docstring is printed. You can learn more about docstrings in the "Defining Functions" section later in this chapter.

Moving Around

At times, it's desirable to change the current working directory within the Python interpreter. This is especially important if the code and data are located in different directories; it might be easier to just switch to another directory as the situation requires.

Suppose you defined a function that accepts a file name as input, reads it, and does some processing. Furthermore, this function was defined interactively, as you were using the interpreter. Now you'd like to run this function on some files, but the path to these files is long and cumbersome. This is a situation where it'd be much easier to switch to the directory where the files reside and execute the function with the relatively shorter file name; that is, you can exclude the path.

Module *os* provides us with this functionality. You've already seen the *os* module in Chapter 1; however, this time we use it to move around the interpreter:

```
>>> import os
>>> os.getcwd()
```

```
'/home/shai/python'
```

```
>>> os.listdir()
```

```
['src', 'data']
```

```
>>> os.chdir('src')
>>> os.getcwd()
```

```
'/home/shai/python/src'
```

```
>>> os.chdir('/home/shai/python/data')
>>> os.getcwd()
```

```
'/home/shai/python/data'
```

```
>>> os.chdir('../src')
>>> os.getcwd()
```

```
'/home/shai/python/src'
```

```
>>> os.listdir('/home/shai/python/data')
```

```
['GPS-2008-06-05-13-02-56.csv']
```

In this listing, I use several functions. The first line imports the *os* module that contains the functions required to move around. I then use several functions from the *os* module:

- The function `os.listdir(path='.')` returns a list of directory contents. The `path` argument is a string with the name of the directory to be listed. If the string argument is not supplied, it is assumed to be a string with a single dot in it (`'.'`); that is, it is assumed to be the current directory, in which case the function returns the contents of the current directory.

■ **Note** When you encounter an argument to a function with an assignment operator, it means that this is the default argument if one is not supplied, as in this example: `os.listdir(path='.')`.

- To figure out your current working directory, issue the command `os.getcwd()`. This function takes no arguments.
- Finally, the `os.chdir(path)` function accepts one string as an argument and, depending on the string, changes directories accordingly. The function accepts both relative directory paths (e.g., `'../src'`) as well as full directory paths (e.g., `'/home/shai/python/data'`).

■ **Tip** In IPython (see Chapter 2), you can use the commands `cd`, `ls`, and `pwd` as you would in any Linux shell instead of using the *os* module functions (they're faster to type!).

Running Scripts

The interactive environment can only get you so far. Eventually, you will want to write programs (scripts) and run them either noninteractively or from within the Python interpreter.

The most common reason to write scripts is that you need to perform a task more than once. Say the accountants in your company use nonlinear depreciation equations, and they ask you (their favorite programmer) for a personal favor, so you decide to write a web-based depreciation calculator. Or the clinical people in your medical device company often require access to log files that are large and require processing, so they ask you to write an end-of-day report per patient summarizing the day's events based on those log files, or…, well, you get the idea.

Typically, I use the interactive environment in parallel to coding the script. That is, I run Python interactively, run a few statements, assign some variables, and plot some graphs; if things look good, I then copy over the commands I issued to an editor where my script resides.

■ **Tip** In IPython you can issue the command `history` to view a list of recently entered commands.

The benefit of coding interactively is that you can examine the variables and data structures of your code, without additional debugging tools. If the script raises an exception, you now have at your fingertips all the variables and data structures: you can reproduce the error and possibly fix the bug.

Once your script is ready (well it's never really *ready*, let's just agree that it's ready to be test-driven), you have several options to run it:

- Run the script from the GUI environment: running IDLE (Python GUI), select File ➤ Open and choose the script to run. This will open the Python script in the IDLE editor (if it's already open, there's no need to reopen it). To run the script, press **F5** or select Run Module from the Run menu. The output should appear in the Python GUI shell.

- Run the script from Python's CLI. This is done by issuing the command `exec(open('scriptname.py').read())`; this is my favorite option when developing. In Python versions 2.x, an alternative is to use `execfile('scriptname.py')`. The reason I prefer this method over the GUI environment is that I like editing my code in an editor that is not part of an IDE.

■ **Tip** If you're using IPython, you can issue the command `run path/filename.py`; the benefits are that you can use character completion to select the file name and that you can supply command-line parameters to the script: `run path/filename.py param1 param2`.

- Invoke the script from the shell or a command window (noninteractive mode).

  Even though you might have developed your script in interactive Python, it's a good idea to test your script in a shell as well, especially if you're distributing your code for others to use: they might not want to run the code interactively. To run the script from a Linux shell or Cygwin, use this command:

  ```
  $ python path/filename.py
  ```

  In Windows, use this command:

  ```
  c:\python33\python.exe path\filename.py
  ```

  In Windows, you could also set the PATH variable to include the Python directory path, c:\python33 (assuming you're using Python 3.3), so invoking the script will not require a full path to the Python executable:

  ```
  path=%path%;c:\python33
  python path\filename.py
  ```

In newer versions of Python, it's possible to set the PATH variable during installation by selecting the option *Add python.exe to Path* (not enabled by default), as shown in Figure 3-1.

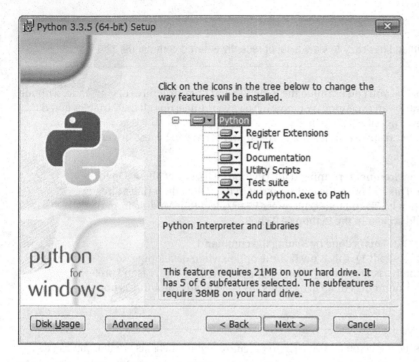

Figure 3-1. Adding python.exe to Path

- Finally, it's also possible to enjoy both worlds: interactive and noninteractive mode! This is done by running the script with the -i switch, which opens up a Python shell *after* the script has run and lets you examine variables, interactively:

```
$ python –i somescript.py
```

■ **Tip** Since the backslash character (\) has a special meaning in strings (we'll get to that later) and is also used as a path separator in Windows, it's best to use the slash (/) character whenever you're working with file names and file paths. If you can, use relative paths (e.g., ../data instead of c:\data); your code will be portable across operating systems and much easier to read.

That's it. I think we're ready for the language itself now.

Data Types

Python data types are similar to data types in other programming languages; you'll see strings and numbers here, just as you would in, say, Basic. But there are some niceties you should know about even in those basic data types; for example, the int data type supports infinite integer precision.

Numbers

We'll start off with numbers. Python natively supports `int`, `float`, and `complex`.

Integers

The data type `int` provides infinite integer precision, so there's no limit to the value of the integers you can use:

```
>>> 2**70
```

```
1180591620717411303424
```

```
>>> 2**700
```

```
5260135901548373507240989882880128665550339802823173859498280903068732154297080822113666536277588451226982968856178217771301943225018380386312781477065188084995522367112844459819166375788432271727129325173578137 6
```

I've introduced the operator power, denoted by **, so 2**70 is 2^{70}.

Other Useful Bases

Bases that are powers of 2 are native to computing systems. One byte is 2^8 as opposed to, say, a power of the decimal system. For this reason, the ability to convert values to and from bases that are powers of 2 (such as the hexadecimal base or the octal base) to the decimal system is important.

■ **Note**   The octal base is less popular nowadays. However, some octal notations are still active, including file permissions in Linux systems.

Hexadecimal values are denoted with a leading 0x. Thus, 0x20 is 32 (decimal). You can use both capital and noncapital letters for digits A–F:

```
>>> 0xaB
```

```
171
```

```
>>> 0xff
```

```
255
```

Octal values are denoted with a leading zero and the character O (i.e, 0o or 0O). Thus 0o20 is 16 (decimal):

```
>>> 0o20
```

16

Notice that in Python 2.x, octal values are preceded only by a zero without the character O.

Similarly, binary values are denoted by a leading zero and the character B (i.e., 0b or 0B). Thus, 0b111 is 7 (decimal):

```
>>> 0b111
```

7

Regardless of how you enter numbers; that is, regardless of what base you've used, they're still retained as numbers in Python. Should you want to look up the different base representation, use the bin(), oct() and hex() function calls. These functions return a string:

```
>>> hex(100)
```

'0x64'

```
>>> oct(100)
```

'0o144'

```
>>> bin(100)
```

'0b1100100'

You can also perform any other base conversion using the function int(str, radix=10), which returns a number, not a string. If radix isn't specified, it is assumed to be 10:

```
>>> int('100')
```

100

```
>>> int('100', 3)
```

9

If you'd like to convert 100 in base 3 to a decimal value, write int('100', 3) or int(str(100), 3). The latter is more useful if you'd like to use a variable; that is, int(str(variable), base). If you pass a floating point value to the function int(), the result is a truncated integer value:

```
>>> int(2.2)
```

```
2
```

It's possible to use higher bases than hexadecimal (base 16), using an increasing number of letters from the alphabet as the new digits for the base. In base 17, the character g is added; in base 18, the character h is used, and so on. So the number 'ggg' in base 17 should is 17^3-1:

```
>>> int('ggg', 17)
```

```
4912
```

```
>>> 17**3-1
```

```
4912
```

This support for bases is up to value 36, corresponding with the character z.

Comparisons

You can compare values using the regular operators: > and < for greater than and less than, respectively. Equality checks are done using a double equal sign (==) to differentiate from the assignment symbol denoted by a single equal sign (=). Inequality is !=, and you can also use >= and <= for greater-than-or-equal and less-than-or-equal comparisons.

```
>>> 2*3 > 5
```

```
True
```

```
>>> 2*3 != 5
```

```
True
```

Some comparisons are not allowed; for instance, you cannot compare a complex number (described in the next section) with an integer value:

```
>>> 1+1j > 2
```

```
Traceback (most recent call last):
  File "<stdin>", line 1, in <module>
TypeError: unorderable types: complex() > int()
```

Bitwise Operations

Bitwise operators are similar to C's bitwise operators, as shown in Table 3-1.

Table 3-1. *Bitwise Operations*

Operator	Description	Example
~	Bitwise not	~0x0ff+0x100 returns 0.
<<	Shift left	1<<8 returns 256.
>>	Shift right	256>>2 returns 64.
^	Bitwise exclusive OR (XOR)	0xff ^ 0xf0 returns 15 (0x0f).
&	Bitwise AND	0xff & 0x0f returns 15 (0x0f).
|	Bitwise OR	0x0f | 0xf0 returns 255 (0xff).

Augmented Assignments

Augmented assignments introduce the operators +=, -=, *=, /=, //=, %=, **=, <<=, >>=, &=, ^=, and |=. This notation is similar to C/C++ syntax. That is, instead of writing a = a+1, you can write a += 1. Similarly, instead of writing a = a >> 1, you can write a >>= 1. Please note that Python does not support the increment operator ++.

Float and Complex

Floating point values have been around for quite some time, and there's no escaping them. Python's float data type is equivalent to C's double, so it's really more accurate than C's float (C's float has less bytes than C's double).

Floating-point values are represented with a dot or with the e or E character denoting exponential notation. If you want to ensure your value is a float, either add a trailing dot (or dot zero, or e/E) or explicitly do so with the function float(). The function float() is also used to convert values to float. This works on strings as well as numbers, as long as the conversion is possible. With the type() function, which returns the type of the variable, function, you can always confirm whether a variable is an integer, a floating point value, or something else:

```
>>> type(2)
```

```
<class 'int'>
```

```
>>> type(2.2)
```

```
<class 'float'>
```

```
>>> float(2)
```

```
2.0
```

```
>>> 1e3
```

```
1000.0
```

```
>>> float('2.5')
```

```
2.5
```

The complex data type represents complex numbers and is composed of two floating-point values, one representing the real part and one representing the imaginary part. The imaginary part is appended with the trailing letter j (or J). Accessing the real and imaginary parts is possible using the imag and real attributes, as follows:

```
>>> a = 1+2j
>>> a.real
```

```
1.0
```

```
>>> a.imag
```

```
2.0
```

You can use most any operator on complex numbers, just as you would on floating-point numbers. Once a computation involving a complex number is encountered, the remaining computation will remain a complex, that is, integers and floating-point values are promoted to complex values. You can convert a number to a complex number using the complex(real[, imag]) function. If imag is provided, it holds the imaginary value of the complex number:

```
>>> complex(10)
```

```
(10+0j)
```

```
>>> complex(10, 2)
```

```
(10+2j)
```

Chapter 7 will discuss the complex data type further, as well as put it to work in some examples.

Strings

Per the classic Python definition, strings are an immutable sequence of characters. This means a string is a sequence of characters that you can't change. I know that this might seem odd at first: you're probably thinking, "How do I work with strings if I can't modify their characters?" The answer is that you create new strings based on your current string.

Expressing Strings

There are several ways to express a string: single quotes, 'string'; double quotes, "string"; and triple-double-quotes, """string""" (phew), to name a few. And there are even more: most notably raw strings denoted by the letter r such as r"string".

To express a basic string, use single quotes as follows:

```
>>> 'split'
```

```
'split'
```

In case your string has a quote in it, you'll have to escape it with a backslash (\):

```
>>> 'it\'s a split'
```

```
"it's a split"
```

The reason we escaped the quote that's part of the word it's is so that the quote before the letter s won't terminate the string.

Single quotes and double quotes are interchangeable. Therefore, we could have achieved the same result, without escaping the quote that's part of the word it's, by replacing the enclosing quote (the ones at the beginning and end) with double quotes:

```
>>> "it's a split"
```

```
"it's a split"
```

But what if we wanted a string that actually does have the backslash before the quote as well—a string that looks exactly like this: it\'s a split? Well, one option is to escape the backslash as well as the quote:

```
>>> 'it\'\\s a split second'
```

```
"it'\\s a split second"
```

```
>>> print('it\'\\s a split second')
```

```
it'\s a split second
```

Notice how the interpreter represents that string differently from how it's printed.

This pattern can keep on going, making things harder to understand. Instead, we could use a raw string:

```
>>> r"it\'s a split second"
```

```
"it\\'s a split second"
```

```
>>> print(r"it\'s a split second")
```

```
it\'s a split second
```

A raw string means that everything following the character r and the starting quote and before the ending quote should be taken literally. When using a raw string, you're basically saying "Have Python escape what needs escaping and return a proper string back to me!"

■ **Note**   Raw strings are common in regular expressions, so as not to escape special meaning characters on several levels. See Chapter 5 for details.

You can enter strings over multiple lines using a backslash:

```
>>> "it's a \
... split second"
```

```
"it's a split second"
```

This obviously could bring about more disasters—what if you *really* wanted that backslash to appear, as well as the line break? Not to worry, it's time to use triple-double-quotes (or triple-single-quotes, they're interchangeable):

```
>>> """it's a split
... second"""
```

```
"it's a split\nsecond"
```

```
>>> print(_)
```

```
it's a split
second
```

If all this sounds too confusing, you're in good company. To acquaint yourself with these caveats, launch Python interactively and experiment! For more information on strings, refer to the online Python documentation available at https://docs.python.org/3.3/library/stdtypes.html#text-sequence-type-str.

Python also supports Unicode strings; I'll touch on those in Chapter 5.

String Operations

So what can you do with strings? Table 3-2 lists some operations that can be performed on strings, along with examples. In the examples, I've selected strings that don't require escaping so they're easier to follow; however, the same can be applied to any string expression described previously.

Table 3-2. *String Operations*

Operator	Description	Example
Adding and Multiplying		
str1+str2	Concatenates strings str1 and str2.	'split '+'second' returns 'split second'.
str*n	Concatenates the str string n times.	'second '*3 returns 'second second second '.
Indexing and Slicing		
n and m are positive integer values less than the length of str. Negative values are counted from the end of the string.		
s[n]	Retrieves the nth character of s.	'split'[3] returns 'i'.
s[n:m]	Retrieves a string slice from nth character to the mth character, excluding the mth character. If n or m are negative, they are counted from the end of the string.	'split second'[6:12] returns 'second'. 'split second'[-6:-2] returns 'seco'.
s[:m]	Equals s[n:m] with n=0.	'split second'[:3] returns 'spl'.
s[n:]	Retrieves a string slice from the nth character to the end.	'split second'[6:] returns 'second'.

You can check whether a character is in a string using the in operator:

```
>>> 'd' in 'abcde'
```

```
True
```

You can count the number of characters in a string using the len() function:

```
>>> len('abcde')
```

```
5
```

Both in and len() operate on other sequences, as you'll soon see.
Chapter 5 discusses strings (including Unicode strings and raw strings) in more detail.

Booleans

I've postponed discussion of Boolean values until now because Booleans values shine in the context of other data types. Booleans can take two values: True (1) or False (0).

```
>>> a = True
>>> a > 1
```

```
False
```

```
>>> a == 1
```

```
True
```

```
>>> type(a)
```

```
<class 'bool'>
```

You can convert a value to a Boolean by using the bool() function. Empty strings, as well as other empty sequences, and the value zero of any form are considered False:

```
>>> bool(0)
```

```
False
```

```
>>> bool(5)
```

```
True
```

```
>>> bool("")
```

```
False
```

```
>>> bool("s")
```

```
True
```

Logical Operations

Logical operations and, or, and not operate on Booleans. I assume you know how to use them. Let's see if you know the answer to the following:

```
>>> 5 > 1 and ((4<3) or 2+4 < 5 and not 6 < 2)
```

(If you're not sure, simply type it in Python and observe the result.)

Data Structures

Python, being a high-level programming language, also provides additional, more complex data types, which I refer to as *data structures*. These include lists, tuples, dictionaries, and sets, to name a few. Data structures make the programming experience a lot more enjoyable. Python documentation does not necessarily differentiate between data types and data structures the way I have. My purpose in this distinction is to split the discussion into two categories: simple *data types*, which you're likely to encounter in popular programming languages (such as C); and more complex data types, or *data structures*, which you're likely to see in higher-level programming languages such as Python and Perl. Regardless of the classification presented in this chapter, both are built-in data types as far as Python is concerned.

In a sense, you've already been exposed to data structures: strings and complex numbers. The string is an immutable sequence, hardly a "simple" data type. By comparison, the C programming language does not support a native string data type, rather, it supports an array of characters, which demonstrates that strings aren't really all that basic. But a string is still limited—it's a sequence of characters. What about sequences of other objects? And what about mutable (changeable) sequences?

Not to worry, Python provides those as well. A *list* in Python is a mutable sequence of arbitrary data types. A *tuple* is quite similar to a list, only it's immutable. We'll also talk about some more complex data structures that can make programming yet more entertaining. You've already seen a *dictionary* object in Chapter 1, and we'll explore that data structure as well as the *set* object. Python is also an object-oriented-programming language; therefore, a discussion of the *class* object will be presented after we have talked about *functions*.

■ **Note**   Python offers additional native data types and structures, but most of them are beyond the scope for this book; they're not a must for data analysis and visualization (with the possible exception of *file* data type, which will be discussed in Chapter 5). For more information, see the Python Standard Library – Built-in Types, https://docs.python.org/3.3/library/stdtypes.html.

Lists

A list is a mutable sequence of objects. A list is denoted by brackets:

```
>>> [1, 'hey', 1+2j]
```

```
[1, 'hey', (1+2j)]
```

You can also create a list using the list() function. This is useful when converting different sequences to a list (e.g., from a string):

```
>>> list('some text')
```

```
['s', 'o', 'm', 'e', ' ', 't', 'e', 'x', 't']
```

A list can be modified. You can add another element to a list by using the + operator. The + operator concatenates lists, so you have to supply another list:

```
>>> [1, 'hey', 1+2j] + ['hey', 'hey']
```

```
[1, 'hey', (1+2j), 'hey', 'hey']
```

The following, however, fails, since you cannot add an integer to a list:

```
>>> [1,2,3] + 2
```

```
Traceback (most recent call last):
  File "<stdin>", line 1, in <module>
TypeError: can only concatenate list (not "int") to list
```

The proper way to do this would be to form another list, made solely of the value 2:

```
>>> [1,2,3] + [2]
```

```
[1, 2, 3, 2]
```

If you're looking to add the value 2 to each and every element of the list [1, 2, 3], that is, to modify the list to [3, 4, 5], you'll get the details for how to do so in the sections "The for Statement" and "List Comprehensions" later in this chapter.

A list is an object too, so you can also have a list inside a list:

```
>>> [[1, 2], [3, 4]]
```

```
[[1, 2], [3, 4]]
```

Now things get trickier, both in describing the object and in actually performing operations. Say you'd like to add another list, [5, 6], to the preceding example. How exactly would you like to add it? Should the updated list be [[1, 2], [3, 4], [5, 6]] or [[1, 2], [3, 4], 5, 6] or [[[1, 2], [3, 4]], [5, 6]] (which really is shamelessly tricky)?

The way I like to describe the data structure [[1, 2], [3, 4]] is as a list of rows. The first row is [1, 2] and the second row is [3, 4].

Here are some of the things you can do to concatenate lists:

```
>>> [[1, 2], [3, 4]] + [5, 6]
```

```
[[1, 2], [3, 4], 5, 6]
```

```
>>> [[1, 2], [3, 4]] + [[5, 6]]
```

```
[[1, 2], [3, 4], [5, 6]]
```

The first line adds the elements 5 and 6. The second line adds the row [5, 6].

Another option is to use a variable to hold the list, L, and use the append() and extend() methods:

```
>>> L = [[1, 2], [3, 4]]
>>> L.append([5, 6])
>>> L
```

```
[[1, 2], [3, 4], [5, 6]]
```

```
>>> L.extend([7, 8])
>>> L
```

```
[[1, 2], [3, 4], [5, 6], 7, 8]
```

The method append() adds an item to the list—in this case, the list [5, 6]. The method extend() adds elements from the sequence one by one to the list—in this case, the elements 7 and 8. It's a bit hard to follow at first, but experiment with lists interactively to get a feel for how to use them properly.

Lists, like strings, can also be indexed:

```
>>> L = [['hey', '1'], [2, 3, 4], '']
>>> L[0]
```

```
['hey', '1']
```

```
>>> L[1]
```

```
[2, 3, 4]
```

```
>>> L[1][1]
```

```
3
```

The last statement, L[1][1], requires some explanation. The statement L[1] returns the second element in the list (indices start at 0, so index 1 is the second element). For our purposes, let's mentally assign L[1] to variable M. However, variable M is a list, as well: [2, 3, 4]. So clearly we also can index M: M[1] is 3. Instead of doing those two steps, we can write this more compactly as L[1][1].

Lists, much like strings, can also be sliced:

```
>>> L = [['hey', '1'], [2, 3, 4], '']
>>> L[0:-1]
```

```
[['hey', '1'], [2, 3, 4]]
```

```
>>> L[:-1]
```

```
[['hey', '1'], [2, 3, 4]]
```

```
>>> L[1:]
```

```
[[2, 3, 4], '']
```

A negative index in a slice means that you count from the end of the list, backwards. Thus, the index -1 means the last element. Also, notice that slicing with a missing index defaults to either zero or to the end of the list, depending on which index is missing.

You can check whether an item is in a list using the in operator:

```
>>> 'hey' in ['hey', 'hey', 'split', 'second']
```

```
True
```

You can count the number of elements in a list using the len() statement:

```
>>> len([['hey', '1'], [2, 3, 4], ''])
```

```
3
```

Since lists are mutable, they can be reassigned:

```
>>> L = [['hey', '1'], [2, 3, 4], '']
>>> L[1] = [4, 5, 6]
>>> L
```

```
[['hey', '1'], [4, 5, 6], '']
```

Lists can also have items removed using the del statement:

```
>>> L = [['hey', '1'], [2, 3, 4], '']
>>> del L[0]
>>> L
```

```
[[2, 3, 4], '']
```

Lists also have methods, functions that operate only on list objects (e.g., append() and extend(), which were shown previously). To use a method, follow the list object with a dot, and then follow the function name with parentheses and parameters within (empty ones in case of no parameters):

```
>>> L = ['hey', 'hey', 'split', 'second']
>>> L.count('hey')
```

```
2
```

```
>>> L.sort()
>>> L
```

```
['hey', 'hey', 'second', 'split']
```

I've used the methods count(), which counts the occurrences of an item in a list, and sort(), which sorts a list. Table 3-3 describes some list methods, along with some examples. In the examples, assume that L is ['second', 'second', 8].

Table 3-3. *List Methods*

Method	Description	Example
append(obj)	Adds an element to the end of a list.	L.append('hey') changes L to ['second', 'second', 8, 'hey'].
count(val)	Returns the number of times val appears in the list	L.count('second') returns 2.
extend(iterable)	Adds elements to the list from iterable (more on iterators and iterables later in this chapter).	L.extend(range(2)) changes L to ['second', 'second', 8, 0, 1].
index(val, [start, [stop]])	Returns the first index of val in the list. If start is supplied, this method returns the first index that is greater than start; if stop is supplied, the index also has to be less than stop.	L.index('second') returns 0. L.index('second', 1) returns 1. L.index('second', 2, 3) returns an exception x not in list.
insert(n, obj)	Inserts an object at index n.	L.insert(2, 'me') changes L to ['second', 'second', 'me', 8].
pop([n])	Returns the nth element in the list and removes it. If n is not supplied, this method returns the last element.	L.pop() returns 8, and the modified list is ['second', 'second']. L.pop(-3) returns 'second', and the modified list is ['second', 8].
remove(val)	Removes the first occurrence of val in x.	L.remove('second') changes L to ['second', 8].
reverse()	Reverses the list.	L.reverse() modifies L to [8, 'second', 'second'].
sort()	Sorts the list. You can supply a sort function to the list; see help(list.sort).	L.sort() raises an exception because sorting a number with a string is not defined. For L = ['zoo', 'a'], L.sort() changes L to ['a', 'zoo'].

Tuples

A *tuple* is an immutable (unchangeable) sequence of objects. A tuple is denoted by parentheses and can be created using the tuple() function:

```
>>> (1, 2, 3)
```

```
(1, 2, 3)
```

```
>>> tuple('hey')
```

```
('h', 'e', 'y')
```

Tuples don't necessarily require parentheses; merely adding a comma suggests the expression is a tuple:

```
>>> 1, 2
```

```
(1, 2)
```

```
>>> 1,
```

```
(1,)
```

```
>>> (1)
```

```
1
```

The expression (1) is not a tuple: it's the value 1 within parentheses, which is treated simply as 1.

Tuples behave much like lists, with this exception: you can't modify a tuple. However, you can create a new one based on an existing one:

```
>>> tuple([1, 2, 3])
```

```
(1, 2, 3)
```

```
>>> _ * 2
```

```
(1, 2, 3, 1, 2, 3)
```

In the first statement, I've created a tuple based on a list. Note that tuple(1, 2, 3) would cause an exception because the function tuple() expects one argument, not three. In the preceding code, I passed a list as an argument: [1, 2, 3]. I could have also written tuple((1, 2, 3)), effectively achieving the same thing: the first outer set of parentheses in the expression is the function parentheses; the inner one is the tuple parentheses. In the second statement listed, I've created a second tuple based on the first one, by multiplying the result variable.

Tuples can contain different data types and data structures:

```
>>> ([1, 2], (3, 4))
```

```
([1, 2], (3, 4))
```

The preceding is a tuple that contains a list and a tuple.

Tuples can also be indexed, similar to lists and strings. Remember that indexing requires brackets, not parentheses:

```
>>> ([1, 2], (3, 4))[0]
```

```
[1, 2]
```

```
>>> ([1, 2], (3, 4))[1]
```

```
(3, 4)
```

```
>>> ([1, 2], (3, 4))[1][0]
```

```
3
```

A tuple can also be sliced, generating a new tuple:

```
>>> ([1, 2], (3, 4))[1:]
```

```
((3, 4),)
```

However, tuples can not be reassigned:

```
>>> a = (['hey', '1'], '')
>>> a[0] = 0
```

```
Traceback (most recent call last):
  File "<stdin>", line 1, in <module>
TypeError: 'tuple' object does not support item assignment
```

But the lists within them *can* be changed, since lists are mutable:

```
>>> a = (['hey', '1'], '')
>>> a[0][0] = 'wow'
>>> a
```

```
(['wow', '1'], '')
```

Checking whether an item is in a tuple can be done using the in operator:

```
>>> 1 in (2, 3)
```

```
False
```

Finally, it's common practice to use tuples to perform multiple assignments, also known as unpacking:

```
>>> a, b = 1, 2
>>> a + b
```

```
3
```

Dictionaries

Dictionaries are mutable sequences that connect a *key* with a *value*. The key must be unique, whereas the value need not be. I like to use a phonebook metaphor when I think about dictionaries. Every phone number (key) has but one entry (value) associated with it, usually a person; however, one person (value) can have several phones (keys). The key and value objects can be most data types, but there are exceptions (e.g., another dictionary).

There are several ways to create a dictionary. For example, you might use the dict() function with a sequence of (key, value) tuples, or you might use the curly braces ({}) with colons separating keys and values:

```
>>> dict((('split', 8), ('second', 1)))
```

```
{'second': 1, 'split': 8}
```

```
>>> {'split':8, 'second':1}
```

```
{'second': 1, 'split': 8}
```

```
>>> type(_)
```

```
<class 'dict'>
```

There are a lot of parentheses in the first expression: the outermost are the parentheses for the function dict(), the innermost are specific tuple pairs, and the ones in between denote a tuple of tuples, because dict() can only accept one argument. A more readable approach would be to pass dict() a list of tuples, instead of a tuple of tuples:

```
>>> dict([('split', 8), ('second', 1)])
```

```
{'second': 1, 'split': 8}
```

You retrieve values from a dictionary using brackets:

```
>>> D = dict([('split', 8), ('second', 1)])
>>> D['split']
```

```
8
```

Checking for membership in a dictionary is done using the in operator, which defaults to checking against the keys of the dictionary, not the values. If you wish to check against the values, use the values() method:

```
>>> D = dict([('split', 8), ('second', 1)])
>>> 'split' in D
```

True

```
>>> 8 in D
```

False

```
>>> 8 in D.values()
```

True

You use brackets to change and assign new values, as well:

```
>>> D = dict([('split', 8), ('second', 1)])
>>> D['python'] = 'snake'
>>> D
```

```
{'split': 8, 'second': 1, 'python': 'snake'}
```

```
>>> D['python'] = 'programming language'
>>> D
```

```
{'split': 8, 'second': 1, 'python': 'programming language'}
```

In the preceding example, the second assignment to the key 'python' overwrites the previous value, 'snake', with the value 'programming language'.

If you think about it, real-world dictionaries may have several entries for one key: the word "python" can mean a nonvenomous, constricting snake or an open source programming language. This behavior can be mimicked in Python dictionaries as well; simply have the value contain a list:

```
>>> D = dict()
>>> D['python'] = ['snake', 'programming language']
>>> D·
```

```
{'python': ['snake', 'programming language']}
```

Dictionaries are implemented using a hashing algorithm. This means that retrieving a value from a key is extremely efficient. There's a lot of information regarding hashing algorithms and hashing functions on the Internet, so look that up if you're interested in knowing how they work (for a good starting point, see https://en.wikipedia.org/wiki/Hash_function). Used properly, a dictionary can simplify your code and make it a lot more efficient. In Chapter 4, I present an example of using a dictionary to locate duplicate files on a hard drive.

Table 3-4 lists dictionary member functions. In the examples in the table, assume D is {'second': 1, 'split': 8}.

Table 3-4. *Dictionary Methods*

Method	Description	Example
Functions		
clear()	Removes all items from the dictionary.	D.clear() changes D to {}.
copy()	Returns a shallow copy of D (see the "Variables" section later in the chapter).	D2 = D.copy().
fromkeys(K[, v])	Creates a dictionary from keys K. If v is provided; all values are set to v.	{}.fromkeys(['split', 'second'], 8) returns {'second': 8, 'split': 8}.
get(k[, def])	Returns the value associated with key k. If k is not in the dictionary, this method returns def if provided.	D.get('first', 1) returns 1.
items()	Returns key-value tuples.	D.items() returns dict_items([('split', 8), ('second', 1)]).
keys()	Returns the list of keys.	D.keys() returns dict_keys(['second', 'split']).
pop(k[, def])	Returns the value associated with key k and removes it from the dictionary. If k is not in the dictionary, this method returns def if provided; otherwise, it raises an exception.	D.pop('split') returns 8 and changes D to {'second': 1}.
popitem()	Returns an arbitrary key-value tuple and removes the pair from the dictionary.	D.popitem() returns ('second', 1) and changes D to {'split': 8}.
setdefault(k[,def])	Returns the value associated with the key k. If k is not in the dictionary, this method returns def if provided and sets D[k] to def.	D.setdefault('hey', 6) returns 6 and changes D to {'second': 1, 'hey': 6, 'split': 8}.
update(e)	Updates the dictionary with data from dictionary e.	See the upcoming example in this section.
values()	Returns the list of values.	D.values() returns dict_values([1, 8]).

While most of these member functions are easy to follow, two require more explanation: update() and get().

The method update() updates the dictionary with key-value pairs from another dictionary. For ease of discussion, I'll refer to the function call D1.update(D2). If a key exists in both dictionaries D1 and D2, the value associated with the key in the dictionary D1 is updated with the value from dictionary D2. If a key from D2 does not exist in D1, it is added to D1 along with its value. The following illustrates this behavior:

```
>>> d1 = {'second': 1, 'split': 8}
>>> d2 = {'second': 3, 'hey': 7}
>>> d1.update(D2)
>>> d1
```

```
{'second': 3, 'split': 8, 'hey': 7}
```

The value associated with the key 'second' was updated, and the key-value pair 'hey': 7 was added.

The next member function I want to talk about is get(). At first, this seems rather odd; how is get() different from simply accessing the key using brackets? The difference is that if you use brackets and the key is not in the dictionary, a KeyError exception is raised. The function get() allows you to check whether a key is in a dictionary; and as a side product, the function also returns a default value if the key is not in the dictionary. A good way to show how this is useful is perhaps with an example.

Consider the function list_gps_commands() presented in Chapter 1 (I've removed the docstring), shown here in Listing 3-1.

Listing 3-1. Function list_gps_commands()

```
def list_gps_commands(data):
    gps_cmds = dict()
    for row in data:
        try:
            gps_cmds[row[0]] += 1
        except:
            gps_cmds[row[0]] = 1
    return gps_cmds
```

To further illustrate the example, let's build a short list of GPS commands, L, to later sort in a dictionary so you can try the example for yourself. First, we execute a set of commands similar to those detailed in the function list_gps_commands():

```
>>> L = ['$GPGSA', '$GPGSV', '$GPGSV', '$GPGSV', '$GPRMC', '$GPGGA']
>>> D1 = dict()
>>> for elem in L:
...     try:
...         D1[elem] += 1
...     except KeyError:
...         D1[elem] = 1
...
>>> D1
```

```
{'$GPGSA': 1, '$GPGSV': 3, '$GPGGA': 1, '$GPRMC': 1}
```

The approach is simple. We first try to access a key in the dictionary. If the key exists, we increment the count. If the key doesn't exist, an exception is raised, which means it's a new entry, so we set it to 1.

A second approach is to check whether a key exists in a dictionary using the in statement and then follow up with an if sentence, as follows:

```
>>> L = ['$GPGSA', '$GPGSV', '$GPGSV', '$GPGSV', '$GPRMC', '$GPGGA']
>>> D2 = dict()
>>> for elem in L:
...     if elem in D2:
...         D2[elem] += 1
...     else:
...         D2[elem] = 1
...
>>> D2
```

```
{'$GPGGA': 1, '$GPGSA': 1, '$GPGSV': 3, '$GPRMC': 1}
```

A more elegant approach would be to use the get() method with a default value of 0:

```
>>> L = ['$GPGSA', '$GPGSV', '$GPGSV', '$GPGSV', '$GPRMC', '$GPGGA']
>>> D3 = dict()
>>> for elem in L:
...     D3[elem] = D3.get(elem, 0)+1
...
>>> D3
```

```
{'$GPGSA': 1, '$GPGSV': 3, '$GPGGA': 1, '$GPRMC': 1}
```

I chose the first approach in Chapter 1 because I think it's clearer to those unfamiliar with the language. However, those familiar with the Python language will probably opt for the last approach presented here; it is clearer and more elegant.

Sets

Our last data structure for now will be a *set*. Sets are sequences of **unique** items. To create a set, use the set() function:

```
>>> set(['split', 'second'])
```

```
{'split', 'second'}
```

```
>>> set(['split', 'second']*8)
```

```
{'split', 'second'}
```

If you pass a duplicate to the set() function, it will not be added to the set. This is shown in the second statement where a list multiplied by 8 is passed as an argument.

In a sense, you've already been introduced to sets: the keys in a dictionary form a set since they are unique items.

Set operations are a bit different from the previous sequences you've seen. They are derived from the math operations and include intersection, union, and difference, to name a few:

```
>>> S1 = set(['split', 'second'])
>>> S2 = set(['split', 8])
>>> S1 | S2
```

```
{8, 'split', 'second'}
```

```
>>> s1.union(S2)
```

```
{8, 'split', 'second'}
```

```
>>> S1 & S2
```

```
{'split'}
```

```
>>> S1 - S2
```

```
{'second'}
```

```
>>> S1.difference(S2)
```

```
{'second'}
```

```
>>> S2.difference(S1)
```

```
{8}
```

The operator | is equivalent to the member function union(). The operator & is equivalent to the member function intersection(). The operator - is equivalent to the member function difference(); and much like regular subtraction, the order is important: S1-S2 is different from S2-S1.

Table 3-5 lists some set functions. In the examples, assume S1 equals set([8, 'hey']).

Table 3-5. *Set Methods*

Method	Description	Example
add(obj)	Adds obj to the set.	S1.add(9) changes S1 to {8, 'hey', 9}.
clear()	Removes all elements from the list.	S1.clear() changes S1 to set().
copy()	Returns a shallow copy of S1 (see a discussion of shallow copy in the "Variables" section later in the chapter).	S2 = S1.copy().
difference(S2)	Returns the difference of two sets. This is equivalent to S1-S2.	S1.difference(set([8])) returns {'hey'}.
difference_update(S2)	Similar to difference() but modifies the set (not merely returns a copy).	S1.difference_update(set([8])) changes S1 to {'hey'}.
discard(v)	Removes the element v from the set. If v is not in the set, nothing happens (no exception is raised).	S1.discard(8) changes S1 to {'hey'}.
intersection(S2)	Returns the intersection of S1 and S2. This is equivalent to S1 & S2.	S1.intersection(['hey']) returns {'hey'}.
intersection_update(S2)	Similar to intersect() but modifies the set (not merely returns a copy).	S1.intersection_update(['hey']) changes S1 to {'hey'}.

(continued)

Table 3-5. (*continued*)

Method	Description	Example
issubset(S2)	Returns True if S1 is a subset of S2 (all elements of S1 appear in S2).	S1.issubset(set(['hey', 8, 'na'])) returns True.
issuperset(S2)	Returns True if S1 is a superset of S2 (all elements of S2 appear in S1).	S1.issuperset(set([8])) returns True.
pop()	Returns an arbitrary element and removes it from the set.	S1.pop() returns 8 and changes S1 to {'hey'}.
remove(val)	Removes val from the set. If val is not in the set, this method raises an exception.	S1.remove('hey') changes S1 to {8}.
symmetric_difference(S2)	Returns the symmetric difference. This is equivalent to (S1-S2) | (S2-S1).	S2 = set(['jude','hey']). S1.symmetric_difference(S2) returns {'jude', 8}.
symmetric_difference_update(S2)	Similar to symmetric_difference() but modifies the set (doesn't merely return a copy).	
union(S2)	Returns the union of S1 and S2 (all unique elements that appear in both sets).	S1.union(set(['na',8])) returns {8, 'na', 'hey'}.
update(S2)	Similar to union() but modifies the set (not merely returns a copy).	S1.update(set(['na', 8])) changes S1 to {8, 'na', 'hey'}.

I find I use sets much less than dictionaries. At times, however, using sets can be quite elegant. Consider the example shown in our previous discussion about dictionaries that enumerates GPS commands. Now suppose you don't care how many times a GPS command appears, only what types of GPS commands exist. You can accomplish this easily with a set:

```
>>> L = ['$GPGSA', '$GPGSV', '$GPGSV', '$GPGSV', '$GPRMC', '$GPGGA']
>>> S = set(L)
>>> S
```

```
{'$GPGGA', '$GPGSV', '$GPGSA', '$GPRMC'}
```

Variables

Variables in Python are similar to variables in most other programming languages. Variable names can consist of characters, digits, and an underscore; however, they have to start with a character or an underscore, and they must not contain spaces. I recommend you avoid odd variable names such as _02 (which is a legitimate variable name) as it might lead to some confusing code. Consider _02 = 3; that just doesn't look right.

An important concept regarding variables of data structures in Python is that of binding. When you assign variable b to be equal to variable a, which we'll suppose is a list, Python does not copy the contents of a to b. Rather, it sets, or *binds*, both a and b to refer to the same object. This is to achieve speed and performance:

```
>>> a = [1, 2]
>>> b = a
>>> b[0] = 'hey'
>>> a
```

```
['hey', 2]
```

```
>>> b
```

```
['hey', 2]
```

In case you do want a real copy of the data structure, and not merely another reference, you have several options:

- Some data structures, such as dictionaries, provide the copy() method.

- In some cases, you can create another item using the constructor, for example, L2 = list(L1).

- You can use the *copy* module from the standard library:

```
>>> import copy
>>> a = [1, 2]
>>> b = copy.copy(a)
>>> b[0] = 0
>>> a, b
```

```
([1, 2], [0, 2])
```

■ **Note** If a variable is a more complex structure (e.g., a list of rows), it's not enough to use copy.copy(), as the newly constructed list still points to the rows in the original list. In this case, you might want to use copy.deepcopy() instead. For more information about shallow copy, deep copy, and lazy copy, see http://en.wikipedia.org/wiki/Object_copy.

Statements

You've already seen statements in action, but Python is a rich language that keeps evolving, so there's plenty more to cover here. To get you going, I've split the discussion into three statement categories: printing, user input, and flow control. We'll also have some off-track discussions about comments, iterators, and list comprehensions along the way.

Printing

One of the basic functions in most programming languages is the print() function. You can use print() to display Python objects:

```
>>> print(2**100)
```

```
1267650600228229401496703205376
```

```
>>> print(1+1j)
```

```
(1+1j)
```

```
>>> print(0x20)
```

```
32
```

```
>>> print("String")
```

```
String
```

```
>>> print(['short list'])
```

```
['short list']
```

```
>>> print(('a', 'tuple'))
```

```
('a', 'tuple')
```

```
>>> print(dict([('hey', 'jude'), (8, 1)]))
```

```
{8: 1, 'hey': 'jude'}
```

```
>>> print(set([1, 2, 1]))
```

```
{1, 2}
```

■ **Tip**   The function `pprint` from module *pprint* provides an alternative to the `print()` function, one that formats the output in a "prettier" fashion, such as avoiding word breaks. This is especially useful if you're displaying large data structures. To use it, `import pprint` and issue the command, `pprint.pprint(object)`.

Suppressing Line Breaks

The default behavior of the `print()` function is to add a newline (line-break) after every print, as follows:

```
>>> for i in [1, 2, 3]:
...     print(i)
...
```

```
1
2
3
```

To suppress the line-break, add the parameter end='' to the print() function:

```
>>> for i in [1, 2, 3]:
...     print(i, end='')
...
```

```
1 2 3
```

Format Specifications

The print() function is similar to C's printf() function in that it accepts format specifications in the form %[flags][w][.pre]type. Other than the % and type fields, all parameters are optional. The simplest use of the format specifications is with the % operator, as follows:

```
>>> print("%d" % 2**4)
```

```
16
```

If more than one specifier is present, provide a tuple after the % operator:

```
>>> print("%d: %s=%d" % (1, 'hey', 8))
```

```
1: hey=8
```

The operator % is present after the string to be printed and before the tuple containing the values to be formatted.

■ **Note**   The function printf() (on which print() is based) is a complex function with a considerable number of options and parameters. This section is quite detailed and should provide most of your daily programming needs. However, should you wish to explore print() and printf() some more, a good source of information is the prinft() manual page (also known as the man page). In any Linux (or Cygwin) prompt, enter man 3 printf for an accurate overview. This is C-level documentation, but C programming skills are not required.

The type field can have several values, but only one is allowed in each specification (e.g., the format specifier %sd will be interpreted as a string, followed by the character d). Table 3-6 provides a distilled list of types.

Table 3-6. *Print Format Specification Types*

Character	Type
d	Integer
e, E	An engineering notation of a floating-point number with e or E, respectively (Mantissa and exponent are always present.)
f	Floating-point number
g	Floating point number in either f or e form, omitting trailing zeros and the decimal point if it's not needed
o	Octal
s	String
x, X	Hexadecimal (lowercase), hexadecimal (uppercase)

The value flags can take several of the following values:

- A number, specifying the number of characters to left-align

- The character +, specifying that in case of a numeric value, the sign must be present (either + or -)

- The character -, specifying that the text should be left-aligned

- The character #, which modifies behavior of some numeric types (out of the scope of this discussion—refer to the documentation)

- The character 0, used to left-pad values with zeros

Here are some examples:

```
>>> print("%d" % 2)
```

```
2
```

```
>>> print("%5d" % 2)
```

```
    2
```

```
>>> print("%+5d" % 2)
```

```
   +2
```

```
>>> print("%-+5d**" % 2)
```

```
+2   **
```

```
>>> print("%05d" % 2)
```

```
00002
```

The value w specifies the minimum width. If the width of the object to print is less than w, the output is left-padded with spaces. If it is greater than w, the value is displayed as-is:

```
>>> print("%10s" % 'Really long string')
```

```
Really long string
```

```
>>> print("%10s" % 'shorter')
```

```
  shorter
```

The value pre is preceded with a dot and specifies the *maximum* number of decimal points in floating-point numbers, the *maximum* number of characters to print in a string, or the *minimum* number of digits in integers:

```
>>> print("%.2f, %.3s, %.4d" % (1/3, 'this will be truncated', 1))
```

```
0.33, thi, 0001
```

You can mix and match format specifiers. Here's a print() call that make use of several format specifiers:

```
>>> print("%+08.3f" % (1/9))
```

```
+000.111
```

The + character forces the sign to appear in the output, the digit 0 takes care of the zero padding, the digit 8 forces the output to be at least eight characters long (the plus symbol, three digits, the dot symbol, and three more digits), the dot followed by 3 ensures at most three digits are displayed, and lastly the character f announces that this is a floating-point number.

Employing print() in this manner is especially useful when you want to create text output that's properly aligned and can be displayed in a report.

Format specifiers, with the use of the % operator, can also be used to format strings, not only print them:

```
>>> s = "%+08.4f" % (1/3)
>>> s
```

```
'+00.3333'
```

User Input

User input in Python is done using the input([prompt]) function (in Python 2.x, the function is called raw_input()). The function prints the prompt string, reads a string from the standard input, and returns it, stripped of end-of-line characters. The prompt argument is optional:

```
>>> s = input("How many times? ")
```

```
How many times? 7
```

```
>>> print("split "*s)
```

```
Traceback (most recent call last):
  File "<stdin>", line 1, in <module>
TypeError: can't multiply sequence by non-int of type 'str'
```

```
>>> print("split "*int(s))
```

```
split split split split split split split
```

The function input() returns a string; thus, even though I've input a numeric value, the function returns the string "7". I've converted the string to a number using the int() function.

In Windows, it's common to see input() at the end of a script. This ensures that the command window stays open, waiting for user input and displaying the results of running the script. The default behavior in Windows is that this box is automatically closed, preventing the user from reading the output, and so input() overrides this behavior.

Python, of course, supports several other sorts of input, such as files and command-line parameters, which you'll learn about in future chapters.

Comments

Comments start at the symbol #, provided it's not part of a string:

```
>>> print("Some text") # This is a comment
```

```
Some text
```

```
>>> # This entire line is a comment
...
>>> print("Text after this sign # is not a comment")
```

```
Text after this sign # is not a comment
```

Flow Control

Flow control statements—such as if, try, for, break, and continue—control the behavior of a script. Python provides several flow control statements, some similar to other programming languages. Typically, a flow control statement is followed by a block, which is indented to the left. This indentation is required because it defines a block. All rows in a block must be indented identically.

if, elif, else

The if statement follows this syntax:

```
if Condition1:
    Block1
elif Condition2:
    Block2
elif Condition3:
    Block3
.
.
.
else:
    ElseBlock
```

If Condition1 evaluates to True, the code in Block1 is executed. Block1 can be more than one line long and must be indented to the same level. If Condition1 is False, Condition2 is evaluated, causing Block2 to be executed if it is True. This continues on to Block3, and so forth. If none of the conditions are met, the ElseBlock is executed.

The statements if, elif, and else should be left-aligned. Statements in each block should be left-aligned to the same indented level. The colon after the if, elif, and else statements is required. Here's an example:

```
>>> if 3 > 10:
...     print("Checked whether 3 is greater than 10")
...     print("It is!")
... elif ord('A') == 65:
...     print("Ordinal of 'A' is 65")
... else:
...     print("All failed, nothing works")
...
```

```
Ordinal of 'A' is 65
```

Other than the if statement, all other statements (elif, else) are optional. In case of a short if statement, you can write the block on the same line as the if statement:

```
>>> if 's' < 't': print("Yeap")
...
```

```
Yeap
```

Conditions can be more complex and can include conditionals such as and and or:

```
>>> x = 25
>>> if x > 20 and x%2 == 1:
...     print("Odd *and* over 20!")
...
```

```
Odd *and* over 20!
```

The pass Statement

The pass statement does nothing and can be used as a placeholder, for example, in multiple if assignments:

```
>>> x = 0.2
>>> if x < 0.1:
...     print("Too small")
... elif x < 0.3:
...     pass
... elif x > 0.5:
...     print("large")
... else:
...     print("huge")
...
```

```
>>>
```

As you can see, nothing happened, which is exactly what I wanted.

Exceptions: try, else, and finally

Exceptions are Python's mechanism of dealing with runtime issues. In Chapter 1 you saw exceptions reported and learned how to catch them; that is, you learned how to prevent them from halting program execution. As you may remember, you can catch, or intercept, exceptions before they stop program execution with the following syntax:

```
try:
    TryBlock
except [ExceptionType1]:
    ExceptBlock1
except [ExceptionType2]:
    ExceptBlock2
finally:
    FinallyBlock
```

If an exception happens inside the TryBlock, ExceptBlock1 is executed. If ExceptionType1 is specified, only exceptions that are of type ExceptionType1 are caught. You can have several except clauses to deal with different types of exceptions. The FinallyBlock is optional and executed after both the try and except section have completed execution.

First, let's see an exception in action, without catching it:

```
>>> str = 'second '
>>> n = '7'
>>> print(str*n)
```

```
Traceback (most recent call last):
  File "<stdin>", line 1, in <module>
TypeError: can't multiply sequence by non-int of type 'str'
```

The reason for this exception is that the operator * doesn't know how to multiply 'second ' by '7' (it does know how to do 'second '*7 but that's a different statement).

As you can see, the exception that was raised was a TypeError exception. Let's catch it and print it:

```
>>> str = 'second '
>>> n = '7'
>>> try:
...     print(str*n)
... except TypeError as e:
...     print("Exception caught!", e)
... finally:
...     print("This will be run regardless")
...
```

```
Exception caught! can't multiply sequence by non-int of type 'str'
This will be run regardless
```

We've caught the exception in the except block printed what the exception was (notice that in Python 2.x the except statement is slightly different and does not use the reserved word as. Instead, it is written as follows: except TypeError, e:). Lastly, the code in the finally block was executed. Let's run it again, this time without triggering an exception:

```
>>> str = 'second '
>>> n = 7
>>> try:
...     print(str*n)
... except TypeError as e:
...     print("Exception caught!", e)
... finally:
...     print("This will be run regardless")
...
```

```
second second second second second second second
This will be run regardless
```

As you can see, the code in the finally block was executed regardless of whether the exception was raised.

Now let's trigger an exception that's not of the TypeError exception. I'll modify the line print str*n to print 1/0, which raises a different exception:

```
>>> try:
...     print(1/0)
... except TypeError as e:
...     print("Exception caught!", e)
...
```

```
Traceback (most recent call last):
  File "<stdin>", line 2, in <module>
ZeroDivisionError: division by zero
```

This time, the exception wasn't caught by the code (it didn't print Exception caught!) and was handled by the interpreter because it wasn't of type TypeError. In order to catch the exception, I should have used ZeroDivisionError exception in my except clause, instead of the TypeError exception.

If you don't specify an exception condition, all exceptions are caught:

```
>>> try:
...     print(1/0)
... except:
...     print("Exception caught!")
...
```

```
Exception caught!
```

As a general rule, try to make your exception specific; that is, try to specify the exception condition. If the list of exceptions is too long, maybe wide-range exception catching (i.e., without a condition) is a better approach.

Exceptions are a fundamental part of flow control. The concept, "It's Easier to Ask Forgiveness than Permission" (EAFP), is demonstrated with the exceptions mechanism. Rather than checking in advance whether the input to the next block of code is OK, it's easier to perform the operation and then, if an error occurs, catch it with an exception.

Exceptions can occur deep within your code. For instance, say function1() calls function2(), which calls function3(). Now let's suppose an exception occurred in function3(). If function3() doesn't handle the exception with the try/except mechanism, the exception moves to function2(). If function2() doesn't handle the exception, function1() has a chance. And finally, if function1() doesn't handle the exception, the interpreter will issue an exception and print the cause.

In the preceding scenario, when function3() does handle the exception, it will not resurface in function2(). However, if you wish to catch an exception *and* pass it to the calling function, you can do that. Although it's beyond the scope of this discussion, you can find more details in the online documentation at https://docs.python.org/3.3/reference/executionmodel.html under the section, "Exceptions."

You can also raise exceptions of your own. This is of value if you write code and want to ensure it's being used properly. Suppose your algorithm works on odd numbers only; a good approach would be to check whether a parameter passed to the algorithm is odd. If not, you raise an exception:

```
>>> n = 6
>>> if not n%2 == 1:
...     raise ValueError("value must be odd")
...
```

```
Traceback (most recent call last):
  File "<stdin>", line 2, in <module>
ValueError: value must be odd
```

In the preceding example, I've used an existing exception, `ValueError`. You can create exceptions of your own or use existing exceptions. For more details and a list of existing exceptions, refer to Python's online documentation: https://docs.python.org/3.3/library/exceptions.html.

Iterators

Before we move to the `for` statement, I'd like to cover an important concept: *iterators*. Iterators are objects that return an element one at a time, instead of returning a full sequence. An object that can be iterated over is known as *iterable*. Using iterators is more memory efficient than using a sequence. For example, the function `range(1000)` creates an iterable object that consumes much less memory than a list: calls to `range()` yield the values from zero to 1000, excluding the value 1000, one at a time.

■ **Note** In Python 2.x, `range()` returns a list of the values and not an iterable object; an iterable object in Python 2.x is generated with a call to `xrange()`. In Python 3.x the function `xrange()` has been removed; to generate an actual list instead of an iterable object, use `list()`, as in this example: `list(range(1000))`.

Python relies heavily on iterators and provides a great number of iterators that work on data structures I've covered. Iterators are best understood in the context of the `for` statement, so let's now take a look at this statement.

The for Statement

The `for` statement is one of the most versatile statements in Python and follows this syntax:

```
for element in sequence:
    ForBlock
```

In the case of a one-line block, the `ForBlock` can appear on the same line as the `for` statement. Indentation rules for blocks are the same as those for `if` statements (and any other block): they must be indented to the same level.

The `for` statement assigns `element` to be a value from `sequence` and executes the `ForBlock`. This happens for all the values in `sequence`:

```
>>> for elem in ['hey', 'jude', 8]:
...     print(elem)
...
```

```
hey
jude
8
```

The for statement can operate on an iterator, as well. If you're interested in a format similar to that of C's for function, use the range() function:

```
>>> for x in range(5):
...     print(x)
...
```

```
0
1
2
3
4
```

It's possible to nest for loops (put one inside the other), as follows:

```
>>> for x in range(5):
...     for y in range(5):
...         print("%4d" % (x*5+y), end='')
...     print()
...
```

```
   0   1   2   3   4
   5   6   7   8   9
  10  11  12  13  14
  15  16  17  18  19
  20  21  22  23  24
```

The for statement shines in the context of iterators. Let's cover a few.

The reversed(seq) iterator returns one element at a time from a sequence in reversed order:

```
>>> for x in reversed(['split', 'second']): print (x)
...
```

```
second
split
```

The iterator enumerate(seq) returns both the index to the item in the sequence and the item, as a tuple:

```
>>> for i, elem in enumerate(['split', 8, 'second']):
...     print (i, "-->", elem)
...
```

```
0 --> split
1 --> 8
2 --> second
```

Here's another example: to go through the (key, value) pairs in a dictionary, use the member function items():

```
>>> d = {'split':8, 'second':1}
>>> for k, v in d.items():
...     print(k, "-->", v)
...
```

```
split --> 8
second --> 1
```

List Comprehensions

List comprehensions apply to lists, but they're rather hard to explain unless you understand for statements. List comprehensions are an efficient method to create lists from lists, but they use a slightly different notation than a regular for loop. List comprehensions follow this syntax:

```
[f(x) for x in list if condition]
```

The condition clause is optional:

```
>>> [x*x for x in range(10) if x > 5]
```

```
[36, 49, 64, 81]
```

```
>>> [x**2 for x in range(6, 10)]
```

```
[36, 49, 64, 81]
```

You can also write a nested list comprehension, similar to nested for loops:

```
>>> [(x, y) for x in range(3) for y in range(3)]
```

```
[(0, 0), (0, 1), (0, 2), (1, 0), (1, 1), (1, 2), (2, 0), (2, 1), (2, 2)]
```

This is a tricky concept, so let's examine what's going on. Mentally replace (x, y) for x in range(3) with inner_statement. The list comprehension now looks like this: [inner_statement for y in range(3)]. Now inner_statement is executed for every value of y that takes the values 0, 1, and 2. However, inner_statement is itself a list comprehension that results in a tuple (x, y) for every value of x that takes the values 0, 1, and 2. The end result: for every value of y, and for every value of x, (x, y) is returned.

You'll encounter numerous uses of list comprehensions throughout the book.

The while Statement

The while statement complements for loops and is best used when a condition has to occur before the loop is terminated. For example, Chapter 1 used a while statement to allow recording of GPS data until a **Ctrl+C** was pressed.

The while syntax is as follows:

```
while condition:
    WhileBlock
```

As long as condition evaluates to True, the WhileBlock is executed:

```
>>> import random
>>> while random.random() < 0.9: print("*")
...
```

```
*
*
*
```

This example will continue printing one star per line for as long as a random number between 0 and 1 remains less than 0.9. I've used the function random() from module *random* (see Chapter 7).

Statements break and continue

The statements break and continue are used to modify behavior within a loop or a block. The statement break exits a flow control block; and the statement continue stops execution of the block, but picks up on the next iteration.

```
>>> for x in range(5):
...     if x == 3: break
...     print(x)
...
```

```
0
1
2
```

```
>>> for x in range(5):
...     if x == 3: continue
...     print(x)
...
```

```
0
1
2
4
```

In the first for statement, I've used the statement break when x is equal to 3, effectively terminating the for loop. In the second for statement, I've merely skipped execution of the block when x is equal to 3, suppressing the print() function, but resuming on the next value.

Some Built-in Functions

Let's now turn to built-in Python functions that weren't covered in any of the previous sections. By built-in, I mean functions that do not require any import command prior to using them. Table 3-7 presents these functions in alphabetical order.

Table 3-7. *Some Useful Python Built-in Functions*

Statement	Description	Example
all(s)	Returns True if all elements of s are not False.	all(['hi', 2]) returns True. all(['', 2]) returns False.
any(s)	Returns True if some elements of s are True.	any(['', 2]) returns True. any([]) returns False.
chr(n)	Returns the Unicode character associated with n.	chr(65) returns 'A'.
ord(ch)	Returns the ordinal value of ch. This is the inverse of chr(n).	ord('A') returns 65. ord(chr(80)) returns 80.
range([i,] j[, k])	Returns a virtual sequence of numbers from i (if supplied; default is zero), ending right before j, with an increment step of k (if supplied; default is 1).	
sorted(s)	Returns the sequence s, sorted.	sorted('hey') returns ['e', 'h', 'y'].
sum(s)	Returns the sum of s.	sum(range(10)) returns 45.
type(obj)	Returns the type of obj.	type(1j) returns <class 'complex'>.
zip(s1[, s2])	Returns a list of tuples, each composed of elements at the same location in the sequences. s2 is optional.	

Some of these functions are very useful. For example, here's how you use the zip() function:

```
>>> for elem in zip(range(2), ['hey', 'jude']):
...     print(elem)
...
```

```
(0, 'hey')
(1, 'jude')
```

Every element in the range(2) (meaning 0 and 1) was matched up with an element from the list ['hey', 'jude']. For an interesting use of the zip() function, turn to the Newton fractal example in Chapter 7.

Defining Functions

Functions are a convenient way to reuse code. Functions in Python are similar to procedures, subroutines, and functions in other programming languages. There's no distinction between a function that returns a value and a function that does not—both are considered functions. (In some programming languages, if a function doesn't return a value, it is named differently: procedure or subroutine, for example.)

Functions are declared as follows:

```
def funcname(arguments):
    FunctionBody
```

The keyword def defines the start of a function. The name of the function is funcname; arguments are optional:

```
>>> def f1():
...     print("F1")
...
>>> f1()
```

```
F1
```

```
>>> def f2(n):
...     print("F2"*n)
...
>>> f2(10)
```

```
F2F2F2F2F2F2F2F2F2F2
```

I've defined two functions: f1() and f2(). Function f1() requires no parameters, while function f2() requires one parameter. Using the functions (calling them) requires the addition of a set of parentheses.

You can also specify optional parameters using an assignment in the list of arguments in the function name, as follows:

```
>>> def f3(n, s="F3"):
...     print(s*n)
...
>>> f3(2)
```

```
F3F3
```

```
>>> f3(2, 'F4!')
```

```
F4!F4!
```

In the first call to f3(), the default value of s is "F3". In the second call, that value is assigned the string 'F4!'.

Functions can return values using the return statement:

```
>>> def f5(n):
...     return "f5"*n
...
>>> f5(5)
```

```
'f5f5f5f5f5'
```

```
>>> a = f5(3)
>>> a
```

```
'f5f5f5'
```

The return statement doesn't necessarily have to appear at the end of the function; however, the function ends execution when it reaches a return.

Functions are typically documented with *docstrings* (which are bold in the following code):

```
>>> def f6(n=1, s="f6"):
...     """Returns a string composed of the string s, repeated n times.
...     n and s are both optional."""
...     return s*n
...
>>> help(f6)
```

```
Help on function f6 in module __main__:

f6(n=1, s='f6')
    Returns a string composed of the string s, repeated n times.
    n and s are both optional.
```

```
>>> f6()
```

```
'f6'
```

The benefit of using a docstring immediately after the function declaration is that executing help(funcname) returns the docstring, which is an excellent way to document a function.

Generators

Generators are functions used to create iterators. The main difference between a generator and a regular function is that generators return one element at a time using the yield statement; however, they can keep on returning values for subsequent calls of the iterator. In contrast to this, functions return only one element using the return statement, and then exit (it could be a sequence or tuple, but it's essentially one object):

```
>>> def odd(s):
...     """A generator function to iterate through odd elements of s."""
...     i = 0
...     while(i < len(s)):
...         yield s[i]
...         i += 2
...
>>> for i in odd(['hey', 'split', 'second', 8]):
...     print(i)
...
```

```
hey
second
```

In the preceding example, I've defined an iterator named odd() that yields the odd elements in a list (i.e., the first, third, fifth, and so on). I've implemented the iterator using a while loop and proper indexing.

There are also other methods I could've used to implement the iterator, but it's important to understand that the motivation behind using an iterator is efficiency. A different implementation could be one that uses the indexing operator with a step value of 2, as follows:

```
>>> def odd(s):
...     """A generator function to iterate through odd elements of s"""
...     for elem in s[::2]:
...         yield elem
```

While this might look like more elegant code, I don't think it's as good. The for loop creates an entire list, s[::2] (albeit half the size), and large lists are not memory efficient.

Generator Expressions

Generator expressions, or *genexps*, are a compact method to implement simple generators. Generator expressions follow this syntax:

```
(f(x) for element in sequence if condition)
```

In a sense, they are very similar to list comprehensions, with the difference being that they are iterators and not lists. Hence, they are more memory efficient. Here's an implementation of the odd() generator function using a genexp:

```
>>> l = ['hey', 'split', 'second', 8]
>>> odd = (x for x in L[::2])
>>> for i in odd:
...     print(i)
...
```

```
hey
second
```

And here's one in one big line:

```
>>> l = ['hey', 'split', 'second', 8]
>>> for i in (x for x in L[::2]):
...     print(i)
...
```

```
hey
second
```

If I were a bit more conscious about memory usage, I'd notice that I've created another list in the for loop: L[::2], which probably is not a good idea (from the perspective of a memory-conscious application). A different approach is to use the range() iterator as follows:

```
>>> L = ['hey', 'split', 'second', 8]
>>> odd = (L[i] for i in range(0, len(L), 2))
>>> for elem in odd:
...     print(elem)
...
```

```
hey
second
```

This might be a bit less clear, but it is a more memory-conscious implementation. Alternatively, you could also use the enumerate() iterator, iterating over list elements and only printing an element if the index is odd. Deciding whether an index is odd or even can be done using the modulo (%) operator, which returns the remainder from dividing by a number—2, in our case:

```
>>> L = ['hey', 'split', 'second', 8]
>>> odd = (elem for i, elem in enumerate(L) if not (i % 2))
>>> for elem in odd:
...     print(elem)
...
```

```
hey
second
```

You should opt for using genexps over list comprehensions if you just want to iterate over items and don't require the list itself. Unless you're using really large data structures (on the order of the scale of the memory you have in your computer), using either is fine.

Object-Oriented Programming

By now you've probably deduced that Python is an object-oriented programming language. You've already seen evidence of this. For example, the data structure list, whose methods are in essence member functions, is an object.

The purpose of this section is to quickly go over the syntax of object-oriented programming and to show how to implement a basic object. The reason I won't be covering Object-Oriented Programming (OOP) in detail is that this book mostly deals with using objects, rather than coding them. If you'd like to know more about coding an object, refer to the online Python documentation and the references at the end of this chapter.

The basic data structure to implement object-oriented programming in Python is a *class*. Classes have functions, called *methods*, and variables, called *attributes*. Here's a simple class named Odd that implements the odd functionality; that is, it retrieves odd elements:

Listing 3-2. Listing of odd.py

```
class Odd:
    def __init__(self, s=[]):
        self.sequence = s
    def odd(self):
        return self.sequence[::2]
```

The first line defines a class named Odd. From here, functions and variables indented per the usual block rules denote functions and variables belonging to class Odd.

I've defined two functions. The first function is the *constructor*, __init__ (double underscores on both sides). The constructor function is called whenever an object is instantiated, or created. To instantiate a class object, call the Odd class with parentheses. Here are some ways you can instantiate the Odd class object (be sure to execute the preceding script first):

```
>>> odd1 = Odd()
>>> odd2 = Odd('a string')
>>> odd3 = Odd(['hey', 'split', 'second', 8])
```

The implementation I chose is that, if a parameter is provided, the variable self.sequence is assigned this parameter. Note the use of the argument self: the word self is a convention and not a reserved word. Whenever you call a class property or method, the argument self is passed automatically, but not spelled out. That is, to instantiate an Odd object, you enter Odd(s) and not Odd(self, s). By passing the argument self (hidden), Python identifies one created object from another. The analogy I like to use is that self is similar to C++'s this statement.

Another important concept here is that of scope. Had I not used the notation self.sequence and written sequence instead, the local variable sequence that is local to the function (and not the class) would have been updated. Once the function returned, that variable would have disappeared. To ensure that the class variable sequence is updated (and not the function's local variable), I've used the notation self.sequence.

The second function I defined is odd(), which returns the odd elements in a sequence. To call the function, use the dot operator after the Odd object, as follows:

```
>>> odd3 = Odd(['hey', 'split', 'second', 8])
>>> odd3.odd()
```

```
['hey', 'second']
```

So far, I've only shown methods, but the class Odd also contains a variable: sequence. To access this variable, you can use the dot operator, as well:

```
>>> odd3 = Odd(['hey', 'split', 'second', 8])
>>> odd3.sequence
```

```
['hey', 'split', 'second', 8]
```

There's a lot more to object-oriented programming in Python, including most of the concepts that appear in other object-oriented programming languages such as inheritance and operator overloading, to name a couple. Again, the references at the end of the chapter should prove valuable resources should you need to learn more about object-oriented programming and design in Python.

Modules and Packages

One of Python's strong suits is the extensive number of packages readily available for it. You've seen how to install packages in Chapter 2; now it's time to learn how to use them.

A module is a set of functions and data structures. In essence, it is similar to a class. Accessing modules is performed using the module's namespace, followed by a dot to access functions and variables. Packages are collections of modules. Accessing modules within packages is performed using the dot operator.

It's also of value to know that it's possible to extend Python with modules from C and C++. From a Python user's perspective, you just import a module and use it as-is, regardless of whether it was written in another programming language.

The import Statement

The import statement loads a module, effectively allowing us to access the functions and variables within the module. You can issue the import statement in several ways:

```
import module
import module as name
from module import function
from module import function as name
from module import *
```

The first method, import module, loads a module with its namespace. To access the module functions, use module.function(). The second method loads the module but renames it; to use its functions, use name.function(). The third statement imports only one function from the module; to access it, simply use its name: function(). You can have multiple functions imported in this manner by separating the functions with commas. The fourth statement is identical to the third, only the name of the function is now name; to call the function, type name(). Lastly, the last import statement loads all functions from a module; to access the functions, you enter their name (without the module name).

You can also import entire packages (replace the module name with the package name) or import modules within packages by using the dot operator, as follows:

```
import package.module
```

Here are some examples:

```
>>> import math
>>> math.pi
```

```
3.141592653589793
```

```
>>> math.sqrt(4)
```

```
2.0
```

```
>>> import math as m
>>> m.pi
```

```
3.141592653589793
```

```
>>> m.sqrt(4)
```

```
2.0
```

```
>>> from math import sqrt
>>> sqrt(4)
```

```
2.0
```

```
>>> from math import sqrt as square_root
>>> square_root(4)
```

```
2.0
```

```
>>> from math import *
>>> sin(0)
```

```
0.0
```

Whether you'll be loading the entire module or just some pieces of the module is totally up to you (and a function of the amount of memory you have). Sometimes, it's easier to load entire modules; other times, it's important to be able to load modules with their namespace, such as when two modules have the same function names (e.g., the modules *math* and *cmath*—see Chapter 7).

Modules Installed in a System

Before you start importing modules and reading about their functions, it would be valuable to know which modules are currently installed and available in your system. Don't forget that the Python standard library is vast, with a substantial number of modules and packages to choose from. Maybe a function you're looking for already exists in the standard library? Of course, you can refer to the online documentation, but you can also refer to the interactive help system.

You invoke the interactive help system by entering help(). At the help prompt, enter modules. This will provide a list of available modules in your system. Enter help(modulename) to read more about that module.

The dir Statement

Another useful statement is the dir statement, which lists the contents of a specific object (for example, a class). In this context, it also lists the methods and properties of a module:

```
>>> dir(math)
```

```
['__doc__', '__loader__', '__name__', '__package__', 'acos', 'acosh', 'asin',
'asinh', 'atan', 'atan2', 'atanh', 'ceil', 'copysign', 'cos', 'cosh',
'degrees', 'e', 'erf', 'erfc', 'exp', 'expm1', 'fabs', 'factorial', 'floor',
'fmod', 'frexp', 'fsum', 'gamma', 'hypot', 'isfinite', 'isinf', 'isnan',
'ldexp', 'lgamma', 'log', 'log10', 'log1p', 'log2', 'modf', 'pi', 'pow',
'radians', 'sin', 'sinh', 'sqrt', 'tan', 'tanh', 'trunc']
```

This is very useful if you're exploring the functions in a module or if you forgot the exact name of a function.

Final Notes and References

It is far beyond the scope of this chapter and this book to cover the entire Python programming language. However, this chapter should get you up and running, and you'll be able to follow through with the rest of the book with very little need for additional references. That said, one of the purposes of the book is to introduce you to the language and provide additional resources should you want to expand your knowledge.

I have found the following references of value, and I hope you find them useful as well:

- "The Python Tutorial" by Guido van Rosso, https://docs.python.org/3.3/tutorial/

- The Python Standard Library, https://docs.python.org/3.3/library/

- *Beginning Python: From Novice to Professional, Second Edition* by Magnus Lie Hetland (Apress, 2008)

- *Dive into Python* by Mark Pilgrim (Apress, 2004; free online version also available at http://www.diveintopython.net/)

- *Python in a Nutshell: A Desktop Quick Reference, 2nd Edition* by Alex Martelli (O'Reilly, 2006)

- *Python Cookbook: Recipes from the Python Community* by Alex Martelli, Anna Martelli Ravenscroft, and David Ascher (O'Reilly, 2005)

CHAPTER 4

■ ■ ■

Data Organization

Organizing Chaos

A preliminary step to designing and programming an algorithm is gathering data and sorting it. When you first test a thesis or write code to analyze network traffic, only part of the information is readily available; some of the data is still unknown. You make initial estimations based on the first set of data files. As data is gathered, you discover new insights and understandings, resulting in possible changes to the processing script and data gathering application, such as adding a previously unlogged parameter and graphing it over time. Some changes may include data gathering over substantially longer time periods than originally anticipated. Consequently, to accommodate for manageable data files, you reduce the sampling rate, implemented by logging only every nth value. Another plausible scenario is that of parsing log files, where the generating application (e.g., a web server) recently went through a software upgrade that altered the file format and the file name scheme.

The situation can get more complex. Some files may have an error due to a hardware malfunction of the recording apparatus; or some portions of the file may be corrupt due to hard drive issues (back up!); or the application that stored the file may have had a bug and generated incorrect data. By now, you realize you need to modify the erroneous data or remove it from your analysis, be it manually or automatically.

In some cases, you may decide to use part of the data as a teacher set to help define the algorithm, while another set of data is used as a tester set to estimate performance. In this case, you may need to feed the algorithm additional information regarding the contents of the files, so that more complex tests can be carried out.

Documenting file contents is important, so that the knowledge of what each file contains is not lost. A few years from now, you may not remember what each and every file is; however, you might be expected to reuse your previous work. So annotating, or note taking, is of value. Ideally you'd like the annotations and documentation to reside with the data, and not in an inaccessible notebook.

By now you have quite a number of different file types: a varying number of parameters, different file lengths, different logging periods, various file formats, several file name schemes, clean and raw data, annotated data, and much more. Ideally, you'd like to use data from all the files, even if some of them have partial information or conform to a different file format; they still hold valuable information. Or it could be that you'd like to use historical information to ensure backward compatibility with older versions of the software.

A lot of the work has many unknowns. Data gathering is an iterative process in nature; if you don't manage your data files properly, you'll lose control. I'm not suggesting that we stop and design an entire data-management infrastructure from the get-go. On the contrary, I think data should be gathered as I've described. However, following some simple guidelines and conventions can make life a lot easier. The purpose of this chapter is to address all these issues: file names, file formats, data organization, data cleaning, and annotation and data documentation. I'll touch on each topic, suggesting guidelines and conventions to help manage data more easily for the programmer and the processing application.

File Name Conventions

The first step in data organization is deciding on a file name convention. You'd be surprised at the odd names people choose for their files. Not because they're not inventive enough, but because they've never given it much thought. They should. File name conventions are of great value when more than one person accesses the data. A good convention will help all data users locate files and manage them: your administrator will find it easier to restore previously backed-up files if he knows the file name pattern. A good naming convention should also have in mind scripts, or programs, so that automation is easier to implement. For example, if the file names contain the day of the week, limit those to three letters (i.e., Sun, Mon, Tue, Wed, Thu, Fri, and Sat) instead of using full day names. This allows the script that processes them to be less complex.

Date and Time in a File Name

We remember a lot based on a date. "Remember that time when we ran that test? That was when you joined the group, about a year and a half ago." One of the best ways to capture date and time information is to use them to name a file. Following this guideline allows easy file searches. Instead of going through the files one at a time, opening them, and looking at the contents, you can browse the directory contents and find data based on a date. Some benefits of using date and time in a file name are:

- The date is useful information. Just looking at the file name tells you a lot about the file.

- File names are almost guaranteed to be unique. This is important when your data logging application is creating file names, because it won't overwrite existing files. If you want to further ensure uniqueness, include the time in seconds along with the date information.

- File names are retained when copying or moving, even if modifying the contents of the files. This is in contrast to relying on the operating system to record the date files are created, as you will find that there are issues with that: copying files using different media and/or over a network might not always retain all the date information (e.g., the creation date). They will, however, retain the file name.

- It's easy to automate and write scripts. A script to display all the graphs from last month is straightforward to implement.

- The convention is easily followed on a wide range of systems and programming languages. The application that records the data can be written in C programming language and not necessarily Python.

As you can see, embedding the date and time (preferably up to the second) is a good scheme to follow. That said, there are a lot of possible ways to denote the date and time. Personally, I follow the date and time format suggested in ISO 8601: YYYY-MM-DDThh:mm:ss (see section "Final Notes and References"), with some modifications, as it is not possible to have a file name with colon (:). Instead of colons, I use a dash (-), making the format YYYY-MM-DDThh-mm-ss. Another possible modification is replacing the letter T used to separate the date and time portions in the ISO standard with a dash, as well (YYYY-MM-DD-hh-mm-ss). The side benefit of those two replacements is that now there's a single field separator that separates year, month, day, hour, minute, and second. This is quite valuable for automation and is easily implemented in most programming languages. Some prefer keeping the character T as it does help remind you where the date ends and when the time starts, and it's not all that complex to implement in Python, either. Leaving the T or replacing it with a dash are both good options; which you should use is mostly a matter of personal preference. As you'll soon see, Python offers a dedicated function for parsing dates, strptime(), that can handle the T quite easily.

Python also provides the split(substr) function, which splits a string into a list of substrings once substr is encountered. In this case, split('-') will split the date-time format:

```
>>> a_date = "2014-05-05-22-17-14"
>>> a_date.split('-')
```

```
['2014', '05', '05', '22', '17', '14']
```

The following example extracts the month as an integer:

```
>>> int("2014-05-05-22-17-14".split('-')[1])
```

```
5
```

In the latter example, I chose to operate directly on the string, not saving it in a variable. The month is the second element in the list; to access it, I index it: [1] (counting starts at 0). The function int() converts the string value to an integer.

If you follow the scheme of using T instead of a dash, you can use the function strptime(), which is part of the *time* module. I assume strptime() is short for string-parse-time; regardless of whether that's true, it helps to remember the function name:

```
>>> from time import strptime
>>> strptime("2014-04-12T09-29-22", "%Y-%m-%dT%H-%M-%S")
```

```
time.struct_time(tm_year=2014, tm_mon=4, tm_mday=12, tm_hour=9, tm_min=29,
tm_sec=22, tm_wday=5, tm_yday=102, tm_isdst=-1)
```

■ **Note** Lowercase and capital letters are used to distinguish between the date and time fields, mainly because the character m can mean both month and minutes. Therefore, the convention is that time is denoted by capitals (HH, MM, SS), and the date is denoted by lowercase letters (yy, mm, dd). There's one exception, and that's the year: when using a four-digit notation (e.g., 2008), the characters are capitalized: YYYY.

As you can see, it's quite easy to extract date and time information in Python from a file name, so long as it conforms to the convention. Processing all the files from, say, April 2014, can be done using a single split() command, followed by an if statement.

Useful File Name Titles

Another important aspect of a file name is a useful title. A short, descriptive title can be a time-saver. You want to describe the system more than the data; the data will speak for itself when you analyze it. SystemY or MarsTelescopeA are good candidates, but you should avoid titles that describe the data such as Logfiles or TemperatureAndFlow. If you do want to describe the data, do so in addition to describing the system: Sys736Logs is a good option. After you come up with a title, pause and think about it a bit. Finding the right balance between a description and ease-of-use can sometimes require revising your idea. Consider these examples:

- `PumpRawData` is lacking a system description. What if you have several pumps you want to test for flow? One alternative is to use the pump's serial number: `Pump472RawData` (assuming 472 is the pump's serial number).

- `VoltageSys2AMay2008` is probably not a good title either. If you append the date to this title, you might end up with a title that looks like this: `VoltageSys2AMay2008-2009-01-01-01-01-01`. So which one is it—year 2009 or year 2008?

- `VoltageCurrentSystem2A` is OK; however, I'd opt to rename it to be *less* specific, or should I say, more general: `ElectricalDataSystem2A`. The reason for the renaming is that it's possible you'll decide to record additional values, (e.g., power, as well as voltage and current); and unless you want to rename your code to look for different headers, having a file name titled `VoltageCurrentSystem2A` that also has power values will be a bit misleading.

File Name Extensions

The last part of the file name convention is an indication of the file format, usually denoted by the file name extension. File name extensions are typically three characters long (some are less, such as `.gz`, and some are longer, such as `.html`). Try to follow a convention of three characters for the extension—again, this will make it easier for the processing application. I suggest thinking about three distinct file name extension subcategories:

- *Known file formats*: Image formats follow very specific extensions: `.jpg`, `.png`, `.bmp`, `.tif`, and more. These file names have a meaning, so if you're recording data in those file formats, use the known extensions. There are also known extensions for compressed file formats, video file formats, and others, so use them accordingly.

- *Text file formats*: Here I suggest either using a `.txt` or a `.csv` extension. If the text file format is not in the Comma Separated Values (CSV) format, use the `.txt` extension; this suggests it is viewable by most text editors. Exceptions to this guideline include files that already have a known extension (e.g., INI files): although they are text files, you really want to capture that they're files holding initialization values. The same would apply to batch files and shell scripts, but those typically are not data files.

- *Binary file formats*: Binary file formats are not as self-descriptive as CSV files. And unlike CSV or plain text files, they are hard to view without knowing in advance the specific file format. For this reason, binary file formats should be accompanied by a header file that describes the contents and format of the binary files. However, it's still valuable to know a bit more about the binary file format even if the exact format is unknown. I suggest this convention: one character denotes whether the data is signed (`i`), unsigned (`u`), or floating point (`f`), followed by the number of bits used to store the data, as described in Table 4-1.

Table 4-1. *Suggested Binary File Name Extensions*

Description	Precision	Extension
Signed integers	8, 16, 32, 64	`.i08`, `.i16`, `.i32`, `.i64` (respectively)
Unsigned integers	8, 16, 32, 64	`.u08`, `.u16`, `.u32`, `.u64` (respectively)
Floating point	32 (single precision)	`.f32`
	64 (double precision)	`.f64`

- *Other binary file formats*: When binary files contain several values of different precisions, the convention described in the Table 4-1 is not feasible, at least not in a three-character extension notation. In that case, use .bin or .x.bin, where x is a number. The reason for the x is that it's conceivable you'll have several file formats of varying precisions, and a good way to tell them apart would be to add an integer prefix. Notice that they still all end with a .bin, enabling easy file distinction.

File Name Convention Recap

Three items are important to file naming conventions: the date and time in a file name, useful and descriptive file name titles, and proper file name extensions. If you follow these conventions, you'll find that writing scripts to manipulate these files is simple.

Using these conventions, we have file names that follow the scheme Title-YYYY-mm-dd-HH-MM-SS.ext, with the placeholders detailed in Table 4-2.

Table 4-2. *Convention Scheme for File Name:* Title-YYYY-mm-dd-HH-MM-SS.ext

Placeholder	Description
Title	A descriptive title of your choice.
YYYY	Year the file was created.
mm	Month the file was created. In the case of January, mm is 01.
dd	Day the file was created. In the case of the 7th, dd is 07.
HH	Hours in 24-hour notation. 11 p.m. would be represented as 23. Values are from 00 to 23.
MM	Minutes. 5 minutes past the hour is 05.
SS	Seconds. 7 seconds past the minute is 07.
ext	An extension describing the file format, three characters long (if possible).

■ **Note** In case of values occupying less than the assigned number of digits, a zero is added. So if the time is 5 minutes past 1 o'clock, the value of hh will be 01 and the value of mm will be 05.

Example: Automating File Name Creation

Once you decide on a file name format, you can implement it using Python. The file name format I chose for this example is SysALogs-YYYY-MM-DDThh-mm-ss.csv. Listing 4-1 presents an implementation of this file name format.

Listing 4-1. Creating a Unique File Name, unique.py

```
from time import localtime
# a script to create unique file names based on title,
# date and time stamp and an extension
datetime_stamp  = '%4d-%02d-%02dT%02d-%02d-%02d' % localtime()[:6]
title = 'SysALogs'
ext = 'csv'
print('Unique filename: %s-%s.%s' % (title, datetime_stamp, ext))
```

Here's the result I got from executing `python unique.py`:

```
Unique filename: SysALogs-2014-05-06T07-26-49.csv
```

> **■ Note** In the example, I assume that files are generated at a slower rate of one file-per-second and that there's only one application logging data; hence, a file name based on seconds is unique. Also, in case of a system time change, there's a chance of files being non-unique. Before creating a file, you could check whether that file exists; but for clarity, this is left out of the example script.

The function `localtime()` is part of the *time* module and provides a structure of values representing the year, month, day of the month, hours, minutes, seconds, week day, day of the year, and daylight saving time (phew):

```
>>> localtime()
```

```
time.struct_time(tm_year=2014, tm_mon=5, tm_mday=6, tm_hour=7, tm_min=28,
tm_sec=7, tm_wday=1, tm_yday=126, tm_isdst=0)
```

```
>>> localtime()[:6]
```

```
(2014, 5, 6, 7, 28, 46)
```

We only require the first six arguments of `localtime()` to create our unique file name. To access the first six elements of the tuple, we use the slicing operator `[:6]`. Thus, `localtime()[:6]` returns the very six elements we're interested in for creating our unique file name.

Next, we use the `%` operator to format the string containing the timestamp: `'%4d-%02d-%02dT%02d-%02d-%02d'`. The substring `'%4d'` means up to four digits, while the substring `'%02d'` means two digits—if there are less than two digits, the digits are padded with zeros. We also use the `%` operator to output the final unique file name, which is composed of the strings stored in variables `title`, `datetime_stamp`, and `ext`. In this case, we use `'%s'` to format strings instead of integers.

Other Schemes

Unfortunately, automating file name creation and using the date and time mostly applies if you're writing the application that generates the data files. That's not always the case: you might be using an embedded system's output files and have no control of the source code. As long as the system generating the files has a real time clock, and assuming you can change the code (or later change the file names), following the preceding convention is doable.

On occasions where a real-time clock is unavailable, you need a different naming scheme. One way to use a timestamp in a file name is as a running index. That's a bit more complex than using the date because now you have to figure out the last index used. That said, it's still a good option: it provides consistency, and unless files are randomly deleted, it also provides some sort of chronological order. Incidentally, that's the scheme used by most digital cameras.

Example: Running Index

Listing 4-2 is a suggested running index implementation. The script will look for files according to a title and extension and determine a running index (up to 999). It will then create a file accordingly. Repeatedly running the script will create files with incrementing index values.

Listing 4-2. Running Index Implementation, index.py

```python
# a script to create unique filenames using a running index
from os.path import exists


index_stamp = 1
max_index   = 999    # maximum number of files
title       = '../data/SysALogs'
ext         = 'txt'

while index_stamp <= max_index:
    unique_filename = '%s-%03d.%s' % (title, index_stamp, ext)
    if exists(unique_filename):
        index_stamp += 1
        continue
    f = open(unique_filename, 'wt')
    f.write("Data")
    f.close()
    break

# report status
if index_stamp > max_index:
    print("Could not create a unique filename")
else:
    print("Created a unique file: ", unique_filename)
```

The general operation of this script is as follows: first, we create a file name string with the current index. Next, we check to see whether the file exists by calling the function exists(), which is part of the *os.path* module (more on *os.path* in Chapter 10). If the file exists, we increment the index and restart the loop; this is done with the statement continue. If the file name we've created does not exist, we proceed with writing the data to the file and breaking out of the while loop. Lastly, if a unique file name is not available (we check up to index 999, per variable max_index), the script reports that a unique file name could not be created.

Notice that we choose to pad the running index with zeros as denoted by the substring '%03d' in the line unique_filename = '%s-%03d.%s' % (title, index_stamp, ext). This is generally a good idea and allows easier processing of file names, as they have identical lengths and the strings representing the file names can be easily sliced.

■ **Note**   If you change the value of max_index, be sure to change the format string accordingly. For example, if max_index is 99999, replace %03d with %05d in the format specifications for unique_filename. This can also be done automatically by calculating the number of digits with int(log10(max_index)+1) and using the result in the format specifications (see the "Example: Searching Inside a Text File" section in Chapter 5). The function log10() is part of the *math* module (see Chapter 6).

File Formats

Up to this point, we've discussed the form of the file names. Now it is time to consider the format of the *contents*; that is, file formats. As previously pointed out, you may not be able to choose the file format used to store the data. Assuming you do have influence over the file format, the question is what format to use. A good file format is portable and easily recognizable. It also does not impact performance drastically, whether from its size or by causing computational overhead, depending on the nature of the application.

When you select a file format, consider the amount of data you'll be dealing with. If you're looking at large amounts of data, you want to be as efficient as possible in both storing the data and accessing it. The trade-off is that you will need to sacrifice a bit of portability and/use a less self-descriptive file format. This means choosing a binary format. If the amount of data is not large, and you want the data to be self-descriptive and as portable as possible, then choose text file formats—specifically, CSV. For large amounts of data, consider the following:

- How much storage space do you have? If you're running a desktop PC, a reasonable size to be dealing with is less than 1 terabyte. Of course, this number is ever-changing as storage space and processing power increase. At times you will find that, due to storage-space limitations, your only option is to go with binary files. The reason for this is that text representation is not as efficient as binary representations. 8-bit integers (characters) require 1 byte of storage in binary form and from 1 to 3 bytes in the text form used in CSV, excluding spaces and commas. Storing floating-point values, which typically require 4 bytes in binary form, will now require a considerably larger amount of bytes. The value 0.00000095367431640625 (which is 2 to the power of minus 20) will now require 22 bytes to represent properly in a CSV file. And that's not counting the separators and delimiters.

- How critical is performance to your application? The smaller the data files, the faster you can process them. There's no need to parse the data; you simply read it. If performance is your major concern, opt for binary file format.

■ **Note** That statement—"the smaller the data files, the faster you can process them"—is not always correct. Compressed files, for example, are smaller, but require more processing to work with; hence, their performance is worse, not better. However, assuming there is no compression, the performance of binary files is usually better.

So from a high-level file format perspective, you want to decide whether you'll be looking at binary data or text data. Table 4-3 lists the pros and cons of using either.

Table 4-3. *The Pros and Cons of Binary and Text File Formats*

	Pros	Cons
Text	Self-descriptive (usually)	Not storage efficient
	Does not require specific knowledge of the file format	Medium read/write access
	Can be viewed by any text editor	Requires "text" parsers
Binary	Relatively small storage space	Not so self-descriptive
	Fast read and write access	Requires knowledge of the file format
		Requires a specific application to view data

Text and binary are high-level categorizations. When dealing with text files, we will mostly limit our discussion to plain text files and CSV files, touching lightly on other file formats. When dealing with binary files, we'll talk mostly about straightforward file formats such as u16 and i32 and not complex file formats such as MP3 and gz that might support compression and/or encryption.

CSV File Format

The CSV file format is a text file format, and it can be viewed by any text editor. Furthermore, most spreadsheet applications are capable of reading and writing CSV files, parsing the values properly into rows and cells. In CSV files, values are separated by commas. In short, values are strings that represent numbers, dates, titles, or any other textual fields. If the string value has a comma in it, quoting is required; that is, the string will have beginning and ending quotes. Alternatively, the comma in the field can be escaped (more on this in Chapter 5). CSV format does not require a fixed number of fields per line (also called a row), which can be quite useful: it allows easy annotation of headers or descriptions of the data, which in turn can later be read by most any spreadsheet and/or editor with all the information recorded still intact and easily accessible.

The following are the contents of a valid CSV file:

```
System A
Data generated by logger1
"Header, 1",Header 2
Value 1,1
Value 2,AA
```

Example: Stock Price Charts

Following a convention that stores a short description of the data in the beginning lines of the CSV files can be very useful for annotating a graph or a report associated with the data in the file.

To follow along with the example, ensure your directory structure is similar to the one presented in Chapter 2 in the "Example: Directory Structure for the Book" section. Use Ch4 as your base directory; within Ch4, include three subdirectories named src, data, and images. If you wish to use a different scheme, be sure to change the file path variable and the call to function savefig() in the script in Listing 4-3, which appears a little later in this section.

Listing 4-3. stock_charts.py, Plotting the NASDAQ charts.xls File

```
from pylab import *
import csv
from time import gmtime, mktime

# modify the following to point to your data file
filepath = '../data/charts.xls'

# read the entire CSV file and store it in an array of lists
# use tab ('\t') as a delimiter
data = []
for row in csv.reader(open(filepath), delimiter='\t'):
    data.append(row)
```

```
# split the data to header and values
header = data[0]
values = array(data[2:])

# the first column is date information in a string format
# we transform it to a day of year format
# notice that this will not work over year boundary (need to add 365)
yearday = zeros(len(values[:, 0]))
for i, day in enumerate(values[:, 0]):
    market_close_time = (int(day[6:]), int(day[:2]), int(day[3:5]), \
        16, 0, 0, 0, 0, 0)
    yearday[i] = gmtime(mktime(market_close_time)).tm_yday

# plot the data
for i in range(1, 5):
    plot(yearday, values[:, i], label=header[i], linewidth=3)

# annotate the start and end dates
text(yearday[0], values[0, 1], values[0, 0], ha='center')
text(yearday[-1], values[-1, 1], values[-1 ,0], ha='center')

grid()
legend(loc='best')
ylabel('Stock price [USD]')
xlabel('Days from start of the year '+values[0, 0][6:])
title('NASDAQ-100 (IXNDX) Stock price, period %s-%s' % \
    (values[-1, 0], values[0, 0]))
savefig('../images/stock_price.png', dpi=150)
```

For this example, you can download data from the NASDAQ stock exchange web site (http://www.nasdaq.com). Select a stock you wish to display, such as the NASDAQ-100 (IXNDX) or your company's stock chart. Select the Interactive Charts option, right-click the chart, and select View Underlying Data. This will present the actual values used to create the chart. You can choose to download the file in Excel format: do so and save the file under Ch4/data/charts.xls.

If you open the file Ch4/data/charts.xls in a text editor, you'll notice that there's header information describing what each column means:

Date	Open	High	Low	Close/Last	Volume
10:24	3598.27002	3599.389893	3587.48999	3598.350098	0
05/05/2014	3566.256	3605.263	3556.403	3605.092	0
05/02/2014	3608.841	3611.563	3578.527	3587.644	0
05/01/2014	3589.659	3613.03	3580.019	3594.362	0
04/30/2014	3556.004	3585.502	3548.11	3582.02	0
04/29/2014	3557.768	3579.03	3538.242	3573.99	0

In reality, the file format is a form of CSV, with the separator being a tab instead of a comma. We can easily overcome this with Python's *csv* module by specifying the delimiter to be tab: '\t'. Listing 4-3 shows our implementation, stock_charts.py, which reads a stock chart file and presents a graph with the header information properly displayed. Be sure to save it in folder Ch4/src. The result will be a PNG image, stock_price.png, in directory Ch4/images.

We start by reading the CSV data file and passing a tab as a delimiter. The first line in variable data is the header information and describes what each column means: Date, Open, High, Low, Close/Last, and Volume. The second line is the current stock price. The remaining lines are the values to be plotted. We therefore split the variable data into header and values, accordingly. We also convert the values to a *NumPy* array using the function call array(). Using a *NumPy* array, the data will easier to process and plot; you will learn more about *NumPy* in Chapter 7.

The following is not so much an explanation of working with CSV files, but it is important to fully understand the script.

Next is the so-called linearization process. Much like in the GPS example of Chapter 1, data in charts.xls is not linear. The information consists of stock prices recorded on a daily basis; however, stocks are not traded every day, with weekends being the prime example, but also holidays. If we plot the information as-is, neglecting these "holes" in the data, the picture presented will be skewed. So instead, we need to choose a different time base, one that will take into consideration nontrade days. I chose to use the day-of-the-year value: January 1 is 1, January 2 is 2, . . . December 31 is 365 (or 366 in a leap year).

Since I don't want to get into the process of determining leap years or summing up the days in each month, I've decided to use the *time* module again. The idea here is to use the function gmtime(); as a side effect, this will retrieve the day-of-the-year value. Function gmtime() receives a value representing the number of seconds elapsed since the epoch, a fixed point in time (see more about the epoch in Chapter 5). While this sounds even more complicated than calculating the day of the year, in reality it's easier because of function mktime(). Function mktime() receives a tuple of nine values, detailed previously, and returns the number of seconds since the epoch. So we first construct a tuple of those nine values, the first three being year, month, and day, which are known to us, and arbitrarily assigning the hour to be 4 p.m. (which coincides with the end of trading day). We leave the remaining fields at zero. We then feed this number to gmtime() and receive a new tuple, now properly populated with the year of day, the eighth element of the tuple, accessible with tm_yday, which we save in vector yearday.

▪ **Note**   The script does not take into account data greater than one year. To accommodate for this, you could take into consideration the number of days in a year (365 or 366, depending on a leap year) and use the lowest year as a baseline.

We then plot the data and annotate the graph. For the legend, we use the header values of the CSV file stored in variable header. We also use actual values from the variable values to annotate the start and end of period on the graph itself, the title, and the x-axis label (see Figure 4-1).

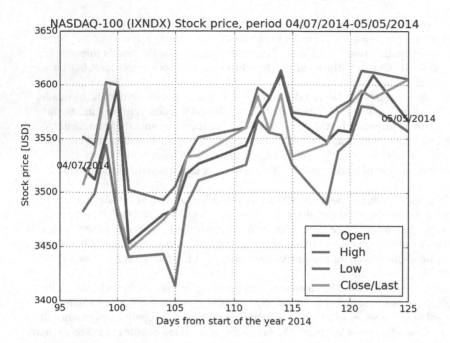

Figure 4-1. *The stock price chart output*

■ **Note** If you look closely at the data in charts.xls, you'll notice that it's reversed; that is, it is backward in time. One of the side effects of using the day-of-the-year value is that values are now plotted from lower to higher values: older times are on the left, and newer events are on the right. If you'd like to reverse this behavior, issue the command gca().axes.invert_xaxis().

Example: Automatically Reading Yahoo! Financial Data

There's an alternative method to manually saving the charts.xls file from NASDAQ. One such option is using the *matplotlib.finance* module. The two core functions that fetch the data and parse it are fetch_historical_yahoo() and parse_yahoo_historical() (although you could easily parse the data yourself). Another function of interest is the candlestick() function, which plots a candlestick graph of the stocks.

Listing 4-4 is a modification of the previous example that uses the functions from the *matplotlib.finance* module. Notice that there are some other minor changes to the code because the data structure is a bit different from the NASDAQ charts.xls file. You can control the stock you wish to view, as well as the start and end dates, by changing the values stock_name, t_start, and t_end.

Listing 4-4. Fetching and Plotting Yahoo! Data yahoo_charts.py

```python
from pylab import *
from matplotlib.finance import *

# stock name and period
stock_name  = '^NDX'
t_start     = datetime.datetime(2014, 1, 1)
t_end       = datetime.datetime(2014, 1, 31)
year_start  = datetime.datetime(2014, 1, 1)

# retrieve and parse stock data
data    = fetch_historical_yahoo(stock_name, t_start, t_end)
y       = array(parse_yahoo_historical(data))

# dates might not be trade days, so update values
# to show actual dates retrieved
t_start = num2date(y[0, 0])
t_end   = num2date(y[-1, -0])

# normalize the x-axis to show values from the start of year
y[:, 0] = y[:, 0]-date2num(year_start)+1

# plot a candlestick graph
figure()
candlestick(gca(), y)

# annotate the graph with additional text
start_str = "%d-%02d-%02d" % (t_start.year, t_start.month, t_start.day)
end_str   = "%d-%02d-%02d" % (t_end.year, t_end.month, t_end.day)
title('Stock: %s, period %s to %s' % (stock_name, start_str, end_str))
xlabel('Days from start of the year %d' % t_start.year)
ylabel('%s Stock price [USD]' % stock_name)
text(y[0, 0], y[0, 1], start_str)
text(y[-1, 0], y[-1, 1], end_str)
grid()
savefig('../images/%s_candlestick_yahoo-%s-%s.png' % \
    (stock_name, start_str, end_str), dpi=150)
```

A couple notes to keep in mind:

- The time base is normalized; that is, the dates are shown from the start of the year 2014 and not the epoch. This is implemented in line y[:,0] = y[:,0]-date2num(year_start)+1.

- The actual dates requested might not be trade days. Therefore, the start and end times are updated after the data is fetched and parsed. This is done in line t_start = num2date(y[0, 0]) and t_end = num2date(y[-1, -0]).

Figure 4-2 shows the results of the example in Listing 4-4.

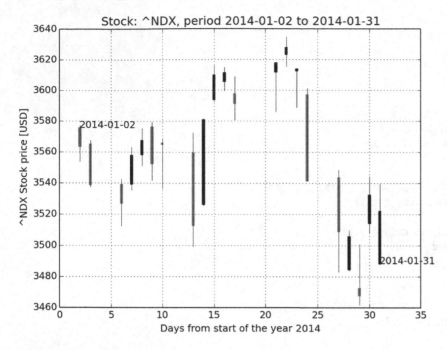

Figure 4-2. *An automatically generated candlestick graph*

Example: Creating a CSV File

If you're creating your own CSV files from scratch rather than downloading the data, you can easily write a list to a CSV file, as shown in this example. I assign some arbitrary mixed data (strings and numbers) to a list named data and write it to file. Try it yourself, and then open the created file, test.csv, to view the file contents:

```
L = [['Time', 'Value', 'Notes'], [0, 20, 'Start point'],\
    [0.1, 'Middle point'], [2]]
import csv
f = open('../data/test.csv', 'w', newline='')
csv.writer(f).writerows(L)
f.close()
```

Here are the contents of the test file, test.csv:

```
Time,Value,Notes
0,20,Start point
0.1,Middle point
2
```

Try changing the values of the list, such as adding a comma to one of the strings. Now open the file in a spreadsheet application: did the application manage to read the comma properly? Next, open the file in a text editor and notice that the string containing the comma is now quoted. The *csv* module took care of adding quotes as required. You'll learn more about the *csv* module in Chapter 5.

USING THE CSV MODULE INSTEAD OF THE SPLIT() FUNCTION

So far, we've used Python's *csv* module liberally. You might be wondering why we're not using the function `split(',')` instead of the `csv.writer` object. The answer is that the *csv* module also addresses special cases, such as a string that includes a comma. Consider the following row:

```
"Surname, Name", 2008, 450
```

Module *csv* will handle this properly and return three elements. However, `split(',')` will return four elements: the quoted string will be broken in two.

CSV Limitations

All's not roses in the world of CSV. Here are some things to consider:

- *Size*: CSV files are typically not size efficient, compared with binary file formats.

- *Performance*: There's also a performance hit with CSV files because they require parsing. An application, be it a spreadsheet application or even our code in Python, calls a function to translate the CSV file into values more easily used by the application. That is, it parses fields and rows and translates from text to integer or floating point, in the case of number values. Running the parser to read the CSV file takes time, so reading a large file will take considerable time. If performance is of importance and your application reads very large files, consider using a binary file format instead.

What to Store

As a general rule, store as much information as possible. Unfortunately, sometimes that ideal is simply not an option. Consider the data rate of an uncompressed HDTV video signal at 1080×720 pixels, 30 frames per second, and true colors (24 bits). That's 1080×720×30×3 bytes-per-second, or roughly 70 megabytes-per-second to store, which is quite a bit to store. (And what if you wanted to store several channels simultaneously?) This means you'll have to discard some of the information or compress it—or get better hardware.

Deciding what to store and what not to store will be very much system dependent. Some opt for decimating the data, which has its implications. Others decide on discarding a parameter they deem less important. Barring file size limitations, consider the following guidelines in deciding what to store:

- Write header file information in the beginning of the file, describing the system and the data, including units of measurement. You can use free-form text for this. Some even go an additional step by adding a special character (e.g., #) at the beginning of every line, ensuring the reader understands those are remarks and not part of the data.

- Include a header for each column, explaining what each column means. It's very useful for both viewing the files using a spreadsheet and for automated scripts to visualize the data.

- Always try to store the time and date. Store the date and time values in the first column. You can follow the ISO 8601 specifications, or you might opt to use a different notation. An alternative valuable notation to ISO 8601 format is to store the number of seconds that have elapsed since the epoch: 1 January 1970 on most Linux machines. That way, you have a number that is very easy to manipulate, as opposed to a date and time that requires parsing. There's also a side benefit: if you have several files, you can use the same time base for all of them. The seconds-since-the-epoch notation is very useful in binary formats.

Here's an example of the contents of a file that follows the preceding guidelines:

```
#Units,Celsius
#Sensor,A1
#System serial number,401
Date and Time,Temperature,Pressure
2005-09-15T01:07:08, 42.0,53.1
2005-09-15T01:07:14, 42.0,53.2
2005-09-15T01:07:19, 39.0,51.8
```

When to Use CSV

Use CSV whenever possible, with the following exceptions:

- Performance is an issue.

- File size is an issue.

- Data is already in a different format.

Binary Files

Binary files are an efficient method of storing data. The term "binary files" means files that are not represented as ASCII text; that is, if you open these files in a text editor, the data will appear to be gibberish. In reality, there's no difference between binary files and text files, other than what the data in the files represents. From the computer's perspective, they're both just files. So in essence, if the file is not a text file, it's a binary file, but that's a loose definition.

As discussed previously, there are merits to using binary file formats, and those are typically size and performance. There's also another reason, and that's the nature of the data. A digital picture is not easily represented as a text file (it can be though—for example, every pixel value is an integer in a CSV file). The same applies for a compressed file, as well. Regardless of the reason, it's almost impossible to avoid using binary files.

In this book, when I refer to binary files, I typically mean one of the following file formats: an array of values, an array of structs, or other commonly used binary file formats.

An Array of Values

The most simple binary file format we'll be using is an array of values, a single data type. The file could be holding signed values or unsigned bytes. The array-of-values file format lends itself nicely to storing simple binary data.

Example: Reading and Writing an Array of Binary Values

The Python array data type (not to be confused with *NumPy*'s array data type) is an ideal candidate for this sort of binary file handling. The array data type is part of the *array* module. To use it, issue the following command:

```
>>> from array import *
```

To create an array, call the `array()` function with the data type and optional initialization parameters, as follows:

```
>>> from array import *
>>> a = array('h') # array of signed numbers, of zero size
>>> a
```

```
array('h')
```

```
>>> b = array('L', [1000, 2000, 3000]) # array of three unsigned numbers
>>> b
```

```
array('L', [1000, 2000, 3000])
```

```
>>> c = array('d', range(10)) # array of floating-points, from 0 to 9 including
>>> c
```

```
array('d', [0.0, 1.0, 2.0, 3.0, 4.0, 5.0, 6.0, 7.0, 8.0, 9.0])
```

The data types listed in Table 4-4 can be used in initializing array objects.

Table 4-4. *Array Data Types*

Data Type	Data Meaning and Minimum Size in Bytes
`'b'`	Signed integer, 1 byte
`'B'`	Unsigned integer, 1 byte
`'u'`	Unicode character, 2 bytes or 4 bytes, platform dependent
`'h'`	Signed integer, 2 bytes
`'H'`	Unsigned integer, 2 bytes
`'i'`	Signed integer, 2 bytes
`'I'`	Unsigned integer, 2 bytes
`'l'`	Signed integer, 4 bytes
`'L'`	Unsigned integer, 4 bytes
`'q'`	Signed integer, 8 bytes
`'Q'`	Unsigned integer, 8 bytes
`'f'`	Floating-point value, 4 bytes
`'d'`	Floating-point value, 8 bytes

Notice how the table header says "Minimum Size in Bytes"? This is because the actual number of bytes might be different and is dependent on the machine architecture; the actual size can be accessed by the `itemsize` array attribute:

```
>>> a = array('L')
>>> a.itemsize
```

On some of my machines, the return value is 8; on others, it's 4.

Writing array values to file is done using the tofile() member function of the array data type:

```
>>> f = open('b.u32', 'wb')
>>> b.tofile(f)
>>> f.close()
```

Reading is performed using the fromfile() member function of the array data type. The function fromfile() also requires the number of values to read. If you supply a number greater than the number of elements in the file, an exception is raised; however, values will still be retrieved:

```
>>> d = array('L')
>>> f = open('../data/b.u32', 'rb')
>>> d.fromfile(f, 3)
>>> f.close()
>>> d == b
```

True

An Array of Structs

A more complex binary data structure we'll be dealing with is an array of structs. The word "struct" is taken from the C programming language and describes a structure combined of several data types.

Suppose data is stored as follows: int, float, float, int, float, float, and so forth. This series can be viewed as an array of structures, with the structure being (int, float, float). In this sense, an array of values, discussed previously, is also an array of structs with the struct being a single data type. If you're familiar with C, the preceding structure might be described as shown in Listing 4-5.

Listing 4-5. A Struct in C

```
struct some_binary_file_format
{
    long epoch;
    float fTemperature;
    float fPressure;
};
```

Note that, unlike our previous binary file formats, this one doesn't lend itself to a nice extension naming convention such as .u16 or .f32, so we simply choose the extension .bin, noting that it's a binary file.

Example: Reading and Writing an Array of Structs

In this example, we'll create a structure containing two data types (int and float), write it to file, and then read it using two different methods: a structure at a time and the entire file at once. You can follow along by entering the commands interactively at the Python shell.

First, we have to import the *struct* module:

```
>>> import struct
```

To illustrate the concept of an array of structs, we'll create a list of rows. Each row is a list of three values: an integer and two floating point values, which represent a C structure. We'll generate a relatively short list, only two rows long:

```
>>> L = [ [ 10, 1.0, 2.0], [20, 0.125, 0.25] ]
```

Next, we define two variables, filename and format, so we don't have to enter them every time:

```
>>> filename = '../data/structs.bin'
>>> format = 'Lff'
```

I'm assuming there's a directory named ../data; if one does not exist, then either create it or change the value of the variable filename accordingly. The format 'Lff' means a 4-byte integer, followed by a float and a float per Table 4-4. Next, we write the list to file:

```
>>> fout = open(filename, 'wb')
>>> for row in L:
...     data = struct.pack(format, row[0], row[1], row[2])
...     num = fout.write(data)
...
>>> fout.close()
```

The first call to open() opens a file in binary mode for writing (the character w in 'wb' stands for write, while the b stands for binary; see the "Files" section in Chapter 5 for more information). We then use a for loop and iterate over the rows in the list L. Every row is packed using the function struct.pack(). The function struct.pack() accepts a format and then the values to pack. The return value is a string that can be written to file. We then write the string to file and store the number of characters read in the variable num. Finally, the last line closes the file.

So now we should have a file named ../data/structs.bin. This file contains the list of values from the list L. Let's read it a struct at a time.

We'll start by defining a variable equivalent to the size of the struct format:

```
>>> struct_size = struct.calcsize(format)
```

The function struct.calcsize() calculates the size in bytes of the format. Armed with the struct size, we start reading the data, a struct at a time:

```
>>> fin = open(filename, 'rb')
>>> data = fin.read(struct_size)
>>> data
```

```
b'\n\x00\x00\x00\x00\x00\x80?\x00\x00\x00@'
```

The first line opens the file for reading in binary mode. We then use the function read(n) to read n bytes and store them in the variable data. So now the variable data holds the first structure from the binary file, but it isn't legible yet. We'll need to unpack it using struct.unpack(); that is, we need to convert it from a string to a tuple of values using the format specifier 'Lff'. But since we'll be reading and unpacking several values, it stands to reason that we should use a while loop, as follows:

```
>>> while data:
...     values = struct.unpack(format, data)
...     print(values)
...     data = fin.read(struct_size)
...
```

```
(10, 1.0, 2.0)
(20, 0.125, 0.25)
```

```
>>> fin.close()
```

The `while` condition evaluates to `True` as long as variable `data` is nonempty; hence, data will be processed until the end of the file. Each struct read is unpacked to a tuple of values using the `struct.unpack()` function. Once a struct is unpacked, we read the next structure. This continues until all the structs are read from the input file. Lastly, we close the file.

The second method we'll examine here is reading the entire file at once. To do so, we first read the entire file to memory, using the `read()` function:

```
>>> data = open(filename, 'rb').read()
>>> len(data)
```

```
24
```

(Note that on some systems, the result might be 32, but this has to do with the underlying OS and shouldn't be a problem). If no parameters are provided for `read()`, the entire file is read into memory until an end of file (EOF) is reached. This might not be a problem with small files, but you should be wary with larger files; your computer might not be able to handle all the data at once, so you will need to read the files in chunks per the previous method. Note that I've chosen not to assign a file handle for the data file; instead, I let Python handle the closing of the file for me.

The function `struct.unpack()` accepts `format` as a parameter and unpacks the data to a tuple. However, we need to unpack the entire array, not just the first structure. We can take the obvious route of using a `for` loop to unpack the binary data a piece at a time. An alternative approach is to change the format value to `unpack()` from a single `'Lff'` to a repetitive `'LffLffLff...'`. This allows unpacking of the entire binary data in one call to `struct.unpack()`. Luckily, Python provides us with a very useful tool for multiplying strings, the multiplication operator:

```
>>> 'Lff'*5
```

```
'LffLffLffLffLff'
```

We can calculate the size of the array we want to unpack by dividing the length of the data by the size of one struct. In our case, that's `len(data)/struct_size`. So, to generate a format to unpack by, we multiply the format by that value, which folds neatly into the following:

```
>>> print(struct.unpack(format*int(len(data)/struct_size), data))
```

```
(10, 1.0, 2.0, 20, 0.125, 0.25)
```

■ **Note** (Advanced readers) This implementation assumes the file is in accordance with the native operating system's byte order. If you try to unpack data in this manner with any of the struct's byte order, size, and alignment format characters such as @, =, <, >, and !, then the function will fail.

OTHER BINARY FILE FORMATS

Binary files can be more complex and can follow a different scheme from the repeating fixed-size structure. Some employ compression, which typically involves a non-fixed-size structure. Others might store data sequentially; that is, using the data of the preceding example, you could write all the integer values, followed by the floating-point values. In that case, a different method to read the file should be employed, but it's quite straightforward if you know the file format. In this book, I'll touch lightly on this topic, specifically about known file types such as pictures and compressed files. Since the number of file formats is virtually unlimited, the topic is too vast for one book to cover.

Header Files

Binary files differ from CSV files in one important respect: you can't really tell whether the information in a binary file is in integer representation, floating point, or an altogether different scheme. This means that you, the programmer, need to know in advance what file format you're dealing with. At first that might not seem such a complex task, but in reality it's not trivial. Even with the same notation that was covered previously in this chapter, say .u16, you still don't know what the values represent. Are they sampled voltage values? Is there a timestamp? And you might have several binary file formats you're dealing with.

To resolve this, we use a header file to describe each file type, or directory, in case all the files conform to the same format. A header file is a text file that describes the format of the binary file. But if we're using a text file, we might as well use CSV!

It's a good idea to have the same base file name for the header file as the binary file (excluding the extension). I typically add an .hdr.csv extension for my header files; for example, for file Lava2001-03-21T08-22-23.f32, I name the header file Lava2001-03-21T08-22-23.f32.hdr.csv.

Here's an example of header file contents for an array-of-structs file format:

```
"Name", "Number of bytes", "Format", "Units"
"Time Elapsed since epoch", 4, "integer", "seconds"
"Temperature", 4, "float", "Degrees Celsius"
"Pressure", 4, "float", "Psi"
```

The nice thing about this structure is that it's quite self-explanatory. It lends itself easily to automation and scripting.

I've also added a column titled Units. This column is obvious; however, you will find later that it's quite useful. Say you know the temperature is an integer, but what exactly does it represent? Degrees? And if so, are those in Kelvin, Fahrenheit, or Celsius?

If the file format is different and does not follow the repeating fixed-size structure format, you can come up with a header that best describes that file format. In the case of sequential data, the header file might look like this:

```
"Name", "Number of bytes", "Format", "Units", "#Values"
"Time Elapsed since epoch", 4, "integer", "seconds", 100
"Temperature", 4, "float", "Degrees Celsius", 100
"Filtered values", 4, "float", "Degrees Celsius", 100
```

This format implies that the data is sequential, having 100 values for each parameter. This is a more complex file format and not at all popular due to the complexity associated with implementing a format that behaves like this; you'd have to remember all the file information and then store it to the file instead of gathering values and storing them one at a time. Again, sometimes you're given data files to work with and can't control the file format.

Readme Files

Readme files are documentation files placed in a directory describing the contents of the files in that directory. There's no clear definition of the contents of Readme files, with this exception: the information should be in clear text, so it can be viewed by any text editor. Some Readme files have directions on what should be run and how to use the software. Others add author information and credits. Using Readme files is an excellent way to document what you've done without the overhead of writing a user's manual. Here are occasions where I found using Readme files of value:

- They are helpful for describing the contents of data in directories: file formats, origin of data, date and time, person in charge, and so forth. See Chapter 1 for an example of a Readme file describing data.

- When directories contain both data and scripts to analyze them, there's bound to be a multitude of scripts. Describing the entry point, or what the user should run first, is a time saver—especially if a process is required before running the scripts (e.g., uncompressing the data). You need to describe that in your Readme file.

Readme files can be as detailed or as cryptic as you'd like. Just remember that they're there to help; include detail in them according to the level of the user or developer, so they understand what's going on.

The common full file name for Readme files is `Readme.txt`.

INI Files

As you add content and capabilities to your scripts, you'll find that you need to control the scripts' behavior using options. For example, you might need to run scripts where you generate only text output, without graphs. Or, you might need to run the scripts on a different set of data points. As the number of options increase, you'll need methods for controlling the options. There are several ways to implement options; some common approaches follow:

- Interactive input from the user, such as "Generate graphs (y/n)?"

- Command-line parameters, such as the `-l` in the command `ls -l`.

- An external configuration file holding the choices and parameters. To change the behavior of the script, the user changes the values in the configuration file. The script reads the configuration file and acts accordingly.

The latter option, a configuration file, is also referred to as an INI file. The reason for this is that, back in the days before the registry was introduced in Windows, applications used to store parameters in files having the application name and ending with an `.INI` extension. In Linux, these are commonly referred to as configurations files; configuration files typically reside in the directory `/etc` and have a `.conf` extension. Python supports INI files natively with the *configparser* module (the module was named *ConfigParser* in Python 2.x).

Much like Readme files describing the data, INI files describe the parameters, options, and choices used to run a script. They provide a clean way of explaining what the options mean. The general markup of an INI file (config file) is a section, denoted by brackets, followed by a list of parameters and their assigned values and optional remarks, as outlined in Table 4-5.

Table 4-5. *INI File Format*

INI/Config Line	Format	Notes
Section	`[section]`	Used to group parameters logically
Parameter	`param1=value1` *or* `param1:value1`	Used to set a parameter to a value
Remark	`; remark` *or* `# remark`	Used to document sections and parameters

Example: Reading and Writing INI Files

Listing 4-6 shows an implementation of writing an INI file using the *configparser* module.

Listing 4-6. Creating an INI (Config) File

```
# creating an INI (config) file
import configparser
options = configparser.ConfigParser()
options['User Options'] = {}
options['User Options']['all_data'] = 'Y'
options['User Options']['graph'] = '1'
options['Plot'] = {}
options['Plot']['grid'] = 'Y'
f = open('../data/options.ini', 'w')
options.write(f)
f.close()
```

First, we import the *configparser* module and create a ConfigParser object. Second, we associate it with the variable options. We then set sections with curly bracers {}, much like dictionaries; there are two sections in this example: 'User Options' and 'Plot'. We set parameters to each section by accessing the section in braces [ ]. For example, options['Plot']['grid'] = 'Y'; in this line, 'Plot' is the section and 'grid' is the parameter (option). Lastly, we create a file and output the ConfigParser object to file, generating an INI file. The following example shows the results from running the script in Listing 4-6:

```
[User Options]
all_data = Y
graph = 1

[Plot]
grid = Y
```

Reading an INI file is even easier. Assuming you have run the previous script, you should now have an INI file named ../data/options.ini. The script in Listing 4-7 will read that file and parse its contents.

Listing 4-7. Reading INI (Config) File

```
# read an INI (config) file
import configparser
read_opts = configparser.ConfigParser()
read_opts.read('../data/options.ini')

# print parameters and values
for section in read_opts.sections():
    print("[%s]" % section)
    for param in read_opts.items(section):
        print(param)
```

The function `ConfigParser.read()` accepts a file name (use `read_file()` if you want to use a file pointer) and parses the INI file with the *configparser* object. The code following the `read()` function call prints the sections, options, and values. Here are the results from running the script in Listing 4-7:

```
[User Options]
('all_data', 'Y')
('graph', '1')
[Plot]
('grid', 'Y')
```

XML and Other Formats

XML, or Extensible Markup Language, has been growing in popularity as a data file format. XML is more descriptive than CSV and definitely more descriptive than binary—hence, its popularity. XML is a very good format for data files, but it has its overhead. Mainly, it requires a complex parser to read the data and check data validity. While that's true for CSV as well, CSV is much less complex.

XML, however, is beyond the scope of this book. This is mainly because CSV provides us with the functionality we require. But this is also because the topic is too large to be addressed properly in this book. If you do require XML support, rest assured that Python has extensive XML support (see `https://docs.python.org/3.3/library/xml.html`). There's also a large selection of books available on XML, and I suggest you consult with them or the Internet should you require XML support.

Beyond XML and the other formats discussed here, there is a large number of other file formats you're likely to encounter, including such image formats as PNG, JPEG, bitmaps and GIF, and compressed file formats such as ZIP or gz. It is far beyond the scope of this book to detail and discuss all these file formats. Two of the benefits of using Python are its popularity and an active developer base with an extensive number of freely available packages contributed by the Python community. There's a good chance there's already a module out there that's suitable for reading different file formats and converting them to programmer-friendly values. For example, a module we'll be exploring in Chapter 9, the *Python Imaging Library (PIL)*, supports most popular image formats.

Locating Data Files

As you gather data, you're bound to end up with files of various types: raw data files, clean data files, processed data files, files of older file formats, and the list goes on. The question is, how do you organize all this data; and furthermore, how do you later locate it for analysis? This section suggests several approaches to organizing files and, more importantly, covers how to maintain well-organized data. One approach is to store files in directories and subdirectories, and we'll discuss methods to locate the files using that approach; another is to use catalog files and annotate them.

Organization into Directories

The most popular method of organizing files is in directories. If you go with this approach, try to have all your subdirectories containing data files in a parent directory named `data` or similar. If you intend to preprocess the data, split the directory into "raw" and "clean" data. The reason you want to do this is that you may find out later that the preprocessing algorithm has a bug or that a different method should be employed to preprocess the data. Or, if you manually preprocessed the data (that is, cleaned up the data files, removed wrong files, edited others, etc.), you may later realize you accidentally erased the wrong data file or that you made a mistake.

From here, there are several options. For example, you might put all the data files in one directory or create subdirectories and organize files there. Personally, I like to split the directories further for several reasons. One is that it gives me greater control over documentation: it's possible to generate Readme files for every directory. The other is that it allows greater control over what files to process. For example, I could process all files from directory systemA. Lastly, it helps provide a more aesthetic view, and that's an important part of any engineering work.

The actual breakdown into subdirectories is very problem specific. It could be based on dates, type of files, contents, and pretty much anything else you would like. However, do try to group the files at least in one top-parent directory, as it will be a lot easier to iterate through the data, as in this example:

```
data
    raw
        systemA
        systemB
        systemC
    clean
        systemA
        systemB
        systemC
```

Searching for Files

If data files are stored in an organized directory, they should be easy to search for. One of the obvious methods for searching for a file is by recursively going through all the subdirectories and looking for files that match a given pattern.

Example: Storing Directory Contents in an Array

When you first look for a file, you don't always find it on your first search, maybe because you chose the wrong file name pattern or because of a simple typo. There's a good chance you'll require additional searches. Now if you have a significant number of data files, it can be tedious to walk the entire directory again. Every search is laborious, and the time spent finding files will increase dramatically. Instead, it's possible to store the intermediate result in a data structure.

Try this yourself. Define the function get_all_files(), as shown in Listing 4-8, and call it interactively in Python by issuing allfiles = get_all_files('some_path'). Observe the results by issuing print(allfiles) at the Python shell.

Listing 4-8. A Function to Retrieve All Files in a Directory and Store It in an Array

```python
import os
def get_all_files(srchpath):
    """Get the names of all the files in a directory, recursively,
    including path, name and size."""
    allfiles = []

    for root, dirs, files in os.walk(srchpath):
        for file in files:
            try:
                pathname = os.path.join(root, file)
                filesize = os.path.getsize(pathname)
                allfiles.append([file, pathname, filesize])
            except FileNotFoundError:
                pass
    return allfiles
```

The function stores an entry to each file in an array of lists. Each entry in the list holds the file name, path name, and file size. A path name is the full path plus a name of a file (e.g., /home/shai/file.txt); a file name is the name of the file excluding the path (e.g., file.txt); and the file size is given in bytes. The function os.walk() was described in Chapter 1 and should not require additional clarifications. I've used the function os.path.getsize() to retrieve the size of a file. I've also used a try/except mechanism to catch an exception that causes issues on some Linux machines.

■ **Note**   In cases where file names contain non-English characters, I've seen the function getsize() raise an exception because it was unable to read the file. If you're dealing with such files, either rename them or add a try/except clause to catch the exception.

Indexing

The act of going through directories and recording file information in an organized manner is called indexing. Done properly, indexing can allow fast searches.

Example: Searching for Duplicate Files

Continuing our previous example, now that we have an array containing all the files in a directory, we can perform fast searches on the array. We can sort the array based on file size and find the ten largest files; or, we can look for files matching a given pattern. In this example, we'll explore a more complex search, one that checks for duplicate files. This is a true need, one that arises especially when dealing with a large number of files.

Assuming you have followed the unique file name convention suggested earlier, there shouldn't be any duplicate file names. However, that's not always the case. Consider the following: data is generated by copying pictures from a digital camera. Many digital cameras follow a simple running index scheme (see the section, "Other Schemes") whereby file names follow the pattern Header0001.jpg, Header0002.jpg, and so on, with each camera having its own Header string. After you copy the files to your computer, you delete the old files in the camera, clearing space for new pictures. New pictures taken by the camera will in turn start from index 1; eventually, as they're copied to your computer, new pictures will have non-unique file names. To ensure files are not accidentally overwritten, you copy over each batch of pictures to a directory of its own, with each directory named uniquely based on a date and time. So it is you end up with several directories, but their contents may contain non-unique file names. Can we clear some up?

Another scenario is that of backups, or that of using several storage locations, such as your laptop and your home PC. You may have copies of data lying around in several spots, and the issue again is whether you have multiple copies of the same data. Of course, if you follow a central server approach and that server is backed up on a regular basis, you'll find that these occasions are rare. Still, it's nice to be able to identify duplicate files, and that's the motivation behind this example.

In the example, we'll confine ourselves to the following: we assume files to be identical if they have the same file name and file size. While this isn't necessarily true, the example can be easily modified to compare contents, as well.

We'll show three different implementations and discuss the best solution of the three. In all three methods, we'll use a dictionary object.

■ **Note**   To be able to follow along, ensure you've defined the function get_all_files() from the previous example. Run it in interactive Python and store the results in an array, as follows: allfiles = get_all_files(pathname).

Method 1: We use the file name as the unique key in our dictionary `mydict1`. The value is a list as follows: `[filepath, filesize]`. At first, `mydict1` is empty. For every entry, we ask whether the file name is a key to the dictionary. If it isn't encountered, we add the list `[filepath, filesize]` as a value, where file name is the key. If the key is in the dictionary, it means that this file name has been encountered in the past. We then retrieve the file size and compare it with the current entry file size. Listing 4-9 shows the implementation.

Listing 4-9. Looking for Duplicate Files, Method 1

```
def find_dupes_1(thefiles):
    """Searches for file duplicates, method 1."""
    result1 = []
    mydict1 = {}

    for filename, pathname, filesize in thefiles:
        if filename in mydict1:
            [dup_file, dup_size] = mydict1[filename]
            if dup_size==filesize:
                result1.append(pathname+filename)
        else:
            mydict1[filename] = [pathname,filesize]
    return result1
```

One of the obvious shortcomings of this method is that there might be several files with the same file name but different sizes; the algorithm might not catch some of them. For example, if the first file is of size A, and several other files have the same file name but are of size B, the algorithm will not identify files of size B as duplicates.

Method 2: This method uses the path name as the unique key in the dictionary `mydict2` and the list `[filename, filesize]` as the value. Since we're using the path name as the key, it's guaranteed to be unique; there are no two files with the same file name and path name. To check whether a file name already exists in the dictionary, we iterate through all the elements in the dictionary using the `items()` method. If the file name and the file size are identical, we announce them to be a duplicate. If not, we add the associated path name as key and the `[filename, filesize]` as a new value to the dictionary (see Listing 4-10).

Listing 4-10. Looking for Duplicate Files, Method 2

```
def find_dupes_2(thefiles):
    """Searches for file duplicates, method 2."""
    result2 = []
    mydict2 = {}

    for filename, pathname, filesize in thefiles:
        for k, v in mydict2.items():
            if v[0]==filename and v[1]==filesize:
                result2.append(pathname+filename)
        else:
            mydict2[pathname] = [filename, filesize]
    return result2
```

This method resolves the shortcoming of method 1 because, if there are several files of the same file name, they will not be skipped. However, the implementation is not a good one. The major issue is that we use a dictionary object to store values and neglect to use the inherent dictionary hashing mechanism properly: we iterate through all the items linearly. We probably could've just as well used an array.

Method 3: This method uses the file name (excluding the path) as the key in the dictionary object mydict3. The difference from method 1 is that, instead of a list holding [pathname, filesize], we now hold an *array* of lists of the form [pathname, filesize] for every key (file name), much like in a real dictionary, where one entry (key) might have several definitions (values). The second change we introduce is that we don't ask whether the file name (key) is part of the current set of keys. Instead, we simply access the dictionary object with the file name using the method get(). If there's an entry, we go through the array of [pathname, filesize] values and check for duplicate files. If one matches, it's a duplicate. If none matches, we append our new [pathname, filesize] to the array of current values. In case there's no entry for the file name, we add it as a new entry to the dictionary object (see Listing 4-11).

Listing 4-11. Finding Duplicate Files, Method 3

```python
def find_dupes_3(thefiles):
    """Searches for file duplicates, method 3."""
    result3 = []
    mydict3 = {}

    for filename, pathname, filesize in thefiles:
        if mydict3.get(filename):
            for [dup_file, dup_size] in mydict3[filename]:
                if dup_size==filesize:
                    result3.append(pathname+filename)
            mydict3[filename].append([pathname, filesize])
        else:
            mydict3[filename] = [[pathname, filesize]]
    return result3
```

Of the three methods, the third one is the best because it uses indexing properly.

To check the performance yourself, copy the function implementations from Listings 4-9, 4-10, and 4-11 to a text editor, save it under cmp_fd.py, and then issue exec(open('cmp_fd.py').read()) (or from cmp_df import *) in an interactive Python shell. Once that's done, use the short set of commands that follow to measure performance. Be sure to change the srchpath variable to point to a directory containing a large number of files, with some duplicates:

```python
>>> srchpath = 'c:/Python33'
>>> allfiles = get_all_files(srchpath)
>>> t = []
>>> from time import clock as clk
>>> t.append(clk()); res1 = find_dupes_1(allfiles); t.append(clk())
>>> t.append(clk()); res2 = find_dupes_2(allfiles); t.append(clk())
>>> t.append(clk()); res3 = find_dupes_3(allfiles); t.append(clk())
>>> len(allfiles)    # number of data files processed
```

8371

```python
>>> print("method 1: %5.5f; method 2: %5.5f; method 3: %5.5f" % \
... (t[1]-t[0], t[3]-t[2], t[5]-t[4]))
```

method 1: 0.02838; method 2: 13.15941; method 3: 0.08488

```
>>> len(res1), len(res2), len(res3)
```

```
(48, 3682, 3682)
```

I've imported the method clock() and renamed it to clk() (to save a few characters). The function clock(), part of the *time* module, returns the system clock and is very useful for comparing performance. Notice how I've entered three function calls in one line. This is important: if you split those into three separate sentences, the time it actually took you to write the command is also added to the time difference, offsetting the results.

■ **Note** Because method 2 is quite inefficient, for a large number of files or a slow machine, it might take considerable time to compute. Although method 1 seems the fastest, in reality it's inaccurate and shouldn't be used.

In the preceding implementations, we do not check the contents of the files to ensure they are indeed identical. It is quite possible to add that check by modifying the functions and comparing the contents of two files, file1 and file2, as well:

```
>>> if open(file1,'rb').read() == open(file2,'rb').read():
...     print('identical files')
```

This method reads the entire files to memory and compares them byte by byte. Note that this is a not a good option if the files are large; reading chunks or using other mechanisms may be better.

Catalogs

We've discussed splitting data files into directories and subdirectories, and we've mentioned that it's a good habit to group files in that manner. While this is an excellent method of maintaining what's what, it's limited to one division. That is, if you'd like to split files into directories based on several criteria, what do you do with a data file that fits several of those criteria? This is where catalogs come in handy.

Catalogs are text files that hold data in columns: the first column contains the file names, and subsequent columns contain subcategories (other criteria). Ideally, you'd like to use CSV because there's a good chance you'll be editing the catalog file manually in a spreadsheet application or automatically with Python; CSV fits that role perfectly.

Once you have a catalog file, it's easy to select only files meeting a specific criteria, and then run a script on those selected files.

Example: Creating a Clean Catalog File

The first step is to generate a basic catalog file, or a clean catalog file. This clean catalog file is generated automatically, using Python. For every file encountered, the full path and the file size are retrieved. Listing 4-12 shows an example of creating a clean catalog of files with extension .py:

Listing 4-12. Creating a Clean Catalog

```
import os, csv

# rename the following to a directory of your choosing
srchpath = '../src'

# the CSV header
catalog = [['Filename', 'pathname', 'size']]

# walk directory tree
for root, dirs, files in os.walk(srchpath):
    for file in files:
        # process only .py files
        if file.lower().endswith('py'):
            pathname = os.path.join(root, file)
            filesize = os.path.getsize(pathname)
            catalog.append([ file, pathname, filesize])

# create the clean catalog
f = open('../data/clean_catalog.csv', 'w', newline='')
csv.writer(f).writerows(catalog)
f.close()
```

To follow along, change the srchpath variable to point to a directory containing Python files, such as the root Python directory (c:\Python33). I chose to list the contents of my ../src directory.

The script walks the search directory looking for Python files (i.e., files ending with the extension .py, case insensitive). For every file encountered, we retrieve the file size. We then store all the information in a CSV file, as shown in previous examples:

```
Filename,pathname,size
get_all_files.py,../src/get_all_files.py,385
read_ini.py,../src/read_ini.py,282
write_ini.py,../src/write_ini.py,330
cmp_fd.py,../src/cmp_fd.py,2285
unique.py,../src/unique.py,273
tips.py,../src/tips.py,151
create_catalog.py,../src/create_catalog.py,595
stock_charts.py,../src/stock_charts.py,1290
yahoo_data.py,../src/yahoo_data.py,1218
read_write_structs.py,../src/read_write_structs.py,795
running_index.py,../src/running_index.py,613
```

Next, you take notes. For example, if a script is a draft, you mark it as such. You can do this either by editing your CSV file with an editor, or by doing so with a spreadsheet. So now you have an additional column: "Draft?" The contents of the catalog file will look something like this:

```
Filename,pathname,size,Draft?
get_all_files.py,../src/get_all_files.py,385,
read_ini.py,../src/read_ini.py,282,
write_ini.py,../src/write_ini.py,330,
cmp_fd.py,../src/cmp_fd.py,2285,Yes
unique.py,../src/unique.py,273,
tips.py,../src/tips.py,151,Yes
create_catalog.py,../src/create_catalog.py,595,
stock_charts.py,../src/stock_charts.py,1290,
yahoo_data.py,../src/yahoo_data.py,1218,
read_write_structs.py,../src/read_write_structs.py,795,
running_index.py,../src/running_index.py,613,
```

For the purpose of this exercise, I chose to use .py files, but you could just as well use it on data files. In this manner, running a script on only clean data from the annotated catalog is manageable and reproducible.

■ **Note**   Maintaining catalog files is a delicate job. Ensure your catalog files are always under version control, or better yet, a software configuration management system (e.g., CVS, Subversion, or Mercurial—see Chapter 2). You will constantly need to re-create clean (unannotated) catalogs if data is added. Consider investing time in maintaining your catalogs to keep them clean and up-to-date. If you find that the number of columns in your catalog files has increased and is unmanageable, consider using a database instead of a CSV file.

Files vs. a Database

There are a lot of pros for using databases over the managing files in directories. If your data becomes too complex to manage, rethinking and redesigning your data infrastructure is not a bad idea. That said, I personally have found that databases do not add to my productivity. In my mind, the reasons are as follows:

- *The nature of the work*: When you design a database, it's important to know a lot of the information up front. A good database relies on a good database design. And good database design relies on knowing the information and structure beforehand. The work described here does not follow that path. As presented in the beginning of the chapter, it's an iterative process; you do not know all the information before you start. And your application is mostly for your usage, not for end users (at least at first). It's not "production-level" code yet. When it does get to production level; that is, when you create an application to be used by end users, rethinking the data organization is a good idea, at which point you should consider using a database, as well.

- *The nature of the data*: The nature of the data described here is somewhat flat. There are not a lot of connections and interconnections and hierarchy and logic. There's simply a lot of data. There's a need to analyze it, fast. Some of the files are quite large, and while it's possible store large files in a database, it's probably not the most efficient way.

- *Overhead*: Databases introduce overhead. Some may argue that it's not significant, and they may be right. However, there's another piece of code, a database engine, that you need to interface with. Yes, Python provides good database support, but it's not the same as opening a file natively in your operating system. The overhead is in several layers: backup is more complex, code writing requires additional libraries, designing databases requires some experience (which you might not have), transferring the work to another computer is not easy, and maintenance is also required.

■ **Note**   It's worth mentioning that the SQLite database module, *sqlite3*, which is part of the Python Standard Library, has very little overhead and is an excellent package for working with databases should you require one.

- *Immediate interaction*: Say you'd like to browse for data and view files. With a database, you'd have to write an application just to extract the data and then to view it. The interaction is less immediate in my mind.

I know I'm not being fair in my analysis; I'm mostly showing the cons of databases. So to offset that, I'll say that databases do have their role. If you feel that you'd like to store your data in a database, you should at least know that Python provides a great number of tools for you to choose from. So even then, Python is the right programming language for you.

Final Notes and References

Data organization is an important part of any serious data analysis and visualization project. If you follow through with the guidelines suggested in this chapter, I believe you will find that the overhead associated with maintaining data coherently is minimal, and furthermore, that it's easy to write scripts to process large sets of data.

I have found the following of great value, when deciding on the file name format or the date and time format in a log file:

- "Numeric representation of Dates and Time, The ISO solution to a long-standing source of confusion," http://www.iso.org/iso/support/faqs/faqs_widely_used_standards/widely_used_standards_other/date_and_time_format.htm.

## CHAPTER 5

Processing Text Files

Text Is Everywhere

A considerable amount of the data we process is text-based. Viewed from a simplistic approach, text files are files that contain characters. The Python scripts we write are text files. The HTML files our web browser receives are text files. The e-mail messages we read are text files. They're simply everywhere. Because of the abundance of text files, you're likely to analyze data that comes in some form of a text file.

But in reality, there's no difference between a text file and another file, say, a binary file. They're both just files that occupy space on your hard drive. The important difference is what text files represent. If you look at data in a text file, a byte at a time, and convert every value using the ASCII table, you will be able to find (usually) intelligible text.

■ **Note** ASCII, short for American Standard Code for Information Interchange, is a 7-bit character encoding. Each character has a number (0–127) associated with it. Characters can also include digits and symbols. To view the ASCII table in Python, issue the following: `for i in range(128): print(i, repr(chr(i)))`. Note that nonprintable characters (usually values 32 and below) will be displayed with their hexadecimal notation.

In a sense, text files are regular files that have information encoded in accordance with a known code. Non-text files (e.g., binary files) will have values that don't necessarily correspond to the ASCII table; if you use the ASCII table to decode a binary file, you'll probably end up with gibberish, not text.

Text files can conform to yet another set of rules, such as the CSV format or the XML markup language. Text files that don't necessarily conform to any mapping other than the ASCII table are called *plain text files*. You'll mostly encounter plain text files and CSV files in this chapter.

This chapter presents the tools needed to work with text, starting with the basics of strings and how to process them, as well as how to read and write to files. We then turn to some topics that are likely to pop up when dealing with text files: handling CSV files, reading date and time information and parsing it, and working with regular expressions, which are powerful tools for processing text. Because date and time are denoted differently around the world (i.e., written differently), we examine how to read data that originated in a different locale. Along the way, we provide plenty of examples to illustrate the concepts discussed.

Text and Strings

Text is nothing more than strings of characters, usually separated by spaces or other separators, such as commas, dots, and punctuation marks. Processing text is therefore based on processing strings.

Although you learned how to slice, index, and concatenate (join) strings in Chapter 3, those examples treated strings as sequences of characters only. In essence, we didn't deal with the string as a text object. You could've just as well thought of the string as a sequence of numbers and the discussion would still be valid. Correct as it may be, that approach is too simplistic. When we view strings that way, we lose important information. Consider this book: it's made of text. But as you read it, there's more information than just a sequence of characters. There are words, lines, and punctuation marks. And even then, there's still yet more information: for example, words that begin with a capital letter have a different meaning. Those distinctions are important to us when we're reading text.

The following section deals with functions and ideas that help us write code to process higher level textual concepts; a "string" is no longer merely a sequence of characters.

Splitting Text

The first tool at our disposal is the split() function, which is a string method:

```
>>> "split second".split()
```

```
['split', 'second']
```

The split() function splits a string into a list of strings once a separator is encountered. The default separator is a whitespace string and is one of the following: carriage return '\r', line feed '\n', tab '\t', vertical tab '\v', form feed '\f', and a space. Vertical tabs and form feeds are used less frequently.

The split() function does not include the separators in the list, nor does it care how long the separator string is. This is especially useful if you're splitting text that's composed of columns, with a varying number of spaces between fields:

```
>>> grocery_list = """Milk   2
... Eggs  12"""
>>> print(grocery_list)
```

```
Milk   2
Eggs  12
```

```
>>> grocery_list.split()
```

```
['Milk', '2', 'Eggs', '12']
```

The separator need not be only a whitespace or a punctuation mark; it can also be an entire string:

```
>>> grocery_list = """Milk   2
... Eggs  12"""
>>> grocery_list.split('ilk')
```

```
['M', '   2\nEggs  12']
```

Much as it's useful to split text on words, it's also useful to split text on lines. The function `splitlines([keepends])` splits a string based on line endings and removes the line endings; that is, it removes the characters `'\n'` or `'\r\n'` if they exist. If the optional value keepends is True, end-of-line characters are retained:

```
>>> grocery_list = """Milk    2
... Eggs  12"""
>>> grocery_list.splitlines()
```

```
['Milk    2', 'Eggs  12']
```

```
>>> grocery_list.splitlines(True)
```

```
['Milk    2\n', 'Eggs  12']
```

Example: Counting the Number of Words and Number of Lines in a String

At times you'd like to count the number of words or the number of lines in a string. This can be done by using the function `len()` to count the number of elements in the lists generated from the calls to functions `split()` and `splitlines()`, as demonstrated in Listing 5-1.

Listing 5-1. Counting the Number of Words and Lines in a String

```
def word_line_count(s):
    """Returns the number of words and the numbers of lines in a string."""
    return (len(s.split()), len(s.splitlines()))
```

The preceding function returns a tuple: the first element is the number of words in the string, and the second element is the number of lines in the string.

Once you define the function, use it as follows:

```
>>> grocery_list = """Milk    2
... Eggs  12"""
>>> word_line_count(grocery_list)
```

```
(4, 2)
```

Joining Strings

Much as you can split a string into a list of strings, you can join a list of strings into a new string using the `join()` member function. Remember, though, that `join()` is a string method. Therefore, you must have a string to operate on to begin with. So, if you'd just like to combine a list of strings with no spaces in between, you should write the following:

```
>>> SOS = ['...', '---', '...']
>>> "".join(SOS)
```

```
'...---...'
```

Converting Strings to Numbers

You typically use the split() function to parse the text and then extract numeric data, which usually comes in the form of a string of digits. Once extracted, the strings representing numbers can be converted to an actual Python numeric representation instead of a sequence of digits.

Converting strings to numbers can be done with float()or int() function calls:

```
>>> float('3.25')
```

```
3.25
```

```
>>> int('100')
```

```
100
```

If you try to convert a string that doesn't represent a number to a number, an exception is raised:

```
>>> float('split')
```

```
Traceback (most recent call last):
  File "<stdin>", line 1, in <module>
ValueError: could not convert string to float: 'split'
```

You can use this to your advantage. For example, say you're looking to print only the number of items from the grocery list in previous examples. Simply employ the EAFP (Easier to Ask Forgiveness than Beg Permission) principle and use the try/except mechanism to convert every string to a number and print it:

```
>>> for item in grocery_list.split():
...     try:
...         print(int(item))
...     except ValueError:
...         pass
...
```

```
2
12
```

In this example, I took special care to discard only ValueError exceptions, which occur in case of a conversion problem.

Example: Base Conversion—Binary, Octal, Decimal, and Hexadecimal

Sometimes, it's useful to convert a number from one base representation to another. If you're dealing with binary octal, decimal, and hexadecimal bases, this is easily achieved using the functions bin(), oct(), int() and hex().

Since we're dealing with representations of numbers, it stands to reason we use strings. I've therefore chosen to define several functions, all of which accept a string as an argument. The functions' names follow the format from2to(), where from is the base to convert from and to is the base to convert to. For example, to convert from octal to binary, the function name is oct2bin(). There are a total of 12 functions for all possible conversions, as shown in Listing 2-2.

Listing 5-2. Base Conversion Helper Functions, base_conversion.py

```python
# base conversion helper functions
def bin2dec(s):
    return str(int(s, 2))
def oct2dec(s):
    return str(int(s, 8))
def hex2dec(s):
    return str(int(s, 16))

def dec2hex(s):
    return hex(int(s))
def dec2oct(s):
    return oct(int(s))
def dec2bin(s):
    return bin(int(s))

def hex2oct(s):
    return dec2oct(hex2dec(s))
def hex2bin(s):
    return dec2bin(hex2dec(s))

def oct2hex(s):
    return dec2hex(oct2dec(s))
def bin2hex(s):
    return dec2hex(bin2dec(s))

def oct2bin(s):
    return dec2bin(oct2dec(s))
def bin2oct(s):
    return dec2oct(bin2dec(s))
```

I've left out the docstrings: I think the function names are documentation enough. The functions do not perform any sort of error checking (e.g., they do not ensure that they received a string as an input).

Each conversion function falls into one of three categories. It is either a conversion *from* decimal (such as dec2bin()), conversion *to* decimal (such as oct2dec()) or *neither* (such as oct2bin()). Conversions *from* decimal are implemented using the functions bin(), oct() and hex(). Conversions *to* decimal are implemented with str(int(s, base)) where base is the target base. Lastly, the third category uses a conversion first *to* decimal, and then *from* decimal. It is implemented using the other two categories, as follows: dec2bin(oct2dec(s)).

Here's a possible use of these functions:

```python
>>> hex2dec('0xffff')
```

```
'65535'
```

```python
>>> oct2hex('0o777')
```

```
'0x1ff'
```

Testing Your Implementation: exec and assert

As you implement the base-conversion helper functions, you'll find that it's quite possible that you've made a mistake. Those are implementations of nested function calls, and they are prone to human error. Python provides several testing modules: *doctest* (https://docs.python.org/3.3/library/doctest.html) and *unittest* (https://docs.python.org/3.3/library/unittest.html). However, I chose a different approach, one that does not use these modules, in hopes of shedding light on a new function, exec(), and a new statement, assert.

The statement, assert, will return an AssertionError if a condition isn't met. This is quite useful for testing purposes:

```
>>> assert 1 == 2
```

```
Traceback (most recent call last):
  File "<stdin>", line 1, in <module>
AssertionError
```

Adding assert statements in your code is a good way to ensure things behave the way you expect them to, such as making certain an argument passed to a function is of a specific type.

■ **Tip**   assert statements are not executed when you run Python with the optimization switch turned on (-O).

The function exec() executes a string as if you type it into the interpreter:

```
>>> exec("print(1+2)")
```

```
3
```

You can use the exec() function for automating command execution.

At first, exec() might not seem such a big deal. But consider those functions in the previous example: there are 12 functions corresponding to all the combinations of base conversions: bin2oct(), bin2dec(), bin2hex(), oct2bin(), and so forth. Testing all these functions is tedious. If you watch closely though, you'll find there's a pattern. And when there's a pattern, it stands to reason we can write a computer program to perform the task for us. This is exactly where exec() comes to life. The idea is to create a list of strings, with each string detailing a function to be executed, and then executing each and every string (see Listing 5-3).

Listing 5-3. Testing Base-Conversion Function Implementations

```
from base_conversion import *
def testbases():
    """Tests implementation of base conversion functions"""
    v0 = { 'bin':'0b0', 'oct':'0o0', 'dec':'0', 'hex':'0x0' }
    v1 = { 'bin':'0b1111', 'oct':'0o17', 'dec':'15', 'hex':'0xf' }

    for v in [v0, v1]:
        perms = [ (a, b) for b in v for a in v if a != b ]
        for (s1, s2) in perms:
            tc = "assert %s2%s(v['%s']) == v['%s']" % (s1, s2, s1, s2)
            exec(tc)
    print('All tests passed')
```

I created two test vectors: v1 and v2. Variables v1 and v2 are dictionaries containing a string that represents the base as the key and a string that represents the number as the value. Because I take care to ensure that the string representing the base names follows the three-letter notations I use for the function names, I can then iterate through my test vector list and execute each test case (tc). Let's break this down into smaller chunks.

I first create a list comprehension named perms that generates all permutations of bases; that is, it generates all the combinations, as long as they're not identical (hence the condition, a != b):

```
>>> v = { 'bin':'0', 'oct':'0', 'dec':'0', 'hex':'0x0' }
>>> perms = [ (a, b) for b in v for a in v if a != b ]
>>> from pprint import pprint
>>> pprint(perms)
```

```
[('hex', 'oct'),
 ('dec', 'oct'),
 ('bin', 'oct'),
 ('oct', 'hex'),
 ('dec', 'hex'),
 ('bin', 'hex'),
 ('oct', 'dec'),
 ('hex', 'dec'),
 ('bin', 'dec'),
 ('oct', 'bin'),
 ('hex', 'bin'),
 ('dec', 'bin')]
```

Because dictionaries don't necessarily return the list of values in a predefined order, the resulting list could be ordered differently (however the conents of the list should be the same).

PERMUTATIONS

The module *itertools* provides functions for creating iterators (see https://docs.python.org/3.3/library/itertools.html). Specifically, *itertools* provides combinatorics generators, including the generator permutations(). Instead of implementing all the permutations using a list comprehension as shown in the example, it's possible to use permutations() like this: permutations(['bin', 'hex', 'dec', 'oct'], 2). Notice that the result is an iterator; to view the entire list, you'll have to generate an actual list from the iterator: list(permutations(['bin', 'hex', 'dec', 'oct'], 2)). The value 2 in the function call tells permutations() to return a tuple of size 2. The module *itertools* provide additional useful generators (e.g., combinations() for all possible combinations and product(), which is equivalent to a nested loop).

To modify this list comprehension to generate actual assertion calls requires some string manipulation; however, you already know how to use format specifiers, so here it is:

```
>>> for (s1, s2) in perms:
...     tc = "assert %s2%s(v['%s']) == v['%s']" % \
...         (s1, s2, s1, s2)
...     print(tc)
...
```

```
assert hex2oct(v['hex']) == v['oct']
assert dec2oct(v['dec']) == v['oct']
assert bin2oct(v['bin']) == v['oct']
assert oct2hex(v['oct']) == v['hex']
assert dec2hex(v['dec']) == v['hex']
assert bin2hex(v['bin']) == v['hex']
assert oct2dec(v['oct']) == v['dec']
assert hex2dec(v['hex']) == v['dec']
assert bin2dec(v['bin']) == v['dec']
assert oct2bin(v['oct']) == v['bin']
assert hex2bin(v['hex']) == v['bin']
assert dec2bin(v['dec']) == v['bin']
```

I've printed a string associated with the command to be executed. The strings represent commands that check the functionality of the base helper functions. Now all that's needed is this: exec(tc).

The nice thing about this implementation is that you can easily add other bases, such as the functions that convert base 5: qui2bin(), qui2oct(), qui2dec(), and so on (I've used the notation qui, which is short for quinary, base 5).

Find and Replace

The next set of interesting functions are find() and replace(). The method find() locates the first occurrence of a substring in a string and takes the general form find(substring [,start [,end]]). The parameters start and end are optional, and they are used to limit the search to indices that are greater than or equal to start and are less than end (if those arguments are provided):

```
>>> grocery_list = "Milk    2\nEggs   12"
>>> grocery_list.find('2')
```

```
7
```

```
>>> grocery_list.find('2', 10)
```

```
16
```

```
>>> grocery_list.find('2', 10, 16)
```

```
-1
```

If a substring isn't found, the return value is -1.

■ **Caution**   If you'd like to check whether the function find() succeeded in finding the search substring, be sure to compare the value of find() with -1, and not with True, as -1 (substring not found) is considered True. That is, instead of writing if str.find(), write if str.find() != -1.

The function replace() doesn't really replace items in a string, as strings are immutable. Instead, it creates a new string, with every occurrence of the old substring replaced with the new substring:

```
>>> grocery_list = "Milk    2\nEggs   12"
>>> grocery_list.replace('Eggs', 'Organic Eggs')
```

```
'Milk    2\nOrganic Eggs   12'
```

The replace() method will replace as many occurrences as possible, unless the count argument is provided, as follows: replace(old, new[,count]). In this case, only the number of values up to and including count will be replaced.

If you'd like to know in advance how many substitutions will occur, you can use the count(substr) method, which counts the number of occurrences of a substring in a string:

```
>>> grocery_list = "Milk    2\nEggs   12"
>>> grocery_list.count('2')
```

```
2
```

```
>>> grocery_list.count('Eggs')
```

```
1
```

The method count() also accepts optional start-of-search and end-of-search indices: count(substr[, start[, end]]); the behavior is similar to that of function find().

Stripping Strings

Stripping strings is the process of removing extra whitespace characters or other sets of characters from a string. The method strip([chars]) removes whitespace characters from both the right side and the left side of a string. If chars is provided, characters from the string chars are used as separators instead of whitespace characters, with each character acting as a separator. Methods rstrip([chars]) and lstrip([chars]) do so on the right or left sides only, respectively:

```
>>> "Hello    ".rstrip()
```

```
'Hello'
```

```
>>> '*-*-* SECTION BREAK *-*-*'.strip('*-')
```

```
' SECTION BREAK '
```

Example: Removing Extra Spaces

In this example, we'd like to remove extra spaces from some text. We could try to use the replace() method, replacing two spaces with one:

```
>>> grocery_list = "Milk   2\nEggs  12"
>>> new_grocery_list = grocery_list.replace("  ", " ")
>>> print(new_grocery_list)
```

```
Milk  2
Eggs 12
```

That didn't work well: there are two spaces between Milk and 2 after the call to replace(). The reason for this is that replace() is not a recursive search-and-replace. After a replacement has been made, the function keeps on looking *forward* for other occurrences. It does not recheck previously replaced strings. For example, consider the case of three consecutive spaces. For the sake of convenience, let's number them space1, space2, and space3. The first two spaces (space1 and space2) are replaced with a single space—let's call this new single space space0. Now the function looks for additional consecutive spaces and finds none because the only one that remains is space3. So in the end, you have space0 followed by space3, which means two consecutive spaces and not one. Of course, you could keep on replacing spaces until there are no more changes to the string, but that's a bit cumbersome.

Another approach is to use the functions split(), splitlines(), strip(), and join():

```
>>> grocery_list = "Milk   2\nEggs  12"
>>> for line in grocery_list.splitlines():
...     clear_line = [s.strip() for s in line.split()]
...     print(" ".join(clear_line))
...
```

```
Milk 2
Eggs 12
```

I've used a for loop to iterate through the split lines. For every line, I've created the list clear_line, where each word is stripped of separators (i.e., extra spaces). I then joined the list of words with a space.

If all this seems like considerable effort to accomplish a simple task, you're absolutely right. There is another, better way, to perform this action: regular expressions. You'll learn more about the topic in the section "Regular Expressions" toward the end of this chapter.

String Formatting

Using format specifiers (see Chapter 3 for more information), you can control string format very accurately. But format specifiers do not take into consideration that we're dealing with text and words; rather, they treat strings mostly as a sequence of characters. The functions presented in this section add string formatting options that are more suited for working with words and text.

The methods upper() and lower() return strings with all characters in uppercase or lowercase, respectively:

```
>>> " Middle of Town ".upper()
```

```
' MIDDLE OF TOWN '
```

```
>>> " Middle of Town ".lower()
```

```
' middle of town '
```

The function `swapcase()` returns a string with the characters' case inverted:

```
>>> " Middle of Town ".swapcase()
```

```
' mIDDLE OF tOWN '
```

The method `capitalize()` returns a string with the first letter in uppercase and the remaining letters in lowercase. Note that this affects only the first character of the string, disregarding English grammar rules or whether there are punctuation marks or line breaks:

```
>>> "first sentence.\nSecond sentence.  Third Sentence".capitalize()
```

```
'First sentence.\nsecond sentence.  third sentence'
```

The method `title()` capitalizes every first letter of a sentence. Again, this isn't in accordance with English grammar rules, as some words in titles should not be capitalized (e.g., "the"):

```
>>> "first sentence.\nSecond sentence.  Third Sentence".title()
```

```
'First Sentence.\nSecond Sentence.  Third Sentence'
```

The method `center(n[, char])` returns a string of length n, with left and right padding of the string with char (default is space), so as to have the string centered in the middle:

```
>>> " Middle of Town ".center(26, '*')
```

```
'***** Middle of Town *****'
```

The methods `ljust(n[, char])` and `rjust(n[, char])` perform left and right justification, respectively, with the optional fill character being char:

```
>>> "East side".rjust(20)
```

```
'           East side'
```

```
>>> "West side".ljust(20, '-')
```

```
'West side-----------'
```

String Conditionals

The following is a set of string conditionals: methods that ask questions about strings. String conditionals are great when you want to check whether the input string fits a certain criteria (e.g., digits only for entering phone numbers, whether upper-case and lower-case letters are used, and so on).

The method endswith(substr[, start[, end]]) returns True if a string ends with substr. The start and end arguments limit the search indices similarly to previously discussed string functions; from now on, I'll refrain from explaining their effect. The endswith() function is useful for checking file name extensions, as in this example:

```
>>> "a20.jpg".endswith('jpg')
```

```
True
```

```
>>> "a20.jpg".endswith('JPG')
```

```
False
```

The second expression evaluates to False because endswith() is case sensitive. However, substr can be a tuple as well, accommodating several condition tests:

```
>>> "a20.JPG".endswith(('jpg', 'JPG'))
```

```
True
```

The method startswith(substr[, start[, end]]) is similar to endswith() only in that it checks the beginning of a string.

The methods isalpha(), isdigit(), and isalnum() return True if all the characters in the string are alphabetic, digits, or both, respectively:

```
>>> "a20.jpg".isalnum()
```

```
False
```

The reason the method isalnum() returns False in the preceding example is that the character '.' (dot) is neither alphabetic nor a digit.

Similarly, the methods islower(), isspace(), istitle(), and isupper() return True if the string is all lowercase, all whitespace, of the title form (first letter in every word capitalized), or all uppercase, respectively:

```
>>> "a20.jpg".islower()
```

```
True
```

■ **Note**   The conditionals starting with is, such as islower(), will return False if the string is empty.

More on Strings

The preceding isn't a full account of strings and string methods. For example, Python 2.6 introduced an additional formatting function, str.format() (see https://docs.python.org/3.3/library/string.html). If your work is text-heavy, have a look at the online documentation for additional information. The discussion that follows relies on the preceding string methods, but not on methods that were not discussed.

Files

Text files are files that contain textual data—that is, text strings. In Python, you access files using the file object. Working with files is quite similar to doing so in other programming languages: open a file and receive a file object; read from the file or write to the file using the file object; and lastly, close the file, again using the file object. You can open a file for reading, writing, or appending; and you can open it in binary mode or text mode.

Opening a File

To open a file, use the open(filename[, mode='r']) built-in function. The function open() returns a file object that is used for subsequent file operations. The first argument, filename, is required. The second argument, mode, is optional, and it can take the values listed in Table 5-1.

Table 5-1. *File Open Modes*

Mode	Description
r	Opens a file for reading. This is the default value if mode isn't specified.
w	Opens a file for writing, overwriting an existing file.
a	Opens a file for writing in append mode; all write operations are performed at the end. If the file doesn't exist, it is created.
x	Create a new file, and open it for reading.
r+	Opens a file for reading and updating. If the file doesn't exist, an exception is raised.
w+	Creates a new file for writing and updating, overwriting an existing one.
a+	Opens a file for reading and writing in append mode. All write operations are performed at the end. If the file doesn't exist, it is created.

Adding the character 'b' to the mode ensures the file is open in binary mode (e.g., 'rb'). Adding the character 't' to the mode ensures the file is opened in text mode (e.g., 'wt'). A file can be opened either in text mode or in binary mode, but not both (the default is text mode).

The difference between binary mode and text mode is whether Python tries to convert line-ending characters it encounters to '\n'. In Windows, the characters '\r\n' are used to denote the end of the line; in Linux, it's just '\n'. To have a consistent method to access text files, use text mode. When dealing with binary files, or when it's important for you to have end-of-line characters unmodified, use the binary mode.

■ **Note** In append mode, write operations are performed at the end of the file, effectively guarding existing data. In write mode, you're allowed to write anywhere in the file, possibly overwriting data.

The open() function accepts additional parameters:

- The parameter buffer determines the file buffering mode. Buffering allows file access with a cache for enhanced performance.

- The parameter encoding allows locale encoding and is available in text files only; you'll see more on locale later in this chapter.

- The parameter newline decides the newline character, which can be None, '', '\n', '\r', or '\r\n'.

For a full account, type help(open).

Closing a File

Contrary to the open() function, which is a built-in function, the close() function is a member function of the file object and not a built-in function. To close files, use the file method f.close() (assuming f is a file object). It's generally good practice to close a file once you're done with it. But if you don't, Python closes the file for you automatically once the file object is no longer in use. The following sample shows how to open and close a file:

```
>>> f = open('somefile.txt', 'wt')
>>> f
```

```
<_io.TextIOWrapper name='somefile.txt' mode='wt' encoding='cp1252'>
```

```
>>> f.close()
>>> type(f)
```

```
<type 'file'>
```

Writing Text

Once a file is open for writing (or appending) and before it's closed, you can write strings to it using the methods write(str) and writelines(strseq).

The method write() writes a string to the file:

```
>>> grocery_str = "Milk    2\nEggs   12"
>>> f = open('../data/tobuy.txt', 'wt')
>>> f.write(grocery_str)
>>> f.close()
```

The contents of the file tobuy.txt are as follows:

```
Milk    2
Eggs   12
```

The method writelines(strseq) writes a sequence of strings to a file:

```
>>> grocery_list = ["Milk", "2", "Eggs", "12"]
>>> f = open('../data/tobuylist.txt', 'wt')
>>> f.writelines(grocery_list)
>>> f.close()
```

The contents of file tobuylist.txt are as follows:

```
Milk2Eggs12
```

Notice how writelines() adds neither spaces nor line breaks. If you do want line breaks or spaces, you can use the join() string method in combination with write(). For example, to add spaces, replace the call to writelines(grocery_list) in the preceding code listing with f.write(' '.join(grocery_list)).

■ **Note** I've assumed you are following the book convention of having your source code reside in directory Ch5/src and your data directory in Ch5/data. If that's not the case, change the path to your data files in the preceding examples.

Reading Text

Once a file is open for reading, you can use the methods read(), readline(), or readlines() to read the file contents. You can also iterate over the file object to read a line at a time. I've found that, when dealing with text files, my code typically falls into one of three categories:

- Reading the entire file at once using the methods read() or readlines(). This option is preferable if the files are not too large.

- Iterating over the file object, reading a line at a time. This option is preferable for larger text files.

- Using a while loop with the method read(n). This option is a good candidate if you don't necessarily want to treat the file as lines of text.

Reading the Entire File at Once

Assuming you're dealing with not-too-large files, using method read() or readlines() to read the entire file at once should be your first choice.

The method read([n]) reads n bytes from the file, returning them as a string. If n is not specified or negative, the entire file is read. For this example, we'll use the file tobuy.txt generated in the previous section, "Writing Text" (the first snippet of code):

```
>>> f = open('../data/tobuy.txt')
>>> text = f.read()
>>> f.close()
>>> print(text)
```

```
Milk    2
Eggs    12
```

155

We can do this more compactly like this:

```
>>> print(open('../data/tobuy.txt').read())
```

```
Milk    2
Eggs    12
```

The method `readlines()` reads the file at once, returning a list of strings:

```
>>> open('../data/tobuy.txt').readlines()
```

```
['Milk    2\n', 'Eggs    12']
```

Iterating Over the File Object

Iterating over the file object is suited for cases when you want to process your file a line at a time, but you don't want to read the entire file at once (e.g., memory constraints might be an issue). Here's an example:

```
>>> for i, line in enumerate(open('../data/tobuy.txt')):
...     print("%d: %s" % (i, line.rstrip()))
...
```

```
0: Milk    2
1: Eggs    12
```

Using a while Loop

Use a while loop in conjunction with `read()` to process chunks of the file at a time. Again, this is best suited for larger files and in cases where you don't want to treat a file as a list of lines:

```
>>> f = open('../data/tobuy.txt')
>>> ch = f.read(1)
>>> while ch != 'k' and ch:
...     print(ch)
...     ch = f.read(1)
...
```

```
M
i
l
```

```
>>> f.close()
```

This example reads the file a byte at a time and stops upon encountering the character `'k'` or an end-of-file where ch would then evaluate to `False`.

Working with Text Files

So far, we have covered the basics of reading and writing files, as well as processing strings. Now it's time to combine these three new skills.

This section is presented as a list of examples. The examples can be used for educational purposes, but they can also be used to form the basis of helper functions for text-based data processing. With time, I hope you modify the code presented here to best fit your needs. For now, it is important that you treat these examples as what they are: examples, not production code. Most of the functions do not perform any sort of error checking or handle exceptions, and they should not be used as-is. When possible, I've added a discussion on how these examples can be improved upon.

To work with files larger than a contrived grocery list, I've chosen to use the electronic version of the book *Flatland*, by Edwin A. Abbott. This book is available for download from Project Gutenberg, located at http://www.gutenberg.org. A direct link to the e-book at the time of the writing of this book is http://www.gutenberg.org/files/45506/45506-8.txt. Once you download the file, save it in the folder data under the original file name, 45506-8.txt. Your directory structure should look similar to that presented near the end of Chapter 2 in the section, "Example: Directory Structure for the Book":

```
Ch5
    src
    data
```

In this directory structure, src is where your code is, as well as your current working directory, and data indicates the location of data files (namely 45506-8.txt—the *Flatland* e-book).

Example: Character, Word, and Line Count

Now you're confronted with the task of counting the characters, words, and lines in a file—and not just a string.

The solution is an immediate extension of the example provided before, using split(), splitlines(), and len(). I've named the function wc(), which is a popular command name on Linux shells: $wc filename (see Listing 5-4).

Listing 5-4. Counting the Number of Characters, Words, and Lines in a File

```
def wc(filename):
    """Returns the number of characters, words and lines in a file.

The result is a tuple of the form (#characters, #words, #lines)."""
    data = open(filename, 'rb').read()
    return (len(data), len(data.split()), len(data.splitlines()))
```

The function returns a tuple of three elements: the first element is the number of characters in the file, the second element is the number of words, and the third element is the number of lines. I've also chosen to open the file in binary mode and not in text mode. This is so that the number of characters will be counted properly, without any conversions of '\r\n' to '\n' that would throw off the numbers count.

■ **Note**   Notice how I've indented the docstring; it's standard practice that, if more than one line is needed to document the function, a blank line is added immediately after the short function description. Subsequent documentation is left justified with no indentation.

It's possible that you're dealing with truly large files, in which case a different approach should be employed: iterating over the file object (see Listing 5-5).

Listing 5-5. Counting the Number of Characters, Words, and Lines in a Very Large File

```python
def wc_large(filename):
    """Returns the number of characters, words and lines in a large file.

The result is a tuple of the form (#characters, #words, #lines)."""
    num_chars, num_words, num_lines = 0, 0, 0
    for line in open(filename, encoding='latin-1'):
        num_chars += len(line)
        num_words += len(line.split())
        num_lines += 1
    return (num_chars, num_words, num_lines)
```

Notice how I've opened the file with the parameter encoding='latin-1'; this encoding maps byte values to the first 256 Unicode code points. You'll learn more about Unicode later in the chapter.

Here are the results from running both functions:

```python
>>> wc('../data/45506-8.txt')
```

```
(210960, 35100, 3776)
```

```python
>>> wc_large('../data/45506-8.txt')
```

```
(210960, 35100, 3776)
```

Example: head and tail

Most Linux system administrators know and love the ***head*** and ***tail*** command-line utilities. It's a fast check on how an installation is coming along, it's great for probing message logs, and it's good for seeing whether any errors occurred during boot time.

The way the head and tail command line utilities work is that they print n lines from the beginning or end of a file, respectively. You'd typically use these commands to look at log files because most log files are plain text files with data written sequentially: a recent event is logged at the end of a file.

The following command will print the last 20 lines from the dmesg log file (a common Linux log file):

```
$ tail -20 /var/log/dmesg
```

Using the method readlines(), both head() and tail() functions are easily implemented in Python, as shown in Listing 5-6.

Listing 5-6. head() and tail() Functions

```python
def head(filename, n=10):
    """Prints the first n lines of the file."""
    for line in open(filename, encoding='latin-1').readlines()[:n]:
        print(line.rstrip())
```

```
def tail(filename, n=10):
    """Returns the last n lines of the file."""
    for line in open(filename, encoding='latin-1').readlines()[-n:]:
        print(line.rstrip())
```

If your files are too large to be read entirely into memory, things get trickier. Implementing the head() function is possible by iterating over the file object, as shown in Listing 5-7.

Listing 5-7. head() Function for Very Large Files

```
def head_large(filename, n=10):
    """Returns the first n lines of a very large file."""
    for i, line in enumerate(open(filename, encoding='latin-1')):
        print(line.rstrip())
        if i == n-1: break
```

You can convince yourself both functions return proper results by modifying the code to return a list and then comparing the returned values from the two functions.

Unfortunately, implementing the function tail() in a similar manner, iterating over the file object, is much more complex. First, you'd have to go through the entire file, reading every line. Remember, this is a large file; therefore, doing this will take considerable time. And even then, the second problem you encounter is that you don't know in advance which line is the last line. A couple approaches might jump to mind. First, you might perform two passes on the file. On the first pass, you'd count the number of lines; and on the second pass, you'd print the last n lines. Second, you might continually store the last n lines read. In both cases, yikes. A third approach is to use random access functions to start reading files at the end and work your way backward. This requires use of the function seek(), which will be covered in Chapter 10.

Example: Splitting and Combining Files

Back in the day, computer users used to transfer files on 360K floppy disks. Since this was rather painful, they opted to use a file compression utility that did both splitting and compressing. Alas, one of the disks always seemed to be misplaced, rendering the data totally useless. Although floppy disks are long gone, the need to split large files into smaller, more manageable ones is still a common task. Each chunk does not necessarily contain legible information, but they will fit on size-limited media (e-mail, flash drive) for transfer. The receiving end will then need to reconstruct the original file from the split files.

The function splitfile() splits a file into n smaller files, each with a modified file name that is composed of the original file name plus the split file index (e.g., 45506-8.txt.1). The function combinefiles() combines several files of the preceding pattern into one, as demonstrated in Listing 5-8.

Listing 5-8. Splitting and Combining Files

```
def splitfile(filename, size=1024**2):
    """Splits a file into n smaller files.

Files are created with a running index."""

    fin, index = open(filename, 'rb'), 0
    data = fin.read(size)
    while data:
        index += 1
        outfilename = filename+'.'+str(index)
        fout = open(outfilename, 'wb')
```

```
        fout.write(data)
        fout.close()
        print("Created file %s, size %d" % (outfilename, len(data)))
        data = fin.read(size)
    return

def combinefiles(filename):
    """Combines a previously split file.

Filename extensions are assumed a running index.
Important note: if a file named filename exists it will be overwritten."""

    fout, index = open(filename, 'wb'), 0
    while True:
        index += 1
        try:
            data = open(filename+'.'+str(index), 'rb').read()
            fout.write(data)
        except IOError:
            break
    fout.close()
    print("Created file %s from %d file(s)" % (filename, index-1))
```

The functions themselves are self-explanatory and should prove easy enough to follow. Here's how you would use splitfile():

```
>>> splitfile('../data/45506-8.txt', 100000)
```

```
Created file ../data/45506-8.txt.1, size 100000
Created file ../data/45506-8.txt.2, size 100000
Created file ../data/45506-8.txt.3, size 10960
```

Now copy the files 45506-8.txt.* located in the ../data directory to a temporary directory, ../data/tmp . You do it this way so that, when you combine the files, the original file will not be overwritten. You can either do this manually, or you can run the following code:

```
>>> import os
>>> src = '../data/45506-8.txt.%d'
>>> dest = '../data/tmp/45506-8.txt.%d'
>>> for i in range(1, 4):
...     os.renames(src % i, dest % i)
>>> os.listdir('../data/tmp')
```

```
['45506-8.txt.1', '45506-8.txt.2', '45506-8.txt.3']
```

I'll cover the module *os* used in the preceding script in detail in Chapter 10.

To combine the files, issue the following:

```
>>> combinefiles('../data/tmp/45506-8.txt')
```

```
Created file ../data/tmp/45506-8.txt from 3 file(s)
```

To satisfy yourself that the files are indeed identical, issue the following:

```
>>> data1 = open('../data/45506-8.txt', 'rb').read()
>>> data2 = open('../data/tmp/45506-8.txt', 'rb').read()
>>> data1 == data2
```

```
True
```

While the topic of this section is text files, the functions `splitfile()` and `combinefiles()` should work on binary files just as well, since we've opened the files in binary mode.

■ **Caution**   The function `combinefiles()` will overwrite an existing file if it already exists.

If you'd prefer `combinefiles()`not to overwrite a file if it exists, you can use the function `os.path.exists()` from the *os.path* module to check for file existence and act accordingly (ask for the user's preference or return without overwriting the file).

Example: Searching Inside a Text File

The examples to this point deal with the files themselves, not really with the information they hold. The examples going forward will look at the contents as well; that is, they will read the file and process text.

A common programming task involves searching for a string inside a file. An even more common task is to search for a string inside multiple files; however, we will leave that to future discussions (see Chapter 10). In Linux, a handy utility achieves this: grep. This utility also provides more complex searches, such as those that include regular expressions. In this example, however, we limit our discussion to simple string searches.

Searching inside a text file is easily implemented in Python, as you can see in Listing 5-9.

Listing 5-9. Searching Inside a Text File

```python
def srchfile(filename, substr):
    """Searches for a substring in a file."""
    for index, line in enumerate(open(filename, encoding='latin-1')):
        if line.find(substr) != -1:
            try:
                print("%4d:%s" % (index, line.rstrip()))
            except UnicodeEncodeError:
                print("%4d: ---encoding error---" % index)
```

I've used the iterator enumerate() to retrieve both the line and the line number, as the line number is displayed by the print() function call later on. I've also used the method rstrip() to remove the extra new-line character. Here's the output from running the command, srchfile('../data/45506-8.txt', 'Guide'):

```
2612:Prostrating myself mentally before my Guide, I cried, "How is it, O
2654:your Wife," said my Guide; "she will not be long left in anxiety;
2699:"Here we descend," said my Guide. It was now morning, the first hour of
2727:to descend at this moment and enlighten them." "Not yet," said my Guide,
2769:absolutely depended on the volition of my Guide, who said in gloomy
3038:"Look yonder," said my Guide, "in Flatland thou hast lived; of Lineland
```

There's room to improve the function srchfile(). First, the function is case sensitive. To allow for case-insensitive searches, I would suggest adding a parameter to the function that controls whether searches are case sensitive or not. In case of a case-insensitive search, srchfile() would use the function upper() (or lower()) and convert both the line to be searched and the search string itself prior to calling find().

Another improvement would be to fix the line-number indentation. Currently, the line number is right-aligned four spaces. If the number of lines is 10,000 or greater, this will create an indentation problem. Changing the implementation to read the entire file at once gives us a total line count, allowing the calculation of the maximum number of digits using the function log10(), which is part of the *math* module (see Chapter 7):

```
>>> numlines = 1234
>>> from math import log10
>>> maxdigits = int(log10(numlines))+1
>>> maxdigits
```

```
4
```

This will only work if you know the line number in advance; hence, the change to the function to read the entire file at once. Listing 5-10 shows a possible implementation of fixing the indentation problem.

Listing 5-10. Searching Inside a Text File (Proper Indentation)

```
def srchfile_ex(filename, substr):
    """Searches for a substring in a file."""
    lines = open(filename, encoding='latin-1').readlines()
    fmt = r'%' + str(int(log10(len(lines)))+1) + r'd:%s'
    for index, line in enumerate(lines):
        if line.find(substr) != -1:
            try:
                print(fmt % (index, line.rstrip()))
            except UnicodeEncodeError:
                print("%d: --- encoding error ---" % index)
```

Notice how I've first created a format specifier, fmt, using a raw string and then used it to print the line number and the string.

Example: Working with Comments

I find that I repeatedly return to code I wrote previously. And what I seem to remember most is the comments. An interesting approach to viewing comments is to think of the comment symbol (#) as a separator. With this in mind, you can implement some interesting searches, as shown in Listing 5-11. For example, you can search inside comments only, or you can perform that search's complement (i.e., *exclude* the comments from your search).

Listing 5-11. Working with Comments

```
def srchcomments(filename, substr):
    """Searches inside Python source comments."""
    for index, line in enumerate(open(filename, 'rt')):
        L = line.split('#')
        if len(L) == 2:
            if L[1].find(substr) != -1:
                print("%5d: %s" % (index, line.rstrip()))
```

This code is hardly foolproof. It assumes that the # symbol appears only once, text before the # is always code, and text after # is a comment. This is not always true; for example, in the fourth line of the preceding code, L = line. split('#'), # is hardly a comment separator. Nevertheless, the function works fine on many occasions.

Using the function in Listing 5-11 as a starting point, you could write a function to convert comments that are not on a line of their own to be single-line comments. For example, the line might initially look like this:

```
port = '/dev/ttyUSB0'  # in Windows, set this to 'COMx'
```

And your function would convert it to something like this:

```
# in Windows, set this to 'COMx'
port = '/dev/ttyUSB0'
```

C++ STYLE COMMENTS

I originally encountered this problem with C/C++. A compiler I was using to write code accepted the C++-style comments, where the behavior is similar to Python's comments (only with the symbols // instead of #). However, another, older compiler was used that didn't accept the C++-style comment, so I had to convert all my single-line comments of the form // comment to C-style comments of the form /* comment */. I used a script similar to the preceding script to do this. Luckily for me, the symbols // didn't appear anywhere in the code other than as part of the comments themselves.

Example: Extracting Numbers from a Text File

Sometimes, it's useful to be able to extract only the numbers in a text file. For example, you might want to create files based on existing ones, for testing purposes. Another scenario might be that you have a system that maintains the number of users in a text file, and you'd like to write a script to increment that number.

The function presented in Listing 5-12 reads a text file and creates a modified version of the file with all the numbers incremented. In this example, numbers are separated by whitespace characters.

Listing 5-12. Incrementing File Contents

```python
def increment_contents(filename):
    """Increments values in a file, creating a new file."""
    data = open(filename).readlines()
    for i, line in enumerate(data):
        for word in line.split():
            try:
                data[i] = line.replace(word, str(int(word)+1))
            except ValueError:
                # uncomment the following if you'd like feedback
                # print(word, " is not a number")
                pass
    open(filename+'.inc', 'wt').writelines(data)
```

The preceding function reads the entire file into memory, and then processes the data a line at a time (it's also possible to achieve the same functionality by iterating over a file object). Every line is split into words. The code then tries to convert every word to a number, and upon success, replaces the number with an incremented value. I've used the replace() method function to do that, which is why you see another str() function call after the increment: the replace() method requires a string, not a number.

In implementing the function, I've tried to convert every single word I've encountered into an int, and then increment it. On success, the data is modified. If a ValueError occurs because the conversion didn't succeed, it means that the string cannot be converted to an int, in which case I've ignored the word.

To test the function, I again resort to the grocery list. Assume the contents of the file ../data/grocery_list.txt are as follows:

```
Milk 12
Eggs 12.0
Olives 1e2
Voodo dolls 1+1j
```

After executing increment_contents('../data/grocery_list.txt'), a new file, ../data/grocery_list.txt.inc, is created with the following contents:

```
Milk 13
Eggs 12.0
Olives 1e2
Voodoo dolls 1+1j
```

The function only increments the value 12 because I've used the function int(). Had I used the function float(), all the first three values would have been properly incremented. However, the first number would then be converted into a float value, and I wanted to leave it as an int.

Handling both float and int values is possible with nested exception handling. First, the function tries to use int(); if int() fails, it tries to use float() (see Listing 5-13).

Listing 5-13. Incrementing File Contents Using float() and int()

```python
def increment_contents_both(filename):
    """Increments values in a file, creating a new file.

Works with both ints and floats."""
    data = open(filename, 'rt').readlines()
    for i, line in enumerate(data):
        for word in line.split():
            try:
                data[i] = line.replace(word, str(int(word)+1))
            except ValueError:
                try:
                    data[i] = line.replace(word, str(float(word)+1))
                except ValueError:
                    # uncomment the following if you'd like feedback
                    # print(word, "is not a number")
                    pass
    open(filename+'.inc', 'wt').writelines(data)
```

The results of running the function increment_contents_both() are as follows:

```
Milk 13
Eggs 13.0
Olives 101.0
Voodoo dolls 1+1j
```

As you can see, both the values 1e2 and 12.0 are now incremented.

Lastly, the functions assume that numbers are always separated by spaces, which might not always be correct. An alternative approach would be to split based on punctuation marks, as well as spaces (see the "Example: Words Used Only Once" section later in this chapter for more on splitting on punctuation marks, as well).

CSV Files

Up to this point, we've been working with plain text files. Plain text files typically do not follow any format, apart from the fact their contents are text-based. But in reality, when you're dealing with data files, they're more structured than plain text files. As discussed previously in Chapter 4, the CSV file format is a good format for structured, text-based data files. The purpose of this section is to provide tools for the more advanced log-file processing that will be presented in the next section.

The *csv* Module

The *csv* module, which is part of the Python standard library, provides simple methods to read and write CSV files. To use the *csv* module, issue import csv; the remaining discussion assumes you've imported the *csv* module properly.

There are two basic objects you'll be working with: the csv.reader and the csv.writer. As their names suggest, one is used for reading, while the other is used for writing.

The `csv.reader` object splits a line of text into a list of words (also referred to as fields). While you might think it's simpler to split the line of text using the `split()` string method, some caveats make this a bit more complex than is readily apparent.

Consider a CSV file with the following contents (assume it is stored in the file, `../data/sometext.csv`):

```
1/1/2000,"Some text, and a comma"
1/1/2000, "Some text, and a comma"
```

If I were to use the `split()` function, I'd get this:

```
>>> L = open('../data/sometext.csv').read().split(',')
>>> from pprint import pprint
>>> pprint(L)
```

```
['1/1/2000',
 '"Some text',
 ' and a comma"\n1/1/2000',
 ' "Some text',
 ' and a comma"\n']
```

This is not really what I wanted, and the fields and rows aren't separated properly. This is because `split()` does not honor string quoting; that is, it will split on a comma, even if it is enclosed in a string.

Using the `csv.reader` object, I get a better result:

```
>>> f = open('../data/sometext.csv')
>>> for line in csv.reader(f, skipinitialspace=True):
...     print(line)
...
```

```
['1/1/2000', 'Some text, and a comma']
['1/1/2000', 'Some text, and a comma']
```

```
>>> f.close()
```

The csv.reader Object

To create a `csv.reader` object, use the following syntax: `csv.reader(f[, dialect='excel'][, params])`. The first parameter, `f`, is the CSV file, but it can also be any iterable object. The second parameter is the `dialect`. Since there are no clear definitions of what constitutes a CSV file (and there are quite a few nuances), you can specify a `dialect`, which is a set of rules instructing the `csv.reader` parser on how to handle those differences. Furthermore, you can use an existing `dialect` and override some parameters of its behavior using the `params` field.

In the previous example, I didn't specify a `dialect`, which defaulted to the `'excel'` dialect. I did provide a format parameter, instructing the `csv.reader` to ignore the space at the beginning of the field (there's an extra space after the comma in the second line of text in my input file). You can view the list of dialects in your system by issuing `csv.getdialects()`.

Once you have a `csv.reader` object, you can iterate through the object and retrieve a list of fields.

The csv.writer Object

The `csv.writer` object complements the `csv.reader` by allowing the writing of CSV files. Creating a `csv.writer` object is similar to creating the `csv.reader` object: `csv.writer(f[, dialect='excel'][, params])`. The difference (aside from the write vs. read operation) is that the `csv.writer` object strictly requires a file, not any iterable object. Once you have a `csv.writer` object, you can use the `writerow()` or `writerows()` methods:

```
>>> lines = [["1/1/2000", "Some text, and a comma"]]
>>> csv.writer(open('../data/outtext.csv', 'w')).writerows(lines)
```

■ **Note** I've created a list of rows (notice the double brackets), even though there is but one row. This is to match the input expected by the `csv.writer` object. If you pass the `csv.writer` object a list, and not a list of rows, the results might not match what you expect.

More CSV Functionality

The *csv* module allows considerable customization, including the use and creation of user-defined dialects. I won't be covering this topic; however, I will be covering some parameters and their meaning.

The `delimiter` specifies the field separator. In other words, the row is split on an occurrence of `delimiter`, provided it is not escaped or quoted. To change the field separator, add `delimiter=char` as an argument to the `csv.reader` object; char must be a character:

```
>>> for line in csv.reader(open('../data/sometext.csv'), delimiter='/'):
...     print(line)
...
```

```
['1', '1', '2000, "Some text, and a comma"']
['1', '1', '2000, "Some text, and a comma"']
```

(In this example, I've chosen to split on a slash for educational purposes; of course, a much better split would be on a comma because that will separate the date from the entry.)

The parameter quotechar specifies the quoting character used to denote a string in a CSV file:

```
>>> lines = [["1/1/2000", "Some text, and a comma"]]
>>> f = open('../data/outtext.csv', 'w')
>>> csv.writer(f, quotechar='|').writerows(lines)
>>> f.close()
```

The preceding example results in the following:

```
1/1/2000,|Some text, and a comma|
```

In this example, the date wasn't quoted, while the text was—the reason being that the text contained the delimiter. To override quoting behavior, change the value of quoting to csv.QUOTE_MINIMAL, csv.QUOTE_ALL, csv.QUOTE_NONNUMERIC, or csv.QUOTE_NONE. The names quite obviously indicate their functionality. If you select a csv.QUOTE_NONE and a field contains the delimiter, you must supply an escapechar, as well:

```
>>> lines = [["1/1/2000", "Some text, and a comma"]]
>>> f = open('../data/outtext.csv', 'w')
>>> cw = csv.writer(f, quoting=csv.QUOTE_NONE, escapechar='~')
>>> cw.writerows(lines)
>>> f.close()
```

The preceding example results in the following:

```
1/1/2000,Some text~, and a comma
```

DictReader and DictWriter Objects

The *csv* module provides us with additional useful objects: the DictReader and DictWriter objects, which are similar to the csv.reader and csv.writer objects. These objects are especially useful for writing and reading dictionary objects, which are ideal data structures to hold comma separated values in Python, once processed.

If you follow the convention that places a header at the beginning of a CSV file—that is, that each column in the CSV file starts with a field name (see Chapter 4 for a discussion of this)—then accessing values can be done by accessing the dictionary with the field name as the key.

Let's turn to an example. To follow along, create the file ../data/tobuy.csv with the following content:

```
Item,Count
Milk,2
Eggs,12
Tomatoes,5
```

Now let's create a DictReader object:

```
>>> import csv
>>> fcsv = open('../data/tobuy.csv')
>>> for row in csv.DictReader(fcsv):
...     print("Please buy", row['Count'], row['Item'])
...
```

```
Please buy 2 Milk
Please buy 12 Eggs
Please buy 5 Tomatoes
```

I've accessed the values in the CSV file using 'Count' and 'Item' as keys to the dictionary object, row: row['Count'] and row['Item']. If columns were switched, the code would still work as expected.

Similarly, you can create a DictWriter object as follows:

```
>>> header = ['Item', 'Count']
>>> rows = [['Organic Eggs', 5], ['Cucumbers', 12 ]]
>>> fcsv = open('../data/tobuy_more.csv', 'w', newline='')
>>> dict_wr = csv.DictWriter(fcsv, header)
>>> dict_wr.writeheader()
>>> for row in rows:
...     dict_wr.writerow(dict(zip(header, row)))
...
>>> fcsv.close()
```

I first created the header, a list of strings, and the data, a list of rows. I then opened a file named fcsv for writing and attached it to a csv.DictWriter object named dict_wr. As you can see, csv.DictWriter requires the header information, as well. Since I want the header to appear in the file as a first row, I call the member function writeheader(), which writes a header row to the file.

Now this is where it gets a little tricky. I'd like to associate each row with the header, so that when I call the writerow() member function, fields will be associated properly. This is achieved by zipping each row with the header, as follows:

```
>>> header = ['Item', 'Count']
>>> rows = [['Organic Eggs', 5], ['Cucumbers', 12]]
>>> for row in rows:
...     print(list(zip(header, row)))
...
```

```
[('Item', 'Organic Eggs'), ('Count', 5)]
[('Item', 'Cucumbers'), ('Count', 12)]
```

Now, all that's required is to do this with the DictWriter object:

```
>>> for row in rows:
...     dict_wr.writerow(dict(zip(header, row)))
```

And here are the contents of the file, ../data/tobuy_more.csv:

```
Item,Count
Organic Eggs,5
Cucumbers,12
```

As you can see, the DictWriter object is not as simple to work with. That's why I rarely use it, although I use DictReader quite a bit. For a full account of DictReader and DictWriter, please consult with the Python Library Reference.

Date and Time

Text files are important, but text isn't really the object of this book, which has more to do with numbers. The most universal form of data you're bound to see when processing data files is the date and time. Text files that record information based on the date and time, especially when recording the events that have transpired, are commonly referred to as *log files*.

I recently performed a search for file names containing the word "log" in my C:\Windows directory. I came up with dozens of files that are indeed log files. I opened some of them in my favorite editor; and of those that did record the date and time, the date and time information was in varying forms.

One file had timestamps that looked like this:

```
06/21/2008 21:57:20: Some text
06/21/2008 21:57:25: Some text
```

Unfortunately, not every line started with a timestamp. Another file looked liked this:

```
2008-10-21    20:37:26 Some text
2008-10-21    20:37:26 Some text
```

And yet another one looked like this:

```
=== Logging stopped: 6/26/2008  15:53:09 ===
Some text [15:53:09:109]: Some text
Some text [15:53:09:109]: Some text
=== Verbose logging stopped: 6/26/2008  15:53:09 ===
```

And still another looked like this:

```
[Thu Aug 12 22:36:49 2004] Some text
[Sat Aug 14 12:54:01 2004] Some text
[Sat Aug 14 13:25:21 2004] Some text
[Sat Aug 14 14:41:48 2004] Some text
```

Of those log files, the ones I particularly like are those that don't save hard disk space and always dump a timestamp in every entry. The reason for this is that parsing the data later can be done without state machines, simplifying the code considerably (for a discussion of state machines, refer to *Text Processing in Python* by David Mertz, Addison-Wesley, 2003 and also online at http://gnosis.cx/TPiP). Log files that sporadically write date-and-time information are even harder to swallow. Clearly, the person writing those did not think of the parsing application—did he assume that a person would actually read this and not a computer?

■ **Tip** When writing log files, start a line of text with the full date and time information. This will allow easier log-file processing.

The *time* module, available as part of the Python standard library, allows easy handling of date and time information.

Time Module

The *time* module provides a set of helper functions and structures that facilitate handling of date and time in a simple manner. A point in time, that is, both date and time, can be represented in one of two ways in the module:

- *A nine-elements tuple*: This tuple includes year, month, day, hours, minutes, seconds, weekday, Julian day and DST (DST stands for daylight savings time). Of this tuple, the values weekday and Julian day are redundant: you can calculate these values based on other values—year, month, and date. We'll refer to this tuple as the struct_time tuple.

- *Number of seconds since the epoch*: The epoch is a fixed time reference point and is system dependent. On my system, the epoch is Thu Jan 01 00:00:00 1970. At times people use the word "epoch" to mean the number of seconds elapsed since the epoch and not the fixed time reference; this is usually done in context and should be easy enough to discern.

Some *time* module functions accept the struct_time tuple, while others accept the epoch. It's not complex to switch representations. With those two notations covered, let's explore the *time* module. But first, to use the module, be sure to issue import time.

The struct_time Tuple

It's possible to access a specific struct_time tuple element by indexing it; for example, if t is a struct_time tuple, t[0] is the year value. However, using indices is quite hard to follow, and you'll constantly have to look up the documentation to figure out which index is the correct index to the specific value you're looking for. Instead, you can use the member variables tm_year, tm_month, tm_day, tm_hour, tm_min, tm_sec, tm_wday, tm_yday, and tm_isdst to retrieve these values:

```
>>> from time import localtime
>>> localtime()
```

```
time.struct_time(tm_year=2014, tm_mon=5, tm_mday=24, tm_hour=17, tm_min=54,
tm_sec=41, tm_wday=5, tm_yday=144, tm_isdst=1)
```

```
>>> localtime().tm_year
```

```
2014
```

```
>>> localtime().tm_yday
```

```
144
```

In this example, I've introduced the function localtime(), which returns the current time as a struct_time tuple.

Parsing and Formatting Date and Time

The functions strftime() and strptime() are the two functions you're most likely to use when dealing with log files. The function strptime(), which was introduced in Chapter 4, accepts a template parse string and the string to parse. It returns a struct_time representation of the time. The function strftime() does the opposite: it transforms a tuple into a string based on a supplied pattern. Both functions use a similar notation to indicate the values in the struct_time tuple, as listed in Table 5-2.

Table 5-2. *Selected Identifiers for strftime() and strptime()*

Identifier	Description	Values Range
%Y	Year with century as a decimal number	
%m	Month as a decimal number	1–12
%d	Day of the month as a decimal number	1–31
%H	Hour as a decimal number	0–23
%M	Minute as a decimal number	0-59
%S	Second as a decimal number	00-61 (61 for leap seconds)
%w	Weekday as a decimal number	0-6 (where 0 is Sunday)
%j	Day of the year as a decimal number	001-366 (366 for leap years)
%z	Time zone field. DST doesn't have an identifier of its own and is part of this field.	
%a, %A	Locale's weekday name, abbreviated and full	
%b, %B	Locale's month name, abbreviated and full	

The full table includes additional identifiers and is available online at https://docs.python.org/3.3/library/time.html.

So let's try to extract the date information from some of the samples I provided at the beginning of the section.

Example: Logging Information with a Date and Timestamp

The purpose of this example is to create a log file in accordance with the tip presented previously in the "Date and Time" section and the ISO time format recommendation (see Chapter 4).

We'll use the function localtime(), which returns a struct_time tuple containing the current time. We then format the current time using the strftime() function:

```
>>> from time import localtime, strftime
>>> strftime("%Y-%m-%dT%H-%M-%S", localtime())
```

```
'2014-05-24T17-57-37'
```

While this notation is handy for file names, in log files you might like to have something a little more self-explanatory. In such cases, you can use the asctime() function:

```
>>> from time import asctime
>>> asctime(localtime())
```

```
'Sat May 24 17:58:45 2014'
```

However, I'll use the following format:

```
>>> from time import strftime, gmtime
>>> strftime('%d-%b-%Y %H:%M:%S', gmtime())
```

```
'24-May-2014 15:00:02'
```

I did this to show formats other than the ISO format and because there's little room to misunderstand it. However, I recommend following the ISO time format whenever possible.

■ **Tip**   The ISO date and time format, in my mind, is the preferred method of writing date-and-time information. It might be a little more cryptic at first, and it might take some getting used to, but it's consistent and very easy to work with. For example, to sort date in ISO time format, you can sort the actual string without converting it to numerical values.

I think the output from `asctime()` adds an unnecessary value—redundant information, if you will: the day of the week. The format I've selected is also problematic in the case of a different locale (see the "Locale" section later in this chapter), but it's pretty hard to get it wrong. It's also probably the most self-explanatory of the formats presented, but that's more a matter of personal taste.

So now that we have the date and time as a string, it's time to write it to a log file. Listing 5-14 presents an example script you can run. This script generates a log file that adheres to the guidelines I've given in this chapter and previous ones.

Listing 5-14.   Creating Log Files

```
from time import strftime, gmtime, sleep
time_str = strftime("%Y-%m-%dT%H-%M-%S", gmtime())
flog = open("../data/LogExample%s.txt" % time_str, 'wt')
for i in range(5):
    sleep(1.7)
    logline = "%s | Some data %d\n" % \
        (strftime('%d-%b-%Y %H:%M:%S', gmtime()), i)
    flog.write(logline)
flog.close()
```

I've introduced another function from the *time* module: `sleep()`. The `sleep()` function accepts as an argument the amount of time in seconds it should sleep and returns once that time period has elapsed. I chose to use a fractional value, so the log file might appear more "real"; that is, it's not in fixed increments:

```
24-May-2014 15:02:26 | Some data 0
24-May-2014 15:02:28 | Some data 1
24-May-2014 15:02:30 | Some data 2
24-May-2014 15:02:31 | Some data 3
24-May-2014 15:02:33 | Some data 4
```

Another benefit of the `strftime()` function is that it adds a leading zero for values that do not require the full length of the field. Thus, 1 a.m. will show as 01 in the hour fields. This is extremely useful when parsing, as the time format has a fixed length and can be string sliced.

One of the problems associated with logging is that, if your program crashes, you might lose important information. To overcome this, you can open and close the log file at periodic intervals (or even every time) when you log data. That way, in the case of a crash, your file is still updated. Another alternative is to use the *logging* module from the Python standard library, which I won't be covering here. Refer to `https://docs.python.org/3.3/library/logging.html` for information about the *logging* module.

Example: Extracting Date and Time Information from File Contents

We've already seen an example of using `strptime()` in Chapter 4. Let's cover it in more detail here. This time, we'd like to parse some of the date and time formats presented at the beginning of the "Date and Time" section.

For the purpose of this example, I'll assign a string to each different time format and parse every string. By now you should be able to write the wrapper functions to implement reading and writing from a file using either the regular file operation or the *csv* module. To show that the format was read properly, I'll print the `asctime()` version of the time:

```
>>> from time import strptime
>>> log1 = '06/21/2008 21:57:20: Some text'
>>> time1 = strptime(log1[:19], '%m/%d/%Y %H:%M:%S')
>>> asctime(time1)
```

```
'Sat Jun 21 21:57:20 2008'
```

If you look at the time information in the string `log1`, it appears to follow a fixed length. That's especially evident because of the leading zero in the month field (06). Therefore, to extract just the information, I sliced the string in the beginning. From there, I used the `strptime()` function to do the rest of the work. If the date had been a value less than or equal to 12, I wouldn't have known in advance whether the field was %m/%d or %d/%m. Furthermore, if the timestamp weren't a fixed-size string, I would have needed to resort to other methods, such as splitting the string and working with fields.

And now let's look at the next string:

```
>>> from time import asctime, strptime
>>> log2 = '2008-10-21\t20:37:26 Some text'
>>> print(log2)
```

```
2008-10-21     20:37:26 Some text
```

```
>>> time2 = strptime(log2[:19], '%Y-%m-%d\t%H:%M:%S')
>>> asctime(time2)
```

```
'Tue Oct 21 20:37:26 2008'
```

This example includes a string with the date and time separated by a tab and a slightly different format. But again, this is hardly a problem for `strptime()`.

Parsing the date and time information of the remaining strings shouldn't be too complex.

The Epoch: "Linearizing" the Time Base

Up to this point, we've been using the `struct_time` tuple exclusively. It's time to talk about the epoch representation. As I mentioned, seconds elapsed since the epoch is the another time representation supported by the *time* module. At times, it's more beneficial to use an epoch representation than a `struct_time` representation.

The first reason that springs to mind is that of visualization. If you want to plot data as a function of time, and your time base is in the form of a struct_time, it's pretty hard to do. You'd have to come up with ways to "linearize" the time base, so that the time base won't be skewed.

You've seen two examples of linearizing the time series data. The first was in Chapter 1, where I manually linearized the time series data by multiplying the hours value by 3600, adding the minutes value multiplied by 60, and then adding the seconds. The second example was given in Chapter 4, where I used mktime() and gmtime() to calculate the day of the year value as my linear time base.

While these are good options, there's a more standardized way, and that is using the epoch notation. As I mentioned previously, the epoch is system dependent and serves as a reference point in time against which time is measured by the total amount of seconds elapsed (fractional values are allowed, as well).

Here's how to figure out the epoch in your system:

```
>>> from time import asctime, gmtime
>>> asctime(gmtime(0))
```

```
'Thu Jan  1 00:00:00 1970'
```

From here on out, you already have a linear time base: the epoch representation.

Let's modify the GPS example from Chapter 1. As you may recall, the time information was as follows: hhmmss.ss, where the second set of ss values after the decimal point represent fractions of a second. Let's consider the values '140055.00' and '140156.00', which are one minute and one second apart. The original calculation used multiplications and additions:

```
>>> vals = ['140055.00', '140156.00']
>>> [float(x[:2])*3600+float(x[2:4])*60+float(x[4:6]) for x in vals]
```

```
[50455.0, 50516.0]
```

```
>>> _[1]-_[0]
```

```
61.0
```

The difference between the two values (and what we're really after, as you recall we set the start of the time base at zero) is 61 seconds—exactly as we would expect. We can alternatively calculate the epoch representation using the function mktime() from the *time* module, and then use that to calculate the time difference:

```
>>> from time import mktime
>>> [mktime((2000, 0, 0, int(x[:2]), int(x[2:4]), int(x[4:6]), \
... 0, 0, 0)) for x in vals]
```

```
[943963255.0, 943963316.0]
```

```
>>> _[1]-_[0]
```

```
61.0
```

Note that I've used filler values for other unknown fields, such as the year, day, and month.

■ **Tip**   The module *datetime*, from the Python standard library, provides functionality that deals with time differences, as well. See: `https://docs.python.org/3.3/library/datetime.html` for additional information.

We get the same result, so what's the benefit of using the epoch-based functions from the *time* module? There are several:

- The preceding example was pretty simple and did not contain date information. Suppose your data recorder also records the date. What happens at midnight? You'll get a rollover if you don't take into account the date, which makes things considerably more complex. Of course, you can add the day into calculations, but what happens when the month changes? That's a bit more complex: months don't have the same number of days in them, so you'd need a lookup table. And what about leap years? You see, it gets complicated. Instead, use `mktime()`, which takes all of these issues into consideration.

- Using the epoch enables sharing a time base across files. This means that you can pull in information from all sorts of data sources and treat them as one.

- If you're dealing with timestamped binary data files, writing the time base can be challenging. Instead of coming up with complex representations for the time base, you can use the epoch representation (see Chapter 10 for a general discussion of binary files and an example of time-based binary files).

Example: End-of-Day Report

The end-of-day report is a summary report of a log file presenting data at the end of the day. Here are two scenarios where this report is useful:

- *Ending quote for a stock*: Suppose you have a log file with the stock prices over a long period of time, such as a month. The end-of-day report prints the stock price at the end of trade days.

- *Patient discharge*: A patient is being treated at the hospital, and during his treatment, all information is logged. You'd like to know the patient discharge state; that is, you want to receive an end-of-day report with the patient's status.

To illustrate the problem, we'll create a log file, `../data/SystemALogs.txt`, that will be composed of timestamps and a log message:

```
Sat Oct 25 08:15:01 2008, Message 1
Sat Oct 25 09:30:31 2008, Message 2
Sun Oct 26 09:19:32 2008, Message 3
Mon Oct 27 08:05:31 2008, Message 4
Wed Oct 29 07:17:40 2008, Message 5
Wed Oct 29 08:44:04 2008, Message 6
Wed Oct 29 09:44:05 2008, Message 7
Wed Oct 29 12:30:50 2008, Message 8
Thu Oct 30 11:22:03 2008, Message 9
```

In this case, the log file is sorted, which is to be expected. But even if that's not the case, the algorithm we employ should still work properly.

To print an end-of-day report, I'll use the following algorithm. A dictionary object stores an end-of-day report per day. The key of the dictionary should uniquely identify a day. I chose to use the tuple (year, day of the year) for that purpose. For the dictionary value, I'll be using a tuple containing the epoch and the message. I'm using the epoch for two reasons. First, I can easily compute it using mktime(). Second, it's a simple value to check against. A larger epoch value means a more recent event.

We process the file line-by-line, extracting the information to create the key and value to access the dictionary. If the key is already in the dictionary, we check whether the information in the current line is from a later time; and if it is, we update the value accordingly. If the key doesn't exist in the dictionary, we add the computed key and value pair to the dictionary. Once we finish processing the file, we print the dictionary object. As you can see, the algorithm doesn't rely on the log file to be sorted to produce correct results.

I've chosen to use the *csv* module to show usage of the module in a full script (see Listing 5-15). In this specific case, a simple split, or string slicing, would've worked just as well.

Listing 5-15. An End-of-Day Report Implementation

```python
# end-of-day report
from time import mktime, strptime, ctime
import csv

d = {}

for row in csv.reader(open('../data/SystemALogs.txt')):
    # t is a struct_time tuple
    t = strptime(row[0], '%a %b %d %H:%M:%S %Y')

    # calculate seconds since the epoch
    t_epoch = mktime(t)

    # construct a key and value
    key = (t.tm_year, t.tm_yday)
    val = (t_epoch, row[1])

    try:
        # do we have a more recent entry?
        if d[key][0] < t_epoch:
            d[key] = val
    except KeyError:
        # current date is not in dictionary
        d[key] = val

for epoch, line in d.values():
    print(ctime(epoch), line)
```

I've also introduced a new function from the *time* module in Listing 5-15, ctime(). The function ctime() accepts the number of seconds since the epoch and prints out a date string representation.

Here are the results from running the script on the preceding log file:

```
Sat Oct 25 09:30:31 2008    Message 2
Thu Oct 30 11:22:03 2008    Message 9
Mon Oct 27 08:05:31 2008    Message 4
Wed Oct 29 12:30:50 2008    Message 8
Sun Oct 26 09:19:32 2008    Message 3
```

The results are correct, but they aren't sorted by date. This can be easily remedied if, instead of printing the files, you were to store them to a list and then call the function sort() to sort the list.

Example: Combining Data from Several Sources Based on the Epoch

One of the benefits of using the epoch is that it is a standard time base to work with. The intention of this example is to combine data from several sources—two log files, in this case—and present a coherent report. For the purpose of this example, we'll split the file SystemALogs.txt from the previous example into two files: SystemBLogs.txt and SystemsCLogs.txt. Our script should combine them back into a sorted log file.

You can see the contents of SystemBLogs.txt here:

```
Sun Oct 26 09:19:32 2008, Message 3
Wed Oct 29 07:17:40 2008, Message 5
Thu Oct 30 11:22:03 2008, Message 9
```

And you can see the contents of SystemCLogs.txt here:

```
Sat Oct 25 08:15:01 2008, Message 1
Sat Oct 25 09:30:31 2008, Message 2
Mon Oct 27 08:05:31 2008, Message 4
Wed Oct 29 08:44:04 2008, Message 6
Wed Oct 29 09:44:05 2008, Message 7
Wed Oct 29 12:30:50 2008, Message 8
```

Trying to sort these lists based on text will generate the wrong results. So, the idea is to convert every timestamp string into an epoch representation and sort based on that value. For this purpose, we'll create a list of rows. Each row will be composed of [t_epoch, line], where t_epoch is the converted time representation, and line is the entire line of text. We then use the sorted() function to sort the lists and dump the data back to file, removing the epoch information (see Listing 5-16).

Listing 5-16. A Script to Combine Two Time-Based Log Files

```
from time import mktime, strptime
data = []
data1 = open('../data/SystemBLogs.txt').readlines()
data2 = open('../data/SystemCLogs.txt').readlines()
fmt = '%b %d %H:%M:%S %Y'
for line in data1+data2:
    # t is a struct_time tuple
    t = strptime(line[4:24], fmt)

    # calculate seconds since the epoch
    t_epoch = mktime(t)

    # append data
    data.append([t_epoch, line])

data = [line[1] for line in sorted(data)]
open('../data/SystemsBCLogs.txt', 'wt').writelines(data)
```

This script assumes you're combining two files. More often than not, if you need to combine log files, you'll need to combine more than two files. Refer to Chapter 10 to learn about working with several input files.

Additional Time and Date Functions

We've covered most of the functionality available in the *time* module. For most of your log file processing needs and other time-based processing requirements, the module is comprehensive and complete. There are additional time- and date-related modules available in Python. The *datetime* module (https://docs.python.org/3.3/library/datetime.html) provides functionality that includes operations on dates using a more object-oriented approach. The *calendar* module (https://docs.python.org/3.3/library/calendar.html) provides general calendar-related operations. Refer to the Python standard library for additional information.

Regular Expressions

Regular expressions are pattern-matching expressions used for searching and replacing text. At times, they are more flexible than the string operations presented previously. To use regular expressions, you'll have to import the regular expression module (named *re*), which is part of the standard library. The module *re* is similar to Perl's built-in support of regular expressions.

Your next step is to design a pattern to match against and decide what function to use on that pattern. The most notable functions are `findall(pat, str)`, which finds all occurrences of a regular expression pattern `pat` in the string `str`; `split(pat, str)`, which splits the string `str` whenever a regular expression pattern `pat` is encountered; and `sub(pat, repl, str)`, which substitutes the occurrence of a pattern `pat` in a string `str` with a supplied substitute, `repl`.

There are additional functions in the module, including `match()`, `search()`, and `compile()` to name a few, but I will not be covering those here. The preceding three functions should take care of most of our data processing needs.

Regular Expression Patterns

A regular expression pattern is basically a string. The pattern can contain both regular characters and special characters. A regular character matches itself. So the pattern `'a'` matches the character `'a'` whenever encountered, and the pattern `'txt'` matches the string `'txt'` whenever encountered:

```
>>> import re
>>> re.split(r'a', 'Flatland')
```

```
['Fl', 'tl', 'nd']
```

```
>>> re.split(r'txt', '45506-8.txt')
```

```
['45506-8.', '']
```

So far, `re.split()` is similar to the `split()` function introduced previously in this chapter. However, the strength of regular expressions lies in the special characters. These characters provide additional functionality to the pattern itself. Let's take a look at some. The first one is the dot character (`'.'`). The dot character matches any single character, except for a new line:

```
>>> re.findall(r'a.', 'Flatland')
```

```
['at', 'an']
```

The character '+' means one or more occurrences of the pattern, the character '?' means zero or one occurrences of the pattern, and the character '*' means zero or more repetitions of the pattern. Note that these are modifiers of the pattern; that is, they change the behavior of the pattern. In contrast, the dot symbol is not a modifier of the pattern, but a part of the pattern. Here are some examples:

```
>>> re.findall(r'.?a', 'Flatland')
```

```
['la', 'la']
```

```
>>> re.findall(r'a.*', 'Flatland')
```

```
['atland']
```

The first example finds the pattern composed of zero or one characters, followed by the character 'a'. The second example matches the character 'a' and can be followed by any number of characters.

One might question why the first pattern matched one character before the character 'a', since obviously zero characters would've worked as well? Similarly, why did the second pattern match the string 'atland' where 'a' would've worked just as well? The answer is that regular expressions are greedy by default; that is, they try to match as many characters as possible. You can turn off the greedy behavior by adding a '?' character after the modifiers presented previously. For example, you could use '??', '+?', and '*?'.

The next special characters are the '^' and '$' characters, which match the start and end of a string, respectively. Here are some examples that demonstrate how to use these special characters:

```
>>> re.findall(r'^.*a', 'Flatland')
```

```
['Flatla']
```

```
>>> re.findall(r'^.*?a', 'Flatland')
```

```
['Fla']
```

```
>>> re.findall(r'a.*$', 'Flatland')
```

```
['atland']
```

These searches can be expressed in English as follows. The first line matches as many characters as possible between the start of the string and the character 'a'. The second line finds as few characters as possible between the start of the string and the character 'a' (notice the nongreedy modifier, '*?'). The third line matches the character 'a' and the remaining characters until the end of the line.

Example: Removing Extra Spaces with Regular Expressions

Previously in this chapter, I explained how to remove extra spaces in a string. We used split() to split the words on spaces and then strip() to remove the excess spaces. We then used join() to combine the list back into a string.

With regular expressions, the same result can be achieved more easily:

```
>>> grocery_list = "Milk    2\nEggs   12"
>>> re.sub(r' +', ' ', grocery_list)
```

```
'Milk 2\nEggs 12'
```

I've used the function sub() with the pattern ' +' (a space followed by the plus sign) to replace one or more spaces with one space.

Special Sequences

Special sequences are used to match some interesting combinations. Here's a short list: '\d' matches a decimal digit, '\s' matches a whitespace, and '\w' matches an alphanumeric character. If you use uppercase, the opposite is achieved; that is, '\D' matches anything but a decimal digit, '\S' matches anything but a whitespace, and '\W' matches anything but an alphanumeric character. Since the '\' character is a modifier, it's a good idea to use the raw string format, r'string', as you've seen previously, so as not to escape characters on several levels (i.e., on the string level and on the regular expression level):

```
>>> grocery_list = "Milk    2\nEggs   12"
>>> re.findall(r'\d+', grocery_list)
```

```
['2', '12']
```

Alternatives

The special character '|' is used to match either pat1 or pat2 in the regular expression, r'pat1|pat2':

```
>>> grocery_list = "Milk    2\nEggs   12"
>>> re.sub(r'Milk|Eggs', 'Chocolate', grocery_list)
```

```
'Chocolate    2\nChocolate   12'
```

Ranges

You can also match a range of values using brackets. The pattern '[12]' will match both the character '1' and the character '2':

```
>>> grocery_list = "Milk    2\nEggs   12"
>>> re.sub('[12]', '0', grocery_list)
```

```
'Milk    0\nEggs   00'
```

You can also denote a range of characters using the '-' character. The pattern '[1-5]' matches any character from 1 to 5, inclusive.

Lastly, follow up with a '^' after the left bracket to negate the range:

```
>>> grocery_list = "Milk   2\nEggs  12"
>>> re.sub('[^0-5]', '*', grocery_list)
```

```
'*******2*******12'
```

When to Use Regular Expressions

It's hard to decide whether to use a regular expression or just plain string operations. Regular expressions are hard to master, but practice makes perfect, as the saying goes. Try solving the same problem with string functions and with regular expressions to get a feel for what's the better approach.

If using string operations makes things more complicated to follow, resolve to regular expressions. Sometimes, a simple regular expression makes the code more readable and elegant. Such a case was presented previously in the example that showed how to remove extra spaces. At other times, it's the other way around. Opt for simplicity and clarity of your code whenever possible.

That said, there is a special case where I've found that using regular expressions is far better than using string methods, and that is when I'd like to split or replace a string based on several options. The main reason is that the string method `split()` requires a separator, and it does not accept several options. With regular expressions, you can provide a range of separators.

Example: Words Used Only Once

We finalize this discussion of regular expressions with an example that uses a dictionary in conjunction with text. The idea is to find words used only once in a file. The motivation behind this example is that words used only once might be typographical errors in source code.

To implement the solution, we'll use a dictionary to count the number of occurrences of each and every word in a file (see Listing 5-17).

Listing 5-17. Finding Words Used Only Once

```python
from string import punctuation, whitespace
import re

def nonce(filename):
    """Returns words used only once in a file."""

    data = open(filename, 'rt').read()
    d, result = dict(), []
    for word in re.split('['+punctuation+whitespace+']', data):
        d[word.lower()] = d.get(word.lower(), 0)+1
    for word, occur in d.iteritems():
        if occur == 1:
            result.append(word)
    return result
```

The function nonce() should prove quite readable. The heart of the script lies in the for loop, which splits the text using a regular expression. This is a prime example where a regular expression is better than the string method split(): the split happens on either a punctuation character or a whitespace character by means of the regular expression range specifier, '[]'.

Bear in mind that this script is good for mostly source code and not plain text English. The reason is that it doesn't take into consideration such things as plural forms (e.g., "girls" and "girl" are considered two different words) and other spoken language characteristics.

Internationalization and Localization

At times you're faced with working with data files that originated in a different locale. This could pose some problems: date and time notations can be different from what your code expects, or the text characters can be of another language.

The purpose of this section is to introduce the topic of internationalization (i18n) and localization (l10n). I'll touch on two topics: the locale and its impact on date notations; and Unicode, which is a convenient method to support different languages, at least when it comes to text files.

■ **Note**   The abbreviation i18n comes from the number of characters between the "i" and the "n" in the string "internationalization," surrounded by the first and last letters of the word. Similarly, the abbreviation l10n refers to "localization."

Locale

In the context of software, *locale* is a set of rules governing the behavior of some functions that are either country or language oriented. From a data analysis perspective, if a log file containing a timestamp of both the date and time is used, and the locale is not identical to the one in use, the function strptime() might fail. For example, some countries use day/month/year notation, while others use the month/day/year notation.

To accommodate for different locales, Python provides support via the *locale* module, which is part of the Python standard library. To use it, issue the command import locale. To set a locale, issue the command locale.setlocale(category, locale). You can either enable the entire set of rules using the category locale.LC_ALL or set specific ones. In our case, we'll be using LC_ALL, which also controls the behavior of the functions strftime() and strptime().

■ **Note**   The *locale* module relies on OS locale support. Different operating systems might have different locale abbreviations. For example, to run the following script on Linux, I had to use the locale 'fr_FR.ISO-8859-1'; on Windows, I've used 'fr'. On some Linux distributions, a list of locale aliases can be found in the file, /usr/share/locale/locale.alias. Unfortunately, I was unable to run the *locale* module properly on Cygwin; some poking around suggests that Cygwin does not currently support locale, other than the basic one (named C, which is to imply the C language implementation).

Generally speaking, you should set your locale upon program entry:

```
>>> import locale
>>> locale.setlocale(locale.LC_ALL, 'french')
```

```
'French_France.1252'
```

If the preceding doesn't work, try replacing `'french'` with `'fr_FR.ISO-8859-1'`, `'fr_FR'` (Mac OS), or `'fr'`:

```
>>> from time import gmtime, strftime, strptime
>>> fmt = '%d-%B-%Y'
>>> strftime(fmt, localtime())
```

```
'24-mai-2014'
```

```
>>> strptime(_, fmt)
```

```
time.struct_time(tm_year=2014, tm_mon=5, tm_mday=24, tm_hour=0,
tm_min=0, tm_sec=0, tm_wday=5, tm_yday=144, tm_isdst=-1)
```

The first line imports the *locale* module. I then set the locale to be `'French_France.1252'`, which basically means the language French, in the country France. It's possible to mix language and country; for example, you can pass the string `'French_Canada'` to set the language to French but the country to Canada. In Windows, I've found the notation `'Language_Country'` to work well, whereas I've had some issues with abbreviations (e.g., `'fr_CA'` didn't work well for me). In Linux, I've found that the notation in the form `'en_US.ISO-8859-1'` works well; so for French Canada, on Linux, I've set the locale to `'fr_CA.ISO-8859-1'`.

For additional information regarding the *locale* module, refer to the Python standard library:

`https://docs.python.org/3.3/library/locale.html`.

We're not done with locale yet; I'll present another example after drilling down a bit on Unicode.

Unicode Strings

The original ASCII table is based on the English language and does not account for a lot of other languages and symbols. Several designs were introduced to try to resolve this, and lately it appears that Unicode (`http://www.unicode.org`) is the industry standard.

The Unicode standard addresses such topics as *character encoding, character properties, visual representation,* and more. From a very simplistic approach, Unicode tries to support characters and symbols from other languages by assigning every character (and there are tens of thousands of those, if not more) a unique integer number, while maintaining compatibility with the ASCII table. This means that some Unicode characters are represented by 4 bytes, not 1 byte.

The problem starts when you want to write your Unicode string to file. Writing 4 bytes instead of 1 every time is space consuming. If the characters you use are simple English characters, they are all well within the ASCII table and thus contain less than 8 bits. To write them, you don't need 4 bytes—1 byte will suffice. In this case, you can choose to *encode* your Unicode string as an 8-bit value, known as UTF-8. UTF stands for Unicode Transformation Format.

If the characters you use are not all from the English alphabet, you might need more bytes to represent your Unicode string. In most cases, 2 bytes is more than enough, which means you can encode your Unicode string using UTF-16 encoding. However, you're also likely to use characters from the English alphabet (or other ASCII symbols), in which case some characters may be encoded with 8 bits. And so some encoding supports those variable size schemes, as well.

For example, let's encode the character "X" using two codes: UTF-8 and UTF-16:

```
>>> "X".encode('utf-8')
```

```
b'X'
```

```
>>> "X".encode('utf-16')
```

```
b'\xff\xfeX\x00'
```

As you can see, the character "X" is encoded differently in UTF-8 and UTF-16. The following section explains Unicode in Python more fully.

From our perspective, it is sufficient to know that Python strings are Unicode strings. And furthermore, we can encode and decode Unicode strings using a host of encoding schemes, including UTF-8 and UTF-16.

Working with Unicode

Unicode strings come to light when you're dealing with non-ASCII characters (i.e., characters for which the ordinal value is above 128).

The value 0xa9 corresponds to © and is pretty hard to type on most keyboards. So instead, I've used its ordinal value in Unicode. Python retains the value as an ordinal value and does not print the symbol associated with it. If we dump the Unicode string to file, it will be possible to view the special characters in most editors or web browsers. In this case, the generated file is ../data/special.txt:

```
>>> u = 'a string\xa9'
>>> u
```

```
'a string\xa9'
```

In Mac or in a Python environment that supports displaying Unicode characters (such as IDLE, see Chapter 2), the previous results show the proper symbol for ©:

```
'a string©'
```

```
>>> open('../data/special1.txt', 'wb').write(u.encode('utf-8'))
```

```
10
```

The write() method accepts only strings, not Unicode strings. So for us to be able to use the write() function and write the Unicode strings to file, we'll have to use the encode() method, which accepts the encoding to be used. In this case, I've selected the UTF-8 encoding, which is widely popular.

Alternatively, you can create a file with an encoding by passing the parameter encoding on file creation. The preceding line would be written as follows:

```
>>> open('../data/special2.txt', 'w', encoding='utf-8').write(u)
```

The function decode() complements encode() and returns the decoded Unicode string:

```
>>> u.encode('utf-8')
```

```
b'a string\xc2\xa9'
```

```
>>> u.encode('utf-16')
```

```
b'\xff\xfea\x00 \x00s\x00t\x00r\x00i\x00n\x00g\x00\xa9\x00'
```

```
>>> u.encode('utf-16').decode('utf-16')
```

```
'a string\xa9'
```

(In an environment that shows Unicode characters properly, '\0xa9' will be replaced with ©.)

Notice how the strings turn to bytes (the leading b). That's because, once you encode strings, you get a sequence of bytes instead of a string.

Example: The Hebrew Alphabet

The purpose of this example is to generate a file with the Hebrew alphabet. If you don't have Hebrew installed on your system (which I suppose is the case for most folks out there), you can try other, more popular characters, as I'll show shortly.

■ **Note**   Alphabet is a Hebrew word. It is composed of the first two letters of the Hebrew language: Aleph and Bet.

The Hebrew alphabet, shown in Figure 5-1, starts with the letter Aleph mapping to the value 0x5D0 and ends at the letter Tav, mapped to value 0x5EA in Unicode. Unless you have the Hebrew keyboard installed on your system, manually typing Hebrew letters is not a trivial task. Therefore, you'll have to construct the alphabet using a Unicode string. Since we don't want (or can't) manually type the values, we'll construct a list of Unicode letters and then generate a string from the list. The function chr() will be used to construct the characters from their ordinal value:

```
>>> letters = [chr(letter) for letter in range(0x5d0, 0x5eb)]
>>> alephbet = ''.join(letters)
>>> open('../data/alephbet.txt', 'w', encoding='utf-8').write(alephbet)
```

27

אבגדהוזחטיכלמנסעפצקרשת

Figure 5-1. *The Hebrew alphabet*

The result is 27, which corresponds to the number of letters in the Alphabet (22 letters plus 5 variants used in the end of a word). Once we have the Unicode string, all that's required is to write it to file. In this case, I've chosen to use the UTF-8 encoding.

The Latin alphabet has special characters, as shown in Figure 5-2: the accented letters, starting at value 0xC0 and ending at 0x0FF. Therefore, you could modify the preceding script to generate the Latin special characters, as follows:

```
>>> letters = [chr(letter) for letter in range(0xc0, 0x100)]
>>> latin = ''.join(letters)
>>> open('../data/latin.txt', 'w', encoding='utf-8').write(latin)
```

64

ÀÁÂÃÄÅÆÇÈÉÊËÌÍÎÏÐÑÒÓÔÕÖ×ØÙÚÛÜÝÞßàáâãäåæçèéêëìíîïðñòóôõö÷øùúûüýþÿ

Figure 5-2. *Some interesting Latin characters*

The result is the number of characters written, 64.

Example: Writing Today's Date in the Current Locale

The purpose of this example is to print the current date and time, in a specific locale, to file. If you're using the English_United States locale, this will be rather boring. So instead, I've decided to use the Hebrew locale again, since we're all familiar with it by now (see Listing 5-18). Since Python doesn't always print other character sets in the interpreter, it's best to write the results to file and view them in a text viewer, editor, or web browser.

Listing 5-18. Today's Date in the Current Locale

```
import locale
from time import strftime, strptime, localtime
from sys import platform
if platform == 'linux' or platform == 'darwin':
    locale.setlocale(locale.LC_ALL, 'he_IL')
elif platform == 'win32':
    locale.setlocale(locale.LC_ALL, 'Hebrew_Israel')
elif platform == 'cygwin':
    raise Exception('Cygwin not supported')
else:
    print("Untested platform: ", platform)
today = strftime('%B %d, %Y', localtime())
open('../data/today.txt', 'w', encoding='utf-8').write(today)
```

At first, I try to guess the encoding for Hebrew based on the current platform using the sys.platform value. As I've mentioned earlier, Linux, Windows, and Cygwin all have different locale abbreviations.

After I set the locale, I can query the preferred locale encoding with the function locale.getpreferredencoding(), which is quite useful in determining how to encode the Unicode string. Unfortunately, I have found that the preferred encoding in the case of Hebrew should be cp1255 and not the one returned by the getpreferredencoding() function. Lastly, I encode the string and write it to file using UTF-8.

187

Figure 5-3 shows the results.

מאי 24, 2014

Figure 5-3. *A date in Hebrew*

More on Unicode

The topic of Unicode is vast, and there are numerous books available that discuss it. As for online information, I have found the Python library reference a valuable resource. If you're looking for information regarding i18n and l10n in general, including code pages and locale information, the following might prove useful:

- *The Unicode Consortium*: `http://www.unicode.org`.

- *Wikipedia*: `http://en.wikipedia.org/wiki/Locale`. Be sure to follow the links to topics such as character encoding and Unicode.

- International Components for Unicode: `http://www.icu-project.org/`.

Final Notes and References

String and text processing is a very large field, especially with the popularity of the Internet and search engines; most of the data available online is in some form of text. This chapter has covered a considerable number of the topics associated with text processing in the context of data analysis.

However, there's a lot more to learn. Two topics presented here were but briefly discussed: regular expressions and i18n and l10n. Considerable documentation is available on the Internet on these two topics, so by all means refer to online resources. At this point, you should know enough of the basics to dive deeper into the subject without much trouble.

The following book is of great value for the topics discussed in the chapter:

- *Text Processing in Python* by David Mertz (Addison-Wesley, 2003)

■ ■ ■

## CHAPTER 6

Graphs and Plots

Visualizing Data

Graphs and plots are efficient methods to present data. Done properly, a graph can convey an idea better than an entire article.

What a graph should portray is a function of your target audience. So when you plot a graph, bear that in mind. If your target audience is technical people, they might require additional technical information. If your target audience is investors, another approach is required. In this chapter, I won't be discussing what to present and what not; instead, I'll show you *how* to present. Examples include how to plot bar charts and pie charts, how to add markers and control line ticks, how to annotate the graphs with text and arrows, and more.

Regardless of your target audience, some ideas and methodologies always hold true. Sources for data should be accurate and verified. Graphs should be easily reproducible by running the code that generated them. (How many times did your boss ask you to modify your last report? If the graph had been generated with a documented script, doing so would have proved easy enough.) And lastly, your graphs should be aesthetically pleasing. Consulting with colleagues could be beneficial as well: what do they understand from the graph? Was the key idea captured? Is the output professional?

In this chapter we'll discuss the basics of creating and annotating graphs. We'll start by exploring the plot() function, continue with text and grid annotation, explore some other types of graphs, and lastly, introduce patches, a method to attach graphical objects to a figure.

The *matplotlib* Package

The *matplotlib* package, available at http://matplotlib.org/, is the main graphing and plotting tool used throughout this book. The package is versatile and highly configurable, supporting several graphing interfaces. *Matplotlib*, together with *NumPy* and *SciPy* (see Chapters 7 and 8), provides MATLAB-like graphing capabilities.

The benefits of using *matplotlib* in the context of data analysis and visualization are as follows:

- Plotting data is simple and intuitive.

- Performance is great; output is professional.

- Integration with *NumPy* and *SciPy* (used for signal processing and numerical analysis) is seamless.

- The package is highly customizable and configurable, catering to most people's needs.

The package is quite extensive and allows, for example, embedding plots in a graphical user interface. Currently, the package supports several graphical interfaces, including wxPython (http://www.wxpython.org/) and PyGTK (http://www.pygtk.org/), to name a couple. However, GUI topics are beyond the scope of the book. We will focus on plotting graphs, rather than discussing the GUI engine itself. For a full account of *matplotlib*, try the online documentation, available as a PDF document, at http://matplotlib.sourceforge.net/Matplotlib.pdf.

Going forward, you should ensure that you have *matplotlib* installed and working properly. Refer to Chapter 2 if you require additional information on installing the package or visit the package's web site.

Interactive Graphs vs. Image Files

There are several ways you can use *matplotlib*:

- Create dynamic content to be served on a web server. For example, you might generate stock price images on the fly or display traffic information on top of a map.

- Embed it in a graphical user interface, allowing users to interact with an application to visualize data.

- Automatically process data and generate output in a variety of file formats, including JPEG, PNG (Portable Network Graphics—see http://www.libpng.org/pub/png/), PDF, and PostScript (PS). This option is best suited for batch processing a large number of files.

- Run it interactively, with the Python shell in X or Windows. This option is good during the development phases of the code.

Of the preceding options, and in view of the book topics, we'll explore two: generating plots of varying file formats and using *matplotlib* interactively. I typically use both options, depending on the stage of my code. In the early stages of development, I work interactively with a small sample of the data: plot, zoom in, change graph parameters, annotate, and then rinse and repeat. Once my code is ready, I let it loose, so to speak, on the full set of data files. Since that might mean tens if not hundreds of graph windows, I prefer to write them as files instead, and then use an image viewer to view the results one at a time.

So let's start. First and foremost, import *PyLab* as follows:

```
>>> from pylab import *
```

As previously mentioned, this imports *matplotlib*, *NumPy*, and *SciPy*. Although, generally speaking, you shouldn't import everything quite so liberally, you should make an exception in the case of *PyLab*: it's considerably easier to work with the entire package loaded into memory; and unless memory is a constraint, the usability is great. Going forward, I'll assume you've imported *PyLab* as just described.

WHERE DOES THIS FUNCTION COME FROM?

A frustration to some, especially those experienced with Python, is that issuing the command `from pylab import *` will import several packages. How do you know whether a specific function is a part of *NumPy* or *matplotlib*? The solution is simple—use `help`! For example, here's the output from `help(diff)`:

```
>>> help(diff)
Help on function diff in module numpy.lib.function_base:

diff(a, n=1, axis=-1)
    Calculate the nth order discrete difference along given axis.
```

As you can see in the first line, `diff()` is a function from the *NumPy* package, or more specifically, `numpy.lib.function_base`.

Our next step is to plot a graph. We'll plot the list, [0, 1, 2]:

```
>>> plot(range(3))
```

```
[<matplotlib.lines.Line2D object at 0x00000000058800F0>]
```

There's no visible output yet (other than *matplotlib*'s response), and the reason for this is that we haven't specified how exactly we want the graph drawn: interactive figures or hard copy files.

Interactive Graphs

Interactive graphs, like the one shown in Figure 6-1, plot the graph in a separate window. If you'd like this option, enter show() at the Python shell or call the function show() in a script.

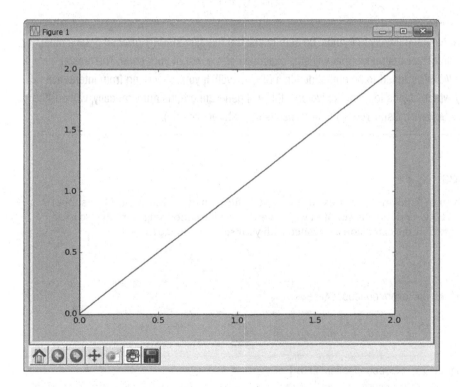

Figure 6-1. *An interactive graph*

The function show() opens up an interactive window. Here are several notes about this window:

- The window is numbered, as you can see by the label 'Figure 1.' This is useful if you have several windows and would like subsequent plots to either override or appear on a specific figure. To switch between figures, use the figure(n) function, where n stands for the figure index. If you'd like a new figure, and don't particularly care about the figure index, issue the command figure(), which will create an empty figure with the next available index.

- The x-axis and y-axis were created automatically to fit the data. In a lot of the cases, *matplotlib* does an excellent job of automatically selecting the right axis (as in this example). However, if you want a different range of values to be displayed, that's doable with the axis() command; you'll learn more about this later in the chapter in the "Axis" section.

- The location of the mouse is printed on the right corner of the figure. This is very useful if you're trying to zoom in on data and find a specific data point. This functionality is not available when you plot graphs to file (i.e., noninteractive mode).

- You have several buttons on the lower-left side of the figure to allow interaction with the graph. The five left-most buttons are used for zooming and zooming history. The first button from the left (with the house icon) is used to change axes to the original plot axes. The left and right arrow buttons cycle backward and forward through previous axes changes. The fourth button allows you to change the origin of the axes, and the fifth button from the left enables zooming. The sixth button from the left controls the margins of the plot with respect to the containing window. Lastly, the seventh button allows you to save the image to disk.

■ **Note**   If you're not using *matplotlib* interactively in Python, be sure to call the function show() *after* all graphs have been generated, as it enters a user interface main loop that will stop execution of the rest of your code. The reason behind this behavior is that *matplotlib* is designed to be embedded in a GUI, as well. If you're working from interactive Python, issue the command ion() which stands for "interactive on"; this will generate graphs automatically, without the need to call show(). To reverse this behavior, issue ioff() (which stands for "interactive off").

Savings Graphs to Files

The function savefig() enables you to write images of varying formats to a file. Out of the box, *matplotlib* supports several file formats, including PDF, PNG, and PS. The simplest way to generate a file containing a graph is to issue savefig(filename), where filename has the extension associated with your selected image format:

```
>>> figure()
```

```
<matplotlib.figure.Figure object at 0x0000000002CAE160>
```

```
>>> plot(arange(3))
```

```
[<matplotlib.lines.Line2D object at 0x000000000826FEF0>]
```

```
>>> savefig('../images/line.png')
>>> from glob import glob
>>> glob('../images/*.png')
```

```
['../images/line.png']
```

I've assumed you're following the directory structure for the book (see Chapter 2) and that you can access the images directory via a relative path: ../images. I've also introduced the *glob* module, which is used to perform wildcard searches of files; you'll learn more about *glob* in Chapter 10.

You should be able to view the figure in most image viewers or your web browser.

■ **Note** *Matplotlib* returns objects as they're created. In the preceding example, the returned plot object is noted by the line, [<matplotlib.lines.Line2D object at 0x000000000826FEF0>]. Going forward, I'll omit these responses to make the interactive code easier to follow.

I called the function savefig() with the file name extension as part of the string holding the file name, instructing savefig() to create a PNG file. Similarly, I could've created a PostScript file by issuing savefig('line.ps').

The dictionary object FigureCanvasBase.filetypes holds a list of supported file types in your system:

```
>>> from pprint import pprint
>>> pprint(FigureCanvasBase.filetypes)
```

```
{'eps': 'Encapsulated Postscript',
 'jpeg': 'Joint Photographic Experts Group',
 'jpg': 'Joint Photographic Experts Group',
 'pdf': 'Portable Document Format',
 'pgf': 'LaTeX PGF Figure',
 'png': 'Portable Network Graphics',
 'ps': 'Postscript',
 'raw': 'Raw RGBA bitmap',
 'rgba': 'Raw RGBA bitmap',
 'svg': 'Scalable Vector Graphics',
 'svgz': 'Scalable Vector Graphics',
 'tif': 'Tagged Image File Format',
 'tiff': 'Tagged Image File Format'}
```

FINDING WHAT YOU'RE LOOKING FOR IN COMPLEX MODULES

So how did I figure out that FigureCanvasBase.filetypes holds the supported file types? Did I read the entire manual? Hardly. Some of the packages we work with are really large, and mastering all the intricacies of variables and objects that control their behavior is not a trivial task. So I use some quick-and-dirty tricks. And although they might not be the "proper" way to do things, they help me get the job done, and that's what really counts. So let me show you what I've done to figure out the available file types.

To figure out the base file types, I issued savefig() with a bogus file format: savefig('a.ext'). The result was, of course, an exception (ValueError); however, I also received some useful information: "Supported formats: eps, jpeg, jpg, pdf, pgf, png, ps, raw, rgba, svg, svgz, tif, tiff." But that's not exactly what I wanted; I wanted an enumeration of the file formats, so I could index them rather than parse a string returned by an exception. So I traced back the source of the error from the exception output: the error originated in the file, C:\Python33\lib\site-packages\matplotlib\backend_bases.py, at line 2070. Next, I opened up the file backend_bases.py, jumped to line 2070, and I started reading the code. Python is a very readable language, and it didn't take me all that long to figure out that the formats are available via `self.get_supported_filetypes()`, which basically just returns the property `filetypes`. Since `self` points to the container object, I scrolled up some more and found that the function `get_supported_filetypes()` is part of the class `FigureCanvasBase`–hence, `FigureCanvasBase.filetypes`.

Reading the exceptions generated by *matplotlib*, along with exploring modules and their names, also helped me find the objects `matplotlib.colors.cnames` and `matplotlib.colors.ColorConverter.colors`, both listing possible colors (see the section "Colors" later in the chapter). That said, reading the manual is also a very viable option.

You can pass an image format argument to `savefig()` to control the output file generated instead of specifying it in the file name string. You can also control other parameters, such as dots per inch (dpi) and face color for the color of the figure. A more general form of `savefig()` is `savefig(fname[, param1=value1][, param2=value2], ...)`. Table 6-1 lists some parameters. In the examples, assume `fn` is a string containing a file name.

Table 6-1. *savefig( ) Parameters*

Parameter	Description	Default Value	Example
dpi	Resolution in dots per inch	None	`savefig(fn, dpi=150)`
facecolor*	The figure's face color	`'w'` for white background	`savefig(fn, facecolor='b')`
transparent	Whether the figure is transparent.	False	`savefig(fn, transparent=True)`
format	File format	`'png'`	`savefig('image', format='pdf')`

* *Refer to Table 6-4 for a list of color values.*

You can combine several parameters, as in this example:

```
savefig('file', dpi=150, format='png')
```

The function `savefig()` supports additional options; see `help(savefig)` for a full account.

■ **Note**   Not all image formats support transparency, especially JPEG. If you require a transparent background, select an image format that supports transparency, such as PNG.

Plotting Graphs

This section details the building blocks of plotting graphs: the `plot()` function and how to control it to generate the output we require. We've used the `plot()` command extensively throughout the book. It's now time to examine it more closely.

The `plot()` function is highly customizable, accommodating various options, including plotting lines and/or markers, line widths, marker types and sizes, colors, and a legend to associate with each plot. The functionality of `plot()` is similar to that of MATLAB (`http://www.mathworks.com`) and GNU-Octave (`http://www.gnu.org/software/octave/`) with some minor differences, mostly due to the fact that Python has a different syntax from MATLAB and GNU-Octave.

Lines and Markers

We'll begin by creating a vector to plot using *NumPy* (see Chapter 7 for a full account of the *NumPy* package):

```
>>> figure()
>>> y = array([1, 2, -1, 1])
>>> plot(y)
>>> show()
```

If you don't have a GUI installed with *matplotlib*, replace show() with savefig('filename') and open the generated image file in an image viewer.

■ **Note**   Going forward, I'll omit the show() call from listings. Be sure to issue show() or savefig() if you'd like to follow along.

I passed the vector y as an input to plot(). As a result, plot() drew a graph of the vector y using auto-incrementing integers for an x-axis. Which is to say that, if you don't supply x-axis values, plot() will automatically generate one for you: plot(y) is equivalent to plot(range(len(y)), y). So let's supply x-axis values (denoted by variable t):

```
>>> figure()
>>> y = array([1, 2, -1, 1])
>>> t = array([10, 11, 12, 13])
>>> plot(t, y)
>>> show()
```

The call to function figure() generates a new figure to plot on, so we don't overwrite the previous figure.

Let's look at some more options. Next, we want to plot y as a function of t, but display only markers, not lines. This is easily done:

```
>>> figure()
>>> plot(t, y, 'o')
>>> show()
```

To select a different marker, replace the character 'o' with another marker symbol. Table 6-2 lists some popular choices; issuing help(plot) provides a full account of the available markers.

Table 6-2. *A Sampling of Available Plot Markers*

Character	Marker Symbol
'o'	Circle
'^'	Upward-pointing triangle
's'	Square
'+'	Plus
'x'	Cross (multiplication)
'D'	Diamond

Much as there are different markers, there are also different line styles, a few of which are listed in Table 6-3.

Table 6-3. *A Sampling of Available Plot Line Styles*

Character(s)	Line Style
'-'	Solid line
'--'	Dashed line
'-.'	Dash-dot line
':'	Dotted line

If you'd like both markers and lines, concatenate the symbols for line styles and markers. To plot a dash-dot line and diamond symbols as markers, issue the following:

```
>>> plot(t, y, 'D-.')
>>> show()
```

Figure 6-2 shows the output of the examples in this section.

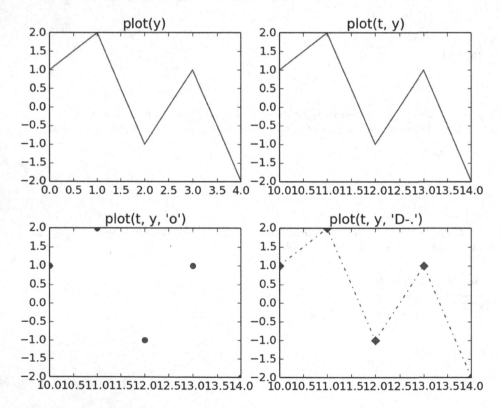

Figure 6-2. *Output of the previous examples: a line plot with no x values (top-left), a line plot with x values (top-right), a marker plot (bottom-left), and a marker and line plot (bottom-right)*

Plotting Several Graphs on One Figure

We use graphs to visualize data and compare it. What's more natural than displaying several graphs in one plot, so we can compare results? There are two ways to do that in *matplotlib*. The first way is to add more vectors to the plot() function:

```
>>> plot(t, y, t, 2*y)
```

You can also do so like this:

```
>>> plot(t, y, '+', t, 2*y, 's-')
```

The second way is by calling plot() repeatedly. Sometimes you might have only partial data to plot. Say you have vector y, but then you modify it and want to print both the original vector and the newly modified vector. What do you do? One option would be to store the intermediate value, but what if you have 20 of those? That would mean calling plot() with some 20+ arguments.

When you call plot() with an already existing figure, there are two possible outcomes. One is that the figure is erased, and the new plot is drawn. The other is that the figure is not erased, and the new plot is added to the figure. This behavior is determined by the hold status of the figure. You can control the hold status with the hold() function: calling hold(True) will ensure new plots don't erase the figure, whereas hold(False) will do the opposite. Issuing the command hold() with no arguments will toggle the hold status. As a general rule, it's best to specify the hold behavior you require and not rely on the default behavior; that is, hold(True) or hold(False).

Line Widths and Marker Sizes

Next, we'll look at controlling line widths and marker sizes. We do so by passing linewidth (or lw for short) and markersize (or ms for short) arguments to plot(), as shown in Listing 6-1. Both arguments accept a floating point value; the default value is 1.

Listing 6-1. Plotting Several Lines in One Graph with Different Line Styles and Markers

```
I = arange(6)
plot(I, sin(I), 'o', I, cos(I), '-', lw=3, ms=8)
title("plot(I, sin(I), 'o', I, cos(I), '-', lw=3, ms=8)")
show()
```

Figure 6-3 shows the results of this example.

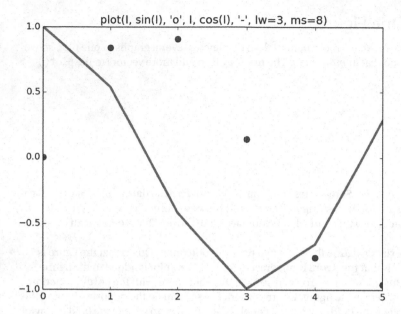

Figure 6-3. *Plotting several graphs in one figure*

When you plot multiple lines in one plot() function call, the parameters linewidth and markersize control *all* the lines in the same plot() command. If you'd like different lines with different line styles or different marker sizes in the same figure, draw each plot with an individual call to the plot() function and use the hold() function, as shown in Listing 6-2.

Listing 6-2. Different Line Widths in One Graph

```
figure(); hold(True)
I = arange(6)
plot(I, sin(I), lw=4)
plot(I, cos(I), lw=2)
show()
```

Colors

Last on our list of plotting basics is controlling color. Just as with marker style and line style, you can control color with one character, according to the list in Table 6-4.

Table 6-4. *The Color Character Look-Up Table*

Character	Color
'b'	Blue
'c'	Cyan
'g'	Green
'k'	Black
'm'	Magenta
'r'	Red
'w'	White
'y'	Yellow

As you might have noticed, *matplotlib* automatically chooses a different color for subsequent line plots if a color is not specified. You can select your preferred color by supplying a color character:

```
>>> figure()
>>> I = arange(6)
>>> plot(I, sin(I), 'k+-', I, cos(I), 'm:')
>>> show()
```

This will plot two lines: the first is a black line with plus markers and a connecting solid line, and the second is a magenta dotted line.

If you'd like a color that does not appear in Table 6-4, you can choose one from the dictionary object, `matplotlib.colors.cnames`. The dictionary contains a better color selection and has more than a hundred values. And lastly, if that dictionary is not enough, you can provide an explicit Red-Green-Blue (RGB) value. If you're using the dictionary values or an explicit RBG value, you have to provide the `color` argument as a parameter to a `plot()` call:

```
>>> plot(randn(5), 'y', lw=5) # 'y' from the color table
>>> plot(randn(5), color='yellowgreen', lw=5) # using matplotlib.colors.cname
>>> plot(randn(5), color='#ffff00', lw=5) # explicit yellow RGB
```

See `help(matplotlib.colors)` for additional color information.

In the preceding example, I've used the function `randn(n)` to generate a random vector of size 5.

Controlling the Graph

For a graph to convey an idea aesthetically, the data, although highly important, is not everything. The grid and grid lines, combined with a proper selection of axis and labels, present additional layers of information that add clarity and contribute to overall graph presentation.

Now that we have the basics of plotting lines and markers covered, let's turn to controlling the figure by controlling the x-axis and y-axis behavior and setting grid lines.

199

Axis

The axis() function controls the behavior of the x-axis and y-axis ranges. If you do not supply a parameter to axis(), the return value is a tuple in the form (xmin, xmax, ymin, ymax). You can use axis() to set the new axis ranges by specifying new values: axis([xmin, xmax, ymin, ymax]). If you'd like to set or retrieve only the x-axis values or y-axis values, do so by using the functions xlim(xmin, xmax) or ylim(ymin, ymax), respectively.

Other than the range limits, the function axis() also accepts the following values: 'auto', 'equal', 'tight', 'scaled', and 'off'. The value 'auto'—the default behavior—allows plot() to select what it thinks are the best values. The value 'equal' forces each x value to be the same *length* as each y value, which is important if you're trying to convey physical distances, such as in a GPS plot. The value 'tight' causes the axis to change so that the maximum and minimum values of x and y both touch the edges of the graph. The value 'scaled' changes the x-axis and y-axis ranges so that x and y have both the same length (i.e., aspect ratio of 1). Lastly, calling axis('off') removes the axis and labels.

To illustrate these axis behaviors, I'll plot a circle (see Listing 6-3).

Listing 6-3. Plotting a Circle

```
R = 1.2
I = arange(0, 2*pi, 0.01)
plot(sin(I)*R, cos(I)*R)
show()
```

The reason I chose a circle of radius 1.2 is that, in the case of a radius with "nicer" numbers (e.g., 1.0 or 2.0), the automatic axis solution works very well, and it's hard to show the effects of the different axis options.

Figure 6-4 shows the results of applying different axis values to this circle.

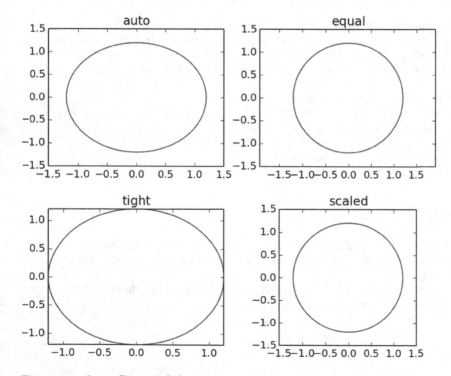

Figure 6-4. *Controlling axis behavior*

Grid and Ticks

The function grid() draws a grid in the current figure. The grid is composed of a set of horizontal and vertical dashed lines coinciding with the x ticks and y ticks. You can toggle the grid by calling grid() or set it to be either visible or hidden by using grid(True) or grid(False), respectively.

To control the ticks (and effectively change the grid lines, as well), use the functions xticks() and yticks(), (see Listing 6-4 and Figure 6-5). The functions behave similarly to axis() in that they return the current ticks if no parameters are passed; you can also use these functions to set ticks once parameters are provided. The functions take an array holding the tick values as numbers and an optional tuple containing text labels. If the tuple of labels is not provided, the tick numbers are used as labels.

Listing 6-4. Grid and Tick Example

```
R = 1.2
I = arange(0, 4*pi, 0.01)
plot(sin(I)*R, cos(0.5*I)*R)
axhline(color='gray')
axvline(color='gray')
grid()
xticks([-1, 0, 1], ('Negative', 'Neutral', 'Positive'))
yticks(arange(-1.5, 2.0, 1))
show()
```

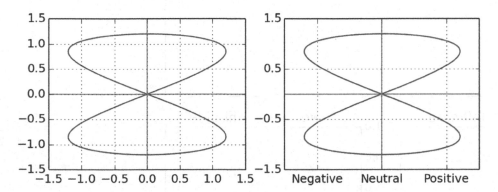

Figure 6-5. *Controlling the grid and axis: the left graph shows the default* xticks()*, while the right graph displays labels*

Figure 6-5 shows the output generated from Listing 6-4 without issuing the last two calls to xticks() and yticks() (left graph) and with xticks() and yticks() calls (right graph). Notice the labels on the x-axis.

I've also used the functions axvline() and axhline(), which plot a line across the x-axis and y-axis, respectively. The axhline() and axvline() functions accept many parameters, including color, linewidth, and linestyle, to name a few.

Subplots

In some of the previous figures in this chapter, I've displayed several smaller graphs in one figure; these are known as *subplots*. The subplot() function splits the figure into subplots and selects the current subplot. The subplots are numbered from left to right, top to bottom, so the upper-left subplot is 1, and the lower-right subplot is equivalent to the number of subplots. Notice that this is different from the default counting behavior used in Python: numbers start at 1 and not at 0.

To split the figure into 2-by-2 subplots and select the upper-left subplot for plotting, issue subplot(2, 2, 1). Alternatively, you can pass the string '221', which does the same thing: subplot('221'). It's also possible to combine subplots of different sizes in one figure. This is a bit tricky and requires subplotting with different subplot sizes. Listing 6-5 shows an example that generates a subplot on the upper half of the figure and two subplots on the lower part of the figure, the results of which you can see in Figure 6-6.

Listing 6-5. Subplots of Varying Sizes

```
figure()
subplot(2, 1, 1)
title('Upper half')
subplot(2, 2, 3)
title('Lower half, left side')
subplot(2, 2, 4)
title('Lower half, right side')
show()
```

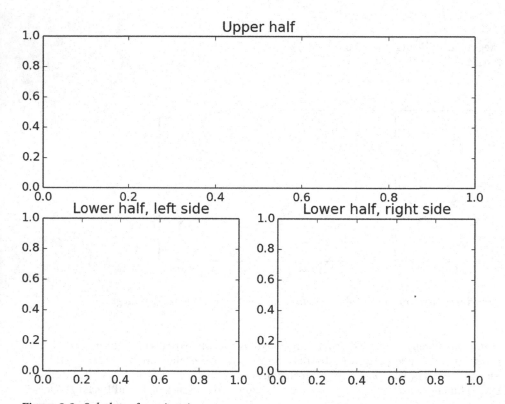

Figure 6-6. *Subplots of varying sizes*

■ **Tip** Subplots are especially useful in visualizing several aspects of the same data. For example, Figure 1-5 in the GPS example in Chapter 1 shows x and y coordinates in one subplot and velocity in another subplot. Events (e.g., speeding) are marked in both, providing a visual link between the two subplots.

Erasing the Graph

The functions cla() and clf() clear the axes and the figure, respectively. These functions are useful when you're working with an interactive environment and would like to clear the current axes (i.e., set the axes to default values and clear the plotted lines). It's also possible to clear the figure altogether, erasing also the axes and subplots, using the clf() function.

Lastly, you can choose to close the figure window altogether; this is done by calling the function close(). If you provide a number to close(), the figure associated with the number is closed. So, close(1) will close Figure 1, leaving the other figures open. If you'd like to close all the figures, issue close('all').

Adding Text

There are several options to annotate your graph with text. You've already seen some, such as using the xticks() and yticks() function. The following functions will give you more control over text in a graph.

Title

The function title(str) sets str as a title for the graph and appears above the plot area. The function accepts the arguments listed in Table 6-5.

Table 6-5. *Text Arguments*

Argument	Description	Values
fontsize	Controls the font size	'large', 'medium', 'small', or an actual size (i.e., 50)
verticalalignment or va	Controls the vertical alignment	'top', 'baseline', 'bottom', 'center'
horizontalalignment or ha	Controls the horizontal alignment	'center', 'left', 'right'

All alignments are based on the default location, which is centered above the graph. Thus, setting ha='left' will print the title starting at the middle (horizontally) and extending to the right. Similarly, setting ha='right' will print the title ending in the middle of the graph (horizontally). The same applies for vertical alignment. Here's an example of using the title() function:

```
>>> title('Left aligned, large title', fontsize=24, va='baseline')
```

Axis Labels and Legend

The functions xlabel() and ylabel() are similar to title(), only they're used to set the x-axis and y-axis labels, respectively. Both these functions accept the text arguments from Table 6-5:

```
>>> xlabel('time [seconds]')
```

Next on our list of text functions is legend(). The legend() function adds a legend box and associates a plot with text:

```
>>> I = arange(0, 2*pi, 0.1)
>>> plot(I, sin(I), '+-', I, cos(I), 'o-')
>>> legend(['sin(I)', 'cos(I)'])
>>> show()
```

The legend order associates the text with the plot. Had I called legend() with the inverted list, the result would be a wrong legend.

An alternative approach is to specify the label argument with the plot() function call, and then issue a call to legend() with no parameters:

```
>>> I = arange(0, 2*pi, 0.1)
>>> plot(I, sin(I), '+-', label='sin(I)')
>>> plot(I, cos(I), 'o-', label='cos(I)')
>>> legend()
>>> show()
```

Figure 6-7 shows the addition of an x-axis label and legend.

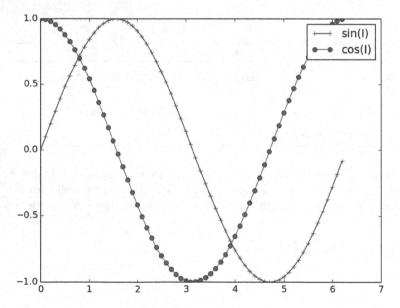

Figure 6-7. *Adding an x-axis label and legend*

You can also control the location of the legend box via the loc parameter. This is important if you don't want the legend text to hide the graph line. loc can take one of the following values: 'best', 'upper right', 'upper left', 'lower left', 'lower right', 'right', 'center left', 'center right', 'lower center', 'upper center', and 'center'. Instead of using strings, you can use numbers: 'best' corresponds to 0, 'upper left' corresponds to 1, and 'center' corresponds to 10. Using the value 'best' moves the legend to a spot less likely to hide data; however, performance-wise there may be some impact.

The function legend() has additional options that let you add a drop shadow and control the spacing between the text within the legend, among other things. Consult with the interactive help for additional information.

Text Rendering

The text(x, y, str) function accepts the coordinates in graph units x, y and the string to print, str. It also renders the string on the figure. You can modify the text alignment using the arguments in Table 6-5. The following will print text at location (0, 0):

```
>>> figure()
>>> plot([-1, 1], [-1, 1])
>>> text(0, 0, 'origin', va='center', ha='center')
>>> show()
```

The function text() has many other arguments, such as rotation (which was used in Chapter 1) and fontsize. See help(text) for a complete list of arguments.

Mathematical Symbols and Expressions

Last on our list of text-related functions is one that renders mathematical symbols and expressions. The syntax to use mathematical symbols provided by *matplotlib* is similar to that of T$_E$X. To render mathematical expressions, use a raw string and enclose your mathematical expression with $ signs. For Greek letters, start with a slash, followed by the name of the letter. So to print Alpha (α), your string should be r'α'. Fractions can be created using the \frac{num}{den} notation; for example, r'$\frac{\pi}{4}$' is the symbol π divided by four. Subscripts are denoted with an underscore, so to render the text a$_i$, write r'a_i'.

It is beyond the scope of the book to cover the entire T$_E$X syntax supported by *matplotlib*. For additional information, refer to the online *matplotlib* web site (at the time of the writing of this book, the following link was available: http://matplotlib.sourceforge.net/users/mathtext.html). That said, whenever you encounter a mathematical expression in this book, you're more than likely be able to figure out how it works with the small subset of commands presented in this section.

Example: A Summary Graph

The example script in Listing 6-6 summarizes the functions we've discussed up to this point: plot() for plotting; title(), xlabel(), ylabel(), and text() for text annotations; and xticks(), ylim(), and grid() for grid control.

Listing 6-6. A Plot Summary Example

```
I = arange(0, 2*pi+0.1, 0.1)
plot(I, sin(I), label='sin(I)')
title('Function f(x)=sin(x)')
xlabel('x [rad]', va='bottom')
ylabel('sin(x)')
text(pi/2, 1, 'Max value', ha='center', va='bottom')
text(3*pi/2, -1, 'Min value', ha='center', va='top')
xticks(linspace(pi/2, 2*pi, 4), (r'$\frac{\pi}{2}$', r'$\pi$', \
    r'$\frac{3\pi}{2}$', r'$2 \pi$'), fontsize=20)
xlim([0, 2*pi])
ylim([-1.2, 1.2])
grid()
show()
```

The result of this example appears in Figure 6-8.

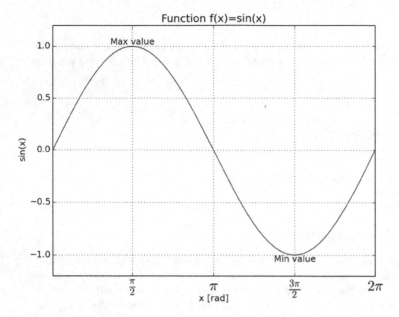

Figure 6-8. *A plot summary example*

More Graph Types

While the regular line and marker plots are excellent visualization tools, they're hardly the only ones. This section provides a quick overview of some other 2-D graph options.

Bar Charts

A favorite of many, a bar chart allows quantitative comparison of several values. To use a bar chart, call the function `bar(left, height)`, where `left` is the x-coordinates of the bar and `height` is the bar height. The function `bar()` allows for considerable customization; issuing `help(bar)` will provide most of the details.

Example: GDP, N Top Countries

For this example, which plots the purchasing power parity (GDP) of various countries, you'll need the CIA GDP Rank Order file, available from the CIA World Factbook (`https://www.cia.gov/library/publications/the-world-factbook/rankorder/rawdata_2001.txt`); this is a tab-delimited file, perfect for easy data processing. I'll assume that you've downloaded the file and saved it in folder `Ch6/data`; the source code resides in `Ch6/src`, and the output files are located in `Ch6/images`.

To begin, we'll define a function to read the data (we will use it in several examples in this chapter). The code in Listing 6-7 should be saved under the file, `src/read_world_data.py`.

Listing 6-7. Function read_world_data.py

```python
import csv, re

def read_world_data(N=10, fn='../data/rawdata_2001.txt'):
    """A function to read CIA World Factbook file.

N is the number of countries to process."""

    # initialize return lists
    gdp, labels= [], []

    # read the data and process it
    for i, row in enumerate(csv.reader(open(fn), delimiter='\t')):
        # remove the dollar, comma and space characters
        gdp_value = re.sub(r'[\$, ]', '', row[2])

        # store data in billions of dollars
        gdp.append(float(gdp_value)/1e9)
        labels.append(row[1].strip())

        # stop analyzing the data after N countries have been processed
        if i == N-1:
            break
    return (gdp, labels)
```

The function reads data from the first N countries and returns their GDP alongside the country names. I've used two modules. The first, the *csv* module, reads the data, which is tab delimited. The second, the *re* module, gets rid of the dollar sign, comma, and space characters in the GDP value field.

Armed with read_world_data() function, we turn to plot the bar chart (see Listing 6-8).

Listing 6-8. Plotting the GDP Bar Chart

```python
# a script to plot GDP bar chart
from pylab import *
from read_world_data import read_world_data

# initialize variables, N is the number of countries
N = 5

gdp, labels = read_world_data(N)

# plot the bar chart
bar(arange(N), gdp, align='center')

# annotate with text
xticks(arange(N), labels, rotation=-10)
for i, val in enumerate(gdp):
    text(i, val/2, str(val), va='center', ha='center', color='yellow')
ylabel('$ (Billions)')
title('GDP rank, data from CIA World Factbook')
show()
```

The script by now should be quite readable. Notice that I've imported the function `read_world_data()` from a separate file, `read_world_data.py`, which was defined in Listing 6-7. I've also chosen to rotate the text labels on the horizontal axis by 10 degrees in the call to `xticks()`. The rotation ensures that the labels for `'United States'` and `'European Union'` do not overlap.

Figure 6-9 shows our bar chart so far.

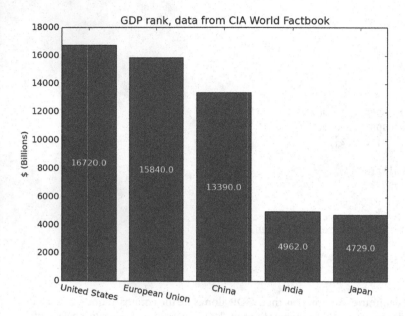

Figure 6-9. *A bar chart showing World GDP rank*

It's also possible to add error bars. To add an error bar equivalent to ±1000 billion dollars (talk about an error, eh?), add this line to the script shown in Listing 6-8, just after the `bar()` function call:

```
errorbar(arange(N), gdp, 1000*ones(N), color='k')
```

Finally, the function `barh()` plots a horizontal bar chart instead of a vertical one, should you require one (but in this case, remember to switch the x- and y-axis labels and ticks).

Histograms

Histograms are charts that show the frequency, or occurrence, of values. In *matplotlib*, the function `hist()` is used to calculate and draw the histogram chart. At a minimum, you must supply an array of values. You can control the number of cells in a histogram by specifying them as follows: `hist(values, numcells)`. Alternatively, you can specify the histogram bins `hist(values, bins)`, where `bins` is a list holding histogram bin values. The return value from `hist()` is a tuple of probabilities, bins, and patches. Patches are used to create the bars; I'll go into more detail in the "Patches" section later in the chapter.

The function `hist()` has other customization options, including the histogram orientation (vertical or horizontal), the alignment of bars, and more. Again, refer to the interactive help: `help(hist)`.

Example: GDP, Histogram

We turn again to the GDP ranks from the CIA World Factbook; this time we want to plot a histogram of the N largest economies. Again, we use the read_world_data() function implemented in the previous example (see Listing 6-9).

Listing 6-9. Plotting a GDP Histogram

```python
# a script to plot GDP histogram
from pylab import *
from read_world_data import read_world_data

# initialize variables; N is the number of countries, B is the bin size
N, B = 20, 1000

gdp, labels = read_world_data(N)

# plot the histogram
prob, bins, patches = hist(gdp, arange(0, max(gdp)+B,B), align='left')

# annotate with text
for i, p in enumerate(prob):
    percent = '%d%%' % (p/N*100)
    # only annotate non-zero values
    if percent != '0%':
        text(bins[i], p, percent,
             rotation=45, va='bottom', ha='center')
ylabel('Number of countries')
xlabel('Income, billions of dollars')
title('GDP histogram, %d largest economies' % N)

# some axis manipulations
xlim(-B/2, bins[-1]-B/2)
show()
```

Figure 6-10 shows the resulting graph.

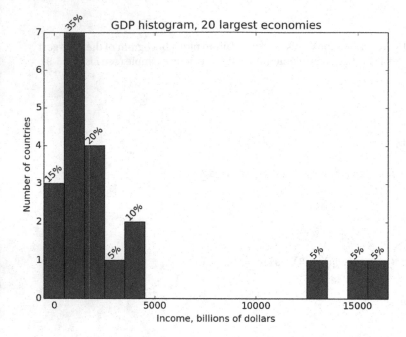

Figure 6-10. *A GDP histogram, with the N largest economies*

Again, the script should prove quite readable. I'd like you to turn your attention to what might appear an odd modification I've made to the x-axis using the call to function xlim(). The purpose of this call is to modify the default behavior of the x-axis ranges. The motivation behind this modification is that, since I've chosen 'center' for the histogram bins, the automatic x-axis range includes negative values. This is because the leftmost bin is centered at zero, but has a width, part of it in the negative x-axis. I didn't like this behavior and chose to override it by manually setting the axis. Instead of setting a fixed number, I've modified the x-axis by subtracting half the bin width, B/2, from the axis.

As a general rule, when you modify default behavior like this, try to use parameters as much as possible (in the preceding example, you would use the parameter B, not the value 1000, and retrieve current values with xlim()); this will allow for more flexible scripts that cater to a wider range of input values.

Pie Charts

Pie charts are as simple to use as bar charts. The function that implements pie charts is pie(x), where x holds the values to be charted.

Example: GDP, Pie Chart

Listing 6-10 presents a script to generate a pie chart, shown in Figure 6-11; again, this example uses the function, read_world_data().

Listing 6-10. Plotting a GDP Pie Chart

```
# a script to plot GDP pie chart
from pylab import *
from read_world_data import read_world_data
```

```
# initialize variables, N is the number of countries
N = 10

gdp, tags = read_world_data(N)

# plot the bar chart
pie(gdp, labels=tags)
axis('equal')
title('GDP rank, data from CIA World Factbook')
show()
```

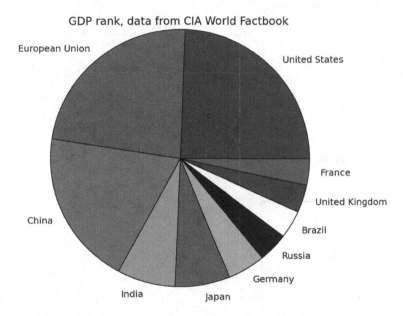

Figure 6-11. *A GDP pie chart, with the N largest economies*

I decided to use the variable tags instead of labels, so that the call to pie() would be a little less confusing. Had I stuck with the original name, labels, the call to pie would've been pie(gdp, labels=labels). This still would've worked, but it would seem a bit confusing, in my opinion.

Logarithmic Plots

The functions semilgox() and semilogy() are used to plot the x-axis and y-axis in a logarithmic scale, respectively. Logarithmic plots of type semilogy() are common when plotting power or intensity values, such as those of the Richter magnitude scale, which measures seismic energy. Likewise, measurements of quantities used with frequencies, for example, are commonly plotted on a logarithmic x-scale denoting octaves and decades. There's also the option of using a loglog() plot, which means that both the x-axis and y-axis are logarithmic. This is the case for Bode plots, which are common in engineering fields.

All three functions, semilogx(), semilogy(), and loglog(), can be modified with arguments similar to those presented with the plot() function.

The function logspace(start, stop, numpoints=50, endpoint=True, base=10.0) can be useful in creating a range of values to be plotted with the preceding functions. The start and stop values are the exponent values. The function logspace() generates logarithmically spaced values between 10^{start} and 10^{stop}. You can decide whether the end value, 10^{stop}, is returned by specifying endpoint = True. If you'd like a base other than 10, set base to the value you require:

```
>>> figure()
>>> I = 2*logspace(1, 5, 5)
>>> I
```

```
array([   2.00000000e+01,    2.00000000e+02,    2.00000000e+03,
          2.00000000e+04,    2.00000000e+05])
```

```
>>> semilogx(I, [20, 19, 8, 2, 2], '+-', lw=2)
>>> title('Logarithmic plot, semilogx()')
>>> xlabel('Frequency [Hz]')
>>> ylabel('Amplitude [dB]')
>>> grid()
>>> show()
```

Figure 6-12 shows the results of the preceding example.

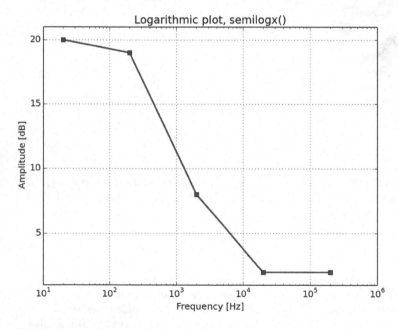

Figure 6-12. *A logarithmic plot*

Notice that, when plotting with `semilogx()`, `semilogy()`, and `loglog()`, the labels are the original values, not the logarithms of the values. If you'd like to print the logarithmic values, you should probably use a regular `plot()` function with `log()` or `log10()` of the values. This is useful, for example, in estimating the energy in decibels (dB):

```
>>> def db(x):
...     """Returns the value of x, in decibels."""
...     return 20*log10(abs(x))
...
>>> plot(db(array([1000, 980, 970, 400, 30, 2, 1, 1])))
>>> title('Logarithmic plot, dB)')
>>> xlabel('Frequency [Hz]')
>>> ylabel('Amplitude [dB]'
>>> xticks(arange(8), 10**arange(8))
>>> grid()
>>> show()
```

Polar Plots

Polar plots draw polar coordinate values: a radius at a given angle. Polar plots are commonly used to draw antenna radiation patterns, as they depict the energy the antenna transmits at any given angle. Polar plots are implemented using the `polar(theta, r)` function.

To set the labels along the radius, use the `rgrids(radii, labels)` function, which works similarly to `xticks()` and `yticks()`. If you don't provide the `labels` value, the `radii` values are used as labels. You can also set the `angle` at which the labels are plotted (the default is 22.5 degrees). Similarly, the function `thetagrids()` plots the angle ticks and labels, as demonstrated in Listing 6-11.

Listing 6-11. A Polar Plot

```
theta = arange(0, 2*pi, 0.01)
polar(theta, cos(theta), theta, -cos(theta))
rgrids([0.5, 1.0], ['Half', 'Full'])
theta_labels = ['0', r'$\frac{\pi}{2}$', r'$\pi$', r'$\frac{3\pi}{2}$']
thetagrids(arange(0, 360, 90), theta_labels, fontsize=20)
title(r'A polar plot of $\pm cos(\theta)$', va='bottom')
show()
```

Figure 6-13 shows the resulting polar plot.

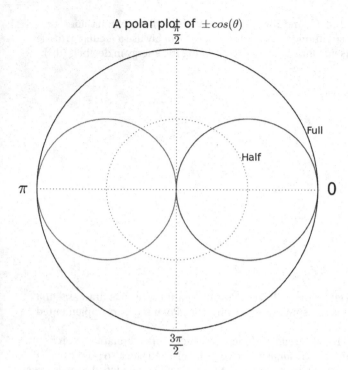

Figure 6-13. *A polar plot*

In the title, I've used the ± symbol denoted by `'$\pm$'`.

Stem Plots

Stem plots draw a vertical line from (x, 0) to (x, y) for every (x, y) value, as well as a marker at (x, y). Stem plots are used to denote discrete data and are popular for plotting filtering windows (see Listing 6-12).

Listing 6-12. A Stem Plot of Filter Windows

```
from pylab import *
N = [4, 8, 16, 64]
for i, n in enumerate(N):
    subplot(2, 2, i+1)
    stem(arange(n), hamming(n))
    xticks(arange(0, n+1, n/4))
    yticks([0, 0.5, 1])
    xlim(-0.5, n+0.5)
    title('N=%d' % n)
show()
```

Figure 6-14 shows the results of this listing.

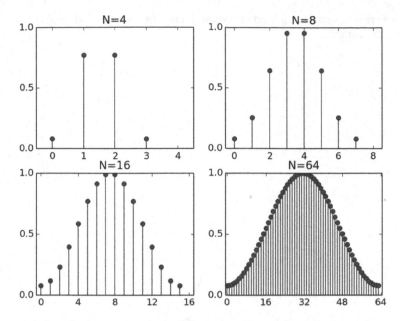

Figure 6-14. *Stem plots of a Hamming window with different N values*

In the preceding example, I've used the hamming() function to create a Hamming window, commonly used in filtering values.

Additional Graphs

Matplotlib also supports a great number of graphs used to depict more complex data. Here's a short list of some of the graphs available:

- The functions contour() and contourf() are used for contour plots. Contour plots draw a line connecting equal (x, y) value pairs. They're used in weather maps, where they detail lines of equal pressure or temperature. In topographical maps, they detail the terrain; and more.

- The function specgram() displays the frequency contents of data over time. specgram() can be used, for example, to plot the frequencies of a sound wave as a function of time.

- Both the contour() and specgram() functions rely on a color map to depict the data. Color maps are a relation between a value and a color. *Matplotlib* provides a set of color maps that include such names as autumn() and hot() to ease the selection of a color map.

- The function quiver() implements quiver plots, which are typically used to describe fields in physics. The quiver plot is a set of arrows that depict the force at each point (direction and magnitude).

Example: Plotting the Frequency Content of a Signal

Sometimes, it's of value to plot the frequencies a signal is composed of as a function of time. For example, in an audio signal, a different frequency means a different note, so plotting frequencies as a function of time is a possible "musical visualization."

In this example, shown in Listing 6-13, we create a signal composed of several discrete frequencies and display those frequencies as a function of time using a specgram().

Listing 6-13. A Specgram of a Signal

```
from pylab import *

Fs = 256
times = [3, 7, 5]
frequencies = [100, 20, 80]

y = array([])
for t, f in zip(times, frequencies):
    x = cos(2*pi*arange(t*Fs)/Fs*f)
    y = append(y, x)

specgram(y, 256, Fs)
xlabel('Time [sec]')
ylabel('Frequency [Hz]')
axis([0, 14.5, 0, 128])
show()
```

I set the frequency of sampling at 256 samples per second and created a signal composed of 100 hertz (Hz) for 3 seconds, 20 Hz for 7 seconds, and then 80 Hz for 5 seconds. I then plotted the signal using specgram(), with the results shown in Figure 6-15.

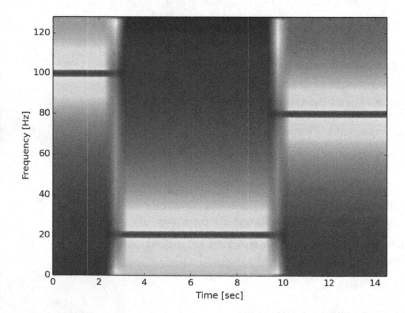

Figure 6-15. A specgram

Figure 6-15 clearly shows that in the first 2 seconds, the frequency is 100 Hz; in the next 8 seconds, the frequency is 20 Hz; and in the last 5 seconds, the signal's frequency is 80 Hz.

■ **Note** If you look closely at the figure, you'll notice there's half-a-second shift in the specgram. This is due to an overlapping window of size 128 samples. See `help(specgram)` for information on the overlapping window.

You can change the colors used to display the specgram using a color map function. Simply issue `hot()` or `autumn()` at the end of the script, and then observe the results. See `help(colormaps)` for a full account of available colormaps.

Example: A Repelling Force Field

The following example illustrates the use of `quiver()` to depict a force field. At each point in the figure, an arrow points at the direction of the acting force, as well as its magnitude, which is denoted by the size of the arrow:

```
from pylab import *

x = arange(-5, 6, 1)
y = arange(-5, 6, 1)

u, v = meshgrid(x, y)
quiver(u, v)

xticks(range(len(x)), x)
yticks(range(len(y)), y)

axis([-1, 11, -1, 11])
axis('scaled')
title('A repelling force field!')
show()
```

I used the function `meshgrid(x, y)`, which generates two matrices: the first is a matrix of repeating values of x, and the second is a matrix of repeating values of y. The output is used to plot the quiver, shown in Figure 6-16. I then updated the axis to reflect the proper ranges.

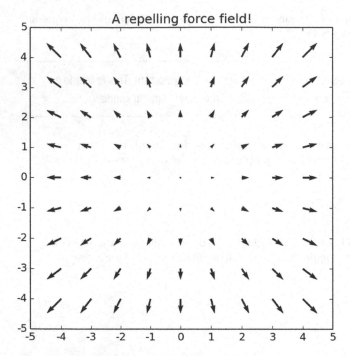

Figure 6-16. *A quiver plot depicting a force field*

Example: A Contour Plot

A contour plot (also known as a contour map) is a plot composed of contour lines. Each contour line joins points of equal value. Examples of contour plots include topographical maps that describe valleys and hills, and meteorological maps that show isobars (lines of equal pressure).

To generate contour plots, you need a matrix corresponding to the function z=f(x, y), where x and y are the independent variables (e.g., latitude and longitude on topographical maps), and z is the function value (e.g., height, in topographical maps).

In the following example, I generate values of x from -5 to 5 with a call to x = arange(-5, 5, 0.1). I do the same with y values. However, the function z=f(x, y) requires a matrix, whereas x and y are vectors. So the next step involves creating a grid from x and y. This is done with a call to u, v = meshgrid(x, y); u corresponds to the x values, while v corresponds to the y values. The beauty of using a grid is that now I can write functions as I normally would—in math. For example, a unit sphere's equation is x²+y²+z²=1, and the half top unit sphere is $z = \sqrt{(1-x^2-y^2)}$. This translates to z = sqrt(1-u**2-v**2) in Python, but you'll have to take care of the square root of negative values (see the "Example: A Non-Rectangular Contour Plot" section later in this chapter). In the contour example, I've chosen an interesting function: z = 2*u**2+v**2-u*v+10*u. Listing 6-14 shows the code and the resulting contour plot.

Listing 6-14. A Contour Map

```
from pylab import *

x = arange(-5, 5, 0.1)
y = arange(-5, 5, 0.1)
u, v = meshgrid(x, y)
```

```
z = 2*u**2+v**2-u*v+10*u
contour(x, y, z, 10)
title('A contour map')
show()
```

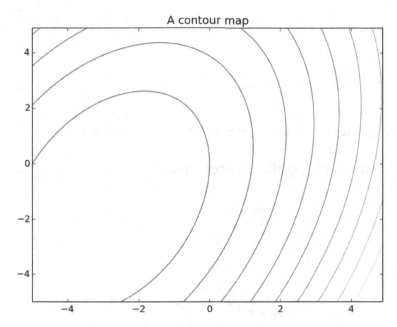

Figure 6-17. *A contour map of the function, z=2x²+y²-xy+10x*

Example: A Non-Rectangular Contour Plot

What if your grid data in the preceding example is not a rectangle? Suppose it's a trapezoid or a circle. In that case, how would you go about generating a contour plot? The trick is to generate an enclosing rectangular grid and set the values that are outside your region of interest to None.

The code in Listing 6-15 generates a filled contour plot using the function contour(). The listing shows both a rectangular grid and a non-rectangular grid of the contours of a sphere. Negative values of $z^2=1-x^2-y^2$ are outside the sphere, and they are either set to zero or not plotted.

Listing 6-15. A Filled Contour Map of a Sphere with a Rectangular Grid and a Non-Rectangular Grid

```
from pylab import *

x = linspace(-1.5, 1.5, 1000)
y = linspace(-1.5, 1.5, 1000)
u, v = meshgrid(x, y)

subplot(2, 2, 1)
z = 1-u**2-v**2
z[nonzero(z<0)] = 0
contourf(x, y, sqrt(z), 10)
```

```
title('A contour map')
axis('equal')
axis('off')

subplot(2, 2, 2)
z = 1-u**2-v**2
z[nonzero(z<0)] = None
contourf(x, y, sqrt(z), 10)
title('Non-rectangular contour map')
axis('equal')
axis('off')
show()
```

Notice how I've used the function nonzero() to set the values of z to either 0 or None per the required grid.

A contour map   Non-rectangular contour map

Figure 6-18. *A filled contour map of a sphere with a rectangular grid (left) and a non-rectangular grid (right)*

Getting and Setting Values

As you start plotting and generating visual output, you'll find that you're using more and more of the "helper" functions, functions that don't necessarily plot the data, but instead control the graph behavior and arrange labels just the way you want them.

So far we've used two methods to modify a plot behavior. One used dedicated functions like axis(), xlim(), and ylim() to control the plot ranges. The other method passed arguments to functions, such as the rotation argument in the text() function.

A third method is available, one that uses the object-oriented design of *matplotlib*. It involves two functions, setp() and getp(), that retrieve and set a *matplotlib* object's parameters. The benefit of using setp() and getp() is that automation is easily achieved.

Up to this point, we've suppressed the output from *matplotlib*, so that the interactive scripts would be easier to follow. But now let's look at those outputs. Whenever you issue a plot() command, *matplotlib* returns a *list* of *matplotlib* objects. This is important; the return value from calling plot() is a list of objects, not the *matplotlib* object itself, even if you only have one line to plot:

```
>>> from pylab import *
>>> p = plot(arange(5))
```

```
>>> type(p)
```

```
<class 'list'>
```

```
>>> type(p[0])
```

```
<class 'matplotlib.lines.Line2D'>
```

The function setp(matobj) prints a list of properties you can set for matobj, where matobj is a *matplotlib* object. The function accepts either a list of *matplotlib* objects or just one object:

```
>>> setp(p[0])
```

```
agg_filter: unknown
alpha: float (0.0 transparent through 1.0 opaque)
animated: [True | False]
antialiased or aa: [True | False]
axes: an :class:`~matplotlib.axes.Axes` instance
clip_box: a :class:`matplotlib.transforms.Bbox` instance
clip_on: [True | False]
```

(Note that additional output of setp() was suppressed.)
If you're not sure of what values a parameter can take, issue setp(p, 'param'):

```
>>> setp(p[0], 'visible')
```

```
visible: [True | False]
```

To hide the plot, you could issue the following:

```
>>> setp(p[0], visible=False)
```

Or you could set the label associated with a line by issuing the following:

```
>>> setp(p[0], label='Line1')
>>> legend()
```

The function setp() also accepts lists of *matplotlib* objects, in which case all the *matplotlib* objects in the list will be set.

■ **Note**   To query acceptable parameters, enclose the parameter to be queried in quotes: setp(p, 'linewidth').
To set a parameter value, do not include the quotes, but do use an assignment: setp(p, linewidth=4).

Similarly, to retrieve values, use the getp() function. The function getp() is a little less forgiving in that it requires one *matplotlib* object, not a list of objects. The variable p that we've been using up to this point is really a list of one *matplotlib* object, so we need to index it:

```
>>> getp(p[0], 'linewidth')
```

```
1.0
```

Setting Figure and Axis Parameters

In the preceding examples, we stored the return value from the call to the function plot(), which is a *matplotlib* object of a line. Specifically, we stored the line we drew—well, a list containing one line. But how do we modify the behavior of the figure or the axis?

The function gcf() returns a handle to the current figure. The function gca() returns a handle to the current axis. Armed with these, we can now modify the axis and figure parameters.

To set the y label, instead of calling ylabel('Y value'), we could issue this command:

```
>>> setp(gca(), ylabel='Y value')
```

But what are the benefits of using setp() in this manner over simply calling ylabel()? The answer is automation. Let's turn to an example.

Example: Modifying Subplot Parameters

Suppose you'd like to write a function that receives a figure number and then modifies all the subplot titles in the figure (if they exist) to numbered titles. For example, for a figure of 2-by-2 subplots in use, you'd like the subplot titles to be from 1 to 4 (if they all exist). In this case, you don't know in advance how many subplots are in a figure.

This is an ideal case for using setp() and getp(), as demonstrated in Listing 6-16.

Listing 6-16. Numbering Subplots

```
from pylab import *
def number_subplots(fignum):
    """Numbers the subplots in a figure."""

    # switch to the requested figure
    figure(fignum)

    fig = gcf()

    for i, fig_axe in enumerate(getp(fig, 'axes')):
        fig_axe.set_title(str(i+1))

    axis()
show()
```

There are a few things to keep in mind regarding the function, number_subplots(). First, we set the focus to the figure we'd like to work on by calling figure(fignum). Next, we retrieve a handle to the figure with gcf(). The following step assumes some knowledge of the *matplotlib* object structure. But even if you're not familiar with the structure, it's pretty simple to figure out what's going on by exploring the objects. To illustrate this, create a simple figure with two empty subplots:

```
>>> figure()
>>> ax1 = subplot(2, 1, 1)
>>> ax2 = subplot(2, 1, 2)
```

Now retrieve the current figure properties with getp(gcf()):

```
>>> getp(gcf())
```

```
agg_filter = None
alpha = None
animated = False
axes = [<matplotlib.axes.AxesSubplot object at 0x00000000...
children = [<matplotlib.patches.Rectangle object at 0x0000000...
```

(I've removed the extra output lines as they're not important for the discussion.)

Now look closely at two properties: axes and children. The parameter axes hold a list of values, and the parameter children holds another list of values. Further examination shows that the axes objects are all contained within the children values. In reality, these are the two axes for the two subplots. So, to get a list of these, we can simply call getp(gcf(), 'axes'), as the code indeed does. We then set the titles and call the axis() function to force a redraw.

There's a caveat in the implementation of the function number_subplots(): numbering is performed in accordance with the creation of the subplots. That is, if the bottom-left subplot was created before the top-left subplot, it will have the smaller title value associated with it and not the regular subplot numbering (left to right, top to bottom). If you'd like to change this, you'll have to look at the positions of the subplots and assign numbers accordingly. This is somewhat more complex and not all that educational, so I've opted to leave it out of the discussion.

A lot of the parameters that are accessible via setp() and getp() are also accessible by means of dedicated functions. Instead of setting the y-axis label parameter with setp(), you can call the ylabel() function. When possible, I prefer using the function version over setp() and getp() because I think it's easier to follow.

Exploring the *matplotlib* object through the dir() built-in function is also a very good method for probing the capabilities of a *matplotlib* object. Most of the functions are self-explanatory and let you set and retrieve values associated with a *matplotlib* object. If you're not sure, use the help() function in an interactive Python session. Based on a partial comparison, I've determined that *matplotlib* object methods are equivalent to the properties available with getp() and setp(). This means you can use either:

```
>>> matobj = gcf()
>>> [func for func in dir(matobj) if func.startswith('get')]
```

```
['get_agg_filter', 'get_alpha', 'get_animated', 'get_axes', 'get_children',
 'get_clip_box', 'get_clip_on', 'get_clip_path', 'get_contains',
 'get_default_bbox_extra_artists', 'get_dpi', 'get_edgecolor', 'get_facecolor',
 'get_figheight', 'get_figure', 'get_figwidth', 'get_frameon', 'get_gid',
 'get_label', 'get_path_effects', 'get_picker', 'get_rasterized',
 'get_size_inches', 'get_sketch_params', 'get_snap', 'get_tight_layout',
 'get_tightbbox', 'get_transform', 'get_transformed_clip_path_and_affine',
 'get_url', 'get_visible', 'get_window_extent', 'get_zorder']
```

A final note: working with setp() and getp() or the set and get methods of the *matplotlib* object is an advanced topic. These functions allow more exact control of the behavior of plots and graphs, but they are not easy to master. Moreover, they require a good understanding of the *matplotlib* object hierarchy. Regardless of the complexity, I believe this is an important concept. As you draw more graphs and deal with more data, you'll find that the default functionality, although great, isn't *exactly* what you want. And in these cases, turning to setp() and getp() is a good option. At this point, I hope you've seen enough of their benefits and how to use them that you will feel comfortable experimenting on your own.

Patches

So far we've worked with text and lines, which are both implemented as *matplotlib* objects. But sometimes those two objects are not enough. A third object, the patch, allows us to draw other types of shapes that don't necessarily fall under the category of a line or text.

To work with patches, you assign them to an already existing graph because, in a sense, patches are "patched" on top of a figure. Table 6-6 gives a partial listing of available patches. In this table, the notation xy indicates a list or tuple of (x, y) values.

Table 6-6. *Available Patches*

Patch	Description
Arrow(x, y, dx, dy)	An arrow, starting at location (x, y) and ending at location (x+dx, y+dy)
Circle(xy, r)	A circle centered at xy and radius r
Ellipse(xy, w, h, angle)	An ellipse centered at xy, of width w, height h, and rotated angle degrees
Polygon([xy1, xy2, xy3,...])	A polygon made of vertices specified by xy points
Wedge(xy, r, theta1, theta2)	A wedge (part of a circle) centered at xy, of radius r, starting at angle theta1 and ending at angle theta2
Rectangle(xy, w, h)	A rectangle, starting at xy, of width w and height h

To use patches, follow these steps:

1. Draw a graph.

2. Create a patch object.

3. Attach the patch object to the figure using the add_patch() function.

■ **Note** This might seem like considerable effort to add an arrow patch, for example; however, these three steps can be folded neatly into one line. To draw an arrow from (0, 0) to (1, 1), issue gca().add_patch(Arrow(0, 0, 1, 1)).

Example: Adding Arrows to a Graph

In this example, we'll draw a graph and connect every two points on the graph with an arrow.

First draw a simple graph:

```
>>> x = arange(10)
>>> y = x**2
>>> plot(x, y)
```

Now create a list of all the arrows:

```
>>> arrows = [(x0, y0, dx, dy) for (x0, y0, dx, dy) in \
... zip(x, y, diff(x), diff(y))]
```

The next part is a bit tricky. First, the function `diff()` creates a difference of every two elements in a vector. For example, `diff([1, 2, 3, 30])` is `[1, 1, 27]`. This is exactly what we need for our dx and dy values for the `Arrow()` function. Second, we combine x, y, dx, and dy using the `zip()` function and return a list of tuples by using a list comprehension. Luckily for us, `zip()` uses the shortest vector, so even though `diff()` vectors are shorter by 1, it's not an issue.

Now all that's left is to iterate through the list comprehension and attach an arrow to the graph:

```
>>> cur_axes = gca()
>>> for x0, y0, dx, dy in arrows:
...     cur_axes.add_patch(Arrow(x0, y0, dx, dy))
>>> title('Arrows!')
>>> show()
```

Figure 6-19 shows the added arrows.

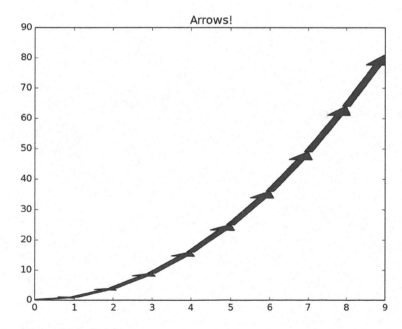

Figure 6-19. *Patching arrows*

Needless to say, `Arrow()` (and other patches) can be customized considerably; you can adjust color, length, width, and more.

Example: Some Other Patches

The code in Listing 6-17 generates a list of patch objects and attaches them to a figure. The figure is originally empty.

Listing 6-17. Some Patches

```
from pylab import *

# Import Ellipse and Wedge to current namespace
from matplotlib.patches import Ellipse, Wedge

# a list of some patches
my_patches = [
    Arrow(0, 4, 0, -4, facecolor='g'),
    Circle([-2, 2], 1.5, linewidth=4, fc='orange'),
    Ellipse([2, 3], 4, 1, 45.0, edgecolor='r'),
    Polygon([[4, 2], [3, 3], [1, -1], [3, -1]], ls='dashed', fill=False),
    Wedge([-1, 0], 3, 200, 300, fc='m', ec='m'),
    Rectangle([1, -2], 3, -2, fill=False, lw=5, ec='r')
    ]

# draw a figure
figure()
axis([-5, 5, -5, 5])

# add the patches
cur_ax = gca()
for p in my_patches:
    cur_ax.add_patch(p)

title('Patches')
show()
```

Figure 6-20 shows the results of the code in Listing 6-17.

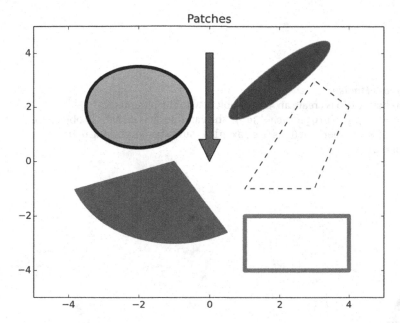

Figure 6-20. *Some patches*

The patch objects `Ellipse` and `Wedge` are not automatically imported to the current namespace when you issue `from pylab import *` (unlike Arrow, Circle, Polygon, and Rectangle). Therefore, I've manually imported them to the namespace with the statement `from matplotlib.patches import Ellipse, Wedge`.

I've also passed arguments to the patches to show how to use them: `facecolor` (or `fc`), `edgecolor` (or `ec`), `linestyle` (or `ls`), `linewidth` (or `lw`), and `fill`.

3D Plots

In the first edition of this book, *matplotlib* did not support 3D plots. With newer versions of *matplotlib* also came 3D plots via the *mplot3d* toolkit (see `http://matplotlib.org/mpl_toolkits/mplot3d/tutorial.html`), which is part of *matplotlib*.

Continuing with our sphere from the "Example: A Contour Plot" section, we now turn to drawing an actual 3D plot of the sphere. The function `plot_surface()` plots a surface in 3D (see Listing 6-18).

Listing 6-18. A 3D Surface Plot of a Sphere

```
from pylab import *
from mpl_toolkits.mplot3d import Axes3D

x = linspace(-1, 1, 100)
y = linspace(-1, 1, 100)
u, v = meshgrid(x, y)

fig = figure()
z = 1-u**2-v**2
z[nonzero(z<0)] = 0
```

```
ax = fig.gca(projection='3d')
ax.plot_surface(u, v, z)
title('A sphere on a plane')
show()
```

After the *PyLab* import, I import the *mplot3d* toolkit.

To generate a 3D plot, the first thing you have to do is create an Axed3D object with the parameter, projection='3d'. You do this in the line, ax = fig.gca(projection='3d'). The variable ax is an Axes3D object; to access the 3D functions, you have to use Axes3D's member functions (e.g., ax.plot_surface() in Listing 6-18).

The resulting 3D plot is shown in Figure 6-21.

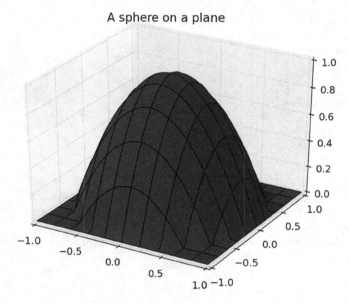

Figure 6-21. *A 3D plot of a sphere on a plane*

Additional 3D plots include contour() and contourf() (simply replace ax.plot_surface() with ax.contour() or ax.contourf() in Listing 6-18). Figure 6-22 shows the 3D contour plots.

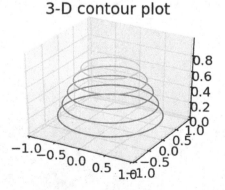  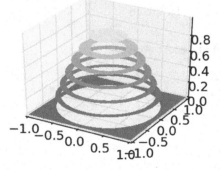

Figure 6-22. *3D contour plots*

The *mplot3d* toolkit also supports plotting 3D line plots (function `plot()`) and scatter plots (function `scatter()`), as shown in Listing 6-19.

Listing 6-19. 3D Line Plots

```
from pylab import *
from mpl_toolkits.mplot3d import Axes3D

N = 50
theta = linspace(0, 2*pi, N)
x = cos(theta)
y = sin(theta)
z = linspace(0, 1, N)

fig = figure()

# first 3D subplot
ax1 = fig.add_subplot(2, 2, 1, projection='3d')
ax1.plot(x, y, z)
title('3D line plot')

# second 3D subplot
ax2 = fig.add_subplot(2, 2, 2, projection='3d')
x = cos(theta) + randn(N)/10
y = sin(theta) + randn(N)/10
z = linspace(0, 1, N)
ax2.scatter(x, y, z)
title('3D scatter plot')
show()
```

In this example I've also introduced 3D subplots. 3D subplots are added with a call to `fig.add_subplot(...,` **projection='3d'**`)`. Notice that to create a 3D subplot, you have to pass the parameter `projection='3d'` when you create the subplot. The results of Listing 6-19 are shown in Figure 6-23.

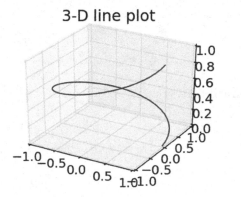
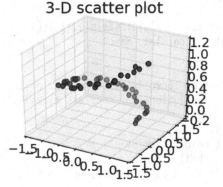

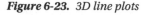
Figure 6-23. *3D line plots*

The Basemap Toolkit

The *basemap* toolkit (see http://matplotlib.org/basemap/) is based on *matplotlib* and enables plotting on 2D data maps in Python. The following section, "Example: French Airports," uses many of *basemap*'s features and should provide enough information to get you up and running with the package. For a full account, refer to *basemap*'s documentation.

Example: French Airports

In this example, I plot the locations of French airports on a map of France. To do this, I use information contained in METAR weather reports. METAR weather reports are used by pilots while preparing for flight. They contain information such as visibility and wind speed. Each station has a designated four-character code, where the two first characters designate the country and the remaining two characters are associated with the airfield. The METAR station codes for France start with LF. For example, LFPB is the station code of the Paris, Le Bourget airport. A full list of these stations is available at the National Center for Atmospheric Research (a direct link: http://weather.rap.ucar.edu/surface/stations.txt). Begin by downloading this file and saving it in the directory, ../data/stations.txt. The code presented in Listing 6-20 assumes the file is available at that directory location. You'll also need to download and install the *basemap* toolkit (http://matplotlib.org/basemap/users/download.html). Refer to Chapter 2 if you require a manual install.

Listing 6-20. French Airports

```
from pylab import *
from mpl_toolkits.basemap import Basemap

# read METAR airport codes, retrieve lat/lon values
airports = {}
metar_codes = open('../data/stations.txt').readlines()
for row in metar_codes:
    code = row[20:24] # METAR code
    if(code.startswith('LF')):
        lat = float(row[39:41])+float(row[42:44])/60
        lon = float(row[47:50])+float(row[51:53])/60
        if(row[53]=='W'): lon = -lon
        if(row[44]=='S'): lat = -lat
        name = row[:20].split('/')[0].strip().title()
        airports[code] = [lon, lat, name]

# draw the map
m = Basemap(llcrnrlon=-5.0, llcrnrlat=41.0, urcrnrlon=10.0, urcrnrlat=51.5,
    projection='merc', resolution='h', suppress_ticks=False)
m.drawcoastlines()
m.bluemarble(scale=0.5)
m.drawmapboundary(fill_color='lightblue')
m.drawcountries(linewidth=1)
m.drawmapscale(-2.0, 41.5, -2.0, 41.5, 500, units='km')
axis('off')

# plot the airports
for site, [lon, lat, name] in airports.items():
    xpt, ypt = m(lon, lat)
```

```
    text(xpt, ypt, ' '+name, va='center', ha='left', fontsize=9,
        color='white')
    plot(xpt, ypt, 'wo')
title('METAR sites in France')
show()
```

First we import *PyLab* and the *basemap* toolkit. Next, we initialize a dictionary object named `airports`. The dictionary object `airports` uses the METAR code as key and a list with the longitude, latitude, and airfield name as a value. We then proceed to read the entire stations.txt file and store it in `metar_codes` variable as a list of strings; each string corresponds to a line in the file. Next, we retrieve the station METAR codes. We do this by slicing each string in `metar_codes` at location 20-24; the value is stored in variable `code`. Since METAR codes for France start with LF (you can verify this by reading the stations. txt file and scrolling to the FRANCE section), we check whether `code` starts with `'LF'`. If it does, we start processing the airfield data. We again use string slicing and convert the strings to float values to store longitude and latitude information. Notice the division by 60; this is needed to translate degrees to fractions of degrees. Also, in case of the Western hemisphere, longitude values are negative; in the case of the Southern hemisphere, latitude values are negative.

Up to this point, I've used basic Python capabilities, but now I will turn to the *basemap* toolkit. First, I create a *basemap* object named `m`, and I initialize that object to show the area of France. The initialization parameter `llcrnrlon` stands for lower-left-corner-longitude; similarly, the initialization parameter `urcrnrlat` stands for upper-right-corner-latitude. I decide on the `'merc'` (Mercator) projection, and that projection determines how to project a sphere (the earth) on a plain (our plot). The full list of projections is available at `http://matplotlib.org/basemap/api/basemap_api.html`. Next, I draw the coastlines (`m.coastlines()`), add blue marble coloring (`m.bluemarble()`), draw the country boundaries (`m.drawmapboundary()`), and then set the map scale to kilometers (`m.drawmapscale()`).

The last part plots the airports in our dictionary object, `airports`. We do this by converting longitude and latitude values with the *basemap* object, `m`, as follows: `xpt, ypt = m(lon, lat)`.

The result is shown in Figure 6-24.

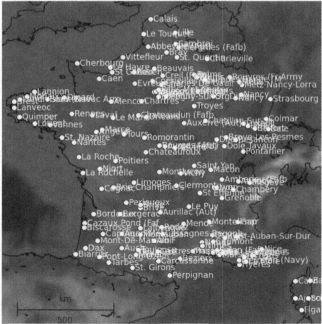

Figure 6-24. *METAR sites in France*

Final Notes and References

We've explored the *matplotlib* package, a rich package that supports plotting in Python. The strong suit of *matplotlib* is that it makes it easy to plot simple and complex graphs with a high number of customization options. If you're not familiar with the package, then try exploring it with IPython's tab completion, complemented by `help()`, trial and error, and the manual. Taken together, these tips should yield excellent results in no time.

The chapter's examples cover a wide range of topics and situations related to graphs and plots. And while your needs may be different, you should now have the tools you need to explore the *matplotlib* package on your own.

The *matplotlib* web site is an excellent source of information, and I encourage you to explore it and learn more about the package:

- The *matplotlib* website, `http://matplotlib.org/`

- The *Mplot3d* toolkit, `http://matplotlib.org/mpl_toolkits/mplot3d/tutorial.html`

- The *basemap* toolkit, `http://matplotlib.org/basemap/`

## CHAPTER 7

Math Games

Preprocessing Data Prior to Visualization

Math is a fundamental tool in data visualization. Python provides outstanding math support, which makes it an ideal development environment for performing analysis prior to visualization. Python's interactive nature makes manipulating data and observing intermediate results easy. Python also makes it easy to modify results and quickly plot them. Another reason I like using Python for data visualization: there are a wide range of popular, freely available, mature numerical packages. Lastly, Python is structured, allowing the development of production-level code for generating quality reports.

In this chapter, we'll explore Python's math capabilities, including its built-in modules *math*, *cmath*, *random*, *decimal* and *fractions*. We'll also look at *NumPy*, an excellent package we'll use extensively (and one we've used in previous chapters). *NumPy* provides powerful n-dimensional arrays, vector and matrix arithmetic, linear algebra, and much more.

Modules *math* and *cmath*

Python provides two flavors of math modules: *math* and *cmath*. The *math* module has functions that are common to most programming languages and essentially uses the C math function calls. Functions from the module *math* return floating point numbers. In the case of improper arguments, an error will be raised:

```
>>> import math
>>> math.sqrt(-1)
```

```
Traceback (most recent call last):
  File "<stdin>", line 1, in <module>
ValueError: math domain error
```

Module *cmath* returns complex results:

```
>>> import cmath
>>> cmath.sqrt(-1)
```

1j

Complex numbers are supported natively in Python with the complex built-in data type. This is probably a contributing factor to Python's popularity as a platform for numerical computation. The imaginary part of complex number has a trailing "j," as shown in the preceding example. Most arithmetic operations and function calls can be performed on complex numbers.

If you do not require complex number support, opt for using *math* over *cmath*. First, it will provide you with valuable exception information if the parameter to a function is out of the domain, as shown previously. Second, *cmath* always returns complex results, even if the results can be represented as noncomplex numbers, in which case the imaginary value will be zero. Lastly, some functions are available in the *math* module only, as listed in Table 7-1.

Table 7-1. *Functions Available Only in the math Module*

Function	Description	Example
atan2(y, x)	Returns the arc tangent of y/x, taking into account the signs and division by zero.	atan2(2, 0) returns 1.5707963267948966 ($\pi/2$). atan2(-1, -1) returns –2.356194490192345 ($-3\pi/4$).
ceil(x)	Returns the smallest integer greater than or equal to x.	ceil(2.5) returns 3. ceil(-2.5) returns -2.
degrees(x)	Convert from radians to degrees.	degrees(1) returns 57.29577951308232.
erf(x)	Returns the error function at x.	erf(2) returns 0.9953222650189527.
erfc(x)	Returns the complementary error function at x.	erfc(2) returns 0.004677734981047268.
expm1(x)	Returns ex-1; avoids loss of precision for small values of x.	expm1(0.01) returns 0.010050167084168057.
factorial(x)	Returns x!	factorial(5) returns 120.
floor(x)	Returns the largest integer less than or equal to x.	floor(2.5) returns 2. floor(-2.5) returns -3.
fabs(x)	Returns the absolute value of x.	fabs(-2.5) returns 2.5.
fmod(x, y)	Returns the remainder of x divided by y.	fmod(2.5, 2) returns 0.5. fmod(-2.5, 2) returns -0.5. fmod(2.5, -2) returns 0.5. fmod(-2.5, -2) returns -0.5.
frexp(x)	Returns the exponent, e, and mantissa, m, such that x=m·2^e.	frexp(2.5) returns (0.625, 2). frexp(-2.5) returns (-0.625, 2).
fsum(iterable)	Returns the sum of the items in iterable.	fsum([0.1, 1.2, -0.6]) returns 0.7.
gamma(x)	Returns the Gamma function at x.	gamma(6) returns 120.
hypot(x, y)	Returns $\sqrt{(x^2+y^2)}$.	hypot(3, 4) returns 5.0.
ldexp(m, e)	Returns m·2^e.	ldexp(0.625, 2) returns 2.5. ldexp(-0.625, 2) returns -2.5.
lgamma(x)	Returns the natural logarithm of the absolute value of the Gamma function at x.	lgamma(6) returns 4.787491742782047.
log1p(x)	Returns the natural logarithm of 1+x; avoids loss of precision for small values of x.	log1p(0.01) returns 0.009950330853168083.

(*continued*)

Table 7-1. (*continued*)

Function	Description	Example
log2(x)	Returns base 2 logarithm of x.	log2(10) returns 3.321928094887362.
modf(x)	Returns the integer and fractional parts of x.	modf(2.5) returns (0.5, 2.0). modf(-2.5) returns (-0.5, -2.0).
pow(x, y)	Returns x^y.	pow(2, 3) returns 8.
radians(x)	Convert from degrees to radians.	radians(1) returns 0.017453292519943295.
trunc(x)	Truncates digits after the decimal point; the return value is an integer.	trunc(2.5) returns 2. trunc(-2.5) returns -2.

The behavior of some of the functions listed in Table 7-1 is different in Python 3.x and Python 2.x. In Python 2.x, the return type is typically a float (even though the actual value is an integer value, it's represented as a float). In Python 3.x, if it's possible to return an integer, the return value is of type int.

For example, In Python 2.7.6, the return type of ceil() is a float:

```
>>> from math import ceil
>>> ceil(2.5)
```

```
3.0
```

```
>>> type(ceil(2.5))
```

```
<type 'float'>
```

Whereas, in Python 3.3.5, the return value of ceil() is an int:

```
>>> from math import ceil
>>> ceil(2.5)
```

```
3
```

```
>>> type(ceil(2.5))
```

```
<class 'int'>
```

Most power, logarithmic, trigonometric, and hyperbolic functions are available in both *math* and *cmath* modules (see Table 7-2). The exceptions are the functions atan2(x, y), hypot(x, y), expm1(x), log1p(x), log2(x) and pow(x, y). These are available only in *math* because they have limited usefulness in complex math.

Table 7-2. *Power, Logarithmic, Trigonometric, and Hyperbolic Functions in the math and cmath Modules*

Function	Description	Example (math)	Example (cmath)
Power			
exp(x)	e^x.	exp(1) returns 2.718281828459045 (e)	exp(pi*1j) returns -1.
sqrt(x)	Square root of x.	sqrt(4) returns 2.0.	sqrt(2j) returns (1+1j).
Logarithmic			
log(x[, base])	Logarithms of x; if base is not specified, defaults to natural logarithms.	log(16, 2) returns 4.0.	log(-1) returns 3.141592653589793j (jπ).
log10(x)	Logarithms of x, base 10.	log10(3) returns 0.47712125471966244.	log10(-1) returns 1.3643763538418412j.
Trigonometric			
sin(x), cos(x), tan(x)	Sine, cosine, and tangent of x.	sin(pi/2) returns 1.0.	cos(1j) returns (1.5430806348152437-0j).
asin(x), acos(x), atan(x)	Arc sine, arc cosine, and arc tangent of x.	asin(1) returns 1.5707963267948966 (π/2).	acos(2) returns 1.3169578969248166j.
Hyperbolic			
sinh(x), cosh(x), tanh(x)	Hyperbolic sine, cosine, and tangent of x.	cosh(0) returns 1.0.	sinh(1j*pi) returns 0.
Constants			
e	2.718281828459045	--	--
pi	3.141592653589793	--	--

FUNCTION ATAN2

Function atan2(y, x) is very useful because it maintains the angle values of a point in a plane, as shown previously in Chapter 1. That is, if x and y represent coordinates in a plane, atan2(y, x) returns the angle from the origin, (0,0). Consider the point located at (1, 1): its angle is 45 degrees (π/4), and point (−1,−1) has an angle of -135 degrees (or 225 degrees). If you were to use atan(y/x), both points (1, 1) and (−1,−1) would yield 45 degrees, losing quadrant information. However, if you use atan2(), the correct values are returned.

A side benefit of atan2(y, x) is that it properly calculates the angle when x is zero, whereas atan(y/x) would raise an exception. Function atan2() is not particularly useful in complex math because values already represent Cartesian points.

Example: Mandelbrot Set

Probably the best known mathematical visualizations, fractals are used by scientists to investigate chaotic systems: systems whose state over time is highly dependent on initial conditions. In the example that follows, we'll use complex math to create a fractal depicting the Mandelbrot set. Along the way, we'll see the capabilities of Python's complex math and explore some ways to visualize data other than a regular plot; fractals and Python are a perfect match.

To generate this fractal, we ask whether repeatedly issuing the operation z=z**2+c for some c, a complex number, generates a bound sequence or not. A bound sequence contains values that are lower than a fixed value, which is 2 in the example. If the sequence is not bound, we write down at point c in the complex plane the number of iterations it took us to decide that the sequence is not bound. Finally, we show the image that originates.

Let's do a manual run:

```
>>> c=0.4+1j*0.5
>>> z=0
>>> z=z**2+c; print(z, abs(z))
```

```
(0.4+0.5j) 0.6403124237432849
```

```
>>> z=z**2+c; print(z, abs(z))
```

```
(0.31000000000000005+0.9j) 0.9518928511129812
```

```
>>> z=z**2+c; print(z, abs(z))
```

```
(-0.31389999999999996+1.0580000000000003j) 1.1035838028894773
```

```
>>> z=z**2+c; print(z, abs(z))
```

```
(-0.6208307900000004-0.16421240000000004j) 0.64218111318053
```

```
>>> z=z**2+c; print(z, abs(z))
```

```
(0.7584651574982646+0.7038962280395922j) 1.0347653332940918
```

```
>>> z=z**2+c; print(z, abs(z))
```

```
(0.4797994952905018+1.5677615269249674j) 1.6395376668399924
```

```
>>> z=z**2+c; print(z, abs(z))
```

```
(-1.827668649625085+2.0044223787089317j) 2.7125784348275634
```

I started by picking an arbitrary point c=0.4+1j*0.5 and then setting the initial value of z to zero. Next, I repeatedly issued the command z=z**2+c and printed the absolute value of z, abs(z). As you can see, the values of abs(z) got increasingly larger; and after the seventh iteration, the value was greater than 2. That means that at the point (0.4, 0.5),

I'll write 7 as the value. If you continue to map out the points c, you'll eventually get the Mandelbrot set fractal (see Figure 7-1). The example requires the *Pillow* module (see Chapter 2 on installing it). Here's the complete listing:

Listing 7-1. mandelbrot.py

```python
from PIL import Image, ImageOps

# creates an image of the Mandelbrot set
res = 400
iters = 200

img = Image.new("L", (res, res), 255)
for im in range(res):
    for re in range(res):
        z = 0
        # a scaling to show the "interesting" part of the Mandelbrot fractal
        c = (re*2/res-1.5)+1j*(im*2/res-1)
        for k in range(iters):
            z = z**2+c
            if abs(z)>2:
                img.putpixel((re, im), 255-k*255/iters)
                break

# create a uniform distribution of gray levels
img = ImageOps.equalize(img)

# save to file
img.save('../images/mandelbrot_%d_%d.png' % (iters, res), dpi=(150,150))
```

Figure 7-1. *A Mandelbrot set, 1000 iterations*

We use the Python Imaging Library, *Pillow* (formerly PIL), to draw the fractal. We start by importing two modules from the package: *Image* and *ImageOps*. From the *Image* module, we use Image.new() to create a new image and Image.putpixel(), to write a single pixel to the image at a specified location. Finally, we use Image.save() to write the image to file. From the *ImageOps* module, we use ImageOps.equalize() to create a uniform distribution of the gray levels, so the fractal image really pops out (see Chapter 9 for a detailed discussion of the *Pillow* package).

We start by creating a gray-level image of size res specifying the fractal's resolution. We then code Mandelbrot's set with a for loop and an if statement to check for convergence. Next, we draw a rectangular area, from -1.5 to 0.5 in the x-axis and from -1 to 1 in the y-axis. You can see this in the line, c = (re*2/res-1.5)+1j*(im*2/res-1). Interesting fractals occur when you zoom in on different areas, so try and look them up.

Next, we map the number of iterations to a specific level of gray. The idea is that k=0 iterations map to 255 (white), whereas k=iters iterations map to the value zero (black). We do this by writing the value 255-k*255/iters to the pixel. Different values for the number of iterations generate interesting results (see Figure 7-2).

Figure 7-2. *A collage of Mandelbrot set fractals with several values for the number of iterations*

Example: A Newton Fractal

With Python and a bit more complex math, you also can create fractals with the Newton-Raphson method, which is also known as Newton's method. Newton's method is an iterative procedure to find numerical solutions, or roots, to an equation of the form f(z) = 0 using an initial guess. One of the characteristics of the method is that, in the case of several solutions, you cannot tell in advance, based on the initial guess, what the converged solution will be (usually). If you were to map out the initial guesses based on the solution, you would find they converge to results in an image known as a Newton's fractal, which is geometrically interesting.

■ **Note** If you'd like to read more about Newton's method, have a look at
`http://en.wikipedia.org/wiki/Newton%27s_method`; there's a lot of additional information available on the Internet.

The function we'll map is f(z) = z**4 + 1. This function has four roots:

```
>>> from cmath import pi, cos, sin
>>> solutions = [ cos((2*n+1)*pi/4) + \
... 1j*sin((2*n+1)*pi/4) for n in range(4)]
```

We can use this statement to verify that these are indeed solutions to the equation:

```
>>> from pprint import pprint
>>> pprint([ z**4 for z in solutions])
```

```
[(-1+4.440892098500626e-16j),
 (-1+4.440892098500626e-16j),
 (-1.0000000000000004+6.661338147750941e-16j),
 (-1+8.881784197001252e-16j)]
```

The imaginary parts are on the order of scale of 10^{-16} and are due to inaccuracies of the trigonometric functions, π, and the floating point representation; the imaginary parts are actually zero.

Newton's method takes an initial guess and calculates the next guess by applying the equation z(n+1) = z(n) – f(z(n)) / f'(z(n)), where f'(z) is the derivative of f(z). In our case, f(z)/f'(z) is z-(z**4+1)/(4*z**3). To check whether the new value is a "good" solution, we reapply it to the original equation and check how close it is to zero. We implement this by checking whether the absolute value is less than delta, a predefined small value. The number of iterations is an indication of how fast the solution was reached. We'll use this to select the color depth of each solution; solutions that converged fast will be brighter. Once our guess converges, we check what solution it converged to and color it accordingly. Since there are four solutions, there will be four colors (at varying color depths) in the fractal. Listing 7-2 generates the example Newton's fractal in the region (0, 0)-(1, 1).

Listing 7-2. newton.py

```
from PIL import Image
from cmath import *

# creates a z**4+1 = 0 fractal using the Newton-Raphson
# root finding method
delta      = 0.000001   # convergence criteria
res        = 800        # image size
iters      = 30         # number of iterations
```

```
# create an image to draw on, paint it black
img = Image.new("RGB", (res, res), (0, 0, 0))

# these are the solutions to the equation z**4+1 = 0 (Euler's formula)
solutions = [cos((2*n+1)*pi/4)+1j*sin((2*n+1)*pi/4) for n in range(4)]
colors = [(1, 0, 0), (0, 1, 0), (0, 0, 1), (1, 1, 0)]

for re in range(res):
    for im in range(res):
        z = (re+1j*im)/res
        for i in range(iters):
            try:
                z -= (z**4+1)/(4*z**3)
            except ZeroDivisionError:
                # possibly divide by zero exception
                continue
            if(abs(z**4+1)<delta):
                break

        # color depth is a function of the number of iterations
        color_depth = int((iters-i)*255.0/iters)

        # find to which solution this guess converged to
        err = [ abs(z-root) for root in solutions ]
        distances = zip(err, range(len(colors)))

        # select the color associated with the solution
        color = [i*color_depth for i in colors[min(distances)[1]]]
        img.putpixel((re, im), tuple(color))

img.save('../images/newton_z4s_%03d_%03d_%03d.png' % \
    (iters, res, abs(log10(delta))), dpi=(150,150))
```

While the iteration is straightforward, deciding which of the four solutions a specific guess converges to and then mapping to the right color and color depth requires some clarifications.

The colors list is composed of the colors red, green, blue and yellow. Each color is represented by a tuple of Red-Green-Blue (RGB) values:

```
colors = [(1, 0, 0), (0, 1, 0), (0, 0, 1), (1, 1, 0)]
```

The variable color_depth is directly responsible for the color depth (or shade) of the displayed color. For a small number of iterations, color_depth is closer to 255; and for a greater number of iterations, this number is closer to 0, resulting in a brighter color for faster converging points (a smaller number of iterations).

Once color_depth is calculated, we find the solution closest to our converging value. Since we're using complex numbers, the closest value is the one with the minimum distance—or in complex math, the one with the smallest value of err = abs(guess-solution).

To implement this, we generate a list of values corresponding to the distances using a list comprehension. Here's an example using an arbitrary root:

```
>>> from cmath import sqrt
>>> z=sqrt(2)/2*(1+1j)
>>> z
```

```
(0.7071067811865476+0.7071067811865476j)
```

```
>>> err = [abs(z-root) for root in solutions]
>>> err
```

```
[1.1102230246251565e-16, 1.414213562373095, 2.0, 1.4142135623730954]
```

Next, we combine these values with the numbers 0-3, which represent the indices to the colors list, using the zip() function:

```
>>> zip(err, range(len(colors)))
```

```
<zip object at 0x0000000002BFAC08>
```

```
>>> list(_)
```

```
[(1.1102230246251565e-16, 0), (1.414213562373095, 1), (2.0, 2),
(1.4142135623730954, 3)]
```

We then find the minimum error by calling the function min(). To find the correct color, we index the color associated with min(distances)[1], which is the second element in the zipped iterable. Maybe it's easier to show this interactively than to explain:

```
>>> distances = list(zip(err, range(len(colors))))
>>> min(distances)
```

```
(1.1102230246251565e-16, 0)
```

```
>>> min(distances)[1]
```

```
0
```

```
>>> colors[min(distances)[1]]
```

```
(1, 0, 0)
```

■ **Note** I've created a list from the zipped values for display purposes. In the code listing, this isn't necessary.

Finally, we use a list comprehension to multiply the RGB values by the color depth. This is because the putpixel() method requires a tuple detailing the RGB values:

```
color = [i*color_depth for i in colors[min(distances)[1]]]
img.putpixel((re, im), tuple(color))
```

■ **Tip** As you experiment with parameters, you may wish to save some of the outputs. These runs can take a considerable amount of time to complete, so it's a good idea to have different file names for the outputs, as opposed to a single file name. This ensures that files are not accidentally overwritten. The outputs of these runs are dependent on input parameters and the code (e.g., the version of the script) that generated them. Therefore, the notation I've used is one that details all the parameters used to create the output within the file name:

```
'../images/newton_z4s_%03d_%03d_%03d.png' % (iters, res, abs(log10(delta)))
```

■ **Note** An even better approach (one that in this case will somewhat disturb the pleasing output) is annotating the images with text describing the parameters used. And lastly, if you use a version control system (see Chapter 2), the version number of the script that generated the output is a very welcome addition either in the file name or in an image annotation.

Figure 7-3 shows a collage of outputs generated by the script with resolution=200 and values of iters ranging from 1 to 9 (the top left is i = 1; the bottom right is i = 9). We'll touch on collages in Chapter 9.

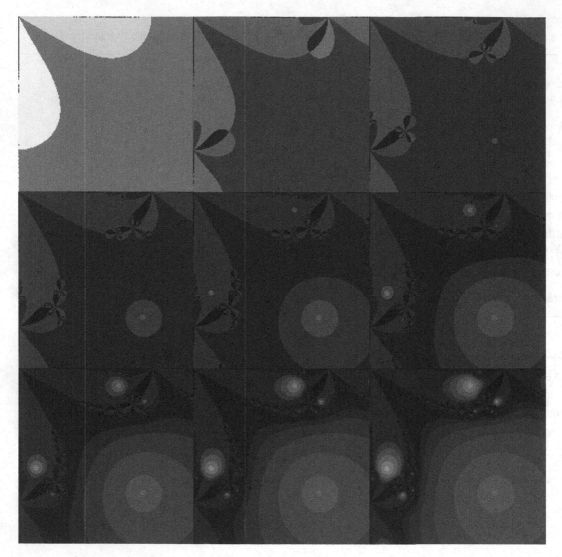

Figure 7-3. *A collage of Newton's fractals with iterations from 1 (top left) to 9 (bottom right)*

Figure 7-4 shows the result of a longer run with `resolution=800` and `iters=30`.

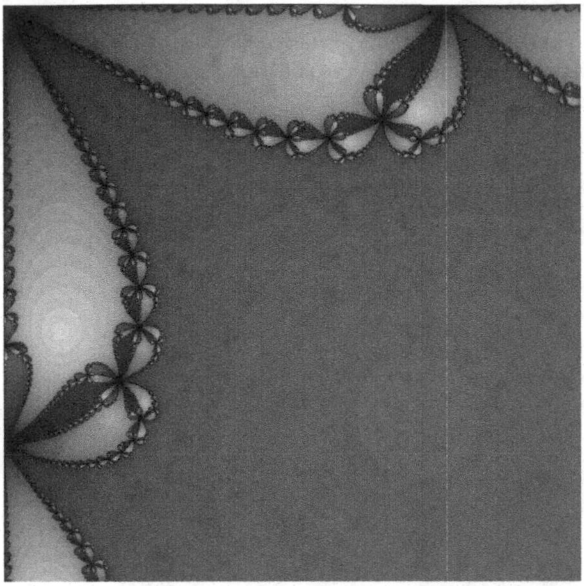

Figure 7-4. *A Newton's fractal with the max number of iterations equaling 30*

■ **Tip** The preceding example explores the region (0, 0) – (1, 1). If you wish to explore around the origin, that is, around (0, 0), change the line `z = (re+1j*im)/res` to `z = ((re-res/2)+1j*(im-res/2))/res`.

Module *decimal*

An interesting module that comes with the Python standard library is the *decimal* module. The module provides support for fixed point and floating point decimals, and it allows arbitrary precision (unlike floating point numbers, which have limited precision). Working with the *decimal* module is a bit less intuitive than regular numbers in Python; however, it's a good option if you require higher precision and are willing to accept some performance loss.

Decimals are generated with the call to `Decimal()`, as follows:

```
>>> from decimal import *
>>> decimal('3.3')
```

```
Decimal('3.3')
```

```
>>> decimal(3.3)
```

```
Decimal('3.29999999999999982236431605997495353221893310546875')
```

The first line creates a decimal with an exact value, 3.3. This is because I've used a string, '3.3'. The second line converts the floating point representation of the number 1/3 to its decimal notation. Usually, you'd want to use strings and not floating point numbers, unless you're converting from floating point numbers to decimals.

You use decimals in the same way you use any other number in Python:

```
>>> a = Decimal('3.3')
>>> a*a
```

```
Decimal('10.89')
```

```
>>> a-13
```

```
Decimal('-9.7')
```

Several mathematical functions are also available to decimals:

```
>>> a = Decimal('3.3')
>>> sqrt(a)
```

```
Decimal('1.816590212458494999253519686')
```

```
>>> exp(Decimal('1'))
```

```
Decimal('2.718281828459045235360287471')
```

For a list of available functions, issue `import decimal`, followed by `dir(decimal)`. For a list of the `Decimal` member functions and attributes, issue `dir(decimal.Decimal)`. You can explore the functions with the `help()` system or the online help available at `https://docs.python.org/3.3/library/decimal.html`.

Module *fractions*

Another interesting module is the *fractions* module, which supports rational number arithmetic. The basic object is the `Fraction` object, which is composed of a numerator and denominator. This object accepts a number of representations, as follows:

```
>>> from fractions import *
>>> fraction(2, 7)
```

```
Fraction(2, 7)
```

```
>>> fraction('2/7')
```

```
Fraction(2, 7)
```

```
>>> fraction(_)
```

```
Fraction(2, 7)
```

```
>>> fraction(1.22)
```

```
Fraction(5494391545392005, 4503599627370496)
```

The first line, Fractions(2, 7) generates a fraction with the numerator 2 and the denominator 7. The second line uses a string to generate a fraction; the third uses another fraction (referred to by _); and finally, the last line uses a floating point number to generate a fraction.

You can use the module to do arithmetic on fractions, as follows:

```
>>> fraction(3, 4)**2
```

```
Fraction(9, 16)
```

```
>>> fraction('3.14')
```

```
Fraction(157, 50)
```

```
>>> fraction(22, 7) - Fraction('3.14')
```

```
Fraction(1, 350)
```

For a list of available functions, issue import fractions, followed by dir(fractions). For a list of the Fraction member functions and attributes, issue dir(fractions.Fraction). You can explore the functions with the help() system or the online help available at https://docs.python.org/3.3/library/fractions.html.

Module *random*

In addition to mathematical functions, Python also provides a rich library for random numbers. Random numbers are important in a variety of software applications. In game programming, random numbers are used to change the behavior of elements in the game to make it more interesting or unpredictable. When writing simulations, random numbers are used to generate data that simulates the real world. Random numbers can also be used to answer probability questions, as you'll soon see.

The *random* module provides random values based on a wide variety of distribution functions, including uniform distribution, Gaussian distribution, and more. The module *random* also supports Python's lists naturally, with *random* functions operating on sequences.

Table 7-3 gives a partial list of some useful random functions.

Table 7-3. *Functions of the Module random*

Function	Description	Example/Note
Integers		
randint(a, b)	Returns a random number between a and b (including a and b).	randint(0, 1) returns 0 or 1 (randomly).
randrange([start,]stop[, step])	Choose a random number from range(start, stop[, step]); does not include the endpoint stop.	randrange(3, 7, 2) returns 3 or 5; 7 is not included.
Floating Point Numbers		
random()	Returns a real value between 0.0 and 1.0 (excluding 1.0).	random() might return 0.11446412321713018.
uniform(a, b)	Returns a real value between a and b (excluding b).	uniform(120, 220) returns a random number between 120 and 220 (excluding 220, excluding rounding).
gauss(u, sigma)	Returns a Gaussian distributed value with u as the mean and sigma as standard deviation.	gauss(1, 2) might return 2.839406209732811.

Module *random* provides several additional random-number distributions, including Log normal and Weibul, to name a couple. Refer to the Python standard library documentation for a full account.

Using Module *random* to Solve Probability Questions

The following examples use the *random* module to solve probability-based questions, numerically.

Example: Hard Disk Head

In this section's first example, we use the *random* module to determine the average distance a hard disk head moves when reading files. We answer the question in two variants. In the first variant, we assume the head moves to the beginning of the hard drive after every read. In the second variant, we assume the head does not move; that is, it stays where it is right after reading the data.

Consider the following (first variant): a hard disk head is normally resting at location 0, representing the start of the disk. Files (of size zero) are evenly distributed between location 0 and 1, where 1 represents the end of the disk. The head is required to access files randomly. After each read, the head returns to location zero. The question is: what is the average distance the head moves?

The answer is not hard: on average, the head moves a distance equivalent to 1. This is because at the lower end, the head starts at location zero and the file requested is also at location zero, meaning the distance travelled is 0. On the upper end, the head starts at location 0 and moves to location 1 and then back again, so the distance travelled is 2. On average, the value is 1. You can easily verify this using a simple script:

```
>>> from random import random
>>> N = 1000 # number of files the head seeks
>>> tot_dist = 0
>>> for i in range(N):
...         tot_dist += random()*2
...
>>> tot_dist/N
```

1.026458180335224

The larger the value of N, the more accurate the result.

Now consider the scenario where the head does not go back to location 0, but instead stays where it is until called on to seek more data (second variant). Finding the average distance the head moves is a bit harder analytically; but numerically, with a simple script, the solution emerges quickly:

```
>>> from random import random
>>> N = 1000 # number of files the head seeks
>>> tot_dist, cur_loc = 0, 0
>>> for i in range(N):
...         new_loc = random()
...         tot_dist += abs(cur_loc-new_loc)
...         cur_loc = new_loc
...
>>> tot_dist/N
```

0.336151105404132

This number turns out to be 1/3.

Example: Friends Meeting

The *random* module is also helpful for probability questions that benefit from visual output. In this example we simulate the timing of two schedules. Although the subject of the example is the arrival of two friends, you could easily apply the same method to the timing of planes, catching a bus, or other converging schedules.

Suppose two friends decide to meet between 8 p.m. and 9 p.m. Once one of the friends arrives at the designated meeting spot, he waits for 10 minutes for his friend to show up. So, if Friend 1 arrives at 8:40, he'll wait until 8:50 for Friend 2 to show up. Friend 1 doesn't know if Friend 2 already showed up earlier (the same is true for Friend 2, he doesn't know if Friend 1 showed up). However, both friends are smart enough to know that if they arrive at 8:55, for example, they only need wait until 9:00 and not 9:05. The question: what's the probability that these two friends meet?

We again turn to the *random* module to help us solve this problem (see Listing 7-3). Only this time, we also visualize the result, hopefully gaining some insight as to how to solve the question analytically.

Listing 7-3. Friends Meeting

```
from random import random
from pylab import *

N    = 40000 # number of events

# generate N events of friends times
friend1, friend2 = [], []
for i in range(N):
    friend1.append(random())
    friend2.append(random())

# find all occurrences of friends meeting
met = array([ (x, y) for (x, y) in zip(friend1, friend2) \
    if abs(y-x) < 1.0/6 ])
not_met = array([ (x, y) for (x, y) in zip(friend1, friend2) \
    if abs(y-x) >=1.0/6 ])

# plot the result, this might shed some light on the problem!
plot(met[:, 0], met[:,1 ], 'y+', mec='y')
plot(not_met[:, 0], not_met[:, 1], 'bo', mec='b')
title("Probability of meeting: %1.3f" % (float(len(met))/N))
xlabel('Time of arrival of Friend 1 [minutes]')
ylabel('Time of arrival of Friend 2 [minutes]')
xticks([n/6 for n in range(7)], [n*10 for n in range(7)])
yticks([n/6 for n in range(7)], [n*10 for n in range(7)])
axis('scaled')
show()
```

The first step is to generate a considerable number of events—40,000 in this case. An event is composed of two numbers: one associated with Friend 1's time of arrival and one associated with Friend 2's time of arrival. We store both their times in lists. The process of generating the events is performed in the first for loop. The function random() returns a value between 0 and 1, which maps to the time of arrival: 0 is 8 p.m., 1 is 9 p.m.

Now that we have a considerable number of events, we ask at what times the friends meet. The friends meet if the difference between their times of arrival is less than 10 minutes, or 10 minutes / 60 minutes * 1.0 = 1/6 (1.0 is the range of random values). But it's also possible that Friend 1 arrives after Friend 2 and not the other way around. Therefore, we should be asking whether friend1–friend2 is less than 1/6, as well as whether friend2–friend1 is less than 1/6. This can be elegantly coded as abs(friend1-friend2) < 1/6.

The actual implementation uses a list comprehension that returns a tuple of (x, y) values that match the condition abs(x-y) < 1/6, which means the friends have met. We then construct an array of these values (a *NumPy* array; more on this shortly) so we can easily access the x and y vectors, without any for loops. We also build a list of times the friends did not meet because we want to plot both, in different colors and markers.

Next, we plot the results and calculate the probability of the friends meeting, numerically, as shown in Figure 7-5.

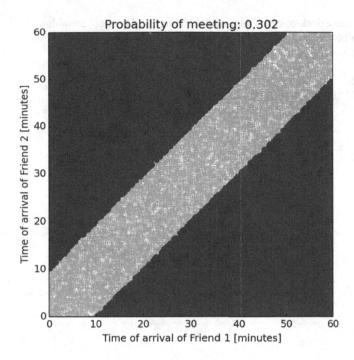

Figure 7-5. *Visualizing friends meeting*

This visualization really helps. The corridor in the middle describes the events corresponding to the two friends meeting. The probability of meeting is the area of this corridor, and it can be calculated by the area of the entire square, minus the area of the top-left triangle and the bottom-right triangle. Each triangle has an area of $0.5 \cdot (5/6)^2$, and the total probability of meeting is $1-(5/6)^2=11/36=0.3055$. This is pretty close to the estimated numerical value (displayed in the figure title).

Random Sequences

The *random* module also offers a set of functions that operate on sequences. These include the functions listed in Table 7-4.

Table 7-4. *Functions from the random Module for Operating on Sequences*

Function	Description
choice(s)	Returns a random element from the sequence s.
shuffle(s)	Shuffles the sequence s.
sample(s, n)	Returns a subsequence of size n from s.

To demonstrate these functions in action, we create a deck-of-cards list using the zip() and range() iterables. Each card is represented as a tuple holding a number between 1 and 13 and a character, 'S', 'H', 'D', and 'C'. These letters correspond to spades, hearts, diamonds, and clubs, respectively:

```
>>> from random import choice, shuffle, sample
>>> cards = list(zip(list(range(1, 14))*4, 'S'*13+'H'*13+'D'*13+'C'*13))
>>> cards[:5]
```

```
[(1, 'S'), (2, 'S'), (3, 'S'), (4, 'S'), (5, 'S')]
```

```
>>> choice(cards)
```

```
(7, 'C')
```

```
>>> shuffle(cards)
>>> cards[:5]
```

```
[(4, 'C'), (10, 'D'), (1, 'C'), (7, 'C'), (12, 'D')]
```

```
>>> sample(cards, 5)
```

```
[(12, 'S'), (12, 'H'), (8, 'C'), (8, 'D'), (5, 'S')]
```

A DECK OF CARDS

You can implement a deck of cards in many ways besides the somewhat tricky method described above. An alternative is to use a double for loop. Not only are for loops more straightforward to implement and read, but you can use full names for the suit of the cards (e.g., 'Spade' instead of 'S'). Or you can use *NumPy*'s ndarray object (discussed in the next section), as in: zip(arange(52)//4+1, 'SHDC'*13).

Which method is best? When deciding this, what should concern you most is the readability of your code. Don't forget that there's a good chance you'll be the person maintaining it, as well. If you're more comfortable with a double for loop, use the for loop approach. If you're more comfortable zipping flat arrays, the options shown in the preceding and following sections are viable approaches. It's a matter of personal preference, as performance is hardly an issue.

That said, you should opt for readability over performance, if possible. After all, Python is a high-level programming language: if you really need code performance, other programming languages might prove a better choice. Even better, you could extend Python with other programming languages.

Module *NumPy*

NumPy's ndarray object is the basic building block for many of the data processing and visualization scripts presented throughout the book. As you've learned in previous chapters, the from pylab import * command imports the *NumPy* package (among others), enabling us to use *NumPy*'s ndarray object without an import call to *NumPy* itself. There's much more to the *NumPy* package, including several functions we'll cover later in this chapter: financial functions, math functions, linear algebra, and more.

NumPy's ndarray object provides substantial added functionality to Python's array object, and it has a lot in common with Matlab's matrix data structure, including matrix operations, linear algebra, signal processing, and more. It also provides the basic building blocks for more complex numerical methods that will be explored in future chapters. "ndarray" stands for N-dimensional array; as its name implies, this object supports N-dimensional arrays. For the remainder of the chapter, I'll use the terms "array" and "ndarray" interchangeably. In both cases I am referring to *NumPy*'s ndarray object—there's little use for Python's array object once *NumPy* is imported.

■ **Note**   *NumPy* is a full and rich package. I will only cover topics that are important for the ideas discussed in the book; and as such, this chapter should be considered a quick introduction to the package. If you'd like to learn more about *NumPy*, consult with the references at the end of the chapter.

Array Creation

Chapter 3 covered Python's built-in data structures, including tuples, lists, and dictionaries. If you recall, there were several methods to create most of these data structures: we've used brackets for lists as well as the list() function, we've used curly braces for dictionaries as well as the dict() function, and so on. Unlike lists, which use the symbols [] to denote a list; and dictionaries, which use the symbols {} to denote dictionaries; *NumPy* arrays have no specific symbol set aside for them. Our options are to use either the array() function or functions that return an ndarray when creating new arrays.

The most straightforward method to create and initialize an array is from a list:

```
>>> from numpy import *
>>> v = array([1, 2])
>>> v
```

```
array([1, 2])
```

```
>>> type(v)
```

```
<class 'numpy.ndarray'>
```

```
>>> m = array([[1, 0],[0, 4]])
>>> m
```

```
array([[1, 0],
       [0, 4]])
```

```
>>> type(m)
```

```
<class 'numpy.ndarray'>
```

Table 7-5 lists several additional array creation methods that are more useful when dealing with larger amounts of data points.

Table 7-5. NumPy's Array Creation Functions

Function	Description	Example
N-Dimensional Arrays		
array(s)	Creates an array based on the sequence s.	array(((1, 2),(3, 4))) returns array([[1, 2], [3, 4]]).
ones(t)	Creates an N-dimensional array initialized with 1s based on the tuple t.	ones(2) returns array([1., 1.]) ones((3,3))) returns array([[1., 1., 1.], [1., 1., 1.], [1., 1., 1.]]).
arange([start,] stop[, step])	Creates an array of values starting at start, ending at (but excluding) stop, and with an increment step. The function arange() can return noninteger values, as well.	arange(1, 2, 0.5) returns array([1., 1.5]).
linspace(start, stop, num=50)	Creates a linearly spaced vector of size num from start to stop including; refer to the interactive help for additional options.	linspace(1, 10, 3) returns array([1., 5.5, 10.]).
logspace(start, stop, num=50)	Similar to linspace(), only values are spaced evenly from 10^{start} to 10^{stop} on a logarithmic scale; refer to the online help for additional options.	logspace(0, 1, 3) returns array([1., 3.16227766, 10.]).

Some additional array creation functions (fromfile(), empty()) exist; but in most cases, you'll find the ones in Table 7-5 sufficient. There's also some redundancy in the functions listed: ones(10) results in the same array as zeros(10)+1.

Slicing, Indexing, and Reshaping

Arrays can be resized using the reshape() and resize() functions, and they can be indexed and sliced using Python's slicing and indexing operators, [] and [:]. The difference between the two functions is that resize() resizes an existing array, whereas reshape() returns a new array based upon the data in the original array:

```
>>> a = arange(12).reshape(4, 3)
>>> a
```

```
array([[ 0,  1,  2],
       [ 3,  4,  5],
       [ 6,  7,  8],
       [ 9, 10, 11]])
```

```
>>> a[1]
```

```
array([3, 4, 5])
```

```
>>> a[-1]
```

```
array([ 9, 10, 11])
```

```
>>> a[1, 1]
```

```
4
```

```
>>> a[:, 1]
```

```
array([ 1,   4,   7, 10])
```

```
>>> a[1, :2]
```

```
array([3, 4])
```

N-Dimensional Arrays

NumPy arrays are N-dimensional arrays, which can be created in the same manner as 1-D and 2-D arrays:

```
>>> ones((2, 3, 4))
```

```
array([[[ 1.,   1.,   1.,   1.],
        [ 1.,   1.,   1.,   1.],
        [ 1.,   1.,   1.,   1.]],

       [[ 1.,   1.,   1.,   1.],
        [ 1.,   1.,   1.,   1.],
        [ 1.,   1.,   1.,   1.]]])
```

A useful operator for N-dimensional arrays is . . ., which means, "all the remaining dimensions" similar to the operator : (colon).
```
>>> a = ones((2, 3, 4))
>>> a
```

```
array([[[ 1.,   1.,   1.,   1.],
        [ 1.,   1.,   1.,   1.],
        [ 1.,   1.,   1.,   1.]],

       [[ 1.,   1.,   1.,   1.],
        [ 1.,   1.,   1.,   1.],
        [ 1.,   1.,   1.,   1.]]])
```

```
>>> a[0,...]
```

```
array([[ 1.,   1.,   1.,   1.],
       [ 1.,   1.,   1.,   1.],
       [ 1.,   1.,   1.,   1.]])
```

```
>>> a[0, 1, ...]
```

```
array([ 1.,   1.,   1.,   1.])
```

How useful are N-dimensional arrays? Some people have little use for N-dimensions, feeling that they do pretty well with one or two dimensions. My experience with N-dimensional arrays is that they provide an excellent data storage when dealing with a combination of several parameters. Consider a simulation with four parameters, each parameter having a range of values. Suppose you want to map out the simulation; that is, you want to calculate the results for every given combination of parameters and also store the results because the running time is long. How would you store the results? One method is to write them to a list, flattening the data. An alternative method is using an N-dimensional array. The following example discusses how to store data as a function of several parameters (typically more than two) using both N-dimensional arrays and flat data structures.

Example: Comparing Mortgages

Since I wrote the first edition of this book, the subprime mortgage crisis has hit the world markets, so I thought it appropriate to give an example that compares different mortgages in this edition. (I'm not financially savvy, so by all means please don't use this as advice in selecting a mortgage!). Let's begin by defining the problem.

Fixed mortgage payments are a function of three parameters: the loan amount (which is also called the present value), the interest rate, and the number of payments. Banks typically have different interest rates as a function of the number of payments, a person's record, and possibly also the loan value. Based on these three parameters (present value, interest rate, and number of payments), we'd like to map out monthly payments—that is, what the expected monthly payment is for every value in the range of parameters.

For this example, assume that we're considering loans in the amounts from $100,000 to $140,000 in increments of $20,000; mortgage interest rates that range from 3 percent to 5 percent in increments of 0.5 percent; and a number of payments that ranges from 60 to 300 in increments of 60 (representing 5 to 25 years in increments of 5 years). We'll use the function pmt(), which is part of the *NumPy* package. The function returns a fixed monthly payment for a fixed-rate mortgage (see http://en.wikipedia.org/wiki/Fixed-rate_mortgage).

We then construct lists representing the range of values we'd like to map out. We implement these lists using the arange() function described previously in this chapter.

THE CONVENIENCE OF USING ARANGE() AND LINSPACE()

Here's another example of why *NumPy* provides convenience over non-math-oriented data structures.
To implement a list of values with noninteger increments, we can use a list comprehension, as in this example:

```
>>> interest_rates = [x/2.0+3 for x in range(5)]
```

While this is perfectly OK, it's less readable than something like this:

```
>>> interest_rates = arange(3.0, 5.5, 0.5)
```

In the former method (using a list comprehension), you'd have to do some math to realize exactly what values are being used. In the second method, they're clearly spelled out: from 3 to 5.5 (excluding 5.5) in increments of 0.5.

I'm assuming the module developer's decision to exclude the edge value (i.e., 5.5, in the above example) in the function arange() is to have it behave in a similar manner to range(). My personal preference would have been to include the edge value.

Alternatively, you could use the linspace() function:

```
>>> interests = linspace(3.0, 5.0, 5)
```

This is awkward in this specific example: the value 5 (the last argument) has to be precalculated to reach an increment of 0.5.

A final note: the values in this mortgage example are annual values; to use them properly you have to divide them by 12 (months) and by 100 (percentage values). Regardless, this is required in both a list comprehension implementation and an arange() implementation. I've left it out, so that the note would be clearer to follow (see the assignment of the variable interests in the code). The ability to multiply (or divide) an array by a value will be shown in the next section.

Next, we iterate over the range of loans, the number of payments, and the interest rates, and then construct a data structure to hold the results: monthly payments. We see the following when we examine the two data structures:

- A flattened list of rows (res1), with each row being a list containing loan size, number of payments, interest rate, and monthly payment. This is a native Python list.

- An N-dimensional array (res2) where each dimension corresponds to a different parameter: loan size, number of payments, interest rate, monthly payment, and cost of loan. This is a 3-D *NumPy* array.

Listing 7-4 compares these two structures.

Listing 7-4. Flattened Data vs. N-Dimensional Data, ndflat.py

```
from numpy import *
loans           = arange(100000, 160000, 20000)
num_payments    = arange(5, 30, 5)*12
interests       = arange(3, 5.5, 0.5)/100.0/12.0

# method 1, storing results in a list
res1 = []
```

```
# method 2, storing results in an array
res2 = zeros([len(loans), len(num_payments), len(interests)])

for i, loan in enumerate(loans):
    for j, num_pay in enumerate(num_payments):
        for k, interest in enumerate(interests):
            res1.append([loan, num_pay, interest, \
                -pmt(interest, num_pay, loan)])
            res2[i][j][k]=-pmt(interest, num_pay, loan)
```

The benefit of using an N-dimensional array is that indexing is a lot easier and faster. For example, assuming loan is fixed and set to 0, the results in the res2 array can be accessed with res2[0, ...]. Achieving the same in a list will probably require iterating over the entire res1 list and comparing the value of the first parameter. There's overhead both in the code and in the actual performance:

```
>>> exec(open('ndflat.py').read())
>>> for row in res1:
...     if(row[0] == 120000 and row[1] == 120):
...         print(row)
...
```

```
[120000, 120, 0.0025000000000000001, 1158.7289363806954]
[120000, 120, 0.0029166666666666668, 1186.6304095428363]
[120000, 120, 0.0033333333333333335, 1214.941657978555]
[120000, 120, 0.0037499999999999999, 1243.6609050842044]
[120000, 120, 0.0041666666666666666, 1272.7861828689065]
```

```
>>> res2[1, 1, ...]
```

```
array([ 1158.72893638,   1186.63040954,   1214.94165798,   1243.66090508,
        1272.78618287])
```

However, the results of the list are much more readable: they show all combinations of parameters in a human readable form. You could do the same with res2, but that requires a for loop:

```
>>> values = res2[1, 1, :]
>>> for i, v in enumerate(values):
...     row = [loans[1], num_payments[1], interests[i], v]
...     print(row)
...
```

```
[120000, 120, 0.0025000000000000001, 1158.7289363806954]
[120000, 120, 0.0029166666666666668, 1186.6304095428363]
[120000, 120, 0.0033333333333333335, 1214.941657978555]
[120000, 120, 0.0037499999999999999, 1243.6609050842044]
[120000, 120, 0.0041666666666666666, 1272.7861828689065]
```

Note that the for loops use enumerate() on the list of values we're iterating over. The reason for this is that *NumPy* arrays require indices (and those are integers), whereas Python lists do not. So in a sense, lists here could be more elegant code-wise (no need to use enumerate()).

Lastly, the list implementation can lend itself very nicely to storage in a CSV file, which is itself a flattened data structure. That said, you could also flatten the array and do the same. Flattening an array can be achieved with an N-dimensional loop or a nested list comprehension. Using our example, the following flattens the 3-dimensional array, res2, using a list comprehension:

```
>>> exec(open('ndflat.py').read())
>>> res2.shape
```

```
(3, 5, 5)
```

```
>>> [n1, n2, n3] = [range(i) for i in res2.shape]
>>> n1, n2, n3
```

```
(range(0, 3), range(0, 5), range(0, 5))
```

```
>>> flat_res2 = [res2[a, b, c] for a in n1 for b in n2 for c in n3]
```

The dimensions of res2 are accessible through res2.shape. We then create three range() iterable objects to iterate over with the line [n1, n2, n3] = [range(i) for i in res2.shape]. Lastly, we use a list comprehension to generate a flattened data structure, in the form of a list, flat_res2.

Although N-dimensional arrays are interesting data structures, most examples in this book are based on 1-D arrays (vectors) and 2-D arrays (matrices), as they cover most anything we might want to do. Even 3-D plots are really represented by 2-D matrices: the indices represent x and y, and the cell value represents z.

Choosing either N-dimensional arrays or flattened data structures is dependent on the exact problem you're trying to solve.

Math Functions

Simple arithmetic operations are possible on arrays, including addition, subtraction, division, multiplication, and exponentiation. You can also use most math functions available in the *math* and *cmath* modules (albeit now they're implemented as part of *NumPy*).

Example: Visualizing Fourier Expansion of a Rectangular Wave

The following example shows a Fourier expansion of a rectangular wave using a sum of sine waves. Fourier expansion is used in numerous applications, ranging from solving differential equations to signal processing. This example will show how we can treat a *NumPy* array as a vector of values and operate on that vector as if it were a function.

The example uses a Fourier expansion of sine waves (*NumPy* arrays) to generate a rectangular wave (another *NumPy* array). Specifically, Listing 7-5 implements the function $4 / (\pi \cdot n) \cdot \sin(2\pi \cdot n \cdot t \cdot N)$, which is a Fourier series expansion of a rectangular wave. The parameter N determines the number of cycles to be expanded, which in the example's case is set to 2, so we can view two cycles. The parameter n determines the frequency of the sine wave; we explore values of n=1, 3, 5 and 7.

Listing 7-5. Visualizing a Fourier Expansion

```
# plots a Fourier expansion of a rectangular wave
from pylab import *

# prepare the plot
figure()
hold(True)

# number of points to display the wave
N = 2**8
t = linspace(0, 1, N)
y = zeros(N)

for n in range(1, 8, 2):
    # the sine waves, added
    y += 4/(pi*n)*sin(2*pi*n*t*2)

    # plot the graph
    plot(t, y)

# annotate the graph
axis([0, 1, -1.4, 1.4])
grid()
xlabel('Time [seconds]')
ylabel('Value []')
title('Fourier expansion of a rectangular wave')
show()
```

Let's walk through the code. First, we import the entire *PyLab* package, which also includes *NumPy* and the plotting commands. Both are required in this example. We then prepare an empty plot: each new calculation of the expansion will be plotted on top of the previous one, so we issue the command hold(True) to ensure subsequent plots do not erase existing ones.

The command t = linspace(0, 1, N) creates the first array object, but we could've also used an arange() function call instead. Array object t is a 1-D array, a vector. All our subsequent operations and math functions will operate on this vector. We then initialize the series expansion variable, y, using the zeros() function. The heart of the computation lies in the for loop. Each sine wave is added to the previous one, and the result is stored in y. The simple line y += 4/(pi*n)*sin(2*pi*n*t*2) is, in reality, operating on entire arrays, which illustrates the strength of the array object.

We then plot y as it is being calculated and annotate the graph once the expansion is complete, as shown in Figure 7-6.

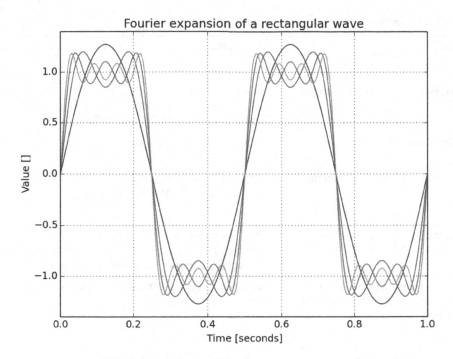

Figure 7-6. *Fourier expansion of a rectangular wave*

Array Methods and Properties

Arrays are objects; as such, they have functions called *methods* and variables called *properties*. Using IPython (see Chapter 2), you can list an object's methods and properties by using character completion, accessible via the **Tab** key. Alternatively, you can issue the following:

```
>>> import numpy
>>> [m for m in dir(numpy.ndarray) if not(m.startswith('__'))]
```

```
['T', 'all', 'any', 'argmax', 'argmin', 'argpartition', 'argsort', 'astype',
'base', 'byteswap', 'choose', 'clip', 'compress', 'conj', 'conjugate', 'copy',
'ctypes', 'cumprod', 'cumsum', 'data', 'diagonal', 'dot', 'dtype', 'dump',
'dumps', 'fill', 'flags', 'flat', 'flatten', 'getfield', 'imag', 'item',
'itemset', 'itemsize', 'max', 'mean', 'min', 'nbytes', 'ndim', 'newbyteorder',
'nonzero', 'partition', 'prod', 'ptp', 'put', 'ravel', 'real', 'repeat',
'reshape', 'resize', 'round', 'searchsorted', 'setfield', 'setflags', 'shape',
'size', 'sort', 'squeeze', , 'std', 'strides', 'sum', 'swapaxes', 'take',
'tofile', 'tolist', 'tostring', 'trace', 'transpose', 'var', 'view']
```

I've used the preceding list to create Table 7-6. Although the table presents only a subset of the methods and attributes, it includes those I feel are the most useful for data processing and visualization. I've also split the methods into categories for easier viewing. Methods are denoted with ( ), while properties do not have a trailing parenthesis. In this table, a refers to an array variable.

Table 7-6. *Array Methods and Attributes (Partial)*

Function	Description	Examples
Logical		
all()	True if all elements of a are true (nonzero).	arange(10).all() returns False (the first element is zero). arange(-5, -2).all() returns True.
any()	True if at least one element of a is true (nonzero).	arange(10).any() returns True.
nonzero()	A tuple of indices to nonzero elements of a.	arange(3).nonzero() returns (array([1, 2], dtype=int64),).
Indexing		
sort()	Sorts elements in a.	a = arange(3, 0, -1) sets a to array([3, 2, 1]). a.sort() changes a to array([1, 2, 3]).
searchsorted(x)	Returns indices to insert x such that the array's order is preserved. Assumes a is already sorted.	arange(4).searchsorted(1.5) returns 2.
Modifying		
clip(min, max)	If an element of a is less than min, returns min; if an element of a is greater than max, returns max; otherwise, returns the element.	arange(5).clip(1, 3) returns array([1, 1, 2, 3, 3]).
compress(cond)	Returns an array whose elements match the condition specified in cond; equivalent to a[cond].	a = arange(10) a.compress(a > 5) returns array([6, 7, 8, 9]). a[a > 5] returns array([6, 7, 8, 9]).
fill(x)	Sets all values of an array to x; equivalent to a[:] = x.	a = zeros([2, 2]). a[:] = -1 sets a to array([[-1., -1.], [-1., -1.]]).
Math		
For math examples, assume a = array([1, 1j, -1]), which can also be expressed as a = exp(1j*pi*arange(3)/2).		
cumprod()	Cumulative product. Each element is the product of the previous elements in the array.	a.cumprod() returns array([1.+0.j, 0.+1.j, 0.-1.j]).
cumsum()	Cumulative sum. Each element is the sum of the previous elements in the array.	a.cumsum() returns array([1.+0.j, 1.+1.j, 0.+1.j]).
real & imag	Real and imaginary values of elements in a.	a.imag returns array([0., 1., 0.]). a.real returns array([1., 0., -1.]).
conj()	Complex conjugate of a (negation of the imaginary part; rows and columns transposed).	a[1].conj() returns -1j.

(*continued*)

Table 7-6. (*continued*)

Function	Description	Examples
max(), min()	Maximum and minimum values of a (performed on real part only).	a.max() returns (1+0j). a.min() returns (-1+0j).
mean()	Mean value of a.	a.mean() returns 0.33333333333333331j (1j/3).
prod()	Product of all the values in a.	a.prod() returns -1j. Note that a.prod() is equal to a.cumprod()[-1].
ptp()	Peak-to-peak value of a; equivalent to a.max()-a.min().	a.ptp() returns (2+0j).
round()	Rounded values of a.	exp(a).round() returns array([3.+0.j, 1.+1.j, 0.+0.j]).
std()	Standard deviation of elements in a.	arange(2).std() returns 0.5.
sum()	Sum of all the values in a.	a.sum() returns 1j. Note that a.sum() is equal to a.cumsum()[-1].
trace([n])	Sum of the diagonal of a 2-D array. If n is provided, sums the offset diagonal.	eye(10).trace() returns 10.
var()	Variance of elements in a.	arange(2).var() returns 0.25.
Shape Related		
flatten()	The values in a as a 1-D array.	eye(2).flatten() returns array([1., 0., 0., 1.])
ndim	Number of dimensions of a.	eye(4, 5).ndim returns 2.
repeat(n)	Copies a over n times, flattened.	eye(2).repeat(2) returns array([1., 1., 0., 0., 0., 0., 1., 1.]).
reshape(d1, d2, ...)	Generates a new array of size (d1, d2, ...).	arange(4).reshape(2, 2) returns array([[0, 1], [2, 3]]).
resize(d1, d2,...)	Resizes the current array to size (d1, d2, ...).	a = arange(4) a.resize(2, 2) sets a to array([[0, 1], [2, 3]])
shape	A tuple representing shape of a.	eye(3, 4).shape returns (3, 4).
transpose()	Transposes a matrix. This is equivalent to conjugate but without negating the imaginary parts.	eye(2, 3).transpose() returns array([[1., 0.], [0., 1.], [0., 0.]]).
Conversion		
tofile(fname)	Writes an array to file (binary).	eye(2).tofile('eye2.bin')
fromfile(fid)	Reads an array from file (binary).	a = fromfile(open('eye2.bin'))
tolist()	Converts an array to a list.	eye(2).tolist() returns [[1.0, 0.0], [0.0, 1.0]]

Example: A Magic Square

A magic square is a square where the sum of each row and column are equal and the same. Typically, magic squares do not allow numbers to repeat. In this example, we'll generate magic squares, populating the values from 1 to N^2 in a square of size N by N. A modern variation on the magic square idea is the Sudoku puzzle game. In fact, you can modify the ideas presented in this example to provide solutions to Sudoku puzzles (see http://en.wikipedia.org/wiki/Sudoku for possible strategies).

We'll create a magic square implementing the De la Loubère method (also known as the Siamese method), which works for squares of odd values of N only. Constructing a magic square is performed by placing the first value, 1, in the middle column at the top. Incremented values are placed diagonally up and to the right. If the spot up and to the right is outside the square, it is wrapped around to the bottom row (if exceeded at the top) or to the first column (if exceeded to the right) or both. If a cell is already occupied, the value moves a row below (again, wrapping if needed). Figure 7-7 illustrates the algorithm with example magic squares of sizes 3 and 5.

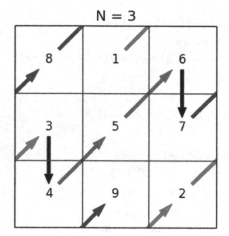
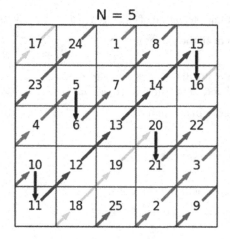

Figure 7-7. *De la Loubère method*

An implementation of the algorithm using an array is presented in Listing 7-6.

Listing 7-6. Creating a Magic Square

```
from pylab import *

def magicsq(n=3):
    """Returns a magic square of size n; n must be odd"""

    if n % 2 != 1:
        raise ValueError("Magic(n) requires n to be odd")
    m, row, col = zeros([n, n]), 0, n//2
    for num in range(1, n**2+1):
        m[row, col] = num        # fill the cell
        col = (col+1) % n
        row = (row-1) % n
```

```
        if m[row, col]:
            col = (col-1) % n
            row = (row+2) % n
    return m

def testmagicsq(m):
    """Returns True if m is a magic square."""
    msum = sum(m[0, :])
    return all(m.sum(0) == msum) and all(m.sum(1) == msum)
```

The main for loop is quite straightforward and follows the algorithm strictly. However, calculation of the column and row values using the modulo (%) operator is tricky and requires some explanation. Consider the way the algorithm is specified: increment the column value and check whether the new value is within the size of the matrix. If it is not, wrap it around to the beginning. A similar approach is taken with the row: decrement and wrap if required. Instead of implementing these two steps, an increment/decrement followed by an if statement, we could use the modulo operation, which captures the idea quite elegantly: col = (col+1) % n.

I've chosen to initialize the variables m, row, and col with a multiple assignment. Multiple assignments can also be used inside the for loop: col, row = (col + 1) % n, (row - 1) % n; however, there's no performance gain or other obvious advantages. For these reasons, my personal preference is to use multiple assignments in initializations and not calculations.

I've defined another function here, testmagicsq(), which checks whether a square is indeed a magic square. The function also works on even values (which is a plus) and uses the sum() member function of the array object. The check is a *naïve* one; that is, the function testmagicsq() tests whether the sum of every row and the sum of every column is identical; it does not check to see whether an element appears only once.

■ **Tip** Python supports testing via several built-in packages, including *doctest* and *unittest*. However, for this example, I've chosen to write a dedicated test function, which will further illustrate the properties of *NumPy* arrays.

The function sum(0) returns an array of the sums of columns (i.e., along axis 0); sum(1) returns an array summing rows (along axis 1). Here's a listing that demonstrates summing along the 0 axis and the 1 axis:

```
>>> exec(open('magic_square.py').read())
>>> a = eye(2, 3)
>>> a
```

```
array([[ 1.,  0.,  0.],
       [ 0.,  1.,  0.]])
```

```
>>> a.sum(0)
```

```
array([ 1.,  1.,  0.])
```

```
>>> a.sum(1)
```

```
array([ 1.,  1.])
```

```
>>> m = magicsq(5)
>>> m.sum(0)
```

```
array([ 65.,   65.,   65.,   65.,   65.])
```

```
>>> m.sum(1)
```

```
array([ 65.,   65.,   65.,   65.,   65.])
```

```
>>> testmagicsq(m)
```

```
True
```

As you can see, the matrix eye(2, 3) has two rows and three columns. Summing along axis 0 via sum(0) returns a 1-D array (a vector) holding the sums of all three columns. Consequently, sum(1) returns a vector holding the sum of the rows. The next lines show how to use this to check whether the square meets the "magic" requirements: both vectors, sum(0) and sum(1), should be equal element-wise to the sum along an arbitrary axis.

In the testmagicsq() function, I've chosen to compare both the sums of columns and of rows with the sum of the first column: sum(m[0, :]). If you compare a vector (1-D array) with a scalar (a single value), the result is a vector with each element compared with the scalar. To ensure all are indeed equal to the required sum, you could use the all() member function. I've opted to use the notation all(m.sum(0) == msum) over (m.sum(0) == msum).all() because I think it's more readable, but that again is personal preference; both do the job.

■ **Note**   In the function testmagicsq(), it's not enough to check that m.sum(0) is equal to m.sum(1) because this only checks whether the sums of the rows is equal to the sums of the columns. However, that's not a sufficient condition. Consider the array [[0, 1], [0, 2]]: it satisfies the condition m.sum(0) == m.sum(1), but it's not a magic square. You might raise the question whether the array eye(N) is a magic square—the function testmagicsq() will return True, but maybe this is a trivial case of a magic square.

One other interesting aspect of the Siamese method is that the sum along the diagonal is also identical to the sum of each row and each column; that's true for both diagonals. The function trace() calculates the sum along the diagonal (top left to bottom right). To calculate the sum of the second diagonal (bottom left to top right), you could use the fliplr() function:

```
>>> m = magicsq(5)
>>> m.trace()
```

```
65.0
```

```
>>> fliplr(m).trace()
```

```
65.0
```

Other Useful Array Functions

In addition to ndarray properties and methods, the *NumPy* package also provides functions that operate on arrays, but are not part of the ndarray object class. For a full account of these, issue the following:

```
>>> import numpy
>>> dir(numpy)
```

As you can see, many functions are available from various fields of interest:

- Vector operations: convolve(), cross(), correlate(), and vdot().

- Matrix operations: diag() and trace().

- Statistical functions: cov(), var(), std(), mean(), and histogram().

- Financial functions: fv(), pv(), and pmt().

- Polynomial operations: polyadd(), polymul(), polydiv(), polyfit(), polyder(), polyint(), and roots().

- Operations that change vector and matrix sizes and orientations: flipud(), fliplr() and rot90().

- Functions that generate windows for filtering: hamming(), hanning(), bartlett(), blackman(), and kaiser().

We'll explore some of these functions in Chapter 8. If you'd like to know more about these functions, issue help(numpy.function). For example, here's a function I particularly like using:

```
>>> help(numpy.diff)
```

```
Help on function diff in module numpy.lib.function_base:

diff(a, n=1, axis=-1)
    Calculate the n-th order discrete difference along given axis.

    The first order difference is given by ``out[n] = a[n+1] - a[n]`` along
    the given axis, higher order differences are calculated by using 'diff'
    recursively.

    Parameters
    ----------
    a : array_like
        Input array
    n : int, optional
        The number of times values are differenced.
    axis : int, optional
        The axis along which the difference is taken, default is the last
        axis.
    Returns
    -------
    diff : ndarray
        The 'n' order differences. The shape of the output is the same as 'a'
        except along 'axis' where the dimension is smaller by 'n'.
```

I use `diff()` to calculate the difference between two consecutive elements in an array. I've used it several times already in the book, including the example: "Adding Arrows to a Graph" in Chapter 6. You could also modify the friends meeting example in this chapter to use `diff()` instead of a list comprehension.

Final Notes and References

NumPy is extremely helpful for a wide range of applications. As evidence of this, you'll find that a considerable number of packages that rely on *NumPy*. And for a good reason: *NumPy* provides a solid base for mathematical arrays.

Should you require additional information on *NumPy* or the other topics discussed in this chapter, I hope you find the following references of value:

- *NumPy* home page, `http://www.numpy.org/`

- The Python Standard Library, `https://docs.python.org/3.3/library/index.html`

- "Mandelbrot set," Wikipedia, `http://en.wikipedia.org/wiki/Mandelbrot_set`

- "Newton's method," Wikipedia, `http://en.wikipedia.org/wiki/Newton%27s_method`

- "De la Loubère Method," Wikipedia, `http://en.wikipedia.org/wiki/Siamese_method`

- "Fourier Series," Wikipedia, `http://en.wikipedia.org/wiki/Fourier_series`

CHAPTER 8

■ ■ ■

Science and Visualization

Numerical Analysis and Signal Processing

I've covered many topics associated with data analysis and visualization: reading and writing files, text processing and converting text to numerical data, plotting and graphing, writing scripts, and implementing algorithms. It's time to take a deeper dive and analyze numerical data.

This chapter deals with two important topics: numerical analysis and signal processing. These two topics appear in many sciences: mathematics, computing, engineering, and more. From a simplistic point of view, *numerical analysis* is concerned with algorithms that yield numerical values: a solution to a nonlinear equation, the decimal representation of π, and so on. *Signal processing* deals with processing signals—that is, values that change over time. Signal processing includes such topics as detection and filtering.

Most universities and colleges offer undergraduate courses that teach these topics. But you don't have to be an engineer or a computer scientist to use the methods and ideas discussed in the chapter; most of the topics are easy to follow. If you have a strong numerical analysis and signal processing background, this chapter should prove a good starting point for these topics in Python. If you're new to the ideas of numerical analysis and signal processing, I hope to shed some light on them, so that you can pick things up from here with relevant scientific literature. In particular, I'd like to point out one of the books that made a great impact on me (and many others): *Numerical Recipes: The Art of Scientific Computing*, Cambridge University Press, 2007 (see the "Final Notes and References" section at the end of the chapter). Although the book implements algorithms using C/C++ (my original copy was in the Pascal programming language), it provides a wealth of information on numerical algorithms and should prove easy enough to port to Python.

In my view, the field of numerical analysis is a cookbook of algorithms to numerically solve mathematical problems. And so in a sense, that's how the chapter is organized as well: as a list of problems and solutions. Each topic will be explored with examples in hopes that you'll modify the examples to fit your needs. And that's also how I suggest you refer to the chapter: as a cookbook of algorithms. While it's quite possible to read through and learn the algorithms one at a time, it's probably easier to read specific sections as you engage problems associated with them in real-life. So my suggestion is this: skim through the table of contents to acquaint yourself with what's available, and then try to solve a specific problem by reading the relevant section.

In this chapter, I've used *SciPy*, *matplotlib*, and *NumPy* extensively. These three packages are rich and complex; and as a result, I was only able to cover some of their functionality, not all of it. I therefore chose to cover topics and show examples of problems I've personally encountered. I hope you'll find the examples of value.

Finding Your Way: Variables and Functions

The *NumPy* package provides us with two useful helper functions. I call them helper functions because they don't fall into any specific numerical analysis or signal processing category.

When one works in an interactive environment, one constantly defines variables. It's hard to remember what variables are defined and what they mean. The function who() prints a list of current *NumPy* arrays:

```
>>> from pylab import *
>>> who()
```

Upper bound on total bytes =   0

```
>>> up, down = arange(10), arange(10, 0, -1)
>>> who()
```

Name	Shape	Bytes	Type
up	10	40	int32
down	10	40	int32

Upper bound on total bytes =   80

The function lookfor() is great for searching inside docstrings. So, to look for functions that perform numerical integration, issue the following:

```
>>> lookfor('integrate')
```

Search results for 'integrate'
----
numpy.trapz
    Integrate along the given axis using the composite trapezoidal rule.

(I've left out some of the output, but there are several functions that have 'integrate' in their docstring.)

SciPy

SciPy (http://www.scipy.org/) is an open source scientific library for Python. The idea of *SciPy* is similar to that of Octave-Forge (http://octave.sourceforge.net/), which provides extra packages for GNU-Octave (http://www.octave.org) and toolboxes that enhance MATLAB (http://www.mathworks.com). *SciPy* is built on top of *NumPy*, so it requires *NumPy* to work properly.

SciPy is organized into several modules, some of which are detailed in Table 8-1.

Table 8-1. *SciPy Packages*

Package	Description
Fftpack	Fast Fourier Transform
Integrate	Integration functions, including ordinary differential equations
Interpolate	Interpolation of functions
Linalg	Linear algebra
Optimize	Optimization functions, including root-solving algorithms
Signal	Signal processing
Special	Special functions (Airy, Bessel, etc.)

We'll be exploring *SciPy* modules that deal with numerical analysis and signal processing. Additional *SciPy* modules include sparse matrices (module *scipy.sparse*), statistics (module *scipy.stats*), and more. And the list continues to grow; however, they will not be covered in this book. For a full account of the available modules, issue `import scipy`, followed by `help(scipy)`.

To import a specific *SciPy* module, issue `import scipy.modulename`. For example, to import *scipy.linalg*, issue:

```
>>> import scipy.linalg
```

You can also accomplish the task this way:

```
>>> from scipy import linalg
```

Personally, I prefer the latter option: `linalg.eig()` is shorter to code than `scipy.linalg.eig()` (plus I think it's easier to read).

Linear Algebra

Linear algebra is a branch in mathematics that deals with matrices, vectors, and solving systems of linear equations. *SciPy* and *NumPy* provide us with many functions to deal with these topics: solving systems of linear equations, matrix and vector operations, and matrix decompositions.

Solving a System of Linear Equations

To solve a system of linear equations, we first write the problem in matrix notation.

```
2 * x + 3 * y = 10
3 * x -     y = -1.5
```

We start by defining a matrix, M, and a vector, V. The matrix is composed of the coefficients of x and y, which are 2 and 3 on the first row, or [2, 3]. They are 3 and –1 on the second row, or [3, -1]:

```
>>> from pylab import *
>>> M = array([[ 2, 3], [3, -1]])
```

Next, we define the vector of the results, [10, -1.5]:

```
>>> V = array([10, -1.5])
```

Now all that's required is to use the function solve():

```
>>> solve(M, V)
```

```
array([ 0.5,  3. ])
```

The result translates into: x is equal to 0.5, and y is equal to 3.

It's also possible to reach the solution by calculating the inverse of the matrix M and multiplying it by vector V:

```
>>> dot(inv(M), V)
```

```
array([ 0.5,  3. ])
```

I've introduced two functions here: inv() and dot(). The function inv() calculates the inverse of a matrix, and the function dot() performs a dot product. Had I multiplied inv(M) with V, I would've received an *element-by-element* multiplication, instead:

```
>>> inv(M)*V
```

```
array([[ 0.90909091, -0.40909091],
       [ 2.72727273,  0.27272727]])
```

Generally speaking, you should use solve() instead of inv(). The function solve() can handle what mathematicians call "less-behaved" matrices—matrices where the determinant is very close to zero. Using inv() on these matrices might produce inaccurate results (i.e., dividing by a number close to zero).

Vector and Matrix Operations

Much like dot(), the function vdot() returns the dot product of two vectors. So if you're only interested in the value of x in the previous example, you can write

```
>>> dot(inv(M)[0], V)
```

```
0.50000000000000022
```

The function inner(v1, v2) will perform an inner product; that is, it will multiply every element in v1 with the corresponding element in v2, and then sum them together:

```
>>> V1 = array([10, -1.5])
>>> V2 = array([1, 2])
>>> sum = 0
>>> for i in range(len(V1)):
...     sum += V1[i]*V2[i]
```

```
...
>>> sum
```

```
7.0
```

```
>>> inner(V1, V2)
```

```
7.0
```

I've implemented an inner product operation with a for loop and compared the results with the results of the function inner(). As you would expect, the results are the same. Note that the function inner() does not multiply an element with its conjugate (negative imaginary part).

The function inner() works on matrices, as well:

```
>>> M = array([[2, 3], [3, -1]])
>>> M
```

```
array([[ 2,  3],
       [ 3, -1]])
```

```
>>> inner(M, inv(M))
```

```
array([[  1.00000000e+00,   1.11022302e-16],
       [  5.55111512e-17,   1.00000000e+00]])
```

Similarly, outer() performs an outer product of two vectors or matrices:

```
>>> V1 = array([10, -1.5])
>>> V2 = array([1, 2])
>>> outer(V1, V2)
```

```
array([[ 10. ,  20. ],
       [ -1.5,  -3. ]])
```

The function transpose() will permute axes, and conjugate() will permute axes and negate the imaginary part of a matrix or vector:

```
>>> V1 = array([10, -1.5])
>>> V2 = array([1, 2])
>>> outer(V1, V2)
```

```
array([[ 10. ,  20. ],
       [ -1.5,  -3. ]])
```

```
>>> outer(V2, V1)
```

```
array([[ 10. ,  -1.5],
       [ 20. ,  -3. ]])
```

```
>>> all(outer(V1, V2) == transpose(outer(V2, V1)))
```

```
True
```

```
>>> conjugate(V1+1j*V2)
```

```
array([ 10.0-1.j,  -1.5-2.j])
```

The function det(M) will return the determinant of matrix M:

```
>>> det(array([[2, 3], [3, -1]]))
```

```
-11.000000000000002
```

Matrix Decomposition

Matrix decomposition is the rewriting of a matrix to a specific form. There are many decompositions including LU decomposition, singular value decomposition, and QR decomposition. *NumPy*'s linear algebra module supports some matrix decompositions via the functions shown in Table 8-2.

Table 8-2. *Some Matrix Decomposition Functions*

Function	Description
cholesky(m)	Cholesky decomposition
eig(m)	Eigenvalue decomposition
qr(m)	QR decomposition
svd(m)	Singular value decomposition

The following code performs eigenvalue decomposition and verifies the results:

```
>>> A = array([[1, 2], [0, 1]])
>>> L, v = eig(A)   # calculate eigenvalues and eigenvectors
>>> det(A - eye(2)*L)   # verify eigenvalues (should be zero)
```

```
0.0
```

```
>>> dot(A, v[:, 0]) - L[0]*v[:, 0]   # verify 1st eigenvector (should be 0)
```

```
array([ 0.,   0.])
```

```
>>> dot(A, v[:, 1]) - L[1]*v[:, 1]   # verify 2nd eigenvector (should be 0)
```

```
array([ 2.22044605e-16,   0.00000000e+00])
```

I've created a matrix (A) and calculated its eigenvalues $\lambda_{1,2}$ (stored in vector L) and eigenvectors $v_{1,2}$ (stored in matrix v); this is done in the line L, v = eig(A). Once the eigenvalues are evaluated, they can be verified by calculating det(A - λ·I), which should be zero; this is done in the line: det(A - eye(2)*L). Also, for every eigenvector λ, λ·v should be equal to A·v; this is verified in the last two lines: dot(A, v[:, 0]) - L[0]*v[:, 0] and dot(A, v[:, 1]) - L[1]*v[:, 1].

We will not be covering other matrix decompositions here; if you require additional information, help() is quite informative.

Additional Linear Algebra Functionality

Additional linear algebra functionality is available with the *scipy.linalg* module. To access *SciPy*'s linear algebra functions, issue import scipy.linalg or from scipy import linalg. *SciPy*'s added functionality includes the following:

- Matrix decomposition functions: lu() for LU decomposition and qr() for QR matrix decomposition, as well as functions for other decompositions.

- Matrix and vector operators such as norm() to calculate a matrix or vector norm, det() to calculate the determinant of a matrix, and inv() to invert a matrix.

- Matrix functions like expm() and tanm(). Matrix function names are similar to regular function names, but with an added character, m.

- Special matrices, such as the Hadamard matrix (hadamard()) used in some error correction codes (see http://en.wikipedia.org/wiki/Hadamard_matrix) and the Hilbert matrix (hilbert()) (see http://en.wikipedia.org/wiki/Hilbert_matrix).

Numerical Integration

Numerical integration is the process of numerically computing a definite integral. There are many occasions where numerical integration is important. Examples include calculating the area of a shape or the area under a graph, as well as solving differential equations.

For this discussion, we'll calculate the area of half a circle of radius 1. We already know this area to be $\pi/2$. So in a sense, calculating the area of half a circle is equivalent to calculating the numerical value of π.

First, we create two vectors: x and y. These two vectors satisfy the circle equation $x^2 + y^2 = 1$. I assume you've already imported *PyLab*:

```
>>> N = 7
>>> x = linspace(-1, 1, N)
>>> y = sqrt(1-x**2)
>>> x**2 + y**2
```

```
array([ 1.,   1.,   1.,   1.,   1.,   1.,   1.])
```

I chose the variable N arbitrarily; N is the number of points in the vectors x and y. The last result shows that all the points in vectors x and y that satisfy the circle equation, $x^2+y^2=1$.

To visualize the numerical integration, I plot rectangles that approximate the area of the circle:

```
>>> figure()
>>> dx = x[1]-x[0]
>>> for i in range(len(x)-1):
...     rect = Rectangle((x[i], 0), dx, 0.5*(y[i]+y[i+1]))
...     gca().add_patch(rect)
...
>>> title('Approximating the area of half a circle')
>>> axis('equal')
>>> show()
```

The area under the curve—that is, the integral—is approximately the sum of these squares. Each square's area is $(y[i] + y[i + 1]) \cdot dx/2$, so the total sum can be written as follows:

```
>>> dx*(sum(y[:-1]+y[1:]))
```

```
2.9175533787759904
```

I've multiplied the result by 2, so we can compare with π instead of $\pi /2$. Obviously, the bigger N is, the closer this number will be to π:

```
>>> for N in [5, 10, 20, 100]:
...     x = linspace(-1, 1, N)
...     dx = x[1]-x[0]
...     y = sqrt(1-x**2)
...     est_pi = dx*sum(y[:-1]+y[1:])
...     print("N=%d, estimated pi is %f" % (N, est_pi))
...
```

```
N=5, estimated pi is 2.732051
N=10, estimated pi is 3.019232
N=20, estimated pi is 3.101560
N=100, estimated pi is 3.138218
```

As you can see, for N = 100, the accuracy is about 1 percent. Figure 8-1 captures this visually (see Appendix A for the full listing.)

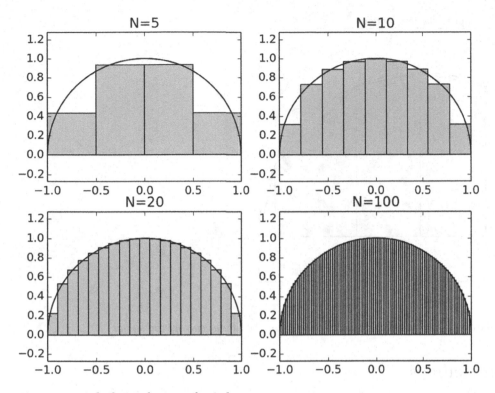

Figure 8-1. *Calculating the area of a circle*

In calculating the area of the circle, I chose values that are evenly spaced. If you'd like to use unevenly spaced values, the implementation is more complex. Also, the method uses rectangles to approximate the area under the curve, but in this particular example (and many others), trapezoidals are probably better suited, which brings us to the function, trapz(y, x). The function accepts vectors y and x and returns the numerical integral. The following performs numerical integration of unevenly spaced x values using the function, trapz():

```
>>> x = array([-1, -0.9, -0.4, 0.0, 0.4, 0.9, 1])
>>> y = sqrt(1-x**2)
>>> trapz(y, x)*2
```

2.9727951234089831

Figure 8-2 shows a visual representation of the trapezoidal integration (see Appendix A for the full listing).

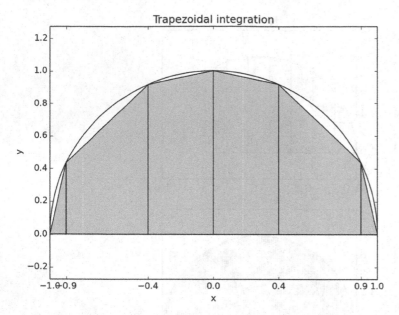

Figure 8-2. *Calculating the area of a circle using the trapezoidal method and unevenly spaced values*

More Integration Methods

Additional integration algorithms are available with the module, *scipy.integrate*. To use this module, issue `from scipy import integrate`.

We'll limit our discussion to the algorithm `quad()`, which uses a Gaussian quadrature to numerically integrate a *mathematical function*. Unlike previous methods such as `trapz()`, using `quad()` requires supplying a mathematical function and not the x and y vectors.

■ **Note**   I've used the term "mathematical function" to differentiate this type of function from a general-purpose Python function. A mathematical function is one that returns a numerical value given an input numerical value, such as y = f(x). In reality, we implement a mathematical function as a Python function.

```
>>> from scipy.integrate import quad
>>> def half_circle(x):
...     return sqrt(1-x**2)
...
>>> pi_half, err = quad(half_circle, -1, 1)
>>> (pi_half*2, err)
```

```
(3.1415926535897967, 1.0002354500215915e-009)
```

I defined a mathematical function `half_circle()` that returns the y-coordinate value of the upper half circle of radius 1, given an x-coordinate value. I then called `quad()` with the arguments `half_circle()`; the function to integrate; and -1 and 1, the range of values to integrate. The function `quad()` returns a value and an error.

The module *scipy.integrate* also supports the solving of ordinary differential equations using functions ode() and odeint(). We will not be discussing these functions. If you're interested in solving differential equations, refer to the *SciPy* home page: http://www.scipy.org/.

Interpolation and Curve Fitting

Interpolation and curve fitting deal with fitting functions to discrete known values. There are several reasons you would want to fit functions to points of data, including the following:

- Fitting a known function to gathered experimental data. This can be helpful in determining other parameters of the experiment.

- Evaluating the numerical values of functions at additional points (other than the given ones).

Interpolation allows efficient implementations that are tailor-made to a specific problem. Instead of writing a lookup table for all the possible values, you could come up with an interpolation polynomial that is more efficient, albeit with a possible loss of accuracy. At other times, you might choose to implement a known function like sqrt() instead of using a library-supplied algorithm to *increase* performance (at the possible cost of accuracy).

INVERSE SQUARE ROOT AND QUAKE III

If you're interested in efficient algorithms to calculate numerical functions, you may find this article of value: "Fast Inverse Square Root" by Chris Lomont at http://www.lomont.org/Math/Papers/2003/InvSqrt.pdf. The article describes a very efficient algorithm to implement the inverse square root of a number that appeared in the source code of the computer game Quake III. The implementation uses the Newton-Raphson method (and not interpolation). The article assumes knowledge of C.

Piecewise Linear Interpolation

Let's turn back to our half-a-circle example. This time, we'll limit ourselves to a quarter of a circle; that is, to positive values of x and y. We start by calculating the y values for x equal to 0, 0.2, ..., 1. We'll store the results in vectors xp and yp:

```
>>> xp = linspace(0, 1, 6)
>>> xp
```

```
array([ 0. ,  0.2,  0.4,  0.6,  0.8,  1. ])
```

```
>>> yp = sqrt(1-xp**2)
```

We'd like to calculate the values of y for x values equal to 0.1, 0.3, ..., 0.9, given xp and yp. We'll use the function interp(x, xp, yp) for this. The function returns the value of the piecewise-linear function defined by xp, yp at a requested point, x. What this means is interp() returns the value of a point on a line connecting two adjacent (xp, yp) points. This is known as piecewise linear interpolation:

```
>>> xi = arange(0.1, 1.0, 0.2)
>>> yi = interp(xi, xp, yp)
```

The vector yi holds the interpolated values at points 0.1, 0.3, . . ., 0.9.

The following visualizes a piecewise linear interpolation for the quarter of a circle:

```
>>> from pylab import *
>>> figure()
>>> hold(True)
>>> x = linspace(0, 1, 500)
>>> y = sqrt(1-x**2)
>>> xp = linspace(0, 1, 6)
>>> yp = sqrt(1-xp**2)
>>> xi = arange(0.1, 1.0, 0.2)
>>> yi = interp(xi, xp, yp)
>>> plot(x, y, 'b', label='ideal')
>>> plot(xp, yp, 'or', label='interpolation points')
>>> plot(xp, yp, '--r', label='piecewise linear function')
>>> plot(xi, yi, 'sg', label='interpolated values')
>>> legend(loc='best')
>>> grid()
>>> axis('scaled')
>>> axis([0, 1.1, 0, 1.1])
>>> title('Piecewise linear interpolation')
>>> show()
```

Figure 8-3 shows the results of this visualization.

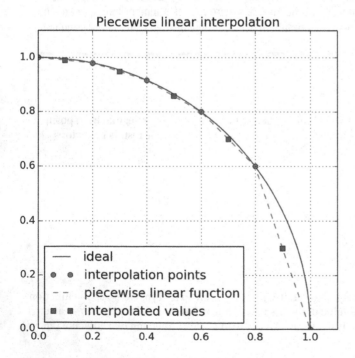

Figure 8-3. *Piecewise linear interpolation*

The values xp and yp are computed in this example; but in reality, these values can originate from sampled data. As you can see from the graph, the interpolated value at 0.9 is considerably less accurate than other interpolated values. Typically, the more points you add, the more accurate the result.

Polynomials

Polynomials are mathematical expressions that involve a sum of integer powers of a variable multiplied by a coefficient. Examples include $2x^2 + x - 1$, as well as x. However, sin(x) is not a polynomial. The reason polynomials are so important is that they involve only basic operations: addition, subtraction, and multiplication (integer power can be implemented with several multiplications). This property makes them very easy to implement in computing. Taylor series expansion (http://en.wikipedia.org/wiki/Taylor_series) is a prime example of transforming a function to a polynomial that is easily computed.

To be able to operate on polynomials with *NumPy* and *SciPy*, we represent a polynomial as a vector. The first element in the vector is the coefficient of the highest power, and the last element in the array is the coefficient of the lowest power, 0. So to express the polynomial $x^2 + 3x + 2$, issue the following:

```
>>> p = array([1, 3, 2])
```

To solve the equation $x^2 + 3x + 2 = 0$, use the function roots(p):

```
>>> roots(p)
```

```
array([-2., -1.])
```

If you'd like to construct a polynomial from its roots instead of its coefficients, use the function poly():

```
>>> p = poly([-2, -1])
>>> p
```

```
array([1, 3, 2])
```

You add and subtract polynomials using polyadd() and polysub():

```
>>> p1 = poly([-2, -1])
>>> p2 = array([1, 0, 0, 0])
>>> polyadd(p1, p2)
```

```
array([1, 1, 3, 2])
```

I've added $x^2 + 3x + 2$ to x^3 and got $x^3 + x^2 + 3x + 2$ as a result.

Multiplying and dividing polynomials is done using polymul() and polydiv(). The return value from polydiv() is a quotient and a remainder:

```
>>> p = polymul(array([1, 2]), array([1, 3]))
>>> p
```

```
array([1, 5, 6])
```

```
>>> polydiv(p, array([1, 3]))
```

```
(array([ 1.,  2.]), array([0]))
```

You perform integration and differentiation on polynomials using the functions `polyint()` and `polyder()`, respectively:

```
>>> p = poly([-1j, 1j])
>>> p
```

```
array([ 1.,  0.,  1.])
```

```
>>> polyder(p)
```

```
array([ 2.,  0.])
```

```
>>> polyint(p)
```

```
array([ 0.33333333,  0. ,  1. ,  0. ])
```

In the first line, I created a polynomial from complex numbers; the polynomial created is stored in p and is $x^2 + 1$. Using `polyder()`, I calculated the derivative of p and got 2x. Using `polyint()`, I calculated the integral of p and got $\frac{1}{3}x^3 + x$.

Uses of Polynomials

So why is all this polystuff important? The main reason is that you can use polynomials to approximate functions both from gathered data and from analytical functions. And since polynomials only require multiplications and additions, implementing polynomials in an embedded system, for example, is straightforward.

You fit polynomials to data using the function, `polyfit(x, y, n)`. Given a vector of x points and a vector of y points, `polyfit()` will return a polynomial of degree n (highest power of x) that best fits the set of data points. Another useful function is `polyval(p, x)`; this function returns the value of the polynomial at x (x can be a vector).

Example: Linear Regression

A known curve-fitting algorithm is linear regression. The idea is to draw a straight line in such a way that the total distance of all the points from the line is minimal.

For this example, we'll create a straight line and then add "measurement noise" to the values. Confronted with the new, "noisy" data, we'll try to evaluate the first order polynomial that fits the data. We'll compare the results with the known true values (see Listing 8-1).

Listing 8-1. Linear Regression with `polyfit()`

```
from pylab import *

# number of data points
N     = 100
```

```
start = 0
end   = 1

A = rand()+1
B = rand()

# our linear line will be y = A*x + B

x = linspace(start, end, N)
y = A*x + B
y += randn(N)/10

# linear regression
p = polyfit(x, y, 1)

figure()
title('Linear regression with polyfit()')
plot(x, y, 'o',
    label='Measured data; A=%.2f, B=%.2f' % (A, B))
plot(x, polyval(p, x), '-',
    label='Linear regression; A=%.2f, B=%.2f' % tuple(p))
legend(loc='best')
show()
```

I've randomly selected values for A (from 1 to 2) and B (from 0 to 1), and then constructed a linear line with noise using randn(). Next, I used polyfit() to fit the data to a first degree polynomial, a straight line. Lastly, I plotted the data along with the newly constructed linear line. Figure 8-4 shows the results of this linear regression.

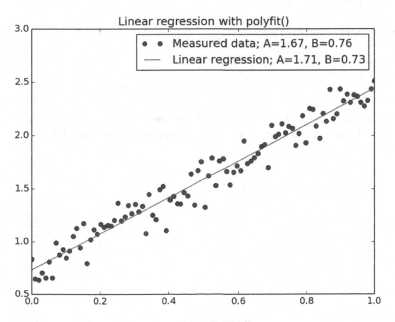

Figure 8-4. *A linear regression with* polyfit()

Example: Linear Regression of Nonlinear Functions

In cases where the function you're trying to fit isn't linear, sometimes it's still possible to perform linear regression, as shown in Listing 8-2.

Listing 8-2. Fitting Exponential Data

```
from pylab import *

# number of data points
N     = 100
start = 0
end   = 2

A = rand()+0.5
B = rand()

# our linear line will be:
# y = B*exp(A*x) = exp(A*x + log(B))

x = linspace(start, end, N)
y = exp(A*x+B)
y += randn(N)/5

# linear regression
p = polyfit(x, log(y), 1)

figure()
title(r'Linear regression with polyfit(), $y=Be^{Ax}$')
plot(x, y, 'o',
    label='Measured data; A=%.2f, B=%.2f' % (A, exp(B)))
plot(x, exp(polyval(p, x)), '-',
    label='Linear regression; A=%.2f, B=%.2f' % (p[0], exp(p[1])))
legend(loc='best')
show()
```

The regression is performed in the call to the function, polyfit(). This time, I've passed x and log(y) as values allowing a linear regression on log(y) or an exponential regression on y. You can see the results of this regression in Figure 8-5.

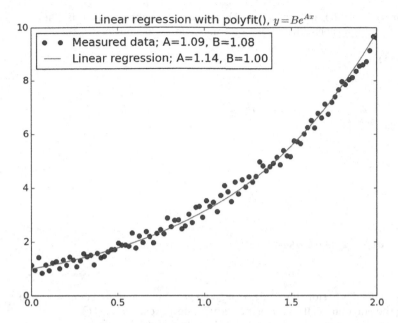

Figure 8-5. *Fitting exponential data*

Example: Approximating Functions with Polynomials

Another set of problems solvable with `polyfit()` is the approximation of functions using interpolation. The motivation behind this is a simple implementation of known functions. For the purpose of this example, we'll approximate the function sin(x).

The idea is to create a polynomial that passes through known interpolation points—that is, to calculate the value of sin(x) for known n values of x, and then to create a polynomial of degree n-1 that passes through all these points.

We start by selecting a set of points from 0 to π/2; these will be our interpolation points. Values outside this range can be computed using trigonometry identities and the interpolation function. We select five points for interpolation, thus deciding the degree of the interpolation polynomial to be 4. Once the points are selected, we calculate the sine of these points.

For the purpose of this example, I've chosen sine values that can be easily computed using the `sqrt()` function. You might argue that I'm cheating here because I'm using a nonlinear function (square root) to calculate sin(x) and not pure polynomials. However, you've already seen how to calculate the square root of a number using Newton's method in Chapter 7.

■ **Note** The selection of interpolation points is an interesting topic, and work by the mathematician Pafnuty Chebyshev has contributed much to the topic. See `http://en.wikipedia.org/wiki/Pafnuty_Chebyshev` and `http://en.wikipedia.org/wiki/Chebyshev_nodes`.

The values I'll select for interpolation are 0, 30, 45, 60, and 90 degrees. The reason I chose these values is that I know their exact sine values: 0, ½, $\sqrt{2}/2$, $\sqrt{3}/2$, and 1, respectively. In vector form, that looks like this:

```
>>> values = [0, pi/6, pi/4, pi/3, pi/2]
>>> sines = sqrt(arange(5))/2
>>> sines
```

```
array([ 0. , 0.5, 0.70710678, 0.8660254, 1. ])
```

Given these, interpolation is straightforward:

```
>>> p = polyfit(values, sines, len(values)-1)
>>> p
```

```
array([  2.87971125e-02,  -2.04340696e-01,   2.13730075e-02,
         9.95626184e-01,   1.52055217e-16])
```

So if you were to implement sin(x), all you need is to store the values of p given previously and then write a simple routine to calculate the value of sin(x) using the polynomial. If you're using *NumPy*, simply call polyval().

Let's plot the difference between our implementation of sin(x) and Python's built-in sin(x) function:

```
>>> figure()
>>> x = linspace(0, pi/2, 100)
>>> plot(x, polyval(p, x)-sin(x), label='error', lw=3)
>>> grid()
>>> ylabel('polyval(p, x)-sin(x)')
>>> xlabel('x')
>>> title('Error approximating sin(x) using polyfit()')
>>> xlim(0, pi/2)
>>> show()
```

Figure 8-6 illustrates this difference.

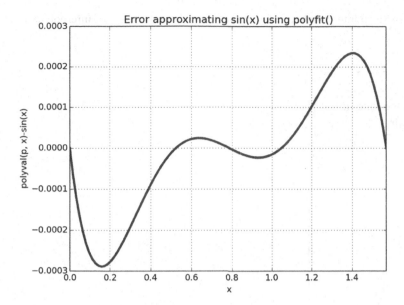

Figure 8-6. *Interpolation accuracy*

The results are quite accurate; the absolute error is less than 0.003.

Spline Interpolation

The *scipy.interpolate* module adds additional interpolation functions. One of these is the spline(xp, yp, x) interpolation function. Notice that the arguments to the function spline() are ordered differently from those of the function interp(). Spline interpolation is a piecewise polynomial interpolation that adheres to specific rules to yield smooth results.

Let's turn to the previous circle example:

```
from scipy.interpolate import spline
from pylab import *

xp = linspace(0, 1, 6)
yp = sqrt(1-xp**2)
xi = linspace(0, 1, 100)
yi = interp(xi, xp, yp)
ys = spline(xp, yp, xi)
figure()
hold(True)
plot(xi, yi, '--', label='piecewise linear', lw=2)
plot(xi, ys, '-', label='spline', lw=2)
legend(loc='best')
grid()
title(r'Spline interpolation of $y=\sqrt{1-x^2}$')
xlabel('x')
ylabel('y')
axis('scaled')
axis([0, 1.2, 0, 1.2])
show()
```

In Figure 8-7, I've compared a piecewise linear interpolation with a spline interpolation. The spline interpolation appears "smoother."

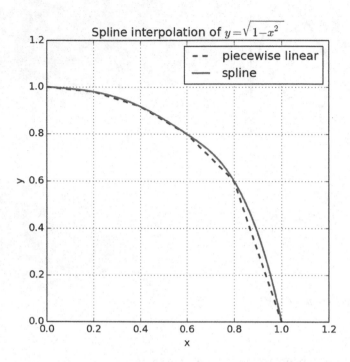

Figure 8-7. *A spline interpolation*

Solving Nonlinear Equations

In Chapter 7 we've talked about Newton's method and used it to draw fractals. Newton's method was used to solve a nonlinear equation.

The module *scipy.optimize* provides us with additional tools to solve nonlinear equations, as well as other optimization routines that will not be discussed here. Of those routines, I'd like to highlight three: fsolve(f, x0), bisect(f, a, b), and newton(f, x0). All these functions try to solve the equation f = 0, where f is a mathematical function implemented in Python.

Suppose we'd like to calculate $\sqrt{3}$ for the previous example. The idea is to construct a function such that the solution will be $\sqrt{3}$. This is easily done by setting $f = x^2 - 3$:

```
>>> def f(x):
...     """Returns x**2-3"""
...     return x**2-3
...
>>> f(10)
```

Let's use the functions fsolve(), bisect(), and newton() to calculate the roots. For fsolve() and newton(), we'll use x0 = 1, which is called the initial guess. The initial guess is a value that is close to the desired result. For bisect(), we need to provide a region for the search. We'll set the region to (1, 2) because we know the square root of 3 is less than 2 but greater than 1:

```
>>> from scipy import optimize
>>> optimize.fsolve(f, 1)
```

```
array([ 1.73205081])
```

```
>>> optimize.newton(f, 1)
```

```
1.7320508075688772
```

```
>>> optimize.bisect(f, 1, 2)
```

```
1.7320508075690668
```

```
>>> _**2
```

```
3.0000000000006564
```

Although in the simple case of square root of 3, all these functions provide accurate results, the algorithms are computationally intensive. In most these functions you can control how accurate you'd like your result to be by passing proper arguments to the functions. Of course, for a question as simple as the one presented here, it's best to use sqrt(3).

Special Functions

The *scipy.special* module provides a host of special functions that surface in higher mathematics and physics. These include the following (and many more):

- Bessel functions, integrals, derivatives, and zeros of Bessel functions
- Airy functions
- Gamma functions and error functions
- Special polynomials: Legendre, Chebyshev

To use the functions, issue the following:

```
>>> from scipy import special
>>> special.chebyt(2)
```

```
poly1d([ 2.00000000e+00,  -4.44089210e-16,  -1.00000000e+00])
```

For a full account, issue help(special).

Signal Processing

Up to this point in the chapter, we've dealt with numerical analysis. Going forward, the topics are related to signal processing. Signal processing is a vast field that deals with signals: values that change over time. Popular signal processing algorithms include the processing of sound, such as an equalizer; others include algorithms for radars, CAT scanning, and many more.

This part of the chapter will cover some of the functionality available with the module *scipy.signal* and complement the discussion with examples. You'll learn about some basic algorithms to detect signals in the presence of noise, as well as some functions to design filters. However, this section is but a taste of the topic, and I encourage you to consult with the references at the end of the chapter and professional literature for efficient signal processing algorithms.

Functions find, nonzero, where and select

The first set of functions we'll cover is `find()`, `nonzero()`, `where()`, and `select()`.

The function `find(cond)` finds the indices to an array for which a condition is met:

```
>>> from pylab import *
>>> squares = arange(10)**2
>>> squares
```

```
array([ 0,  1,  4,  9, 16, 25, 36, 49, 64, 81])
```

```
>>> I = find(squares<50)
>>> I
```

```
array([0, 1, 2, 3, 4, 5, 6, 7])
```

```
>>> squares[I]
```

```
array([ 0,  1,  4,  9, 16, 25, 36, 49])
```

We created a vector holding the squares of the numbers 0-9, and then found all the indices to the vector that satisfy the condition that the values are less than 50. Notice that the return value is a vector of indices; if you require the values and not the indices, you have to access the original array, which is `squares[I]` in the preceding example.

The function `nonzero(seq)` returns nonzero elements of seq. This is similar to `find(seq!=0)`. However, the function `nonzero()` returns a 2-D matrix, whereas `find()` returns indices to the flattened sequence, `seq`. This makes it hard to use `find()` in the kind of 2-D matrices used in images; in that case, `nonzero()` is the better option:

```
>>> A = eye(3)
>>> A
```

```
array([[ 1.,  0.,  0.],
       [ 0.,  1.,  0.],
       [ 0.,  0.,  1.]])
```

```
>>> I1 = find(A!=0)
>>> I1
```

```
array([0, 4, 8])
```

```
>>> A[I1]
```

```
Traceback (most recent call last):
  File "<stdin>", line 1, in <module>
IndexError: index 4 is out of bounds for axis 0 with size 3
```

```
>>> A.ravel()[I1]
```

```
array([ 1.,   1.,   1.])
```

```
>>> I2 = nonzero(A)
>>> A[I2] = 3
>>> A
```

```
array([[ 3.,   0.,   0.],
       [ 0.,   3.,   0.],
       [ 0.,   0.,   3.]])
```

I've created a 2-D matrix, A, and used find(A!=0) to find nonzero elements in A. Notice that the return value, I1, is a 1-D array; this means that indexing a 2-D array. Therefore, issuing A[I1] raises and exception. To access the values of A, I must first flatten the matrix A using a call to ravel(). However, if I use the function nonzero(), I can access 2-D elements seamlessly, as shown in the code of line A[I2]=3.

The function where(cond, x, y) accepts three arrays of the same size: cond, x, and y, and then evaluates every element in cond. If the element evaluates to True, the return value is the corresponding element from x. If the return element evaluates to False, the return value is the corresponding element from y:

```
>>> up = arange(10)
>>> up
```

```
array([0, 1, 2, 3, 4, 5, 6, 7, 8, 9])
```

```
>>> down = arange(10, 0, -1)
>>> down
```

```
array([10, 9, 8, 7, 6, 5, 4, 3, 2, 1])
```

```
>>> highest = where(up > down, up, down)
>>> highest
```

```
array([10, 9, 8, 7, 6, 5, 6, 7, 8, 9])
```

The function select(cond, vals, default=0) adds functionality to the function where() by allowing for several conditions. The function accepts a list of conditions specified in cond and returns the corresponding element associated with vals if a condition is met; if none of the conditions is met, the default value is selected:

```
>>> up = arange(10)
>>> ramp = select([up < 4, up > 7], [4, 7], up)
>>> ramp
```

```
array([4, 4, 4, 4, 4, 5, 6, 7, 7, 7])
```

The first three elements of up are less than 4, so the condition up < 4 is met, causing the selection of value 4. The last three elements are greater than 7, causing the selection of the value 7. Values greater than or equal to 4 yet less than 7 are retained as-is because the default is set to be equal to up. As a matter of fact, this functionality is called *clipping* and is available as both a method of the *NumPy* ndarray object and as a stand-alone function, clip().

So now that you know about the functions find(), nonzero(), where(), and select(), what can you do with them? The answer is simple: they're great for picking up values, what we call *detection* in signal processing.

Example: Simple Detection of Signal in Noise, Part 1

The detection of signals in the presence of noise plays an integral role in a great number of applications. For example, it is used in communication systems in the detection of signals such as radio or television broadcasts and to help differentiate them from noise. It is also used in medicine with the detection of an ECG signal, as well as in many other fields.

For this example, we'll first construct a clean signal. By a signal, I mean a one-dimensional array (vector), where values are stored as a function of time. Our purpose will be to detect "events," which will be represented by narrow triangles placed randomly in time. There can be several events in a signal.

To generate a triangular pulse, I'll use the signal.triang() function. This is really a window function (you'll learn more about such functions in the "Window Functions" section of this chapter). The function generates a triangular window of a specified size. We randomly place triangular pulses in the signal vector, as shown in Listing 8-3.

Listing 8-3. Randomly Placing Triangular Spikes

```
from pylab import *
from scipy import signal

# parameters controlling the signal
n = 100
t = arange(n)
y = zeros(n)
num_pulses = 3
pw = 11
amp = 20

for i in range(num_pulses):
    loc = floor(rand()*(n-pw+1))
    y[loc:loc+pw] = signal.triang(pw)*amp

# add some noise
y += randn(n)
```

```
figure()
title('Signal and noise')
xlabel('t')
ylabel('y')
plot(t, y)
show()
```

First, I defined some parameters I'll be using. The number of points in the signal is n and is equal to 100. The number of triangular pulses I'll place is 3, denoted by num_pulses. Each triangular pulse will be generated using pw=11 points. The maximum value for the triangular spike will be amp, which denotes amplitude.

Once I have all the parameters defined, I create two vectors: the time vector, t, and the values vector, y. The vector t is some arbitrary timestamp; in this example, it increments values starting at zero and ending at n–1. The vector y is initially set at zero.

Next I randomly place triangular spikes. The location, loc, where the triangular spike will be placed, is randomly generated with the call to the function rand() that generates a value between 0 and 1. So, I randomly pick a value between 0 and n – pw + 1 to ensure spikes aren't placed outside the vector y. Once I have all the spikes placed, I add noise with the function randn(), which generates normally distributed noise. This is also known as Gaussian distribution, or "white noise." I've chosen to use a normal distribution with variance 1 and mean 0. Notice that randn() is different from rand().

Figure 8-8 shows the generated signal.

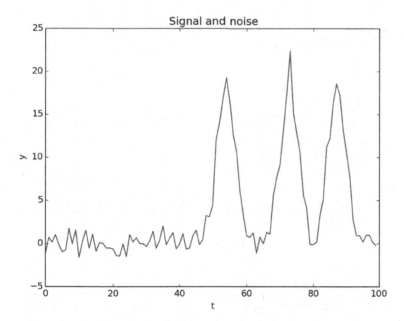

Figure 8-8. *Three triangular spikes with noise*

I did not check to see that spikes do not overlap. So, as you run the script, sometimes you'll view one or two spikes instead of three. This is fine, since we want to add some randomness to the example.

So far we've just created the signal. Now let's detect it. For detection, we'll use a simple algorithm: whenever a value is above a set threshold, we'll declare this as an event, or detection. We'll set the threshold at amp/2 and use the function find(), as shown in Listing 8-4.

Listing 8-4. Detecting Signals (a Continuation of Listing 8-3)

```
# detect signals
thr = amp/2
I = find(y > thr)

# plot signal with noise plus detection
figure()
hold(True)
plot(t, y, 'b', label='signal with noise')
plot(t[I], y[I], 'ro', label='detections')
plot([0, n], [thr, thr], 'g--')

# annotate the threshold
text(2, thr+.2, 'Threshold', va='bottom')

title('Simple signal detection in noise')
legend(loc='best')
show()
```

Figure 8-9 shows the result.

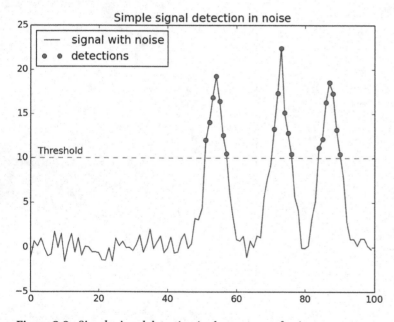

Figure 8-9. *Simple signal detection in the presence of noise*

Functions diff and split

Another set of functions that's useful in signal detection is `diff()` and `split()`. The function `diff(v)`, which was introduced in previous chapters, returns a vector composed of the differences of the elements in v. The function `split(v, indices)` splits a vector on indices:

```
>>> v = arange(10)
>>> split(v, [4, 8])
```

```
[array([0, 1, 2, 3]), array([4, 5, 6, 7]), array([8, 9])]
```

Example: Simple Detection of Signal in Noise, Part 2

In the previous example, you saw how to perform simple detection using `find()`. We've displayed all points that were above a specific threshold. In many occasions, we're less interested with points above a threshold because the threshold is arbitrarily chosen; we're more interested with the highest points above a threshold.

Here we pick up from the previous example. This time, we'd like to spot the peak in each detection. Listing 8-5 presents the code to do that.

Listing 8-5. Peak Detections

```
# peak detections
J = find(diff(I) > 1)
for K in split(I, J+1):
    ytag = y[K]
    peak = find(ytag==max(ytag))
    plot(peak+K[0], ytag[peak], 'sg', ms=7)
```

The implementation is a bit tricky, so let's walk through it. The idea is this: we split the detections into separate groups; and in each group, we find the peak and plot it.

■ **Note**   Because the both noise and signal are randomly selected, your actual numerical values might differ from those presented in this section. Nevertheless, the concepts and ideas are still valid.

The first problem of splitting detections uses the indices of detected values. A group is considered one detection if the indices are consecutive. Whenever there's a jump in indices, it means a new group:

```
>>> I = find(y > thr)
>>> I
```

```
array([51, 52, 53, 54, 55, 56, 57, 71, 72, 73, 74, 75, 76, 84, 85, 86, 87, 88, 89, 90])
```

So the group [51, 52, 53, 54, 55, 56, 57] is one group, the group [71, 72, 73, 74, 75, 76] is the second group, and the group [84, 85, 86, 87, 88, 89, 90] is the last group.

The function `diff(I)` returns values other than 1 whenever there's a new group. Whenever the difference is greater than 1, it means the start of a new group:

```
>>> diff(I)
```

```
array([ 1,  1,  1,  1,  1,  1, 14,  1,  1,  1,  1,  1,  8,  1,
        1,  1,  1,  1,  1])
```

```
>>> J = find(diff(I)>1)
>>> J
```

```
array([ 6, 12])
```

So we'd like to split on the sixth element (denoted by 6) and the twelfth element (denoted by 12). We do this with the `split()` function:

```
>>> split(I, J+1)
```

```
[array([51, 52, 53, 54, 55, 56, 57]),
 array([71, 72, 73, 74, 75, 76]),
 array([84, 85, 86, 87, 88, 89, 90])]
```

All we need to do now is find the peak, which is coded as `find(ytag == max(ytag))`. In Figure 8-10, peak detections are marked by squares.

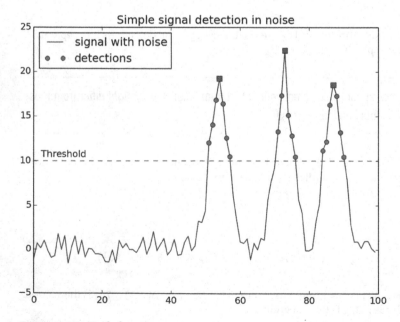

Figure 8-10. *Peak detections*

Waveforms

Additional *SciPy* functionality includes several waveforms that can be used when you're designing a signal processing algorithm or testing it. These include sawtooth(), square(), gausspulse(), and chirp():

```python
from pylab import *
from scipy import signal

cycles = 10
t = arange(0, 2*pi*cycles, pi/10)

waveforms = ['sawtooth', 'square']

figure()
for i, waveform in enumerate(waveforms):
    subplot(2, 2, i+1)
    exec('y = signal.' + waveform + '(t)')
    plot(t, y)
    title(waveform)
    axis([0, 2*pi*cycles, -1.1, 1.1])
show()
```

Figure 8-11 shows the resulting waveforms.

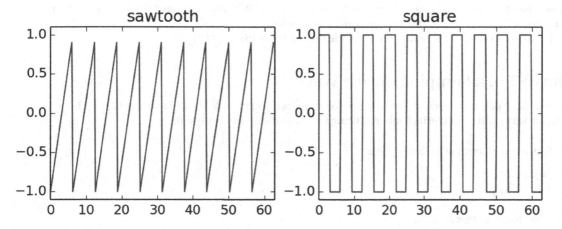

Figure 8-11. *Some waveforms*

The difference between waveforms and the triangular window used earlier is that they're repetitive, whereas triang() generates a single window.

The functions gausspulse() and chirp() are a bit more specialized; refer to the interactive help for information on using them.

Fourier Transform

Fourier transform is a linear operation that transforms a function from the time domain to the frequency domain. Much as the sound you hear can be viewed as an amplitude as a function of time, it can also be viewed by its frequency components: basses are the low frequencies of audio, for example.

The topic of Fourier transforms is quite large and requires some mathematical rigor. I will not be trying to address the topic in depth here; instead, I will show how you can use *PyLab* to perform Fourier transforms on sampled data.

To convert a signal from a time domain to a frequency domain, use `fft(x)`. FFT, which stands for Fast Fourier Transform, is an efficient implementation of the transformation. Generally speaking, if the number of elements in x is a power of 2, the results are quite fast:

```
>>> from time import time as t
>>> t1 = t(); dummy = sum(fft(arange(2**21))); print(t()-t1)
```

```
0.20280003547668457
```

```
>>> t1 = t(); dummy = sum(fft(arange(2**21-1))); print(t()-t1)
```

```
1.0452020168304443
```

(Your actual result might differ due to the processing power of your CPU). The first `fft()` was performed on a vector the size of 2^{21}, which is a power of 2; the second one was performed on a *shorter* vector, but it took longer to compute (more than twice as long, actually) because it is not a power of 2. In the example, I've used the function `time()` from module *time*, to measure the time the calculations take.

To transform data from the frequency domain to the time domain, use `ifft(x)`.

Example: FFT of a Sampled Cosine Wave

A cosine wave is made of one frequency (actually, two frequencies if you include the negative frequency). Let's generate a cosine wave and calculate its frequency using `fft()`, as shown in Listing 8-6.

Listing 8-6. Fourier Transform of a Cosine Wave

```
from pylab import *
from scipy import signal

N = 2**9    # we prefer powers of 2
F = 25      # a wave at 25 Hz
t = arange(N)/float(N)  # sampled over 1 second
x = cos(2*pi*t*F)   # the signal
figure()
p = subplot(2, 1, 1)
plot(t, x)
ylabel('x []')
xlabel('t [seconds]')
title('A cosine wave')
grid()
```

```
p = subplot(2, 1, 2)
f = t*N
xf = fft(x)
plot(f, abs(xf))
title('Fourier transform of a cosine wave')
xlabel('f [Hz]')
ylabel('xf []')
xlim([0, N])
grid()
show()
```

I began by defining a few parameters: N is the number of points in the signal, and f is the frequency of the cosine wave. I then created a time vector, t, which is composed of evenly spaced samples between 0 and 1, representing 1 second. I then calculated the sampled cosine wave and plotted it, along with its Fourier transform. I've chosen to plot the absolute of the transformed signal because Fourier transforms return complex values (albeit in this case those complex values are zero). Figure 8-12 shows the results.

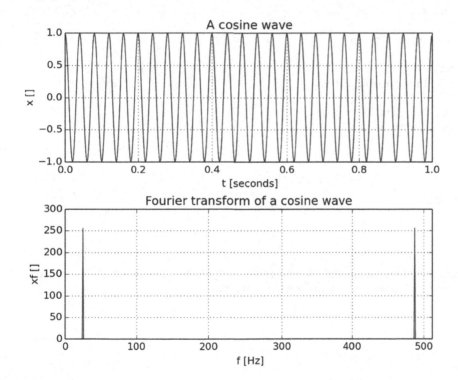

Figure 8-12. *FFT of a signal*

▬ **Note**   There's a frequency content at 25 Hz (the left spike), but there's also another one at 487 Hz. That's really the value corresponding to (–25) Hz; that is, (512 – 25) Hz. If you'd like to view the frequency domain centered around 0 Hz, use the function fftshift().

Window Functions

In the FFT example, I carefully chose a cosine wave that will have a full number of cycles in 1 second, which is basically any integer number for the frequency value. If I had chosen a noninteger value, I would've ended up with a signal that does not have full wave cycles. The problem with this signal is that, when you perform the FFT of the signal, you'll start seeing other frequencies—and not just the frequency of your original signal. The reason for this is, in essence, that FFT assumes the signal is repetitive; that is, it's not just from 0 to 1 second, but from minus infinity to infinity. And so it treats the signal as if it's copied left and right an infinite number of times. If the signal has an integer number of cycles, it will nicely fit when copied left and right. But in reality, you can't guarantee an integer number of waves in your sampled signal, so you'll start seeing these sampling effects. To minimize the effect, we can use a window function.

Several window functions such as hamming(), hanning(), bartlett(), and kaiser() help minimize this effect, but at a cost: the signal itself is also distorted. To use a window, multiply it by the time-domain vector, as shown in Listing 8-7.

Listing 8-7. A Hamming Window

```
N = 2**9    # we prefer powers of 2
F = 25.5   # wave frequency
t = arange(N)/float(N)   # sampled over 1 second
f = t*N
x = cos(2*pi*t*F)   # the signal
xh = x*hamming(512) # multiply with a hamming window
figure()
plot(f, abs(fft(x)), 's-', label='original')
plot(f, abs(fft(xh)), 'o-', label='with Hamming')
xlim([0, 50])
xticks(arange(0, 55, 5))
legend()
grid()
title('Signal with Hamming window')
xlabel('Frequency [Hz]')
ylabel('Amplitude []')
show()
```

I've plotted the FFT of two vectors: the original and the one with a Hamming window. In Figure 8-13, you can see I've zoomed in on the 25.5 Hz frequency to show the effects of the window function.

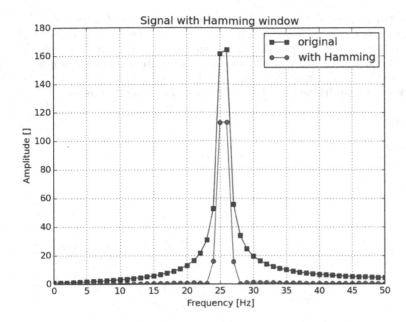

Figure 8-13. *Viewing a signal with a Hamming window*

The *scipy.signal* module provides additional window functions. To access these, issue the following:

```
>>> from scipy import signal
>>> help(signal)
```

Now scroll down to the window functions section.

Filtering

One of the reasons to transform a time-domain signal to a frequency-domain signal is that filtering in the frequency domain is, at times a, lot simpler. A filter is an operation that changes a signal. Much like filters in your kitchen sink, filters let some frequencies pass (water), while stopping other frequencies (large food remains). Filters are used in a variety of applications, ranging from audio to radar systems.

Filters are categorized by their behavior. A filter that lets through low frequencies and stops high frequencies is called a low-pass filter (LPF). Similarly, a high-pass filter (HPF) will allow only high frequencies to pass. There are also other categorizations, such as band-pass filters (allows only a specific band of frequencies), band-stop filters (allows anything but a specific band of frequencies), and notch filters (suppresses very few frequencies).

Filters are further categorized by their behavior to an impulse input; in other words, they are categorized by the output of the filter as a function of time, assuming you were to input a short spike to the filter. Filters that eventually forget the impulse are known as finite-impulse-response (FIR) filters, and filters that never forget are known as infinite-impulse-response (IIR) filters. From a very simplistic approach, if a filter does not rely on previous outputs (no feedback), it is considered an FIR; otherwise, it's an IIR.

Filter Design

Assuming you know what filter you wish to design, this section will help you do so. Filter design is an advanced topic (see http://en.wikipedia.org/wiki/Filter_design); and as such, this section is meant for those who require a few pointers on designing filters in Python with *SciPy*.

The *scipy.signal* module includes several functions to help design a filter. The function iirdesign() is used for designing an IIR filter. It is quite complete, and it's best to read the online help and follow it through. Other useful IIR design filters include butter(), cheby1(), cheby2(), and ellip(). FIR filter design functionality is provided with functions remez() and firwin(). I won't be covering those, but should you need to use them, the *SciPy* online help is quite informative. Finally, if you'd like to view the frequency response of a filter, use the functions freqz() and freqs().

The code in Listing 8-8 creates a low-pass Butterworth filter (an IIR filter) and plots its frequency response.

Listing 8-8. The Frequency Response of a Filter

```
N = 256      # number of points for freqz
Wc = 0.2     # 3dB point
Order = 3    # filter order

# design a Butterworth filter
[b, a] = signal.butter(Order, Wc)

# calculate the frequency repsonse
[w, h] = signal.freqz(b, a, N)

# plot the results
figure()

subplot(2, 1, 1)
plot(arange(N)/float(N), 20*log10(abs(h)), lw=2)
title('Frequency response')
xlabel('Frequency (normalized)')
ylabel('dB')
ylim(ylim()[0], ylim()[1]+5)
grid()

subplot(2, 1, 2)
plot(arange(N)/float(N), 20*log10(abs(h)), lw=2)
title('Frequency response (3dB point)')
xlabel('Frequency (normalized)')
ylabel('dB')
text(Wc+.02, -3, '3dB point', va='bottom')
ylim([-3, 0.1])
grid()
show()
```

I've used two functions: butter() and freqz(). The function butter() designs an IIR filter with specified parameters (order and cutoff frequency), and the function freqz() returns a frequency response. Note that the frequency response is a complex number, so I've plotted the amplitude in dB of the absolute value: 20*log10(abs(h)), as shown in Figure 8-14.

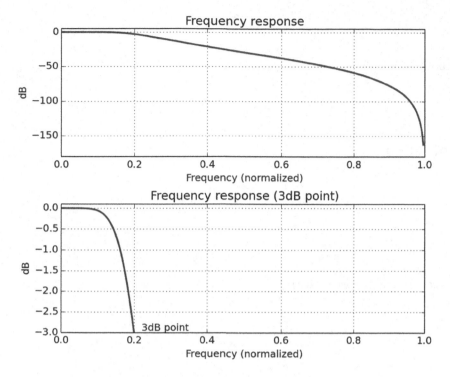

Figure 8-14. *The frequency response of a low-pass filter*

To filter data, given a known filter, use the function, `scipy.lfilter(b, a, x)`. Let's turn to an example.

Example: A Heart-Rate Monitor

For this example, I'll generate a signal that simulates the data generated from a heart-rate monitor connected to a patient. Please do not use this in any sort of production system; it's merely for educational purposes.

The patient walks around, and as a result, two signals are picked up: the heart signal and a signal associated with the patient's movement, or what is typically referred to as a movement artifact. Listing 8-9 shows these signals in my simulation.

Listing 8-9. A Heart Rate Simulation

```
# heart signal simulation
N = 256     # number of samples per second
T = 2       # number of seconds
hr = 1.67   # 100 beats per minutes
F1 = 0.5    # movement frequency

t = arange(T*N)/float(N)
y1 = 5*sin(2*pi*t*F1)      # movement artifact
```

```
# add heart signals
y2 = zeros(size(y1))
for i in range(int(T*hr)):
    y2[i*N/hr:i*N/hr+10] = signal.triang(10)

# combine movement with beats
y = y1+y2

# create a high-pass filter
[b, a] = signal.butter(3, 0.05, 'high')

# filter the signal
yn = signal.lfilter(b, a, y)

# plot the graphs
figure()

subplot(2, 1, 1)
title('Heart signal with movement artifact (simulation)')
plot(t, y, lw=2)
xlabel('t [seconds]')
ylabel('Amplitude []')

subplot(2, 1, 2)
title('Filtered signal')
plot(t, yn, lw=2)
xlabel('t [seconds]')
ylabel('Amplitude []')
show()
```

I've defined several parameters that control the script. The value N is equal to the number of samples per second (some are used to naming this value Fs, which stands for frequency of sampling). The value T is the total number of seconds; in this case, 2 whole seconds. The value hr is the patient's heart rate, 100 beats per minute: 100 / 60 = 1.67 Hz. Lastly, I defined the movement artifact frequency at 0.5 Hz. I then constructed a time vector, t, and a movement artifact vector, v1, and added "beats" with triangular waveforms using the signal.triang() function.

Now that I have a heart signal with a movement artifact, I turn to filter out the movement artifact. I design a second-order Butterworth HPF to do so via the call to signal.butter(), and then use the filter parameters to filter the signal with signal.lfilter(). Figure 8-15 shows the resulting plot.

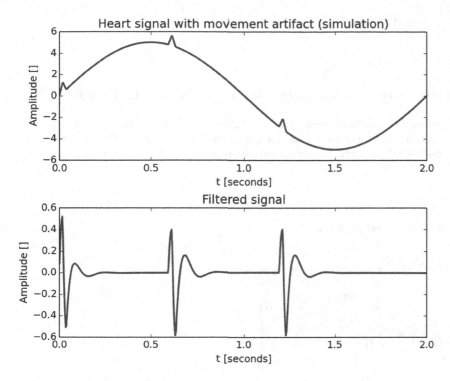

Figure 8-15. *Filtering a signal*

Example: Moving Average

On many occasions, filtering is used to "smooth" a signal. A simple algorithm is that of a moving average. For every two consecutive points, we calculate the average and use that value instead. The points are overlapping, so a result of using the algorithm on the vector [1, 2, 0, 2] would be [1.5, 1, 1]. But why stop at two samples? Moving average can be performed on several points, returning the average of those points. Listing 8-10 shows how this could be written with *SciPy* in Python.

Listing 8-10. A Moving Average

```
from pylab import *
N = 512
t = linspace(0, 10, N)
x = 1-exp(-t) +randn(N)/10
W = 32  # num points in moving average
xf = zeros(len(x)-W+1)
for i in range(len(x)-W+1):
    xf[i] = mean(x[i:i+W])

plot(t, x)
hold(True)
plot(t[W-1:], xf, lw=3)
title('Moving average')
```

```
legend(['signal with noise', 'filtered signal'])
xlabel('t [seconds]')
ylabel('x []')
show()
```

This is a straightforward implementation using a for loop. The input to the filter is arbitrarily chosen as $1-e^{-t}$, plus noise.

There is an easier approach. A moving average is a FIR filter with all its elements equal to 1/W; where W is the length of the moving average window. In this case, a quick-and-simple way to implement a moving average filter instead of the for loop is by calling the signal.lfilter() function and passing ones(W)/W as the filter values:

```
>>> from scipy import signal
>>> xf = signal.lfilter(ones(W)/W, 1, x)
```

Figure 8-16 shows the results of plotting a moving average.

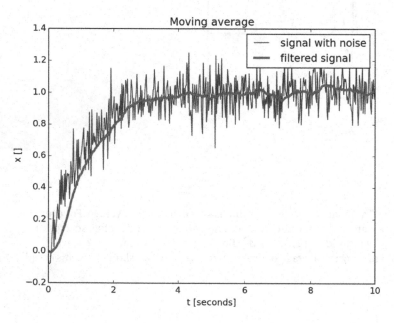

Figure 8-16. *A moving average*

Final Notes and References

The purpose of this chapter is to serve as a cookbook of algorithms in numerical analysis and signal processing. I took great care to limit the amount of math used in the examples and yet still be informative.

Even so, the topics covered in the chapter are far too many to be explored in one book, let alone one chapter. If you find these topics of interest, the following may provide additional information:

- *Numerical Recipes: The Art of Scientific Computing, Third Edition* by William H. Press, Saul A. Teukolsky, William T. Vetterling, and Brian P. Flannery (Cambridge University Press, 2007; for more information, see http://www.nr.com)

- *SciPy*, http://www.scipy.org/

CHAPTER 9

■ ■ ■

Image Processing

Two-Dimensional Data

Up to this point we've mostly dealt with one-dimensional data. That is, we've covered graphs and data that are essentially composed of a series of values. We've plotted the data, analyzed it, and created an image that was later saved to file or displayed to screen.

However, an image data file, or the image on your screen, is two dimensional. It is composed of pixels (which is short for picture elements). Each pixel has a location in two dimensions, x and y, and a value corresponding to the color. In this chapter, we will turn to manipulating images on the pixel level; that is, we'll operate on the two-dimensional matrix of pixels.

Operations on images are similar to operations performed on one-dimensional data. Slicing a 1-D array of values and adding those values to another array is equivalent to copying and pasting images. Saving an array to file is equivalent to writing images in TIFF or JPEG format. And so on.

Copying and pasting, resizing, and cropping are all simple operations supported by most GUI-based graphics applications. But with a GUI application, it's harder to perform these operations in a systematic and automated manner. For example, you might resize several images, and then combine them together to form a collage of images. It's doable in GUI applications, but it's typically not as easy and requires some user skills. Other simple image operations include converting file formats, rotating images, and cropping them. I'll cover these image operations, as well as how to automate them, so the results are consistent.

I'll show you how to deal with data on a numerical level, including reading the image, transforming it into a *NumPy* 2-D array, and then operating on the array itself. I'll also show you how to implement some interesting algorithms that involve image processing. Lastly, I'll touch on some more complex topics like filtering, which is the act of modifying a picture to enhance the visual output.

The basic package we'll use for all these operations is a fork of the Python Imaging Library (PIL), named *Pillow*. Be sure to install *Pillow* per the guidelines in Chapter 2. We'll also be relying on *NumPy* and *matplotlib*.

Make sure you read Chapters 6 and 7 before continuing with this chapter; the concepts taught in those chapters are required to follow along with this chapter.

Reading, Writing, and Displaying Images

The Python Imaging Library provides us with several classes that enable image processing. The basic class, `Image`, supports image operations such as reading an image from file, writing an image to file, copying and pasting, resizing, and rotating. To use *Pillow*, we issue the import statement: `import PIL` (notice that it's `PIL` and not `Pillow`).

Reading Images from File

Let's get started. To use the Image class, import it as follows:

```
>>> from PIL import Image
```

■ **Note**   Going forward, I'll assume you've issued `from PIL import Image`, and I will refrain from mentioning the `import` statement.

Our first operation is reading an image file. Since we currently don't have any images, let's generate an image and read it from file. We'll use *matplotlib* patches for this, as shown in Listing 9-1. (If you're not familiar with *matplotlib* patches, refer to Chapter 6.)

Listing 9-1.   Creating an Image

```
>>> from pylab import *
>>> figure()
>>> gca().add_patch(Circle((0, 0), 1))
>>> axis('off')
>>> axis('scaled')
>>> savefig('../images/circle.png')
```

I've used *matplotlib* to create an image file to work with, but you just as well could use any image file, for example, a JPEG picture you took with your digital camera. The code in Listing 9-1 draws a filled circle and saves it to file `../images/circle.png`.

■ **Note**   In accordance with the directory structure presented in Chapter 2, I assume that you're currently running from directory `Ch9/src` and that directory `Ch9/images` holds image files. If that is not the case, be sure to change the path to the images in the examples provided in this chapter.

Our first operation is to read the file and attach it to an Image object:

```
>>> im = Image.open('../images/circle.png')
```

Image Attributes

Now that we have an Image object associated with an image file, we can query the object's attributes:

```
>>> im.size
```

```
(800, 600)
```

```
>>> im.info
```

```
{'dpi': (100, 100)}
```

```
>>> im.mode
```

```
'RGBA'
```

```
>>> im.format
```

```
'PNG'
```

```
>>> im.filename
```

```
'../images/circle.png'
```

This is quite a bit of information. We know that the image size is 800×600 pixels wide, the resolution is 100 dpi, the mode is RGBA (we'll get to modes a little later in this chapter's "Creating New Images" section), the image format is PNG, and the file associated with the object we've created is ../images/circle.png.

Example: Image Catalog

My experience with analyzing image data is that images are not always taken in a consistent manner. This means that you, the programmer, have to manually crop, resize, enhance, or even delete images. This also translates into maintaining a catalog file of some sorts. An approach I find helpful is to create an automated catalog file and then annotate the information as I work with the data (see Chapter 4 for a discussion of catalog files).

The purpose of this example is to create a basic image catalog file (see Listing 9-2). The script uses the Image attributes presented in the previous section and creates a CSV catalog file in the parent directory of the searched directory. The catalog file has an extension of .cat.csv. That is, if you're searching /home/user, a catalog file will be created and named /home/user.cat.csv. The catalog file includes the name, size, format, and resolution of each image.

Listing 9-2. Creating an Image Catalog

```
from PIL import Image
import os, csv

def image_catalog(srchpath):
    """Creates a catalog file named srchpath.cat.csv."""

    # the CSV header
    catalog = [['Filename', 'Pathname', 'Format', 'Size', 'Resolution' ]]

    # walk directory tree
    for root, dirs, files in os.walk(srchpath):
        for file in files:
            pathname = os.path.join(root, file)
            try:
```

```
            img = Image.open(pathname)
            filesize = os.path.getsize(pathname)
            catalog.append([file, pathname, img.format,
                img.size, img.info])
        except IOError:      # not an image
            pass

    # create the clean catalog
    f = open(srchpath.rstrip('/')+'.cat.csv', 'w', newline='')
    csv.writer(f).writerows(catalog)
    f.close()
```

The script defines a function named image_catalog(), which accepts the directory to search and produces an image catalog file in CSV format. The variable catalog is a list of rows containing image information. We iterate through the directory and look for images with the Easier to Ask Forgiveness than Permission (EAFP) approach: try to open a file as if it were an image file. If we succeed, the catalog is updated. If the file is not an image, the exception IOError is raised, and we pass this file.

■ **Note**   If your directory is supposed to contain strictly images, you might want to add a print statement before the pass, notifying the user that a non-image file was encountered.

Here are the results I got from running the script in the directory images (the contents of the file, images.cat.csv):

```
Filename,Pathname,Format,Size,Resolution
nightsky1.png,../images/nightsky1.png,PNG,"(800, 600)","{'dpi': (100, 100)}"
nightsky2.png,../images/nightsky2.png,PNG,"(800, 600)","{'dpi': (100, 100)}"
circle.png,../images/circle.png,PNG,"(800, 600)","{'dpi': (100, 100)}"
nightsky.png,../images/nightsky.png,PNG,"(800, 600)","{'dpi': (100, 100)}"
collage.png,../images/collage.png,PNG,"(600, 600)",{}
```

Displaying Images

You can view an image by calling the Image method show(), or Image.show(). The method in turn calls the operating system's default image viewer, which is usually provided by the OS. To use a different viewer from the one supplied by the OS, associate the image with an image viewer you desire. The following will display the image ../images/circle.png, which was created previously:

```
>>> Image.open('../images/circle.png').show()
```

Converting File Formats

One of the common operations to perform on images is to convert the image file format. Perhaps you want to store images in a more efficient format using compression, or maybe the application you're using requires the image in a different format than you received it in. No matter what your reason, the Image method save() enables saving an image to file in a specified image format. There are two approaches for specifying a format: by using a file name extension or by explicitly specifying the format argument.

Assuming you've created an image file `../images/circle.png` per the previous listing, you can read the image and convert the file format to a JPEG file format, as follows:

```
>>> im = Image.open('../images/circle.png')
>>> im.save('../images/circle.jpg')
>>> import os
>>> os.listdir('../images')
```

```
['circle.jpg', 'circle.png']
```

In this particular example, you're not really converting the file, but creating another file with a different image format (converting it would mean that you also delete the original file).

Or, you could create a function to convert an image to JPEG format, as shown in Listing 9-3.

Listing 9-3. A Function to Convert an Image to JPEG Format

```
from PIL import Image
from os.path import splitext

def ConvertToJpeg(filename):
    """Convert an image file to a Jpeg file."""

    jpegname = splitext(filename)[0]+'.jpg'
    Image.open(filename).save(jpegname)
```

In the preceding example, I've used the `splitext()` function, which is part of the *os* module to replace the original extension with a `.jpg` extension. The `.jpg` extension instructs the `save()` function to create a JPEG file.

As mentioned previously, you can also explicitly specify a format:

```
>>> im = Image.open('../images/circle.png')
>>> im.save('../images/circle', format='Jpeg')
>>> import os
>>> [fn for fn in os.listdir('../images') if fn.startswith('circle')]
```

```
['circle.png', 'circle', 'circle.jpg']
```

In this case, `save()` does not add an extension to the file name (that is, the file created is `circle`, not `circle.jpg`) because that is the filename passed to it: `circle`.

PIL supports a large number of file formats, and the `Image` class can read most popular image formats. Furthermore, most images can be saved using known file formats, including JPEG, TIFF, and PNG. However, some image formats can only be read. Other formats such as MPEG (video files) are supported in identify mode only. For a full account, refer to the *Pillow* reference: `http://pillow.readthedocs.org/en/latest/reference/index.html`.

Example: A Function to Convert All Images in a Directory to JPEG Format

A direct continuation of the idea of converting an image file format is to write a function that iterates through a directory and converts all images to JPEG format, as shown in Listing 9-4. We'll also keep the original image because JPEG uses a lossy compression algorithm, which might lower the original image quality. However, you can easily modify the example to remove the original images.

Listing 9-4. Converting All Images in a Directory to JPEG

```python
import os, csv
from PIL import Image

def ConvertDirToJpeg(srchdir):
    """Converts all images in a directory to a jpeg file."""

    # walk directory tree
    for root, dirs, files in os.walk(srchdir):
        for file in files:
            # pathname holds the image filename
            pathname = os.path.join(root, file)
            try:
                # convert the file to a Jpeg file
                img = Image.open(pathname)
                jpegname = os.path.splitext(pathname)[0]+'.jpg'
                if os.path.exists(jpegname):
                    print("Did not create %s; file already exists." % jpegname)
                else:
                    img.save(jpegname)
                    print("Created file ", jpegname)
            except IOError:      # oops, not an image
                pass
```

Again, the preceding script uses the EAFP approach: try to open a file as an image, and if all goes well, convert it to a JPEG image. To run the function, enter `ConvertDirToJpeg(dirname)`.

■ **Note**   If the function `ConvertDirToJpeg()` is called with a non-existent directory, no output is generated, not even a warning message. If you require such functionality, be sure to modify the function and include it.

Image Manipulation

So now we can read images, display them, and convert file formats. But in converting file formats (and provided we do not use a lossy compression algorithm), we haven't really changed the images; we've merely saved them in a different format.

In this section, we'll turn to performing basic image manipulations. In other words, we'll modify the contents of an image by cutting and pasting, cropping, and rotating it.

Creating New Images

Pillow provides us with the ability to create images, not just read them from files. This is especially useful when you want to copy and paste images from other sources to a new image. The syntax for creating a new image is `Image.new(mode, size, color=0)`. The `mode` argument can take one of the values listed in Table 9-1.

Table 9-1. *Image Modes*

Mode	Description
'1'	1 bit per pixel; useful for black-and-white images.
'L'	1 byte per pixel (values from 0 to 255), black and white; useful for working with a one color band (see a discussion about color later in the chapter).
'RGB'	Red, green, and blue, 1 byte per color, also known as true color. RGB is common when the image background is black, such as on a screen monitor.
'RGBA'	Red, green, blue, and a transparency mask, 1 byte per color; common in several file formats, including PNG.
'CMYK'	Cyan, magenta, yellow, and black, 1 byte per color. CMYK is common in print.

There are additional image modes, but I won't be covering them in this chapter. To view the list of available modes, issue the following:

```
>>> from PIL import Image
>>> Image.MODES
```

```
['1', 'CMYK', 'F', 'I', 'L', 'LAB', 'P', 'RGB', 'RGBA', 'RGBX', 'YCbCr']
```

Refer to the *Pillow* web site for additional information:
http://pillow.readthedocs.org/en/latest/handbook/concepts.html.

The size argument in the Image.new() function is a two-element tuple describing the width and height of the image. The color argument is a function of the mode. For example, in the case of an RGB image, the color is a tuple in the form (red, green, blue); in the case of CMYK, the color takes the form (cyan, magenta, yellow, black):

```
>>> im1 = Image.new('L', (800, 600)) # black, one-band image
>>> im2 = Image.new('CMYK', (800, 600), (0, 255, 0, 0)) # magenta image
>>> im3 = Image.new('RGB', (800, 600), (255, 0, 0)) # red image
```

You can view the images by calling the show() method e.g., im1.show().

Copy and Paste

The methods copy() and paste() let us copy images and paste images into other images, respectively. The method copy() requires no parameters and creates a copy of the current image. The method paste(im, xy) pastes the image im into the current image; the xy argument is a tuple indicating the (x, y) location to paste (top left). Let's turn to an example that uses the paste() method.

Example: Fractal Collage

In this example, we'll use the functions new(), open(), paste(), and save() to create a collage of images. To follow along, you'll need to modify the fractal script presented in Chapter 7, so that it's a function instead of a script (see Listing 9-5). Once you create the function, save it under Ch9/src/fractal.py.

Listing 9-5. A Function to Create Fractals

```python
from PIL import Image
from cmath import *

def fractal(delta=0.000001, res=800, iters=30):
    """Creates a z**4+1=0 fractal using the Newton-Raphson method."""

    # create an image to draw on, paint it black
    img = Image.new("RGB", (res, res), (0, 0, 0))

    # these are the solutions to the equation z**4+1=0 (Euler's formula)
    solutions = [cos((2*n+1)*pi/4)+1j*sin((2*n+1)*pi/4) for n in range(4)]
    colors = [(1, 0, 0), (0, 1, 0), (0, 0, 1), (1, 1, 0)]

    for re in range(0, res):
        for im in range(0, res):
            z = (re+1j*im)/res
            for i in range(iters):
                try:
                    z -= (z**4+1)/(4*z**3)
                except ZeroDivisionError:
                    # possibly divide by zero exception
                    continue
                if(abs(z**4+1) < delta):
                    break

            # color depth is a function of the number of iterations
            color_depth = int((iters-i)*255.0/iters)

            # find to which solution this guess converged to
            err = [abs(z-root) for root in solutions]
            distances = zip(err, range(len(colors)))

            # select the color associated with the solution
            color = [i*color_depth for i in colors[min(distances)[1]]]
            img.putpixel((re, im), tuple(color))

    return img
```

Armed with the function fractal(delta, res, iter), we create a fractal collage, as shown in Listing 9-6.

Listing 9-6. A Collage of Fractals

```python
from PIL import Image, ImageOps

# import the fractal function, from fractal.py file
from fractal import fractal

fsize = 200      # small fractal image width and height
nx = 3           # number of images, width
ny = 3           # number of images, height
```

```
collage = Image.new("RGB", (fsize*nx, fsize*ny))
for i in range(ny):
    for j in range(nx):
        im = fractal(0.000001, fsize, i*nx+j+1)
        print("Processing image %d of %d" % (i*nx+j+1, nx*ny))
        collage.paste(im, (fsize*j, fsize*i))

collage.save('../images/collage.png')
```

The script generates fractals with increasing numbers of iterations and pastes them into an image that serves as the image collage. The arguments to the paste() method are chosen so that the images are pasted from the top left to the bottom right. I've saved the image to file ../images/collage.png.

The result from running this script is shown in Figure 7-3 in Chapter 7.

Crop and Resize

Cropping and resizing modify an existing image. The function crop() selects part of the original image, and the function resize() resizes an existing image; that is, it scales it so it fits the new size.

Assuming you have run the previous collage example, you should now have a file named collage.png. The function crop() accepts a tuple of four values, detailing the box to crop: (x0, y0, x1, y1). Let's read the collage.png file and crop it to show only 2 by 2 images from the fractal collage:

```
>>> img = Image.open('../images/collage.png')
>>> img.size
```

```
(600, 600)
```

```
>>> cropped_img = img.crop((0, 0, 400, 400))
>>> cropped_img.size
```

```
(400, 400)
```

```
>>> cropped_img.show()
```

Suppose you want to show the entire image, but scaled to size (400, 400); in this case, you'd use the resize(xy) function, where xy is a two element tuple detailing the width and height of the resized image:

```
>>> img = Image.open('../images/collage.png')
>>> img.size
```

```
(600, 600)
```

```
>>> resized_img = img.resize((400, 400))
>>> resized_img.show()
>>> resized_img.size
```

```
(400, 400)
```

You can also use the method thumbnail(), which is similar to resize(). The difference is that resize() returns a modified image copy, whereas thumbnail() modifies the image itself.

```
>>> img.thumbnail((400, 400))
>>> img.size
```

```
(400, 400)
```

In both the resize() and thumbnail() methods, you can provide a filter argument that determines the method of resampling. The acceptable values are Image.NEAREST (default), Image.BILINEAR, Image.BICUBIC, and Image.ANTIALIAS (best quality); see http://pillow.readthedocs.org/en/latest/handbook/concepts.html for details. Antialiasing has the best results, but it might take longer to compute:

```
>>> img.thumbnail((400, 400), Image.ANTIALIAS)
```

Rotate

Last on our list of basic operations is the rotate() function. The function rotate(theta) rotates an image theta degrees.

From a user's perspective, rotating is a basic operation, such as when rotating a scanned document by a few degrees so it's properly displayed. But in reality, rotation isn't such a basic operation; it requires changing the width and height of the image. In the case of rotating by multiples of 90 degrees, the rotate() function knows to swap the x-axis and the y-axis; however, in the case of other rotation values, both axes change, so the total area of the image changes. You can control whether you want rotate() to expand the image so it includes the entire rotated image or not by passing expand=True or expand=False, respectively:

```
>>> img = Image.new('RGB', (200, 300), (0, 255, 255))
>>> img30 = img.rotate(30)
>>> img30.show()
>>> img30.size
```

```
(200, 300)
```

```
>>> img30e = img.rotate(30, expand=True)
>>> img30e.show()
>>> img30e.size
```

```
(324, 360)
```

In the first line, I've created a simple blue image that is 200 pixels wide and 300 pixels high. I've then rotated the image 30 degrees with and without expanding. The results are shown in Figure 9-1.

Figure 9-1. *Rotated images: the left is not expanded, while the right is expanded*

Image Annotation

Annotating images is just as important as annotating graphs. It gives extra, important information. When was this picture taken? What camera was used? And so on. However, in some cases, annotating an image with text disrupts the pleasing visual result. That's probably why it's less common in pictures. There's also the issue of what color to choose. In cases where the picture is mostly white, you probably want to choose nonwhite annotation.

In this section we'll cover text annotation, as well as geometrical shapes to highlight specific image features.

Annotating with Geometrical Shapes

Pillow provides us with the `ImageDraw` object, which allows us to annotate an existing image. To import the `ImageDraw` object, issue `from PIL import ImageDraw`. To use the `ImageDraw` object, attach it to an existing image:

```
>>> from PIL import Image, ImageDraw
>>> img = Image.new('RGB', (200, 300), (0, 0, 255))
>>> draw = ImageDraw.Draw(img)
```

I've created an `ImageDraw` object named `draw` and attached it to the image, `img`. Going forward, operations performed with the `ImageDraw` object will be performed on the Image object:

```
>>> draw.line((100, 100, 200, 200))
>>> img.show()
```

This will draw a line from (100, 100) to (200, 200).

You can use the functions in Table 9-2 to annotate an image. In the table, assume `draw = ImageDraw.Draw(Image)`.

Table 9-2. *Some ImageDraw Functions*

Function	Description	Example
arc(xybox, start, end)	Draws an arc, a part of the circle bound by the rectangle, xybox (a tuple of four elements), starting at angle start and ending at angle end.	draw.arc((100, 100, 200, 200), 90, 180) will draw a quarter of a circle.
chord(xybox, start, end)	Similar to arc(), only it draws a line connecting the arc edges.	draw.chord((0, 0, 100, 100), 90, 180)
ellipse(xybox)	Draws an ellipse bound by the four-element tuple xybox. If you'd like a circle, use a square for the xybox values.	draw.ellipse((50, 50, 150, 100))
line(xyseq)	Draws lines connecting elements in the sequence, xyseq.	draw.line([0, 0, 10, 10, 20, 10, 20, 20])
point(xy)	Draws a point at location, xy.	draw.point((40, 40))
polygon(xyseq)	Draws a polygon connecting elements in the sequence, xyseq. The difference from the line() function is that the polygon is always a closed shape, allowing the use of the fill argument.	draw.polygon([10, 20, 40, 40, 50, 30, 70, 80])
rectangle(xybox)	Draws a rectangle specified by the four-element tuple, xybox.	draw.rectangle((20, 60, 80, 140), fill=128)

The ImageDraw annotation functions accept the following optional arguments: fill, which determines the color of the annotation or the fill object (similar to the facecolor argument in *matplotlib*); outline, which determines the line to draw the object (similar to the *matplotlib* edgecolor argument); and font, in the case of text annotations.

Text Annotations

Other than geometrical shapes, ImageDraw also provides text annotation with the function, text((x,y), string):

```
>>> from PIL import Image, ImageDraw
>>> img = Image.new('L', (160, 160), 255)
>>> draw = ImageDraw.Draw(img)
>>> draw.ellipse((0, 0, 160, 160), fill=128)
>>> draw.text((80, 80), 'A long string')
>>> img.show()
```

Originally, I had intended to have the text centered horizontally. However, the text string has a width, so I require a method to calculate the width and height of the text in pixels. Once I have the width and height, I can draw the text at location (80 – width/2, 80 – height/2). This is done using the function, textsize():

```
>>> from PIL import Image, ImageDraw
>>> img = Image.new('L', (160, 160), 255)
>>> draw = ImageDraw.Draw(img)
>>> draw.ellipse((0, 0, 160, 160), fill=128)
>>> s = 'A long string'
>>> width, height = draw.textsize(s)
```

```
>>> width, height
```

```
(78, 11)
```

```
>>> draw.text((80-width/2, 80-height/2), s)
>>> img.show()
```

Figure 9-2 shows the results with and without taking into consideration the string width and height.

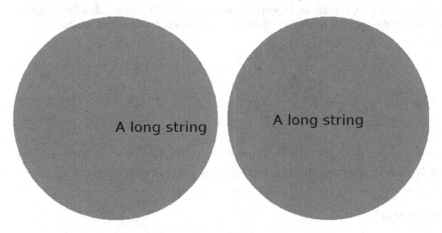

Figure 9-2. *Text annotation using* text() *and* textsize()

Fonts

It's also possible to use other fonts with the text() function. To do so, first create an ImageFont object. The ImageFont object is part of *Pillow*; to import it, issue from PIL import ImageFont. Once ImageFont is imported, you can use a font with a call to ImageFont.truetype(fontname, size). The returned ImageFont object can be passed as an argument to the text() function by means of the font argument.

Of course, before you can use fonts, they must first be installed in your system. Windows and MacOS typically come with built-in fonts; and on Linux, fonts are usually installed with X (as well as other applications). You can also use fonts from the GNU FreeFont project (http://www.gnu.org/software/freefont/).

However, font and font names are different on varying systems, and not just different operating systems: my Windows system might have different fonts than your Windows system. This means calling ImageFont.truetype(fontname, size) might work on one system and not on another. To overcome this problem, I use the function findfont(), which is part of the *matplotlib.font_manager* module. The function findfont() returns a string with the location of a font that best matches the requested font.

The following script annotates text with the Vera font using the findfont() function:

```
>>> from matplotlib import font_manager
>>> from PIL import Image, ImageDraw, ImageFont
>>> img = Image.new('L', (250, 100), 255)
>>> draw = ImageDraw.Draw(img)
>>> font_str = font_manager.findfont('Vera')
>>> font_str
```

```
'C:\\Python33\\lib\\site-packages\\matplotlib\\mpl-data\\fonts\\ttf\\Vera.ttf'
```

```
>>> ttf = ImageFont.truetype(font_str, 54)
>>> s = 'ABCabc'
>>> (w, h) = draw.textsize(s, font=ttf)
>>> draw.text(((250-w)/2, (100-h)/2), s, font=ttf)
>>> img.show()
```

The first two statements import the proper objects from *Pillow*, as well as *matplotlib*'s font manager. I then create a one-band image of size (250, 100), followed by the instantiation of an ImageDraw object attached to the image.

Next, I use *matplotlib*'s findfont() function to find a font that's closest to the font named Vera. The path to the font is stored in the string, font_str. Following that, I create an ImageFont object named ttf and use that font object to render the text. I then calculate the size of the text and render it in the middle of a white background, as shown in Figure 9-3.

ABCabc

Figure 9-3. *Font rendering*

■ **Note**   To use a font, you must supply the font argument in calls to two functions, text() and textsize().

Example: Thumbnail Index Image

In a previous example (Listing 9-2), we created a catalog of images. While that catalog is quite useful, it doesn't show the contents of those images. Perhaps a more useful catalog would be a collage of the images annotated with text showing each image's file name (see Listing 9-7).

Listing 9-7. A Thumbnail Index Image

```
# thumbnail index
import os
from PIL import Image, ImageDraw

def thumbnail_index(dirpath):
    """Create a thumbnail index from images in dirpath."""

    num_images = 5
    thumb_size = (128, 96)
    cat_size = (num_images*thumb_size[0], num_images*thumb_size[1])

    fn_index = 0            # filename index
    img_index = 0           # image index

    # go through all the pictures in a directory
    for file in os.listdir(dirpath):
        # get the pathname for the file
        pathname = os.path.join(dirpath, file)

        try:    # is this an image file?
```

```
        # open the image file
        img = Image.open(pathname)

    except IOError:
        print(file, "is not an image file")
        continue

    # create a thumbnail
    img.thumbnail((thumb_size), Image.ANTIALIAS)
    draw = ImageDraw.Draw(img)
    draw.text((2, 2), file)

    # do we need to create a new catalog image?
    if img_index == 0:
        thumbs_img = Image.new('RGB', cat_size)

    # calculate the location for this image
    x = img_index % num_images
    y = img_index // num_images

    # paste the thumbnail
    thumbs_img.paste(img, (x*thumb_size[0], y*thumb_size[1]))

    # increment the image index
    img_index += 1

    # have we reached the end of the catalog image?
    if img_index==num_images**2:
        img_index = 0
        thumbs_img.save('%s-%03d.cat.jpg' % (dirpath, fn_index))
        fn_index += 1

# save the last catalog file
if img_index:
    thumbs_img.save('%s-%03d.cat.jpg' % (dirpath, fn_index))
```

The function thumbnail_index() accepts a directory and produces a thumbnail index image. Figure 9-4 shows the result from running the function on a collection of images my daughter particularly likes.

Figure 9-4. A thumbnail index image

For the purpose of this example, I decided not to use os.walk() to iterate through the directory listing. Instead, I used os.listdir(). I defined two parameters: num_images, which holds the number of images on either x- or y-axis; and thumb_size, which holds the thumbnail width and height. Next, I composed a list of all the files in the requested directory. For every file, the script tries to open the file as if it were an image file. If a file is indeed an image file, a thumbnail of the image is created and pasted to the index image. Additionally, the thumbnail is annotated with the file name in the top-left corner. There's some indexing used to determine the exact location of an image in the thumbnail index image, as well as to create a new thumbnail index image once the current one has filled up.

■ **Tip** An alternative approach to displaying the text directly on the thumbnail image is to display it below the image. You can do this by adding a stripe of black (or white) between rows of images.

Image Processing

So far, we've performed tasks that can also be performed by most GUI-based image editing applications, including GIMP, the GNU Image Manipulation Program (http://www.gimp.org/). However, GUI-based applications have a GUI user in mind and are not easily automated. We now turn to explore possibilities of writing scripts to automatically perform operations on images.

Furthermore, as you start thinking about higher-level image processing algorithms, you may realize you require access to the actual data, the numbers that represent the image. In this section, we'll also show how this can be achieved.

A word of caution: image processing is a vast field. I won't be covering even the basics here; instead, I'll show that, if you do have an image processing algorithm, it's quite likely you can implement it in Python.

Matrix Representation and Colors

An image can be represented by a matrix, with each (x, y) point corresponding to a column and row in the matrix, and the value corresponding to the color.

The color value is a function of the mode (see Table 9-1 earlier for details). For example, in the case of an RGB image, each value of the matrix is a tuple of 3 bytes, with each byte representing a different color. In a sense, you can think of the entire image as three matrices, with each matrix corresponding to the colors red, green, and blue, which are also known as color bands, or channels.

Furthermore, each image can be split into these colors (depending on the mode, of course—there's no splitting of a 1-bit image into individual colors). You can do this with the Image method, split():

```
>>> from PIL import Image
>>> im = Image.open('../images/circle.png')
>>> im.mode
```

```
'RGBA'
```

```
>>> R, G, B, A = im.split()
>>> R.mode, G.mode, B.mode, A.mode
```

```
('L', 'L', 'L', 'L')
```

■ **Note** I've assumed you have followed along with the chapter and created a file named ../images/circle.png; if not, follow Listing 9-1 to create a circle.png image.

Each split image is an image by itself, but it now contains only one-color information—hence, its mode is 'L', not 'RGBA'.

To retrieve the *data* associated with the color—that is, the actual values—call the function, getdata(). We can then transform the values to a *NumPy* array for some interesting numerical processing. The following continues on the previous listing:

```
>>> from pylab import *
>>> data = array(R.getdata())
>>> type(data)
```

```
<class 'numpy.ndarray'>
```

```
>>> data.size
```

```
480000
```

```
>>> data.shape
```

```
(480000,)
```

The image data is stored as a list of all the values in the image, not a matrix representation of the image. To change it to a matrix, we use the *NumPy* method, reshape():

```
>>> im.size
```

```
(800, 600)
```

```
>>> data = data.reshape(im.size)
>>> data.size    # size should be the same
```

```
480000
```

```
>>> data.shape    # reshaped as a matrix
```

```
(800, 600)
```

Now that we have the data as a matrix, we can operate on the matrix instead of the image. This gives us great flexibility. Say we want to arbitrarily draw a magenta stripe in the middle of the circle; all we need to do is modify the matrix associated with the red channel, and then merge it to form a new, modified image.

■ **Tip**   Why does changing the red channel generate a magenta output? The way I'm going to modify the matrix is by setting the red channel to 255. This means that my previously blue circle will now be a combination of blue and red, which is magenta, while the rest of the background, which is white, will remain white.

Let's do this a step at a time, from the top:

```
>>> from pylab import *
>>> from PIL import Image
>>> im = Image.open('../images/circle.png')
>>> im.mode
```

```
'RGBA'
```

```
>>> im.size
```

```
(800, 600)
```

```
>>> R, G, B, A = im.split()
>>> data = array(R.getdata()).reshape(im.size)
>>> (w, h) = data.shape
>>> data[w/2-100:w/2+100, :] = 255*ones((200, h))
>>> R.putdata(data.reshape(h*w))
>>> new_img = Image.merge('RGB', (R, G, B))
>>> new_img.show()
```

The first line reads the image from file and displays some image information. I then split the image into four channels: red, green, blue, and the transparency mask. From here on, I'll restrict myself to dealing with the red channel only. First, I retrieve the actual numerical values associated with the red channel. This is done with a call to getdata(). In the same line, I also transform the data into a *NumPy* array and reshape the list to a matrix form.

Next I change the data values associated with 200 rows in the middle and set their value to 255. This effectively creates the magenta stripe. I then update the red channel with the modified data by calling the function, putdata(). The function putdata() complements getdata() and expects a list, not a matrix, so I reshape the data back to a 1-D array.

Finally, I create a new image, this time in RGB mode (I don't require transparency) by combining the original green and blue channels with the modified red channel. This is done by calling the merge() function, which is the opposite of the split() function. Figure 9-5 shows the results.

Figure 9-5. *A circle with a stripe*

■ **Note**   It's also possible to perform this task using the `ImageDraw` object.

So far we've covered an interesting number of functions that enable working on images with numerical values: `split()`, `merge()`, `getdata()`, and `putdata()`. Next, we'll use some of them in a more complex example.

Reading an Image to a *NumPy* Array

An alternative method to using *Pillow*'s Image object and converting it to a *NumPy* array is to directly read the image as a *NumPy* array. You can do this by using *NumPy*'s `imread()` function. To save a *NumPy* array as an image, use `imsave()`. Finally, to view the image represented by the *NumPy* array, use *matplotlib*'s `imshow()`. Notice that *matplotlib* will display a 2-D image, along with the image's axis and its title; if you don't want the axis to show, you can remove it by issuing `axis('off')`.

The following shows how to read the image `../images/circle.png` using *NumPy* and display it using *matplotlib*:

```
>>> from pylab import *
>>> data = imread('../images/circle.png')
>>> data.shape
```

```
(600, 800, 4)
```

```
>>> data.size
```

```
1920000
```

```
>>> data.max()
```

```
1.0
```

```
>>> data.min()
```

```
0.0
```

```
>>> imshow(data)
>>> axis('off')
```

```
(-0.5, 799.5, 599.5, -0.5)
```

Notice that the shape of the variable data, as shown in `data.shape`, is `(600, 800, 4)`; this is to show that the *NumPy* array is a 3-D array, pixels are 800×600, and there are 4 channels: R ,G, B and A.

The next thing to notice is that `imread()` scales the pixel values from 0 to 1. This is shown in the results printed from `data.max()` and `data.min()`.

Now, let's modify the image by operating on the `data` array. In the following example, I invert the values of the channels R, G and B, and then write the result to file: `../images/inverted_circle.png`:

```
>>> data[..., :3] = 1 - data[..., :3]
>>> imshow(data)
>>> imsave('../images/inverted_circle.png', data)
```

If you're working on an algorithm, and you want *NumPy* and *SciPy* functionality (i.e., to operate on *NumPy* arrays), then I suggest you read the image directly to a *NumPy* array with the function shown in this section. If you require actual image operations (e.g., image filtering, image rotation, and so on), I would advise you to use *Pillow* instead.

Example: Counting Objects (Five Parts)

The following example is rather long and deals with an interesting aspect of image processing: counting objects in an image. The idea is to write a script that counts the number of elements in a picture. Counting elements is a complex task, even for the human mind: What objects should I count? What constitutes an object? And so on.

The task of counting objects is very useful in a wide variety of applications, as indicated by just a few examples:

- *Biology*: Estimating the number of bacteria in an image from a microscope
- *Medicine*: Counting the number of axons in a tissue cross-section
- *Electronics board manufacturing*: Counting the number of imperfections in a printed circuit board or counting the number of resistors
- *Astronomy*: Counting the number of stars

For the purpose of this example, we'll create an image of the sky at night, with stars placed randomly. We'll then write a script to count the number of stars. We'll have a very sterile image, one that has a very clean background (black, night sky) and most information in one channel. However, we'll add a bit of complexity by varying shapes and sizes of stars.

Once we have an image of the sky at night, I'll talk a bit about recursion, a topic I have been avoiding thus far. Recursion will be used to implement an algorithm to fill an image. Lastly, I'll discuss some ideas and methods you could use to expand upon this example and add more capabilities to the algorithm.

Part 1: Twinkle, Twinkle, Little Star

First, we create the stars for our image of the sky at night. The night sky will be composed of white stars and a black background. Since we want the stars to be of varying sizes and shapes, we'll create a function named `star()` that creates a *matplotlib* patch object (see Listing 9-8).

Listing 9-8. A Star Patch, the Source of `star_patch.py`

```
# create a star patch object
from pylab import *

def star(R, x0, y0, color='w', N=5, thin=0.5):
    """Returns an N-pointed star of size R at (x0, y0) (matplotlib patch)."""

    polystar = zeros((2*N, 2))
    for i in range(2*N):
        angle = i * pi/N
```

```
        r = R*(1-thin * (i%2))
        polystar[i] = [r*cos(angle)+x0, r*sin(angle)+y0]
    return Polygon(polystar, fc=color, ec=color)
```

The values that control the star patch are R, which determines the star's radius; x0 and y0, which control the star's location; color, which determines both the fill and edge color; N, which controls the number of pointy edges a star has; and thin, which controls how thin or thick a star is (on the range of 0 to 1, with 1 being very thin).

■ **Tip** The default star patch is white because we'll be using it for the night sky. Be sure to change it to a different color if you're using a white background.

I've used the Polygon object to create the star patch, with some mathematical trickery. The idea is this: I place N pointy edges on a circle of radius R with the center at (x0, y0) at fixed angle increments. I then place another set of points at a smaller radius to serve as the inner edges of the star, again at fixed angle increments, but shifted so that each inner point resides exactly in the middle of the outer edge's points. The thin parameter determines the radius of the inner circle: the larger the value, the smaller the radius, and the "thinner" the star is. Lastly, I draw a line connecting all these points using the Polygon patch object.

■ **Note** Be sure to save the star patch listing as file star_patch.py; we'll use it in future scripts.

USING A LIST COMPREHENSION

It's also possible to implement the star patch with list comprehensions. The idea is to zip together the elements in the polygon list:

```
def another_star(R, x0, y0, color='w', N=5, thin = 0.5):
    """Returns an N-pointed star of size R at (x0, y0)."""

    a = arange(0, 2*pi, 2*pi/N)
    r = (1-thin)*R
    polystar = array(list(zip(R*cos(a)+x0, R*sin(a)+y0, \
        r*cos(a+pi/N)+x0, r*sin(a+pi/N)+y0)))
    return Polygon(polystar.reshape(N*2, 2), fc=color, ec=color)
```

Some prefer this implementation over the for-loop implementation. Personally, I think both are fine; choose whichever is easier for you to follow.

It's also possible to code the entire function as a single return statement, but I strongly recommend against it, as the code would be hard to understand.

The script in Listing 9-9 generates some interesting stars.

Listing 9-9. Generating Some Interesting Stars

```
# show some star examples
from pylab import *
from star_patch import star

examples=[
    "star(10, 0, 0, 'k')",
    "star(10, 0, 0, 'k', 10)",
    "star(10, 0, 0, 'k', 5, 0.2)",
    "star(10, 0, 0, 'k', 3, 0.9)" ]

for i, example in enumerate(examples):
    subplot(2, 2, i+1)
    exec("new_star="+example)
    gca().add_patch(new_star)
    title(example)
    axis('scaled')
    axis([-10, 10, -10, 10])

show()
```

In this script, I've decided to iterate over a list of strings and use the exec() function. The same string used for the exec() function is also used to create the title for the subplots (see Figure 9-6).

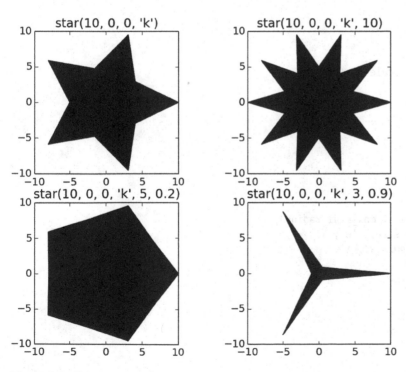

Figure 9-6. *Some star patches*

There's room for additional work on the star() patch object; for example, you could add a rotation parameter, rotating the entire star by rotation degrees. This can be done by changing the argument to the functions sin() and cos() in the star() function. Another modification could include a hollow star, implemented by splitting the edgecolor and facecolor functionality.

Armed with the star patch, let's turn to the second part of this example: creating an image of the sky at night.

Part 2: The Sky at Night

To create a simulated image of the night sky, we use the script in Listing 9-10. The script places 25 stars of random shape at random locations, and then stores the result in the image file, nightsky.png.

Listing 9-10. Creating an Image of the Sky at Night, nightsky.py

```python
# create a fictitious night sky
from pylab import *
from random import randrange as rr
from star_patch import star

# parameters for the simulated night sky image
img_size  = 800
num_stars = 25

# star parameters: number of pointy edges and radius
min_num_points  = 5
max_num_points  = 11
min_star_radius = 2
max_star_radius = 10

# star parameter 'thinness' is on a scale of 1 to 10
min_thin = 5
max_thin = 9

# draw the night sky
figure(facecolor='k')
cur_axes = gca()

# patch stars
for i in range(num_stars):
    new_star = star(rr(min_star_radius, max_star_radius),
        rr(0, img_size) , rr(0, img_size), 'w', \
        rr(min_num_points, max_num_points), \
        rr(min_thin, max_thin)/10.0)
    cur_axes.add_patch(new_star)

# modify axis behaviour
axis([0, img_size, 0, img_size])
axis('scaled')
axis('off')

# save the figure without the extra margins
savefig('../images/nightsky', facecolor='k', edgecolor='k')
```

I've imported the function randrange() from the module *random* and renamed it to rr(), which I think is clearer to read. I then define a set of values you can tweak and observe the results. The values are self-explanatory and include such values as the image size and number of stars in the image.

The patching of stars is done in the for loop, which creates a new star with random values and adds it to the current figure. I then follow up by updating the image size and removing the axes. Finally, I save the image to file, ../images/nightsky.png. Figure 9-7 shows random output from the simulated night sky.

Figure 9-7. *A simulated (random) night sky*

Part 3: Flood Fill and Recursion

We now turn to something completely different: recursion. *Recursion* describes a scenario where a function calls itself. Some known recursion algorithms implement the factorial operation and Fibonacci sequences. We'll use recursion for image processing, specifically to fill an image using a flood fill algorithm.

Flood fill, sometimes also referred to as *bucket fill*, is an algorithm to fill a closed area of a specific color with a different color. This is a quite common operation in most image processing applications. Kids love to use it to paint digital coloring images.

To implement flood fill, we'll use recursion. In this implementation, we'll assume that the image to fill is given to us as a *NumPy* array, and more specifically as a 2-D array (i.e., a matrix). It's also possible to manipulate a *Pillow* Image object, but I prefer using a matrix for two reasons:

- It's more generic. I can port the flood-fill algorithm to other objects, as long as I can convert the objects to a *NumPy* array (matrix).

- It's easier to view the code by indexing over matrix elements than to use the getpixel() and setpixel() methods provided by the Image object.

So how does flood fill work? Flood fill starts by receiving a point to start filling from. If the point is the color to be converted, flood fill will change the color to the desired color. It then moves to a point adjacent to it—say, to the right—and calls itself. As the process continues, points to the right will start filling up with the new color. If the point to the right is not in the desired color (that is, it shouldn't be painted), the point to the top is checked, and the process resumes. This process is repeated for left and bottom points surrounding each point. The end process is a filled, closed object.

FLOOD FILL AND MINESWEEPER

The flood-fill algorithm can also be used in the coding of the game Minesweeper (shipped with Windows). You can use the algorithm to expand an area and reveal points adjacent to mines. The algorithm will follow a similar path, and one option would be to create a matrix of values corresponding to whether a square is empty (value 0) or adjacent to a mine (value equal to the number of mines it is adjacent to), with a different value indicating a mine (say, value -1). When the user clicks a square, the flood-fill algorithm kicks in and decides how many squares to reveal. If you're not familiar with Minesweeper, I suggest you *refrain* from trying it; the game is addictive!

Listing 9-11 presents a simple flood-fill implementation.

Listing 9-11. A Flood-Fill Implementation Using Recursion, flood_fill.py

```
from numpy import *
from sys import getrecursionlimit

def flood_fill(x, y, m, total):
    """A function to flood fill an image (matrix)."""

    if total > getrecursionlimit():
        return total

    # nothing to fill
    if m[x, y] != 1.0:
        return total

    m[x, y] = 0.5
    if(x-1 >=0):
        total = flood_fill(x-1, y, m, total+1)
    if(x+1 <= m.shape[0]-1):
        total = flood_fill(x+1, y, m, total+1)
    if(y-1 >=0):
        total = flood_fill(x, y-1, m, total+1)
    if(y+1 <= m.shape[1]-1):
        total = flood_fill(x, y+1, m, total+1)
    return total+1
```

The function flood_fill() is an implementation of the flood-fill algorithm described previously. I've indicated where recursion actually happens (the function calling itself) with boldface type.

The function accepts the values x and y, denoting the point to fill; m, which is the *NumPy* matrix; and total, which is a variable used to keep track of the recursion depth (i.e., how many times a function calls itself repeatedly).

I've chosen to fill all values corresponding to 1.0 with 0.5. Essentially, this means that, if the object is fully red (or green or blue, depending on the band selected), it will be changed to "half" red. You can modify the function flood_fill() to accept an original color and a new color as parameters; I chose not to do so because I think the code looks clearer that way.

Every time a function is called in a recursion, additional memory is consumed. Python limits the recursion depth with the value, sys.getrecursionlimit(). If the running code exceeds this limit, a recursion exception is raised. It's possible to increase this number by calling sys.setrecursionlimit(), but that's only a small fix; inevitably, you'll reach a memory limit, which might cause a system crash.

Therefore, it's best if your code can detect these events beforehand and alert the user if such an event transpired. I have chosen to do so by returning the value `total`. If `total` is greater than the maximum recursion depth, I can notify the user of the event.

It's also important to note that, if your night sky image gets larger or the size of stars get larger (e.g., a larger radius)—or if you save the image at a higher resolution (more points per star)—inevitably you will hit a recursion limit because the areas to fill get larger and larger. So while this is a viable option to fill objects, maybe a different algorithm should be employed for production-level code, so as to avoid the recursion limit (which you wouldn't want in production level code). For example, you might use ImageDraw's `floodfill()` method, instead.

USING IMAGEDRAW FOR FLOOD FILL

The `ImageDraw` object also provides a `floodfill()` function, which may be used for the algorithm presented here. There are several reasons I chose to implement `flood_fill()` instead of using the `ImageDraw` function:

- I wanted to talk about recursion.

- `ImageDraw`'s `floodfill()` doesn't return information like the size of the filled region, which can be used to enhance the algorithm. That said, it's quite possible to use other methods to complement this, such as comparing the image before and after flood filling it.

- I wanted to show you how to tweak flood fill, for example, to include diagonals cells as adjacent cells (and not just up, down, left, and right).

So now that we have the `flood_fill()` function, how does that help us count the number of stars at night?

Part 4: Counting Objects

Counting objects is easy, once you've implemented `flood_fill()` (see Listing 9-12). The idea is simple: go through every point in your image and fill it. The return value from `flood_fill()` is the actual number of points filled. If there was nothing to fill, the value will be zero; but if `flood_fill()` fills an object, the return value will be nonzero, which indicates that `flood_fill()` found and filled an object. Future calls to `flood_fill()` for that pixel will not fill the object, as it is already filled. Now all that's required is to count the number of times `flood_fill()` returns a nonzero value, and you have the number of objects!

Listing 9-12. Counting Objects in a Picture

```
from pylab import *
from PIL import Image
from sys import getrecursionlimit
from flood_fill import flood_fill

# read the image, and retrieve the Red band
data = imread('../images/nightsky.png')[..., 0]
rows, cols = data.shape

# set all values that are nonzero to 1.0
# (could be values due to antialiasing)
data[nonzero(data)] = 1.0

# count the stars
count, recursion_limit_reached = 0, 0
```

```
for i in range(rows):
    for j in range(cols):
        tot = flood_fill(i, j, data, 0)
        if tot > getrecursionlimit():
            recursion_limit_reached += 1
        elif tot > 0:
            count+=1

if recursion_limit_reached:
    print("Recursion limit reached %d times" % recursion_limit_reached)
print("I counted %d stars!" % count)

imshow(data)
```

The script is an implementation of the preceding algorithm. We start by importing the necessary modules, as well as the module flood_fill.py, which contains the flood_fill() function implementation. Next, we open the image of the sky at night using *NumPy*'s imread() and select the red band with the indexing [..., 0]. I decided to work strictly on the red band; however, because we were dealing with black-and-white pictures, I could just as well have chosen any other channel (other than the transparency).

Next, I implement a simple threshold. What I do is change all nonblack values to white by setting all nonzero (i.e., not black) values to 1.0 (i.e., black); this is done using the nonzero() function call as follows: data[nonzero(data)] = 1.0. Other algorithms use a different approach, such as setting all values above and including 0.5 to 1.0 and all values below 0.5 to 0. In this particular case, the results would be very similar.

Now, I focus on using the flood_fill() function. I go through every pixel in the matrix and call the function flood_fill(). If the return value is greater than the recursion limit, I increment the number of times a recursion limit has been reached. If the return has not reached the recursion limit and is nonzero, I increment the count of objects.

Lastly, I report my results: the number of recursions that exceeded the maximum allowed value (for debugging purposes more than anything) and the number of stars counted. Here's a result from running the script on the night sky image presented earlier:

```
I counted 23 stars!
```

(We'll get to why that number is not 25 in the next section; your result may vary.)

To be sure I counted all the stars in the night sky picture—and to also be sure that I did not accidentally count objects that are not stars—I decided on some sort of visual feedback of the result. I do this in my last two line of code with a call to imshow().

Part 5: Optimizing the Algorithm

So why did the algorithm return 23 stars and not 25? (See the num_stars value in Listing 9-10.) A plausible reason is that several stars overlapped. This would cause the algorithm to combine several objects into one. In real pictures (nonsterile, as presented in the example), there could be other reasons, and this is where you can start tweaking your image-processing algorithm.

But as you start working with "real" data, you'll find that sometimes the opposite happens; that is, the algorithm counts more objects than there really are. The reason for this could be because the images are not ideal, and even small specks, or noise, could throw off the number count. In that case, a possible solution would be to count only elements where the size is greater than a fixed value. That is, when reading the value returned by flood_fill(), you would discard objects where the size is too small. Another option would be to preprocess the image using a filter (see the "Image Filtering" section later in this chapter).

Another improvement to the algorithm could be giving it the capability to find the largest object. Again, this is quite possible by reading the value returned from the function flood_fill() and then sorting the results or finding the maximum.

And you can also try to evaluate the luminosity of the night sky, by counting the areas of all the stars. You might use this to estimate how clear the skies are. Or, in the case of a microscopic image, you could use this approach to help determine whether the size of a bacteria colony has changed.

Some real images might have objects so small that you'll need to think about flood filling diagonals, as well. For example, consider the character "x" drawn on a 3×3 pixel grid: there's no pixel that's adjacent to another unless you count diagonals. Modifying flood fill to include diagonals will combine the pixels that make up this "x" into one object.

The point of the matter, now that data is accessible as a *NumPy* matrix, is that you can implement whatever algorithm or image-processing idea you might have. In many cases, you don't even have to resort to the matrix level; *Pillow* provides a good number of support functions.

Image Arithmetic

Pillow provides a set of arithmetic operations via the module *ImageChops* (Chops is short for channel operations). In the night sky example, some people would prefer working on a white background; this could save quite a bit of ink if you're printing the images (see Figure 9-8). Per the previous section, you could transfer the image to a *NumPy* array and then convert it; but in such a simple case, it makes more sense to use the *ImageChops* invert() function:

```
# display an image and its inverse
from PIL import Image, ImageChops
im = Image.open('../images/nightsky.png')
new_img = Image.new('RGB', (im.size[0]*2, im.size[1]))
new_img.paste(im, (0, 0))
new_img.paste(ImageChops.invert(im), (im.size[0], 0))
new_img.show()
```

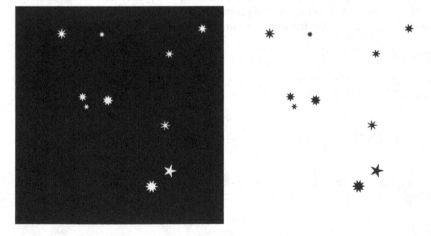

Figure 9-8. *Inverting an image: the original is on the left, and the inverted image is on the right*

In Figure 9-8, I've used the image generated by the script nightsky.py (see Listing 9-10) with num_stars=10, min_star_radius=10 and max_star_radius=30 to show a more pronounced effect of the image inversion.

Table 9-3 lists some additional *ImageChops* operations. Notice that *ImageChops* operations operate only one channel (L) or RGB images.

Table 9-3. *Some ImageChops Operations*

Function	Description
add(img1, img2, scale=1.0, offset=0)	Adds two images as follows: (img1+img2)/scale+offset. The default values of scale and offset mean a simple addition.
constant(img1, value)	Returns an image of size img1 filled with color value.
darker(img1, img2)	Returns an image with the darker pixel from both images. This a minimum of the two images, on a pixel-by-pixel level.
difference(img1, img2)	Returns the absolute difference of two images. This is abs(img1-img2), on a pixel-by-pixel level.
lighter(img1, img2)	Returns an image with the lighter pixel from both images. This a maximum of the two images, on a pixel-by-pixel level.
subtract(img1, img2, scale=1.0, offset=0)	Subtracts two images as follows: (img1-img2)/scale+offset. The default values of scale and offset mean a simple subtraction.

There are additional functions available in *ImageChops*; to learn more, check out either help(ImageChops) or the *Pillow* web site (http://pillow.readthedocs.org/en/latest/reference/ImageChops.html).

You can create some interesting effects using these simple operations. And these effects can in turn be used for some fast image-processing algorithms. Listing 9-13 presents a script that uses the lighter() method on two night sky images. To follow along, run the nightsky.py script and rename the generated file images/nightsky.png to images/nightsky1.png. Now do it again, this time renaming the generated image to images/nightsky2.png.

Listing 9-13. Using lighter() on Two Images

```
from PIL import Image, ImageDraw, ImageFont, ImageChops
from matplotlib import font_manager

# read the images
img1 = Image.open('../images/nightsky1.png')
img2 = Image.open('../images/nightsky2.png')

# create a new image, made of the lighter of the two
img3 = ImageChops.lighter(img1, img2)

# create a collage of three images
width, height = img1.size
delta = 10
img = Image.new('RGB', (width*2+delta, height*2+delta), (255, 255, 255))
img.paste(img1, (0, 0))
img.paste(img2, (width+delta, 0))
img.paste(img3, ((width+delta)//2, height+delta))
```

```
# annotate the images with text
font_str = font_manager.findfont('Vera')
ttf = ImageFont.truetype(font_str, 54)

draw = ImageDraw.Draw(img)
draw.text((delta, delta), 'Night Sky (1)', fill='white', font=ttf)
draw.text((delta*2+width, delta), 'Night Sky (2)', fill='white', font=ttf)
draw.text(((width+delta)//2+delta, height+delta*2), \
    'Combined', fill='white', font=ttf)

# display the final image
img.show()
```

I've made a collage and separated the images with a white delta band. Figure 9-9 shows the result.

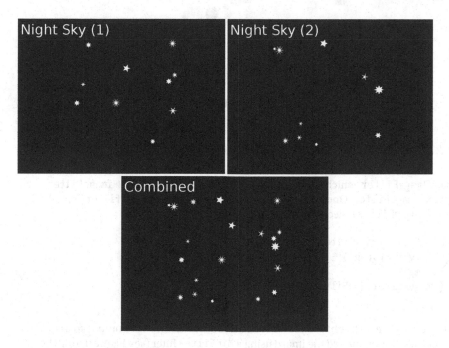

Figure 9-9. *Using lighter( )*

It's interesting to note that, in this specific case, using the function add( ) would have resulted in a similar image.

Image Filtering

Most GUI-based image-processing applications come with bundle of image filters. There's a wide variety of filters available, and different applications group them into different categories. Some of the common filtering categories are blur, enhancement, edge detection, and so on.

From an image-processing standpoint, *image filters* are known operations that help us achieve a specific effect. For example, I once used the counting objects algorithm (see Listing 9-12) to count the number of bubbles in a printed circuit board soaked in water. As you probably realize, pictures obtained from a real-life image are not as sterile as those presented in the sky at night example. And so, prior to using the algorithm, I had to clean up the images. By "clean up," I mean I had to filter the image using known filters. I ended up using a threshold combined with a median filter, and then converted the image to a 1-bit (black-and-white) version prior to running the algorithm.

The following text assumes you have some background in image filtering. If not, my suggestion is that you experiment with a GUI application such as GIMP to get a feel for what filters you can use and how they can help you with basic image processing. Once you have the preprocessing figured out; that is, once you know what filters you want to run on your image prior to the final algorithm, you can implement the filters with a Python script that uses *Pillow* filters (see Figure 9-10). (You might not even require a final algorithm if you select the proper filters.)

Figure 9-10. *Filtering an image: left is the original, and right shows the image filtered with a* MinFilter *set to 15*

Pillow provides us with the class ImageFilter, which supports a good number of filters. To use ImageFilter, import it as follows: from PIL import ImageFilter. Once you've imported ImageFilter, call the filter() method that's part of the Image object (not the ImageFilter object) to filter an image:

```
>>> from PIL import Image, ImageChops, ImageFilter
>>> img = Image.open('../images/nightsky.png')
>>> inv_img = ImageChops.invert(img)
>>> filt_img = inv_img.filter(ImageFilter.MinFilter(15))
>>> filt_img.show()
```

In the preceding example, I've used the night sky images you've seen before and inverted the output so as to work on black stars over white background. I then filtered the image using a MinFilter filter (see Figure 9-10). The MinFilter works on a pixel-by-pixel level. For every pixel, it returns the minimum pixel from the square of size n (15, in the example) centered on the given pixel. As you can see, even from this small example, there's quite a bit to be gained by working with image filters.

ImageFilter provides *fixed* image-enhancement filters that are easily distinguished by their capitalized names:

```
>>> from PIL import ImageFilter
>>> [filt for filt in dir(ImageFilter) if filt.isupper()]
```

```
['BLUR', 'CONTOUR', 'DETAIL', 'EDGE_ENHANCE', 'EDGE_ENHANCE_MORE', 'EMBOSS',
'FIND_EDGES', 'SHARPEN', 'SMOOTH', 'SMOOTH_MORE']
```

By *fixed*, I mean that the filters accept no parameters. To use these filters, call the `filter()` method with the fixed filter, as follows:

```
>>> new_img = img.filter(ImageFilter.CONTOUR)
```

The names of these filters should provide direction as to what action they perform.

ImageFilter also provides nonfixed filters (i.e., filters that accept parameters). Table 9-4 lists some additional filters supported by the ImageFilter object.

Table 9-4. *Some Image Filters*

Function	Description
MaxFilter(size=3)	For every pixel in the original image, returns the pixel with the maximum value from a square of width size placed around the original pixel. size must be odd (3, 5, 7, . . .).
MedianFilter(size=3)	For every pixel in the original image, returns the median pixel from a square of width size placed around the original pixel. size must be odd (3, 5, 7, . . .).
MinFilter(size=3)	For every pixel in the original image, returns the pixel with the minimum value from a square of width size placed around the original pixel. size must be odd (3, 5, 7, . . .).
ModeFilter(size=3)	For every pixel in the original image, returns the most common pixel from a square of width size placed around the original pixel. size must be odd (3, 5, 7, . . .).

Making Movies

Making movies is a somewhat advanced topic, and here I'll assume you have some basic knowledge of movie formats.

Movies are sequences of images. Once you know how to operate on an image, you can easily apply that knowledge to operate on a movie, as well.

Splitting Movies

The method I'll present here involves splitting a given movie into individual images, operating on these images, and then combining the images again to create a movie. Of course, if you wish to create a movie from a sequence of images, the first step (splitting a given movie) is not required. It should also be noted that movies also contain a sound track; in this discussion, the sound track (audio) is discarded.

To be able to follow along, you will need to download and install an application that has the ability to split a movie into individual frames. It should also be able to do the opposite: create a movie from a sequence of images. I chose to use the MPlayer application, The Movie Player, available at `http://mplayerhq.hu`.

■ **Caution**   Be sure you download the MPlayer application from the official web site (`http://mplayerhq.hu`) to avoid any malware issues. If possible, use the OS package manager (Linux) to install the proper application.

If you use Linux or Mac, once you have MPlayer installed, you can easily access it via the terminal since it will be available to all users. However, in Windows, the location of MPlayer is important, and you should remember where MPlayer is installed. In this section, I assume the location is at c:\mplayer.

To split a movie named movie.avi to individual images, use the following command line in a Linux/Mac terminal. Note that this will discard any audio information:

```
$ mplayer -vo png movie.avi
```

In Windows, this looks slightly different:

```
C:\mplayer> mplayer -vo png movie.avi
```

In Windows, if you're running scripts outside the c:\mplayer directory, you will need to provide to full path to mplayer.exe or add it to the path, as follows:

```
C:\> path=%PATH%;c:\mplayer
```

The result is a sequence of indexed PNG images, generated in the working directory, as follows: 00000001.png, 00000002.png, and so on.

Creating Movies from Images

Combining images into movies is similar to splitting a movie into images, only in reverse. To generate a video from images, we use the MEncoder utility. This utility is part of the MPlayer application, so there's no need to install additional software.

To generate a movie in Mpeg4 format from a list of images, issue the following:

```
mencoder mf://*.png -mf type=png fps=25 -ovc lavc -o new.avi
```

I chose some command-line options in this example. First, I chose the frame rate, fps (which stands for frame-per-second), which I set to 25. I also chose to use a movie codec, Mpeg-4, as evident in this option: vcodec=mpeg4. For a full account of these options, refer to MPlayer's web site (a direct link: http://www.mplayerhq.hu/DOCS/HTML/en/menc-feat-enc-images.html) or consult with the online help.

Example: A Fractal Movie

In this example, we create a sequence of images from the Mandelbrot fractal presented in Chapter 7.

The example is straightforward. We generate fractal images with an increasing number of iterations. We store the images to the files mandelbrot0001.png, mandelbrot0002.png, and so on. Once we're done, we use the *os* module to execute a few shell commands. We do this with a call to os.system() with the command to execute (calling MEncoder; calling MPlayer) as a string. First, we change to the directory where the images are stored. Next, we call MEncoder to encode files. Once the encoding is complete, we use MPlayer to view the file. We can also view the file manually by opening the generated file, Mandelbrot.avi. Lastly, we change to our previous working directory. Listing 9-14 shows the entire script to generate a Mandelbrot fractal movie.

Listing 9-14. The Mandelbrot fractal movie

```
from PIL import Image, ImageOps
import os

# creates an image of the Mandelbrot set
res = 400
```

```python
for iters in range(50):
    img = Image.new("L", (res, res), 255)
    for im in range(res):
        for re in range(res):
            z = 0
            # a scaling to show the "interesting" part of
            # the Mandelbrot fractal
            c = (re*2/res-1.5)+1j*(im*2/res-1)
            for k in range(iters):
                z = z**2+c
                if abs(z)>2:
                    img.putpixel((re, im), 255-k*255/iters)
                    break

    # create a uniform distribution of gray levels
    img = ImageOps.equalize(img)

    # save to file
    img.save('../images/mandelbrot_%04d.png' % iters, dpi=(150,150))

last_path = os.getcwd()

# handle Linux/Mac and Windows properly
os.chdir('../images')
if os.sys.platform.startswith('win'):
    mee = 'c:/mplayer/mencoder '
    mep = 'c:/mplayer/mplayer '
else:
    mee = 'mplayer '
    mep = 'c:/mplayer '

# encode the movie
os.system(mee+'mf://mandelbrot*.png -mf type=png -ovc lavc -o mandelbrot.avi')

# play the movie
os.system(mep+'mandelbrot.avi')
os.chdir(last_path)
```

Combining these two abilities (splitting movies and generating movies from sequences of images) with the image-processing methods shown previously in this chapter will get you started on movie processing in no time.

Final Notes and References

Image processing is a large field, and it is gaining more and more popularity as computers increase in performance. And image processing is only two dimensional; nowadays we see more and more 3-D data processing, as well, including video.

Armed with Python, the Python Imaging Library, and *NumPy*, you can prototype even complex image-processing tasks. However, image processing requires a great deal of memory and processing power; as you work with images, you'll realize you may require faster tools, and you may even need to port parts of your code to a lower-level programming language such as C to gain performance. Nevertheless, Python is an excellent prototyping environment; it provides fast responses in an interactive environment, and it can help you define your image-processing algorithm.

Additional information can be found at the following sites:

- The Python Imaging Library, `http://www.pythonware.com/library/pil/handbook/`

- GIMP, `http://www.gimp.org/docs/`

- MPlayer, The Movie Player, `http://www.mplayerhq.hu`

CHAPTER 10

■ ■ ■

Advanced File Processing

More on Files

A common task of programmers is to work with files. Programmers do more than read and write files; they also organize them, move them around, delete them, compress them, archive them, and more. To accomplish these tasks, I often find myself borrowing code from my previous projects, especially code that deals with reading and parsing files, typically via copy and paste. But that seems such a waste—why not come up with a library of functions that addresses these common needs?

Other programmers must have felt the same way, and so they turned to writing modules, libraries of functions to perform these tasks. And many of these libraries are now included with the Python standard library; more libraries are added on a regular basis.

This chapter examines such file-related topics. Expanding on ideas discussed in Chapters 4 and 5, this chapter also builds on some previous examples to create more reusable code. The examples include reading and writing *NumPy* arrays directly to files, reading and writing MATLAB files, reading data from multiple files, reading command-line parameters, manipulating directories, comparing files, and more.

Binary Files and Random Access

The term *binary file* describes a non-text file, whether an executable file, an image file, or simply a data file. In this section I'll show you some methods of dealing with binary data files, including random binary file access, reading and writing numerical data to binary files using the *struct* module, and reading and writing MATLAB binary files.

Previously when working with text files, we've used readline() or read(n) to read chunks of data from a file. The function readline(), in a sense, splits the file into smaller chunks of data (i.e., lines of text).

With binary files, it's more common to see random access; that is, to see arbitrary reading of chunks of data from anywhere in the file. With text files, this is a bit harder because you don't know in advance how many characters and words are in a line, so randomly picking the nth line is not a trivial task. With binary files composed of fixed-length records, random access allows you to access to an arbitrary field.

The methods seek(offset[, whence]) and tell() are random access file functions. To better understand what these functions do, you need to understand the concept of file pointers. A *file pointer* points to a location in the file: subsequent read or write operations will happen at that specific location (assuming the file was opened in a mode that allows random access read and/or write). Whenever we read or write data from the file, the file pointer is incremented accordingly.

■ **Note**   As in previous chapters, I assume you're running an interactive Python session in directory Ch10/src and that directory Ch10/data exists.

The function seek() sets the file pointer to a value of our choosing; subsequent calls to read() will pick up from the newly "seeked" location. The function tell() returns the current file pointer value in bytes. Here's a short interactive Python session describing the works of seek() and tell():

```
>>> f = open('../data/example.bin', 'wb')
>>> f.tell()
```

```
0
```

```
>>> f.write(b'0123456789')
```

```
10
```

```
>>> f.tell()
```

```
10
```

With the preceding code, I created a binary file. When you first do so, the file pointer associated with the file is set to 0, as shown by the result from f.tell(). After writing ten values, the file pointer is at 10. Notice the leading b character before the string, b'0123456789'; this is so that the string is encoded as bytes (i.e., each character is encoded as its ASCII value):

```
>>> f.seek(5)
>>> f.write(b'0123456789')
```

```
10
```

```
>>> f.tell()
```

```
15
```

```
>>> f.close()
```

I've changed the file pointer to point to location 5 and then rewrote the same ten values. As a result, the file pointer has changed to 15. Let's print the contents of the file:

```
>>> open('../data/example.bin', 'rb').read()
```

```
b'012340123456789'
```

As expected, the result is the string b'0123456789', which is overlapped by another copy of the same string at location 5, resulting in the string b'012340123456789'.

The argument whence in the function seek(offset[, whence]) indicates how the offset should be calculated. If whence is 0 (the default), seek() moves offset bytes relative to the start of the file. If whence is 2, seek() moves the file pointer offset bytes relative to the end of the file. Notice that in order to change the file pointer to n bytes before the end of the file, you must pass a negative value as an offset. On many systems, it's possible to seek past the end of the file (which is a feature, not a bug, as you'll soon see). If whence is equal to 1, seek() moves relative to the current location. Again, both negative and positive values are allowed. Negative values for seek() are not allowed if whence is 0. Let's continuing with our previous example:

```
>>> f = open('../data/example.bin', 'rb')
>>> f.seek(-2, 2)
```

```
13
```

```
>>> print(f.read())
```

```
b'89'
```

```
>>> f.close()
```

I've set the file pointer to 2 bytes (negative 2) before the end of the file and printed the contents of the file from that point forward. As expected, the result is two bytes long and corresponds to b'89'.

Example: Reading the Nth Field

The functions seek() and tell() are especially useful for accessing large binary files that contain fixed-length records. Unlike text files, with binary files of fixed-length records you can calculate in advance the location of a field in the file. Combined with seek(), it's possible to read a single field. This is especially important in large files where reading the entire file or even reading the file a value at a time (without seeking directly to the required field) can take a considerable amount of time.

In the example shown in Listing 10-1, we combine seek() and tell() with the *struct* module (see Chapter 4).

Listing 10-1. Reading the Nth Field

```
import struct
from math import sqrt
from random import randrange

# binary filename
bin_fn = '../data/large_file.bin'

Nfields = 1000      # number of fields
N = 766             # field to retrieve
fmt = 'cdL'         # format: byte, float, 4-bytes

fmt_size = struct.calcsize(fmt)
```

```
# create a random binary file
fout = open(bin_fn, 'wb')
for i in range(Nfields):
    data = struct.pack(fmt, bytes([randrange(32, 128)]), sqrt(float(i)), i)
    fout.write(data)
fout.close()

# read the nth value
fin = open(bin_fn, 'rb')
fin.seek((N-1)*fmt_size)
data = fin.read(fmt_size)
(c, d, l) = struct.unpack(fmt, data)
print("At location %d, I read:" % (fin.tell()/fmt_size), (c, d, l))
```

The first part of the script creates a binary file with some made-up data. Notice the line, data = struct.pack(fmt, bytes([randrange(32, 128)]), sqrt(float(i)), i), as it requires some explanation. The function struct.pack() accepts a format specifier, in our case 'cdL', which stands for a one-byte integer, a double floating-point value, and a 4-byte integer, and then the actual values: a byte, a double, and a 4-byte integer. While generating a double and a 4-byte integer is straightforward in Python (the default size for a floating point value and the default size for an integer), generating a one-byte integer is a little more complex. To generate a single-byte value, I use the function bytes(). The function bytes() returns an immutable sequence of bytes and has several flavors. The one I chose to use accepts an iterable and generates a byte array from that iterable. In this case, the iterable is simply a list with one value, which is generated from the function randrange(). Therefore, the statement bytes([randrange(32, 128)]) turns a 4-byte integer into a 1-byte integer.

The next part of the code reads a single field at location 766 without reading the entire file. This is done by changing the file pointer to point to location (N-1)*fmt_size and reading only one field.

Here's a result from running the script:

```
At location 766, I read: (b'[', 27.65863337187866, 765)
```

Example: Efficient Tail Implementation

In Chapter 5 you saw a possible implementation of head-and-tail functionality. The tail functionality was harder to implement for a very large file. To implement tail functionality, you have to know in advance the number of lines in a file. This forces you to either read the entire file, perform two passes, or keep a buffer of the last lines (for more details, see Chapter 5, "Example: head and tail"). In this example, we turn to implement tail functionality for large files with use of seek() and tell(), as demonstrated in Listing 10-2.

Listing 10-2. A tail() Function for Large Files

```
from os.path import getsize

def tail_large(filename, n=10):
    """Returns the last n lines of a very large file."""

    N, data = 1024, b''

    # open the file and retrieve its size
    f = open(filename, 'rb')
    fsize = getsize(filename)
```

```
# seek to the end of file
f.seek(0, 2)

for i in range(fsize-N, -N, -N):
    # read the next chunk of data
    f.seek(max(i, 0))

    # store read data, reversed order
    data = f.read(N)+data

    # do we have enough lines?
    if data.count(b'\n') > n:
        break

# print the last n lines
lines = data.splitlines()
for line in lines[-n:]:
    print(line)
```

The idea is this: read N bytes from the end and store the result in data. The parameter N is an arbitrary number and describes the number of bytes to read in one chunk. I've set it to 1024. If data contains more than n lines (simply count the number of times '\n' is encountered), break out of the for loop and print the last n lines of data. If data does not contain n lines, read the next chunk of N bytes (i.e., backward) and add the read bytes to data. In a sense, we're going backward from the end of the file, reading chunks of N=1024 bytes, and then counting whether we encountered enough line breaks. If we have, we print those lines; if we haven't, we keep reading more data until we either have read the required number of lines or have reached the beginning of the file.

This implementation is not as straightforward as the one presented in Chapter 5. However, there is a substantial performance gain for large files. The reason for this is that you don't read the entire file, which can be very time consuming for large files; instead, the code starts at the end of the file, going backward, and only reads the requested lines.

Example: Creating a Fixed Size File

Dealing with binary files, you may need to create a large file (of non-initialized values) at times, such as to set aside storage for future data to be written to it.

A trick I use when creating a file is to seek past the end of the file to a location equivalent to the required length minus one, and then write 0 and close the file. This creates a file of the required size (in many systems).

The following creates an uninitialized file of size 1GB (2^{30} bytes):

```
>>> f = open('../data/1gb_file.bin', 'wb')
>>> f.seek(2**30-1)
```

```
1073741823
```

```
>>> f.write(bytes([0]))
```

```
1
```

```
>>> f.close()
```

Now you need to ensure that the file was indeed created:

```
>>> from os.path import getsize
>>> getsize('../data/1gb_file.bin')
```

```
1073741824
```

■ **Note**   The ability to seek past the end of a file is system dependent and not supported by all systems.

Example: Recording Time-Based Binary Data

When recording time-based binary data, a method I particularly like is using the epoch notation (see Chapter 5). For this example, I'll be using functions from the *time* module and from Python's *array* module (not to be confused with *NumPy*'s array object).

If you're simply recording a variable as a function of time, it's easier if the recorded variable is in floating-point notation because now both the time and the value use the same data type. This allows for a simple use of the *array* module, as shown in Listing 10-3.

Listing 10-3. Writing Epoch-Based Data in Binary Form

```
import random, time, array

N = 10
fname = '../data/binary_data.f64'
data = array.array('d')

# create data
for value in range(N):
    time.sleep(random.random())
    data.append(time.time())
    data.append(value)

# store data to file
f = open(fname, 'wb')
data.tofile(f)
f.close()
```

The script runs five seconds on average and generates timestamps and values. I've used the `array` method `tofile()` to store binary values to file.

Retrieving data from the binary file is simple as well, as you can see in Listing 10-4.

Listing 10-4. Reading Binary Data Stored with Epoch Notation

```
import random, time, array

N = 10
fname = '../data/binary_data.f64'
data = array.array('d')
```

```
# read data
f = open(fname, 'rb')
data.fromfile(f, N*2)
f.close()

# display data
L = data.tolist()
for t, val in zip(L[::2], L[1::2]):
    print(time.ctime(t), val)
```

Most of the work is performed in the line data.fromfile(f, N*2), which reads values and stores them in a Python array. I then rearrange the data and display the results:

```
Sun Jun 22 23:25:58 2014 0.0
Sun Jun 22 23:25:59 2014 1.0
Sun Jun 22 23:25:59 2014 2.0
Sun Jun 22 23:26:00 2014 3.0
Sun Jun 22 23:26:00 2014 4.0
Sun Jun 22 23:26:01 2014 5.0
Sun Jun 22 23:26:02 2014 6.0
Sun Jun 22 23:26:02 2014 7.0
Sun Jun 22 23:26:02 2014 8.0
Sun Jun 22 23:26:03 2014 9.0
```

I've used a trick to rearrange the data. When I convert the data from an array to a list, L, the values are interlaced: time, value, time, value, and so on. To print values, I can just iterate through L, converting to a time format every odd value. Here I've opted to zip slices of even and odd values. The following code illustrates this:

```
>>> L = [1, 'Value', 2, 'Another value', 3, 'Last value']
>>> L[::2]    # these are the odd values
```

```
[1, 2, 3]
```

```
>>> L[1::2]   # these are the even values
```

```
['Value', 'Another value', 'Last value']
```

```
>>> list(zip(L[::2], L[1::2]))
```

```
[(1, 'Value'), (2, 'Another value'), (3, 'Last value')]
```

```
>>> for i, s in zip(L[::2], L[1::2]):
...     print(i, s)
...
```

```
1 Value
2 Another value
3 Last value
```

Reading MATLAB Files as *NumPy* Arrays

Many *PyLab* users will find reading and writing MATLAB-style .mat files an important capability. This enables easy transfer of data from MATLAB to Python and vice versa. MATLAB is a popular mathematical programming language and environment; for more information, see http://www.mathworks.com. If you do not use MATLAB files, you can skip this section.

MATLAB-style .mat files are binary files with a specific binary format. To read and write mat files, we use *scipy.io* module. To read files, we use savemat(filename, dict); to write files, we use loadmat(filename), as follows:

```
>>> from pylab import *
>>> from scipy.io import savemat, loadmat
>>> a = arange(10)
>>> savemat('data.mat', {'a': a})
>>> del a
>>> a
```

```
Traceback (most recent call last):
  File "<stdin>", line 1, in <module>
NameError: name 'a' is not defined
```

```
>>> loadmat('data.mat')
```

```
{'__header__': b'MATLAB 5.0 MAT-file Platform: nt, Created on:
Sun Jun 22 23:43:58 2014', '__globals__': [], '__version__': '1.0',
'a': array([[0, 1, 2, 3, 4, 5, 6, 7, 8, 9]])}
```

```
>>> data = loadmat('data.mat')
>>> data['a']
```

```
array([[0, 1, 2, 3, 4, 5, 6, 7, 8, 9]])
```

At first, I create a *NumPy* array, a. I then use savemat() to write the array to a mat file. Notice how savemat() requires a filename and a dictionary composed of variables names and the actual values. In this case, the variable name is a; hence, the dictionary object is {'a': a}.

Reading mat files is similar. The result is a Python dictionary, data, which can be accessed using the variable name, a, as the key: data['a'].

■ **Note**   Not all MATLAB files versions are supported, so consult with the SciPy web site: http://www.scipy.org/.

Reading Text Files Directly to *NumPy* Arrays

It's also possible to read and write *NumPy* arrays directly as text files with the functions loadtxt() and savetxt(), respectively. These are highly versatile functions especially well-suited for the task of reading and writing text files containing numerical data.

The function loadtxt(fname) accepts the parameters listed in Table 10-1.

Table 10-1. *Optional Parameters for loadtxt()*

Parameter	Description
Comments	The character used to indicate the start of a comment. Comment lines will be ignored.
Converters	A dictionary detailing the function used to convert each column (e.g., converters='{0: datestr2num}'). It will convert column 0 (the first column) using the function datestr2num().
Delimiter	The character used to separate values. The default is any whitespace character.
Dtype	Data type. The default is float.
Ndmin	Forces the returned array to be n-dimensional; n can be 0, 1, or 2.
Skiprows	The number of rows to skip; the default is 0.
Usecols	A sequence containing the columns to read. For example, usecols=(2, 3) will read the 3rd and 4th columns (counting starts at zero).
Unpack	A Boolean flag indicating whether the read array should be transposed.

Example: Reading and Writing Text Files to NumPy Arrays

For this example, we use the file charts.xls from "Example: Stock Price Charts" in Chapter 4. I assume you have followed the directory structure used in the book (see Chapter 2) and that the file is located in the directory, ../data/charts.xls.

The file charts.xls looks like this:

```
Date         Open          High          Low           Close/Last    Volume
10:24        3598.27002    3599.389893   3587.48999    3598.350098   0
05/05/2014   3566.256      3605.263      3556.403      3605.092      0
05/02/2014   3608.841      3611.563      3578.527      3587.644      0
05/01/2014   3589.659      3613.03       3580.019      3594.362      0
```

(The listing is truncated.)

Since the first row of charts.xls is a header row, and the second row is yet another header row (but in a different format), we'd like to skip these two rows; hence, skiprows=2. Furthermore, the first column consists of dates. Dates are not numbers, so they cannot fit into *NumPy* arrays. To overcome this, we can simply ignore the first column if we're not interested in date information by specifying usecols=(1, 2, 3, 4, 5) (notice the missing 0 column). Alternatively, we can use a converter to convert the date to a number, as follows:

```
>>> from pylab import *
>>> def co(x):
...     return datestr2num(x.decode('utf-8'))
...
```

```
>>> data = loadtxt('../data/charts.xls', skiprows=2, converters={0:c0})
>>> data
```

```
array([[ 735358.   ,   3566.256,   3605.263,   3556.403,   3605.092,
              0.   ],
       [ 735355.   ,   3608.841,   3611.563,   3578.527,   3587.644,
              0.   ],
       [ 735354.   ,   3589.659,   3613.03 ,   3580.019,   3594.362,
              0.   ],
       [ 735353.   ,   3556.004,   3585.502,   3548.11 ,   3582.02 ,
              0.   ],
```

(The output is truncated.)

I've defined a function named c0() which is the converter function for column 0; all other columns will be of type float by default. The function c0() uses the function datestr2num(), which is a *NumPy* function to convert a string to a number. Since datestr2num() expects a string and not an array of bytes, I've used decode('utf-8') to convert from an array of bytes to a string.

■ **Tip** The function genfromtxt() is similar to loadtxt(), and it can handle missing data. For a full account, issue help(genfromtxt).

To write *NumPy* arrays to text files, we use the savetxt() function:

```
>>> savetxt('../data/charts_mod.txt', data)
```

Object Serialization

When working with an interactive session in Python, sometimes it's useful to be able to save variables to file. Prior to writing them to file, variables should be serialized; that is, they should be converted into a stream of bytes. The stream of bytes can then be written to file and later retrieved.

The *Pickle* Module

Instead of creating dedicated file formats to deal with all sorts of variable types (lists, strings, *NumPy* arrays, and the like), Python provides us with a built-in object serialization module that is ideal for this purpose: *Pickle*.

To use *Pickle*, first issue import pickle. The function pickle.dump(obj, file[, protocol]) serializes an object and writes it to file. The protocol argument can take the values 0 for ASCII (the default), 1 for binary, and 2 to indicate support for new Python objects. Both protocols 1 and 2 create binary files. If you provide a negative value for dump(), the highest version protocol will be used. This is to account for future protocol versions of *Pickle*. The function pickle.load(file) will read an object from file.

The function pickle.dumps(obj[, protocol]) serializes the object and returns its string representation without writing it to file. Similarly, pickle.loads(str) creates an object from a string.

Example: Saving and Retrieving Python Session Variables

Listing 10-5 uses the *Pickle* module to write variables of varying data types to file.

Listing 10-5. Pickling Several Objects to File

```python
import pickle
from numpy import *

fname = '../data/mysession.pickle'
a = 3
b = "A string"
c = {'dict': 10}
d = eye(3)

fout = open(fname, 'wb')
for var in [a, b, c, d]:
    pickle.dump(var, fout)
fout.close()
```

To "pickle" objects (i.e., serialize them) and write them to file, I've used the function `pickle.dump(var, file)`. You can issue subsequent calls to `pickle.dump()` to store additional values to file.

To read the objects from file, use Listing 10-6.

Listing 10-6. Reading Objects from a File

```python
import pickle

fname = '../data/mysession.pickle'
fin = open(fname, 'rb')
var_index = 0

while True:
    try:
        var_index += 1
        exec("v_%d = pickle.load(fin)" % var_index)
        exec("var_type = type(v_%d)" % var_index)
        print("Read v_%d, type is: %s" % (var_index, var_type))
    except EOFError:
        break
```

Whenever you issue a call to `pickle.load()`, the return value is a Python object (unless the end of file is reached). However, the name of the object is not stored. Therefore, I've used the `exec()` built-in function to create variables named v_1, v_2, and so forth to store the objects.

Here are the results from running the script:

```
Read v_1, type is: <class 'int'>
Read v_2, type is: <class 'str'>
Read v_3, type is: <class 'dict'>
Read v_4, type is: <class 'numpy.ndarray'>
```

```
>>> v_4
```

```
array([[ 1.,  0.,  0.],
       [ 0.,  1.,  0.],
       [ 0.,  0.,  1.]])
```

If you're using *NumPy* arrays, you can use the functions save() and load() provided by *matplotlib*. These functions accept a file name and read and write a *NumPy* array object to and from file:

```
>>> from pylab import *
>>> fname = '../data/session.npy'
>>> save(fname, eye(3))
>>> load(fname)
```

```
array([[ 1.,  0.,  0.],
       [ 0.,  1.,  0.],
       [ 0.,  0.,  1.]])
```

If the file name used in save() and load() ends with .gz, gzip compression is automatically used (see the "File Compression" section later in this chapter).

Command-Line Parameters

This section, which covers command-line parameters, may seem to be a bit of an off-topic discussion. Before we get into the details of the *FileInput* module, however, you need to understand command-line parameters. As you'll soon see, the *FileInput* module makes more sense in the context of command-line parameters. In essence, command line parameters enable us to pass along parameters directly, via the command-line, to an application, in order to control its behavior.

A possible progression from an interactive Python session is to create a stand-alone utility or application—that is, to create a Python script callable from the shell, be it the command prompt in Windows or a command shell in Linux. One of the options of interacting with such a script is by passing command-line parameters, or command-line arguments. For example, in the tail command-line utility, a command-line parameter could be the number of lines tail will display. So, to list the last 20 lines of a file, you would write the following:

```
$ python tail.py -n 20 filename
```

argv

The *sys* module enables command-line processing with the sys.argv variable, as shown in Listing 10-7. sys.argv is a list of strings containing the entered split shell command. The value in sys.argv[0] is the name of the Python script.

Listing 10-7. Command-Line Arguments

```
import sys
for i, cmd in enumerate(sys.argv):
    print("argv[%d] = '%s'" % (i, cmd))
```

Save the file as parse_args.py and run python parse_args.py 20 myfile in a shell or a command prompt (ensure the Python executable is in your path). Here are the results:

```
argv[0] = 'parse_args.py'
argv[1] = '20'
argv[2] = 'myfile'
```

Example: Creating a Fixed Size File (a Stand-Alone Script)

Now we turn to modify the code from the "Example: Creating a Fixed Size File" section. The goal is to create a stand-alone script callable from a CLI (shell or command window). The script, shown in Listing 10-8 (empty_file.py), accepts the number of bytes and a file name, and then creates a file of specified name and size.

Listing 10-8. Creating a Fixed-Size File (Stand-Alone Script), empty_file.py

```
from sys import argv, exit

usage = "Usage: python empty_file.py nbytes filename"

# we expect three arguments: script name, size and file name
if len(argv) != 3:
    print("Improper number of arguments.")
    print(usage)
    exit()

# is size an integer?
try:
    nbytes = int(argv[1])
except ValueError:
    print("First argument is not an integer number.")
    print(usage)
    exit()

# retrieve the requested file name
filename = argv[2]

# can we create the file?
# here a failure could be due to a non-existing path
try:
    f = open(filename, 'wb')
except IOError:
    print("Unable to create file", filename)
    print(usage)
    exit()
```

```
# finally! create the file
f.seek(nbytes-1)
f.write(b'0')
f.close()
print("Successfully created file %s of size %d." % (filename, nbytes))
```

I've carefully checked the parameters passed by the user to determine whether there are an adequate number of parameters and if those values are valid. I took special care to ensure that the file can indeed be created. Finally, the code that generates the empty file is simple.

I've also introduced the function exit(), provided with the *sys* module. The function is especially useful when you're writing a stand-alone script, as it exits the script immediately.

The *optparse* Module

Enforcing a strict syntax for command-line parameters renders a script less user friendly. For instance, in the previous example, you might want the script to automatically create a file of default size, say 1KB, in case no length is provided. Or you might want to add additional parameters with default values, further controlling the behavior of the script so that it creates a path to the file name if it does not exist.

Accommodating additional options as well as default options will cause the code in the previous listing to grow larger and less maintainable. When the number of options increases, consider using the *optparse* module; the *optparse* module is designed to address command-line parameters in an easy set of library functions.

■ **Tip**   The module *getopt* (http://docs.python.org/library/getopt.html) is an older module that also provides functions to parse command-line options.

To use the *optparse* module, follow these steps:

1.   Import the *optparse* module: import optparse.

2.   Create an OptionParser object.

3.   Add options to the parser using the add_option() method.

4.   Parse the command-line arguments using the parse_args() method.

The first step is obvious: import the module. The second step requires you to instantiate an OptionParser object by setting parser = OptionParser(). Adding options is a bit more complex as there are many possibilities to choose from (as you'll soon see). The last step is calling the function parse_args(), which returns a list of command-line options.

The return value of parse_args() is a tuple of options and arguments. The difference between an option and an argument is that options are, of course, optional, and arguments (positional arguments per *optparse* documentation) are required.

Example: Processing Command-Line Parameters

We'll modify our previous example so that now the number of bytes per file is an option followed by the requested number of bytes (i.e., -n 1000), as in Listing 10-9 (empty_opt.py). Furthermore, we'll add an option switch, also known as an option flag, indicating whether a .bin extension should be added to the file name. The existence of the option flag -x instructs the script whether to create the extension; there's no additional value following this flag.

Listing 10-9. *Processing Command-Line Parameteres Using optparse, empty_opt.py*

```python
from optparse import OptionParser
from sys import exit

usage = "Usage: python empty_opt.py [options] filename"

# create an OptionParser instance
parser = OptionParser(usage)

# these are the options
parser.add_option("-n", "--numbytes", dest="nbytes",
    type = "int", default=1000, help="number of bytes in file")
parser.add_option("-x", "--ext", dest="ext",
    action="store_true", default=False,
    help="adds 'bin' extension to filename")
(opt, args) = parser.parse_args()

# must have a filename
if len(args) != 1:
    print("Improper number of arguments.")
    exit()

# append extension if switch is on
filename = args[0]+'.bin' if opt.ext else args[0]

# create the file
try:
    f = open(filename, 'wb')
except IOError:
    print("Unable to create file", filename)
    exit()

f.seek(opt.nbytes-1)
f.write(b'0')
f.close()

print("Successfully created file %s of size %d." %
    (filename, opt.nbytes))
```

The preceding listing begins by importing the *optparse* module. I then instantiate an `OptionParser` object and provide it with the default usage string. The `usage` string will be displayed as the first line whenever the user issues the command-line switch -h or –help, which looks like this: `python empty_opt.py -h`.

I then add options using the `add_option()` method. The `add_option()` method has many parameters to control how options should be parsed. In my first `add_option()` call, I've set how the user invokes this option: by entering either `-n NBYTES` or `--numbytes NBYTES`. I set the destination for this option to be named nbytes. This means that, after the option is parsed, I can access the option value through variable, `opt.nbytes`. The type of variable is an int, as detailed by the `type` argument, and the default value is 1000, in case nbytes isn't provided by the user. Lastly, the help string associated with this option is detailed: `help="number of bytes in file"`.

Similarly, I set another option named ext. This option is a switch, and the user invokes the switch simply by entering -x or --ext; there are no additional values following the switch (in contrast, the -n option was accompanied by an NBYTES value). The action argument instructs *optparse* to treat this as a positively acting switch: if -x is provided, set the flag to True. Lastly, I've set the default value to False and added a help string: help="adds 'bin' extension to filename".

Parsing the command-line options is performed with the call to parse_args(). Both the options and arguments are then retrieved. The options are accessed via a class parameter, and the arguments are provided in a list. Following that is the actual creation of the file.

The following are the results from running the script with various options in a bash shell:

```
$ python empty_opt.py
```

```
Improper number of arguments.
```

```
$ python empty_opt.py -h
```

```
Usage: python empty_opt.py [options] filename

Options:
  -h, --help            show this help message and exit
  -n NBYTES, --numbytes=NBYTES
                        number of bytes in file
  -x, --ext             adds 'bin' extension to filename
```

```
$ python empty_opt.py file1
```

```
Successfully created file file1 of size 1000.
```

```
$ python empty_opt.py -x file1
```

```
Successfully created file file1.bin of size 1000.
```

```
$ python empty_opt.py -n 2000 --ext file1
```

```
Successfully created file file1.bin of size 2000.
```

```
$ python empty_opt.py -n 2000 --ext file1 file2
```

```
Improper number of arguments.
```

```
$ python empty_opt.py -n 2a --ext file1
```

```
Usage: python empty_opt.py [options] filename

empty_opt.py: error: option -n: invalid integer value: '2a'
```

The script expects an input as follows: `[options]` `filename`. Calling the script with the command-line parameter `-h` or `--help` prints out the usage help message. This is implemented automatically when you use the *optparse* module. Next, I've issued some valid command-line parameters and some invalid ones. For example, *optparse* handles the parsing of the values, while my code handles the number of arguments (only one: `filename`). I've also called the script with full option names (`--ext`) and abbreviated option names (`-x`).

The module *optparse* is a rich module with many features. Refer to the online help at `https://docs.python.org/3.3/library/optparse.html` for a detailed description of the module.

■ **Tip**   As the number of options increases, consider using the *configparser* module instead. See Chapter 4 for an introduction to *configparser* and the online help (`https://docs.python.org/3.3/library/configparser.html`).

The *FileInput* Module

We'll close our command-line parameters discussion with the *FileInput* module. This module provides an easy method for accessing several files (or streams) passed by the command line (i.e., `python somescript.py file1 file2 file3`). To use the module, issue `import fileinput`.

Using the module is straightforward: iterate over `fileinput.input()`. The result from the iteration is the next line in the current file. Once the end of file is reached, the next file is opened automatically, and the process resumes until all lines from all files have been iterated over.

Table 10-2 lists some useful *FileInput* methods that can be used to further enhance scripts that use the module.

Table 10-2. *Some Useful FileInput Methods*

Method	Description
`fileinput.close()`	Ends the processing, closing all opened files.
`fileinput.filelineno()`	Returns the line number in the current file.
`fileinput.filename()`	Returns the name of the file currently being read.
`fileinput.fileno()`	Returns the index of the current file.
`fileinput.isfirstline()`	Returns True if this is the first line in a file.
`fileinput.lineno()`	Returns the cumulative line number of all lines read from all the files.
`fileinput.nextfile()`	Stops processing the current file and jumps to the next file.

Let's turn to an example.

Example: Combining Data from Several Sources Based on the Epoch

Next, we'll pick up from an example previously presented in Chapter 5 in a section with the same title as this one. This time, Listing 10-10 allows for more than two files to be combined, based on the epoch.

Listing 10-10. Combining Several Files Based on the Epoch, combine_epoch.py

```
import fileinput
from time import mktime, strptime
data = []
fmt = '%b %d %H:%M:%S %Y'
for line in fileinput.input():
    data.append([mktime(strptime(line[4:24], fmt)), line])
for line in sorted(data):
    print(line[1], end='')
```

The contents of the files are detailed in Chapter 5. Use the script as follows: python combine_epoch.py file1 file2 .... This code reads line after line from all the input files (using the module *fileinput*), appending each line read to a list, data. The last couple of lines of code print the array of lines, sorted by the epoch, and then generate a combined, time-synchronized output.

Example: Searching for Text in Multiple Files

Again, Listing 10-11 builds on an example previously shown in Chapter 5, "Example: Searching Inside a Text File." As in the previous example, we want to search for text in multiple files. To use the script, srchfile.py, issue the command python srchfile.py search_string file1 file2 ....

Listing 10-11. Searching for Text in Multiple Files, srchfile.py

```
import fileinput, sys

# string to search is the first argument
for line in fileinput.input(sys.argv[2:]):
    if line.find(sys.argv[1]) != -1:
        print("File %s, #%d: %s" % (fileinput.filename(),
            fileinput.filelineno(), line.rstrip()))
```

The main difference from the example in Chapter 5 and this one is that now the first parameter is the string to search instead of a file. Therefore, I access the command-line parameters and pass the values from the third parameter onward (sys.argv[2:]) to fileinput.input(). Doing so will skip the script name (argv[0]) and the search string (argv[1]).

The module also provides support for modifying files as you process the lines via the inplace argument. Refer to the online help for more on this: https://docs.python.org/3.3/library/fileinput.html.

File and Directory Manipulation

In addition to reading and writing files and processing command-line parameters, manipulating files is also a task commonly required of a developer. You've seen the *os.walk* module and some directory operations in previous chapters; here I expand on those, as well as file operations: deleting files, moving files, and more.

Module *glob*

The *glob* module enables searching for files when given a file-name pattern. The function glob(pattern) will return a list of all the files matching pattern; the function iglob(pattern) returns an iterator (as opposed to a list in glob()) of all the files matching pattern. I usually just use the list version, glob(pattern):

```
>>> from glob import glob
>>> glob('*.py')
```

```
['combine_epoch.py', 'empty_file.py', 'empty_opt.py', 'import sys.py',
'parse_args.py', 'srchfile.py']
```

glob() accepts shell-like wildcards, such as * (matches a string of characters), ? (matches one character), [chars] (matches any character from a list of characters) and [!chars] (matches anything but those characters listed). The following will match a file name that ends with py and contains a number:

```
>>> glob('*[0-9]*py')
```

```
['extract3.py']
```

This snippet will match a file name that ends with py and does not start with c:

```
>>> glob('[!c]*py')
```

```
['extract3.py', 'tail_large.py']
```

Please note that glob expressions contain shell wildcards, so they are not regular expressions.

■ **Tip** You should also see the module, *fnmatch* (https://docs.python.org/3.3/library/fnmatch.html).

Additional *os* Module Functionality

You've already seen a considerable number of functions from the *os* and *os.path* modules (see the "Moving Around" section in Chapter 3). Table 10-3 lists a few more, not mentioned earlier, that are especially useful for manipulating files and directories. In the table, assume the current working directory is /home/user and that the file in the directory is file.ext.

Table 10-3. *os Module Functions for Manipulating Files and Directories*

Function	Description	Example
os.chmod(path, mode)	Change file permissions (in Windows, only the read and write permissions are changed; all else is ignored).	os.chmod('file.ext', 0777) changes the file permissions to read, write, and execute for all.
os.remove(pathname), or os.unlink(pathname)	Delete the file specified in pathname.	os.unlink('file.ext') deletes the file, file.ext.
os.rmdir()	Remove a directory if it's empty.	os.rmdir('/home/user') removes the directory /home/user if it's empty.
os.mkdir(path)	Create a directory.	os.mkdir('another') creates the directory, /home/user/another.
os.makedirs(path)	Create a directory as well as any intermediate subdirectories.	os.makedirs('dir1/dir2') creates the directories /home/user/dir1 and /home/user/dir1/dir2.
os.rename(old, new)	Rename a path or file.	os.rename('file.ext', 'file2.ext') renames the file file.ext to file2.ext.
os.renames(old, new)	Rename a path or file, including the creation of intermediate directories and the removal of empty ones.	os.renames('/home/user', '/home/user2/dir1/dir2') renames the directory /home/user to /home/user2/dir1/dir2. It also creates subdirectories that do not exist and removes the directory /home/user if it's empty.

Additional *os.path* Module Functionality

The module *os.path* provides functions that help manage file names and file paths. Table 10-4 lists some useful *os.path* functions. In the table, assume the current working directory is /home/user and that the file in the directory is file.ext.

Table 10-4. *Some Useful os.path Functions*

Function	Description	Example
os.path.abspath(s)	Returns the absolute path of a file.	os.path.abspath('file.ext') returns '/home/user/file.ext'.
os.path.basename(s)	Returns the file name, excluding the path.	os.path.basename('/home/user/file.ext') returns 'file.ext'.
os.path.dirname(s)	Returns the directory name of a path.	os.path.dirname('/home/user/file.ext') returns '/home/user'.
os.path.exists(s)	Returns True if the path or file specified by s exists.	os.path.exists('/home/user') returns True.
os.path.getatime(s)	Returns the last access time of a file.	time.ctime(os.path.getatime('/home/user/file.ext')) prints the access time (ctime() is part of the time module).
os.path.getctime(s)	Returns the creation time of a file.	Similar to os.path.getatime() example.
os.path.getmtime(s)	Returns the last modification time of a file.	Similar to os.path.getatime() example.
os.path.getsize(s)	Returns the file size in bytes.	os.path.getsize('file.ext') returns the size of file file.txt in bytes.
os.path.isabs(s)	Returns True if the path specified by s is an absolute path.	os.path.isabs('file.ext') returns False os.path.isabs('/home/user/file.ext') returns True.
os.path.isdir(s)	Returns True if s is a directory.	os.path.isdir('/home') returns True.
os.path.isfile(s)	Returns True if s is a file.	os.path.isfile('file.ext') returns True.
os.path.join(base, seq)	Joins two or more paths, adding slashes as needed.	os.path.join('/home/user', 'file.ext') returns '/home/user/file.ext'. os.path.join('/home', 'user', 'file.ext') returns '/home/user/file.ext'.
os.path.split(s)	Splits a pathname, returning the path and the file name.	os.path.split('/home/user/file.ext') returns ('/home/user', 'file.ext').
os.path.splitext(s)	Splits a pathname returning the extension, including the dot.	os.path.splitext('/home/user/file.ext') returns ('/home/user/file', '.ext').

Module *shutil*

The *shutil* module provides higher-level functions for copying, moving, and renaming files. Of those, we'll explore the following: copy(src, dest), copytree(src, dest), rmtree(path), and move(src, dst). For a full account of the module, refer to https://docs.python.org/3.3/library/shutil.html.

I assume a file named file1.txt exists in the current directory. If yours doesn't have this file, create one if you wish to follow along.

First, let's create a directory with subdirectories and copy file1.txt to the newly created directory:

```
>>> import shutil
>>> from os import makedirs
>>> from glob import glob
>>> makedirs('dir1/dir2/dir3/dir4')
>>> shutil.copy('file1.txt', 'dir1/dir2/dir3/dir4')
```

```
'dir1/dir2/dir3/dir4/file1.txt'
```

```
>>> shutil.copy('file1.txt', 'dir1/dir2/dir3/dir4/file2.txt')
```

```
'dir1/dir2/dir3/dir4/file2.txt'
```

```
>>> glob('dir1/dir2/dir3/dir4/*')
```

```
['dir1/dir2/dir3/dir4/file2.txt', 'dir1/dir2/dir3/dir4/file1.txt']
```

First, I imported several modules and functions: *shutil*, *os*, and *glob*. I then created a directory (as well as its parent directories): dir1/dir2/dir3/dir4. I used the function copy() in two ways: first, to copy the file file1.txt to the newly created directory; and second, to copy the file file1.txt to the same directory under a different name, file2.txt:

```
>>> shutil.move('dir1/dir2/dir3/dir4/file2.txt', 'dir1/dir2')
```

```
'dir1/dir2/file2.txt'
```

```
>>> glob('dir1/dir2/*')
```

```
['dir1/dir2/dir3', 'dir1/dir2/file2.txt']
```

```
>>> glob('dir1/dir2/dir3/dir4/*')
```

```
['dir1/dir2/dir3/dir4/file1.txt']
```

I've moved the file filet2.txt to directory dir1/dir2. The results from glob() confirm the move.
Next, I copied the entire directory leaf under dir1 to a new directory named Dir_1:

```
>>> shutil.copytree('dir1', 'Dir_1')
```

```
'Dir_1'
```

```
>>> glob('Dir_1/dir2/dir3/dir4/*')
```

```
['Dir_1/dir2/dir3/dir4/file1.txt']
```

And lastly, it's time for cleanup—I removed both directories, as well as their subdirectories:

```
>>> shutil.rmtree('dir1')
>>> shutil.rmtree('Dir_1')
>>> glob('dir1')
```

```
[]
```

File Compression

File compression is the process of representing a file in fewer bytes. Compression is typically divided into two categories: lossy compression and nonlossy compression. In lossy compression, the compressed data is not identical to the original data; data is lost in the process of reducing the file size (hopefully unimportant information is lost). Nonlossy compression uses clever schemes to represent data in a way that is more efficient. For example, instead of writing a hundred identical values to file, a nonlossy compression scheme might be to write the value 100, representing the count, and then the repeat value.

Python provides us with several compression and archiving modules (see Table 10-5). We use archiving modules to create compressed files, but we use compression modules to deal with the compression itself. We can use compression on files, as well as strings. The distinction between archiving and compression is somewhat blurred because some modules perform both compression and archiving. The names of the packages are also the import names; so to use *gzip*, issue `import gzip`.

Table 10-5. Python Standard Library Compression and Archiving Modules

Module name	Functionality	Documentation link
bz2	Nonlossy compression	`https://docs.python.org/3.3/library/bz2.html`
gzip	Nonlossy compression	`https://docs.python.org/3.3/library/gzip.html`
zlib	Nonlossy compression	`https://docs.python.org/3.3/library/zlib.html` `http://www.zlib.net/`
tarfile	Archiving	`https://docs.python.org/3.3/library/tarfile.html`
zipfile	Archiving and compression	`https://docs.python.org/3.3/library/zipfile.html`

There are some differences between the different modules in terms of compression ratio, performance, and popularity. However, they're all easy to use and provide excellent results. In this section we'll explore the *tarfile* module.

Example: A Compressed tar File

In the open source community, it's common to see files distributed with the extensions `.tar.gz` or `.tar.bz2`. These are compressed *tar* files; tar stands for tape archive, but in reality there's no need for tapes. The example in Listing 10-12 creates several files, archives them, and then retrieves them from the archive.

Listing 10-12. Creating an Archive

```
import tarfile, glob, os.path

# create some files
for i in range(5):
    f = open('../data/file%d.txt' % i, 'w')
    # write some data
    for j in range(100):
        f.write('Some data: %d\n' % j)
    f.close()

# archive the files using bz2 compression
tf = tarfile.open('../data/files.tar.bz2', 'w:bz2')
for filename in glob.glob('../data/file*'):
    tf.add(filename, os.path.basename(filename))
tf.close()
```

The first section of the script generates five files with some made-up data. Once the files are created, I create a tar file for archiving. The file mode is specified as `'w:bz2'`, which stands for writing (creating) a tar file compressed with compression algorithm bz2. Other modes include `'w:gz'` for gzip compression and `'w'` for no compression. Similarly, opening an archive can be done by specifying `'r'`, `'r:gz'`, or `'r:bz2'`.

Once the `tarfile` object is created, we add files to the archive using the `add(path, arcname)` method. If you provide a directory to `add()`, the entire directory is added to the archive.

I've decided to add the files one at a time in case other files exist in the directory that I don't wish to include. I've also set the archive name by calling `os.path.basename()` function to split the filename from the relative path; this is so that future calls to `extract()` will create a file in the current working directory and not the relative path, `../data`. Finally, I close the tar file, effectively creating the file, `files.tar.bz2`.

Retrieving files from an archive is simple as well, as demonstrated in Listing 10-13. The method `extractall()` extracts all files from an archive. The method `extract(member, path)` extracts a file that is a member of the archive to a location specified by `path`. The method `getmembers()` lists the members (files) in an archive.

Listing 10-13. Extracting All Files from an Archive

```
import tarfile, os

tf = tarfile.open('../data/files.tar.bz2', 'r:bz2')
tf.extractall('../data/new/')
tf.close()
```

Listing 10-14 shows how to extract just the first three files in the archive.

Listing 10-14. Extracting the First Three Files from an Archive

```
import tarfile, os

if not os.path.exists('../data/new'):
    os.mkdir('../data/new')

tf = tarfile.open('../data/files.tar.bz2', 'r:bz2')
for member in tf.getmembers()[:3]:
    tf.extract(member, '../data/new')
tf.close()
```

I've use the method `getmembers()` to retrieve the list of files in the archive, and then indexed only the first three files.

Comparing Files

Ensuring two files are identical is a common task. In the case of input data files, it means we can remove the copy, and our script will both run faster and provide better statistics because now the data isn't used twice. The reasons for duplicate files can be numerous, as discussed in Chapter 4.

A simple mechanism for comparing two files can be to open both files, read the entire files to memory, and then compare the values:

```
>>> data1 = open('../data/file1.txt', 'rb').read()
>>> data2 = open('../data/file2.txt', 'rb').read()
>>> data1 == data2
```

```
True
```

The main benefit of this method is that it's simple. However, there are several shortcomings:

- *Inefficiency*: Suppose one file is of size 10GB and other file is 1 byte long. By looking at the file sizes, it's possible to tell the files are not identical. On the other hand, reading a 10GB file to memory can bring the system to a crawl.

- *Lack of information*: If two files are not identical, what exactly are the differences?

Modules *filecmp* and *difflib* from the Python standard library provide us with functionality to compare files and find the differences.

Module *filecmp*

The module *filecmp* provides functions for file and directory comparisons. The method cmp(file1, file2[, shallow]) compares file1 with file2. If shallow is not provided (or is True), files that have the same *stat* signature are considered equal. In other words, files that have the same system information, such as size, creation date, and more (see https://docs.python.org/3.3/library/os.html for an explanation of stat), are considered equal. If shallow is False, files are also compared for content:

```
>>> filenames = ['../data/file1.bin', '../data/file2.bin']
>>> for fn in filenames:
...     f = open(fn, 'w')
...     f.write('some data')
...     f.close()
...
```

```
9
9
```

```
>>> import filecmp
>>> filecmp.cmp(filenames[0], filenames[1])
```

```
True
```

The class dircmp(dir1, dir2) enables the comparison of directories dir1 and dir2. The comparison includes all subdirectories, as well. The method report() will print the result from comparing both directories.

For the following example, I assume you've created the file files.tar.bz2 in the previous compression example. Here, we create two directories, new1 and new2. Directory new1 contains the extracted files from the archive; directory new2 contains the extracted files from the archive, as well as another subdirectory, new3, which also contains the contents of the archive. Let's compare the directory contents (see Listing 10-15).

Listing 10-15. Comparing Directories

```python
import tarfile, os, filecmp

if not os.path.exists('new1'):
    os.mkdir('new1')

if not os.path.exists('new2/new3'):
    os.makedirs('new2/new3')

tf = tarfile.open('files.tar.bz2', 'r:bz2')
tf.extractall('new1')
tf.extractall('new2')
tf.extractall('new2/new3')
tf.close()

cmp = filecmp.dircmp('new1', 'new2')
cmp.report()
```

The results are as follows:

```
diff new1 new2
Only in new2 : ['new3']
Identical files : ['file0.txt', 'file1.txt', 'file2.txt',
'file3.txt', 'file4.txt']
```

As you can see, comparing directory contents using the *filecmp* module is easy and simple.

Module *difflib*

The module *difflib* provides several objects and functions to help compare lists of strings (e.g., text files). Several functions provide a diff result in different formats. These include context_diff(), ndiff(), and unified_diff(). In this section, we examine context_diff(f1, f2[, fromfile][, tofile]); other functions have similar behavior.

First, we create two files, ../data/file1.txt and ../data/file2.txt. These files have similar, but not identical, content, as shown in Listing 10-16.

Listing 10-16. Creating Files for Comparison

```python
import difflib

content = """A string
123, 456
789
some text\n"""
```

```
fname1 = '../data/file1.txt'
fname2 = '../data/file2.txt'

f1 = open(fname1, 'w')
f1.write('before\n')
f1.write(content)
f1.close()

f2 = open(fname2, 'w')
f2.write(content)
f2.write('after\n')
f2.close()
```

The two files differ in that the first file contains an extra line in the beginning, and the second file contains an extra line at the end. We call context_diff() to display those differences (see Listing 10-17).

Listing 10-17. Comparing File Contents

```
import difflib

fname1 = '../data/file1.txt'
fname2 = '../data/file2.txt'

lines1 = open(fname1).readlines()
lines2 = open(fname2).readlines()
for line in difflib.context_diff(lines1, lines2, fname1, fname2):
    print(line, end='')
```

I've include the name of the files as parameters to context_diff(); this will generate a report that displays the file names in the header information. Here are the results:

```
*** ../data/file1.txt
--- ../data/file2.txt
***************
*** 1,5 ****
- before
  A string
  123, 456
  789
  some text
--- 1,5 ----
  A string
  123, 456
  789
  some text
+ after
```

A section starting with *** means that the report addresses the file, `../data/file1.txt`; a section starting with `---` means that the report addresses the file `../data/file2.txt`. A line starting with a - sign implies that the line is missing from the current file; a + sign means that the line is included in this file, but not the other one. The output is similar to output generated by UNIX diff command-line utilities.

Additional *difflib* functionality can be found online at `https://docs.python.org/3.3/library/difflib.html`.

Final Notes and References

Python provides a wealth of libraries that deal with common programming tasks: file processing, command-line parameters, file and directory manipulation, compressing and archiving files, and many more. There are a great number of additional modules available with the Python standard library:

- The Python Standard Library, `https://docs.python.org/3.3/library/index.html`.

APPENDIX

■ ■ ■

Additional Source Listing

This appendix is a collection of source listings that didn't quite belong in the chapters themselves, but nevertheless might be of interest to you.

Nudge Subplots

In generating subplots of size 2 by 2 for this book, I noticed that the text for the x-axis of the top subplots clashes with the titles of the lower subplots. To overcome this, I defined nudge_subplot(), a function designed to modify the location of subplots within a figure (see Listing A-1).

Listing A-1. Source Listing of nudge_subplot()

```
def nudge_subplot(sp, dy):
    """A helper function to move subplots."""

    sp_ax = sp.get_position()
    sp.set_position([sp_ax.x0, sp_ax.y0+dy,
        sp_ax.x1-sp_ax.x0, sp_ax.y1-sp_ax.y0])
```

To use the function, store the return value from subplot() and then "nudge" it by calling nudge_subplot(sp, dy), as shown in Listing A-2, where sp is the subplot and dy is the amount to nudge (a value of 0.02 for dy usually works well).

Listing A-2. Using nudge_subplot()

```
from pylab import *

# values to plot
t = arange(5)
y = array([1,  2, -1,  1, -2])

plot_cmds = [
    "plot(y)",
    "plot(-y)",
    "plot(y**2)",
    "plot(sin(y))"
    ]
```

```
figure()
for i, plot_cmd in enumerate(plot_cmds):
    sp = subplot(2, 2, i+1)
    if i == 1: nudge_subplot(sp, 0.02)
    if i == 3: nudge_subplot(sp, -0.02)
    exec(plot_cmd)
    title(plot_cmd, fontsize='large')
    xlabel('x values')
show()
```

In this code, I've nudged the rightmost subplots and left the left ones as-is, as you can see in Figure A-1.

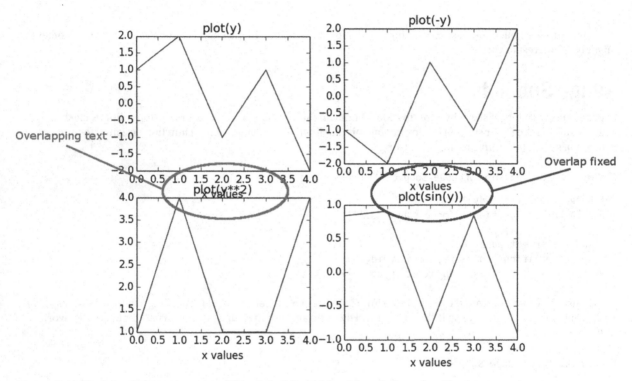

Figure A-1. *The left subplots are unmoved (the default), and the right subplots are nudged*

Magic Square Arrows

In Chapter 7, I presented a figure describing the magic square algorithm. I used *matplotlib* patch arrows embedded in the algorithm to plot that figure. Listing A-3 is the source code used to generate the diagram.

Listing A-3. Magic Square Diagram Creation

```
from pylab import *

def magicsq(n=3):
    """Returns a magic square of size n; n must be odd"""
```

```python
    if n % 2 != 1:
        raise ValueError("Magic(n) requires n to be odd")
    m, row, col = zeros([n, n]), 0, n//2
    for num in range(1, n**2+1):
        m[row, col] = num        # fill the cell
        col = (col+1) % n
        row = (row-1) % n
        if m[row, col]:
            col = (col-1) % n
            row = (row+2) % n
    return m

def testmagicsq(m):
    """Returns True if m is a magic square."""
    msum = sum(m[0, :])
    return all(m.sum(0) == msum) and all(m.sum(1) == msum)

def magic_arrow(x,y,str, n,c, d=0.15):
    my_colors='rgbym'
    mc='k' if c == 'k' else my_colors[c%len(my_colors)]
    if mc == 'y':
        mc = '#dfdf00'
    if str == 'top-right':
        gca().add_patch(Arrow(x+0.5+d,n-y-0.5+d,1-2*d,1-2*d, width=0.2,
            fc=mc, ec=mc))
    elif str == 'down':
        gca().add_patch(Arrow(x+0.5,n-y-0.5-d, 0, 2*d-1, width=0.2,
            fc=mc, ec=mc))
    else:
        raise ValueError("Unsupported arrow direction: "+str)

def show_alg(n=3):
    """Draws a magic square, n must be odd"""
    if n % 2 != 1:
        raise ValueError("Magic(n) requires n to be odd")
    if n<1:
        raise ValueError("Magic(n) requires n to be positive")
    axis('scaled')
    axis([0, n, 0, n])
    altc=0
    m, row, col = zeros([n,n]), 0, n//2
    for num in range(1, n**2+1):
        m[row,col] = num
        text(col+0.5,n-row-0.5, '%d' % num, va='center',ha='center')
        pcol,prow = col,row
        col = (col+1) % n
        row = (row-1) % n
        if m[row,col]:
            col = (col-1) % n
            row = (row+2) % n
```

```
            if col-pcol == 1 and prow-row == 1:
                magic_arrow(pcol,prow, 'top-right', n,altc)
            elif pcol == col and num != n**2:
                magic_arrow(pcol,prow, 'down', n,'k')
                altc += 1
            elif col-pcol == 1 and prow-row != 1:
                magic_arrow(pcol,prow,'top-right',n,altc)
                magic_arrow(pcol, n,'top-right',n,altc)
            elif col-pcol != 1 and prow-row == 1:
                magic_arrow(pcol, prow, 'top-right', n, altc)
                magic_arrow(-1, prow, 'top-right', n, altc)
            elif num == n**2:
                pass
            else:
                raise ValueError("Woah")

    for i in range(n):
        plot([0, n], [i, i], 'b')
        plot([i, i], [0, n], 'b')
    xticks([])
    yticks([])
    title('N=%d' % n)

def show_some():
    figure()
    for i in range(2):
        subplot(1, 2, i+1); show_alg(2*i+3); title('N = '+str(2*i+3))

show_some()
show()
```

Here, I defined the function `magic_arrow()` that draws an arrow at a given position using a *matplotlib* arrow patch. The arrow's direction is determined by comparing the current location with the previous location. Other than that, the code is similar to the code discussed in Chapter 7. The result is shown in Figure A-2.

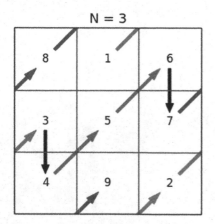
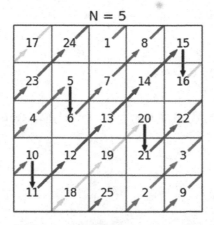

Figure A-2. *A visualization of the magic square generating algorithm*

Numerical Integration Visualization Source Code

In Chapter 8, I used graphs to illustrate numerical integration. Listing A-4 shows the source for the graph in Figure 8-1; Listing A-5 generates Figure 8-2.

Listing A-4. A Numerical Integration in Chapter 8, Figure 8-1

```
from pylab import *
N=1000
x1 = linspace(-1, 1, N)
y1 = sqrt(1-x1**2)
for i, N in enumerate([5, 10, 20, 100]):
    subplot(2, 2, i+1)
    x = linspace(-1, 1, N)
    y = sqrt(1-x**2)
    dx = x[1]-x[0]
    for i in range(len(x)-1):
        gca().add_patch(Rectangle((x[i], 0), dx, 0.5*(y[i]+y[i+1]),
            fc='lightblue'))
    axis('equal')
    title('N=%d' % N)
    plot(x1, y1, 'k', lw=1)
show()
```

Listing A-5. A Numerical Integration in Chapter 8, Figure 8-2

```
from pylab import *

figure()
title('Trapezoidal integration')
xlabel('x')
ylabel('y')

# plot the "ideal" circle
N = 1000
x_circle = linspace(-1, 1, N)
y_circle = sqrt(1-x_circle**2)
plot(x_circle, y_circle, 'k', lw=1)

# non-evenly spaced values
x = array([-1, -0.9, -0.4, 0.0, 0.4, 0.9, 1])
y = sqrt(1-x**2)
for i in range(len(x)-1):
    # add trapezoids
    gca().add_patch(Polygon([[x[i], 0], [x[i], y[i]], [x[i+1],y[i+1]], \
        [x[i+1], 0]], fc='lightblue'))
xticks(x)
axis('equal')

show()
```

Fractal Function Source Code

In Chapter 9, I used a variation of Chapter 7's fractal script to create a collage by wrapping it within a function. Listing A-6 shows the function used in creating the fractal collage in Chapter 9.

Listing A-6. A Fractal Collage Function

```
from PIL import Image
from cmath import *

# creates a z**4+1=0 fractal using the Newton-Raphson
# root finding method
delta      = 0.000001    # convergence criteria
res        = 200         # image size
iterations = range(1,10)  # number of iterations

for iters in iterations:
    # create an image to draw on, paint it black
    img = Image.new("RGB", (res,res), (0,0,0))

    # these are the solutions to the equation z**4+1=0 (Euler's formula)
    solutions = [cos((2*n+1)*pi/4)+1j*sin((2*n+1)*pi/4) for n in range(4)]
    colors = [ (1,0,0), (0,1,0), (0,0,1), (1,1,0) ]

    for re in range(0, res):
        for im in range(0,res):
            z = (re+1j*im)/res
            for i in range(iters):
                try:
                    z = z-(z**4+1)/(4*z**3)
                    if(abs(z**4+1)<delta):
                        break
                except ZeroDivisionError:
                    # possibly divide by zero exception
                    continue

            # color depth is a function of the number of iterations
            color_depth = int((iters-i)*255.0/iters)

            # find to which solution this guess converged to
            err = [ abs(z-root) for root in solutions ]
            distances=zip(err, range(len(colors)))

            # select the color associated with the solution
            color=[ i*color_depth for i in colors[min(distances)[1]]]
            img.putpixel((re,im), tuple(color))
```

```python
        img.save('../images/fractal_z4s_%03d_%03d_%03d.png' % \
            (iters, res, abs(log10(delta))))
        print('wrote ../images/fractal_z4s_%03d_%03d_%03d.png' % \
            (iters, res, abs(log10(delta))))

collage = Image.new("RGB", (res*3,res*3))
for x in range(3):
    for y in range(3):
        im = Image.open('../images/fractal_z4s_%03d_%d_005.png' \
                % (x*3+y+1, res))
        collage.paste(im, (res*y, res*x))
collage.show()
```

Index

Get the eBook for only $10!

Now you can take the weightless companion with you anywhere, anytime. Your purchase of this book entitles you to 3 electronic versions for only $10.

This Apress title will prove so indispensible that you'll want to carry it with you everywhere, which is why we are offering the eBook in 3 formats for only $10 if you have already purchased the print book.

Convenient and fully searchable, the PDF version enables you to easily find and copy code—or perform examples by quickly toggling between instructions and applications. The MOBI format is ideal for your Kindle, while the ePUB can be utilized on a variety of mobile devices.

Go to www.apress.com/promo/tendollars to purchase your companion eBook.